M000047972

THE RHIZOMATIC WEST

POSTWESTERN HORIZONS

General Editor
William R. Handley
University of Southern California

Series Editors
José Aranda
Rice University

Melody Graulich
Utah State University

Thomas King
University of Guelph

Rachel Lee
University of California, Los Angeles

Nathaniel Lewis
Saint Michael's College

Stephen Tatum
University of Utah

The Rhizomatic West

Representing the American West in
a Transnational, Global, Media Age

Neil Campbell

UNIVERSITY OF NEBRASKA PRESS • LINCOLN AND LONDON

© 2008 by the
Board of Regents
of the
University of Nebraska
All rights reserved
Manufactured in the
United States of America
∞

Library of Congress
Cataloging-in-Publication Data
Campbell, Neil, 1957–
The rhizomatic West:
representing the American West
in a transnational, global,
media age / Neil Campbell
p. cm.—(Postwestern horizons)
Includes bibliographical references and index.
ISBN 978-0-8032-1539-9 (cloth: alk. paper)
ISBN 978-0-8032-4393-4 (paper: alk. paper)
1. West (U.S.)—In art.
2. Place (Philosophy) in art.
3. Identity (Philosophical concept) in art.
4. Arts, Modern—20th century.
I. Title.
NX653.W47C36   2008
700.45878—dc22
2008001903

Photo on pages ii–iii
© iStockphoto.com/Robert van Beets.
Set in Quadraat by Bob Reitz.
Designed by R. W. Boeche.

CONTENTS

ILLUSTRATIONS

ACKNOWLEDGMENTS

Many people have helped, in many different ways, with the writing of this book. I would like to begin by thanking Stephen Tatum for his generous advice and understanding of my work, for his friendship and great company in diverse western places. Also a big thank you to fellow scholars and friends in the field of western studies, many of whom I have met through the wonderful Western Literature Association: José Aranda, John Beck, Frank Bergon, Krista Comer, Nancy Cook, Steve Cook, David Fenimore, Audrey Goodman, Melody Graulich, Richard Hutson, Michael K. Johnson, Susan Kollin, Nat Lewis, Susan Maher, Martin Padget, Zeese Papanikolas, Ladette Randolph, Forrest Robinson, Alan O. Weltzien, and many others. Special thanks go to Susan Bernardin for her advice on chapter 6, and to Paul Groth for his permission to use the J. B. Jackson photographs from his personal collection. For specific help with chapter 5, thanks go to Andrew Cross, Nick Waplington, and Jason Shenai and Niall O'Leary at Millennium Images.

For financial help to create time to write this book and to travel to the American West, I would like to thank the Arts and Humanities Research Council, the British Academy, and the University of Derby research awards scheme. Finally, as ever, my last words are for my wife, Jane, for all her love, tolerance, and company along the way.

INTRODUCTION
Theorizing the Rhizomatic West

Nothing less is asked of the thinker today than that
he should be at every moment both within things and outside them.
Theodor Adorno

Culture is contested, temporal, and emergent. Representation and
explanation—both by insiders and outsiders—
is implicated in this emergence.
James Clifford

There's nothing more unsettling
than the continual movement of something that seems fixed.
Gilles Deleuze

A System of Westness

"Like people and schools of criticism, ideas and theories travel—from person to person, from situation to situation, from one period to another. Cultural and intellectual life are usually nourished and often sustained by this circulation of ideas, and whether it takes the form of acknowledged or unconscious influence, creative borrowing, or wholesale appropriation, the movement of ideas and theories from one place to another is both a fact of life and a usefully enabling condition of intellectual activity." Edward Said's words suggest how ideas and theories travel or are borrowed and used in different places for different purposes: "For borrow we certainly must if we are to elude the constraints of our immediate intellectual environment."[1] I take this as a starting point for this book's project, the examination of a traveling or mobile discourse, the American West, while avoiding certain constraints in its examination. In this I am exploring an anomaly in western studies between the "lines of flight"—that is, mobility and migration existing both as ideas and as the material conditions that transformed the region as tribes, immigrants, nomads, conquerors, traders, trappers, farmers, and many other forms of transient peoples passed through—and the mythic quest for rootedness, settlement, and synthesis so often accepted as the outcome, the final point, and the essential identity of this fluid movement. The desire for fixity, belonging, and integration has an impressive presence in the narratives of the West relating both to the needs of a modern state to present a solidity and unity at its heart—the foundation of national identity—and to the developing discipline of western studies itself. This zealous mission has the quality of a form of "intra" imperialism amplified by the West's "self-representation as the fount of Americanness," a unified, coherent metanarrative in which a singular, national identity is explained and justified.[2] Such ideological weight remains in political rhetoric and representation, whether through Ronald Reagan assuming the role of wood-chopping rancher in California or George W. Bush defining foreign policy as a simplistic sheriff/outlaw screenplay. It is sedimented in historiography through the Turner thesis, the art of Bierstadt and Russell, the western novels of Wister or Grey, the western films of John Ford, the photographic epics of Ansel Adams, the fashion iconography of Ralph Lauren, and the advertising of Marlboro, all constructing interrelated aspects of a westward creation story. In the West, it claims, is the evidence of a nation forged out of the intense and diverse experiences of the so-called open, vacant frontier, transforming encounter and contact into a closed, destined relationship of evolution and progress toward the production of an essentially rooted American character. Settling the West has been for so long a key trope of how that land, that space, that political complexity has been discussed. Putting down roots, building communities, taming the land, removing the indigenous populations with their itinerant ways, assimilating the immigrant into the nation, and asserting a national narrative have been intrinsic to westernness. However, as West-based writer Charles Bowden comments, these mythic frameworks act as a screen, and "we hide behind the feel and the image of the taking, the days of the pioneers, the vestments of the cattle industry, the pageants of the Neolithic cultures we gutted, the image of the gun, the memory of the roar of our firepower when the trigger was pulled." These frameworks, he goes on to argue, must be broken and questioned, because "We need to look at ourselves, with love, with doubt, with clear eyes."[3]

To borrow from James Clifford, one might argue, therefore, that conventional narratives have "privileged relations of dwelling over relations of travel," despite the fact that travel was central to the processes that brought people to the West in the first place. As it was for Clifford's anthropologists, it is more ideologically convenient to study rooted communities in the field (so-called fieldwork) as fixed and unitary, and consequently "to marginalize or erase several blurred boundary areas, historical realities that slip out of the *ethnographic frame*" (emphasis added). Often excluded in such a narrow and particular focus on the local is "the wider global world of intercultural import-export in which the ethnographic encounter is always already enmeshed."[4] Applying Clifford's perspective to the West might allow for some productive rethinking of how western space has been viewed over time—to displace fieldwork with what Paul Gilroy terms "route work" and to consciously step outside the frame of settled community to perceive other forces at work in cultural space now viewed as a contact zone where "disparate cultures meet, clash and grapple with each other."[5] As Clifford writes, the ethnographer, like the western historian or writer, "has localized what is actually a regional/national/global nexus" and marginalized "external relations and displacements," when according to Mary Louise Pratt's definition of "contact zones," what is significant are "copresence, interaction, inter-locking understandings and practices."[6] Too often, however, the West has been seen from within the West by westerners creating "naturalized affiliations between subject and object," as Paul Giles puts it, defining a space in which American concerns are at the fore and where settlement is the key to the understanding of social and cultural forces and where identity has been shaped by restricted local parameters.[7] However, the West has always had a global dimension as a geographical, cultural, and economic crossroads defined by complex connectivity, multidimensionality, and imagination, even if these have often been elided in favor of a more inward-looking and emotive vision. To view the cultures of the West more globally alters this point of vision, "putting pressure on the conceptual frameworks by which we have traditionally grasped the social world."[8] If, therefore, the culture of the West is viewed globally, it can be detached from its isolation as purely American, a "fixed locality" of "boundedness and coherence," requiring us, as Clifford says, to "step away from notions of separate, integral cultures" and see culture as traveling with "multiple external connections . . . a shifting paradox, an ongoing translation," refocusing the West as "encounters, co-productions, dominations, and resistances" with the emphasis shifted to "hybrid, cosmopolitan experiences as much as on rooted, native ones."[9] Thus the concept of the local and the regional so often at the heart of western studies is put under question or opened out until it is interrupted and interfered with by international (or rather outer-national forces), global flows that rupture the "self-perpetuating circuit which tries simply to appropriate the authenticity of the land to underwrite certain forms of social authority or aesthetic closure."[10]

To examine the West in the twenty-first century is to think of it as always already transnational, a more routed and complex rendition, a traveling concept whose meanings move between cultures, crossing, bridging, and intruding simultaneously. Rather than the assumption that "roots always precede routes" in the definition of culture, one might rethink "any local, national, or regional domain," such as the West, as an inter-active process of constitutive contacts and mobilities.[11] In these terms, the work of Said and Clifford encourages a reorientation of culture as both roots and routes, both dwelling and traveling, which has much to offer western studies, providing an alternative framework that deterritorializes established traditions, displacing static myths with complex, intersecting strands.[12] Such theoretical concepts, as so often, find better expression in different forms, and for me it comes via Bowden, first, at the opening of *Blood Orchid*, his scathing, broken "unnatural history of America," where he writes that "I seek roots, just as long as they can accommodate themselves to around seventy-five miles an hour and no unseemly whining about rest stops or sit-down dinners," defining himself as "A person fated never to settle yet always seeking the place to settle"; and second, toward the end of the book, which consistently critiques the mythic frame of nationhood as embodied in the American West with its imposed ideology of "one big tribe, the rainbow tribe," which he tries to comprehend and discovers only the following: "We are embedded in this thing called the West but we cannot see it. It is always . . . over the next hill, the far side of the mountain, up the farthest canyon, something that slipped away yesterday, last week, twenty years ago, the last century. . . . Or it never was at all. . . . I can't find the West . . . and nobody is likely to frame an elegant map of it and put it on the wall. . . . It's a kind of secret thing."[13]

To comprehend what Bowden calls this "secret thing" is the skeptical action of route work, following ever-multiplying paths without re-sorting to any established vision—a vision he describes as "a world left mumbling to itself, a perfect garden with the dreaded outside, the fabled Other held at bay and the neat rows of cultures and genes safe behind some hedgerow." Bowden's work is about "vitality, rough edges, torn fences, broken walls, wild rivers, sweat-soaked sheets," a disorderly as-sault on the perfect, mythic, and essentialized spaces of western mythol-ogy in writing that he parallels with graffiti in its capacity to "speak for the mongrel, the mestizo, the half-breed, the bastard, the alley cat, the cur, the hybrid, the mule . . . that pounds against all the safe and disgust-ing doors." If, as Bowden suggests, the West is too often represented as some "perfect garden . . . safe behind some hedgerow" of stories and established iconographies, then the task of critical regionalists is to disrupt this flow of ideas through the activation and articulation of the "dreaded outside."[14] To think of the American West more as fluid graf-fiti and less like a determined "rooted body that grows, lives, dies" is to open it up more sharply as "constructed and disputed historicities, sites of displacement, interference, and interaction" in which the cultural archi-tecture of the West is consistently remodeled and expanded.[15]

All the "routes" by which we might travel are, of course, no longer tied to physical movement, to bourgeois privileges of a white middle class, since every billboard, every commodity purchased, every radio, iPod, CD player, TV, and PC permits "travel" to some extent, however virtual, creating a movement that affects the local and interferes with perceptions of where and what we are.[16] Traversing the West as tourist site, website, advertising imagery, fiction, theme park, film, or immi-grant experience—all of these are continuations of the processes that constructed the American West like those described in a novel that in many ways has come to encapsulate a myth of settlement, The Virginian (1902). In one scene in Owen Wister's classic novel, the West is seen as exactly a space of difference being transformed into "America," forg-ing the East (the "tenderfoot" narrator) and the South (the traveled Virginian) with the "rainbows of men-Chinese, Indian chiefs, Africans, General Miles, younger sons, Austrian nobility, wide females in pink." As Wister writes, "Our continent drained prismatically through Omaha once." In this space, this prism, language and meanings collide and refract as the cosmopolitan "bill-of-fare" announces "salmis, canapés supremes," and "Frogs' legs à la Delmonico," while the owner speaks of eggs as "white wings" and rare beef as "slaughter in the pan." In this prismatic, hybrid mix Wister captures a vision of a diasporic West full of encounter, contact, and fusion, a vision he is swift to consign to the past, like the Indian and the buffalo, referring only to the palace as a lost, nostalgic memory of another West already being overtaken. This is a revealing episode, demonstrating a consistent pattern in Wister's novel whereby an awareness of and fascination for ideas of cultural mixing, of a subject-in-process, and of the West as diasporic are tempered and retreated from by a more conventional belief in and desire to institute an essentialized American identity as the "natural" product of the social evolution of the fittest.[17]

In Wister's metanarrative, national identity is forged by melting down exterior differences into a "new product," as Frederick Jackson Turner called it, a composite American self, formed out of a migratory westward journey, contact with the rigors of climate, geology, and indigenous populations, and the consequent realignment of European values in the soil of the frontier: "a people composed of heterogeneous materials, with diverse and conflicting ideals and social interests, having passed from *the task of filling up the vacant spaces of the continent*, is now thrown back upon itself, and is seeking an equilibrium. *The diverse elements are being fused into national unity*" (emphasis added).[18] In displacing the uncertainty and fluidity of migration and movement he asserts a rhetoric of interiority, of essential, rooted identity as the focus for the epic narrative giving coherence and authority to the westward urge of nation building, providing America with a distinct creation myth, or what Bowden called the "perfect garden." Indeed, Turner's use of organic, corporeal images suggests that the very lifeblood of this settled America, its "body politic," emerged by transforming "the slender paths of aboriginal intercourse," broadening them for an "ever richer tide" far more "complex" than the "originally simple, inert continent." Fluidity is thus converted into solid "organs" and rooted, settled identity, metaphors of glaciation halted to become stable human landscape.[19] As Richard Slotkin has written, "myth-making is simultaneously a psychological and a social activity . . . its function is *to reconcile and unite* . . . individualities into a collective identity" (emphasis added).[20] The multiplicities and mobilities of the prismatic West momentarily acknowledged by Wister and Turner are brought under control in the service of a coherent national narrative with a gridlike neatness revealing its mythic (rooted, treelike) structure. What it glosses over are the very complex relations and contacts that actually existed in the various spaces of the West, as well as the multiple ways in which the West spilled out beyond its immediate geographic boundaries, becoming a global, transnational phenomenon.

In the theory of Gilles Deleuze and Félix Guattari, the tree typifies this limited, rooted model, "hierarchical" and working "along preestablished paths," and appropriately, Bowden's commentary on American history in *Blood Orchid* utilizes the organic image of the orchid and its roots as a bloody metaphor for destructive, rapacious possession: "The roots get thicker by the year, at first fine lines like lace on the bark of our lives, the skin of our life, the hopes of our life, and then coarsening as more and more wealth and power surges through and at first the roots begin to look like snakes, then like cables and later like giant aqueducts . . . nothing but blood, thick, sticky, virulent."[21] In contrast to arborial rootedness, Deleuze and Guattari propose the grasslike rhizome as an alternative image of thought, since "Thought is not arborescent, and the brain is not rooted or ramified matter . . . the brain is much more grass than tree."[22] As John Rajchman reminds us, a "given society or culture is never exhausted by its constitutive relations or distinctive divisions; on the contrary, it is always 'leaking' (*en fuite*), and may be analysed or 'diagrammed' in terms of its 'lines of flight' (*lignes de fuites*)."[23] Spaces are always far more complex than the East-West frontiers defined by Turner (or the western grid I will discuss in detail), and it is in studying these rhizomorphic "leakages" or "lines of flight" that don't tally with the official, mythic images that we might produce a different and more sophisticated "diagram" of the West. This is the aim of *The Rhizomatic West*.

Against Turner's notion of a blank page upon which America wrote its new identity in the West, one can posit another vision and style of language, of the West as a more complex text like that defined by Roland Barthes as "made of multiple writings, drawn from many cultures and entering into mutual relations of dialogue, parody, contestation . . .

[where] a text's unity lies not in its origin but in its destination."[24] This is like Wister's hybrid text uncontained by his imposed mythic grid of nationalism, maintaining "dreaded outside" perspectives on the West from within and from without: found in ethnic voices, the discounted, awkward and delinquent, the foreigner and the "minor," and in all the panoply of "fugitive poses" that in themselves unsettle or rupture the orderly segmentations and definitions of established "westness."[25] Kathleen Stewart, writing about another American region, defines Appalachian culture as a complex system that is "not either/or but both/ and: both global and local, both tactile and imaginary, both set and fleeting, both one thing and another . . . [where] moments of cultural naturalization and denaturalization are interlocked . . . a place where centripetal and centrifugal forces . . . form a unity of opposed forces."[26] This "insurrection of knowledges," as Foucault terms them, is close to the sense of the West that I wish to explore in this book, a mobile genealogy of westness, a cultural discourse constructed through both national and transnational mediations, of roots and routes, with its territories defined and redefined (deterritorialized) from both inside and outside the United States.[27]

In his explication of Deleuze's thought, Rajchman writes: "If, then, segmentation of social space permits a geometry of horizontals and verticals within which to chart or locate all social 'movement,' minorities and becomings work instead with 'diagonals' or 'transversals,' which suggest other spaces, other movements. To 'diagram' a space is to expose such diagonal lines and the possibilities they open up . . . a map that is not the 'tracing' of anything prior, but which serves instead to indicate 'zones of indistinction' from which becomings may arise."[28] In western terms, these "other spaces" of "minorities and becomings" refute the neat narrative lines that join point to point, frontier to frontier, as in Turner's "cord of union"; on the contrary, they suggest the intersections of many tangled lines, like those in westerner Jackson Pollock's paintings, always bifurcating and crossing others, forming and deforming, making more lines rather than reaching some final, settled point.[29] Turner's "fluidity of American life" that begins his thinking about expansion and frontier mobility falters because it follows only a "single line" (the frontier), believing it leads inevitably to one destination (nationhood, union, a fixed identity). To rethink the West rhizomatically, beyond its function as national unifier—"a holding together of a prior or virtual dispersion"—is to view it as unfinished, multiple, and "open" and to recognize that "beneath . . . official histories and divisions there exist other powers, actualised through other kinds of encounter and invention," tracing divergent, entangled lines of composition that both interconnect and split apart constantly.[30]

Deleuze's processive philosophy exemplifies the approach I intend to take to "westness," defining it as an *art brut*—a sort of outsider's art with its "own raw materials that permit it to enter into external relations . . . with other disciplines," while "the whole is not given, and things are always starting up again in the middle, falling together in another looser way . . . [with] nothing of the well-planned itinerary; on the contrary, one is taken on a sort of conceptual trip for which there preexists no map—a voyage for which one must leave one's usual discourse behind and never be quite be sure where one will land." His desire is to get outside preexistent forms, narratives, and assumptions and all the mechanisms that contain, enframe, and delimit possibilities in order to present and explore alternative "voyages" for which the "map" (or "diagram") is ever forming and deforming. In these metaphors of mobility, spatiality, and outsideness, of going "off the map" via encounters and reinventions, Deleuze offers a process and approach I wish to apply, in varying ways, to understanding the overcoded West not as a single region but as a mutating multiplicity, a "way of departing from the compartmentalization of knowledge, yet without recourse to an organic unity (Romantic nostalgia for its loss)."[31]

Testing the Grid

One of the defining geometrical images of thought in the United States has been the grid as an organizing principle for settlement of towns and cities, then outward into the control, possession, and acculturation of nature itself, and more generally as a metaphor for contained, boundaried ways of thinking. One cannot think of the West as rural or urban space without visualizing the powerful checkerboard symmetries of the meshlike grid as it arrests and orders space, seemingly cutting up and arranging nature into culture, ordering chaotic flows into a defined "schedule."[32] The underlying conceptualization of space that produced the grid historically and translated it so prominently onto American soil relates, I believe, to a certain approach to complex, multiple spaces that aligns this material practice to a whole way of thinking that Deleuzian theory helps me to unravel or unfold. William L. Fox writes that the grid system of mapping and land division "lead[s] us to believe that we understand where we are" and helped to "create a series of assumptions" about possession built around the visual control gridding appears to supply. This "cartographic imperative is a direct corollary to the doctrine of Manifest Destiny, which . . . held that the land was ours for the taking," providing a "cocoon" of "customary perceptual protocols" through which we contain the landscape.[33] President Jefferson, himself a surveyor, understood in his 1785 Land Ordinance the power of the grid as a tool of mapping empire so that mass emigration might follow to secure and unify the central West against the British and Spanish. As Fox writes, "To map the land, therefore, was in no small measure to claim it," for "the grid exercises authority over space by applying a ruler to it in all senses of the word. It stretches out a straight edge across unenclosed space and automatically extends a map to the romantic horizon."[34]

As Fox points out, the gridding of the West gave rise to the division of farmland and the transfer of "straight corridors" to the railways (and later the freeways), and it guided transcontinental telegraph lines, then the routes of power lines, telephone wires, and fiber-optic cables; therefore, to comprehend the impact of such a project was to uncover "the national nervous system." The grid, in Fox's analysis, becomes a meme, an "idea that survives, as if it were an independent organism, by replicating itself in different forms from mind to mind," but its overwhelming function as map and cartographic segmentation "abstracted us away from looking at land."[35] As J. B. Harley writes, "The steps in making a map—selection, omission, simplification, classification, the creation of hierarchies, and 'symbolization'—are all inherently rhetorical . . . they signify subjective human purposes . . . the map maker merely omits those features of the world that lie outside the purpose of the immediate discourse." Cartography, therefore, controls and orders the world, disciplines and normalizes it, becoming "a silent arbiter of power," like the surveyors who helped "construct" the West as "a whorl of contour

1. John Brinckerhoff Jackson, untitled (date unknown). Used courtesy of Paul Groth.

lines, turning chaos into cosmos . . . *reframing* observed information into a scale model of a geographic reality" (emphasis added).[36] The central controlling device of mapmaking is here articulated as framing and reframing, that is, of taking the complex, multiple nature of the world and translating it into another language and then containing and limiting it within a gridded space. This is illustrated well in J. B. Jackson's aerial photograph of the grid (see figure 1).

At the beginning of his *PrairyErth* (1991), William Least Heat-Moon seeks to counter this cartographic fixture with what he terms a "deep map" of place taking him beyond the gridded frames of Chase County, Kansas, and into a richer, more complex understanding of the West. He begins his study at Roniger Hill in the Flint Hills, the "buckle cinching East to West," a point he stands upon "as if atop a giant map of the United States," and quickly contrasts this experience with another as he spreads twenty-five maps of the area over the carpet of his room to create a "paper land." Both the real experience and the paper version reveal the dominance of the grid shape that has come to define the spatial representation of the West, "arbitrary quadrangles that have nothing to do with the land, little to do with history, and not much to do with my details . . . a system of coordinates that have allowed the wildness to be subdued." For Least Heat-Moon his book will "test the grid" by thinking "what's under them, their depths and their light and darkness," by "digging, sifting, sorting, assembling shards" and following an "arbitrary course" like a Japanese person reading a book "up to down, right to left."[37]

According to these ideas, the grid and the map act centripetally to reduce the complex West to a contained and framed object, a controlled architecture (like a house with its walls, ceilings, and windows that shelter and contain), yet from another perspective the grid can work centrifugally, acting to remind us of all that exists outside the mapped frame. As Rosalind Krauss has written, grids in modernist art are "cheerfully schizophrenic," presenting "a tiny piece arbitrarily cropped from an infinitely larger fabric" and so operating "from the work of art outward, compelling our acknowledgement of a world beyond the frame."[38] This might be paralleled with a painting's frame, which both contains the "inside" of the art and is itself a part of the experience, a porous interface, a border between the inside and the outside. As Deleuze and Guattari put it, "The frame or the picture's edge is, in the first place, the external envelope of a series of frames or sections that join up by carrying out counterpoints of lines and colors, by determining compounds of sensations. But the picture is also traversed by a deframing power that opens it up onto a plane of composition or an infinite field of forces . . . diverse . . . irregular forms, sides that do not meet . . . all of which give the picture the power to leave the canvas. The painter's action never stays within the frame and does not begin with it."[39]

Thus the frame, like the grid, while enclosing, is also "deframed" by the forces from outside as well as those simultaneously exploding outward from inside and pointing beyond its restrictive space. To bring this back to the West is to recognize the discursive "frames" imposed around it as image (film, literature, art), geography (maps, sections, territories, states), experience (frontier, Manifest Destiny), culture (cowboy myths, nation building, univocity), and real and imagined space (vacancy, Paradise, Americanization) and to employ the immanent "field of forces" from within and without as a source of creative "deframing" "in order to open it onto the universe." Rather than defining the West narrowly, Deleuze and Guattari encourage us to think of it as "opening, mixing, dismantling, and reassembling," or as they put it, like Bakhtin's concept of the novel, as "contrapuntal, polyphonic, and plurivocal." The "house" (an image Deleuze and Guattari use a lot) has to be opened up (unhoused), as in the example of music, with its rigid enframing forms like the sonata ("an entire house with its rooms") that can nonetheless express variation, a "deframing," a "disaggregation of the tonal frame." Thus the territory (whether house, music, or region) becomes deterritorialized as the frame or the grid is extended and fractured.[40] As Fox argues, to study the grid and to contrast it with all that is outside it is to see its limitations, creating a cognitive dissonance and "a new viewpoint" so that we "see where we live—and therefore ourselves-from a new angle," and, as in Krauss's analysis, create a vision more capable of seeing "both ways at once."[41]

Creative engagements in art, writing, film, and critique will, according to Fox, "mitigate against the grid," opening up and unhousing, disassembling, reassembling, and routing its previously static and rooted forms. To make their point, Deleuze and Guattari recall D. H. Lawrence's essay "Chaos in Poetry," which argues that mankind "must wrap himself in a vision, *make a house of apparent form and stability and fixity*," "putting up an umbrella between himself and the everlasting whirl" and on its underside painting a firmament (emphasis added).[42] Poets and artists, claims Lawrence, those enemies of convention, make slits in the umbrella, tearing open the firmament itself "to let in a bit of free and windy chaos," slits that others will "patch over" and upon which they will redraw the fixed stars.[43] However, new artists must come to cut through once more, for a "glimpse of chaos is a vision, a window to the sun" that questions and "deframes" the umbrella's sheltering and comforting assertions, just as a fugitive voice might challenge the stable and cozy definitions of the West's "umbrella" of fixed myth, convention, and sustaining national narrative.[44] As the West becomes framed by its own approved and established orthodoxies (canonical and noncanonical, Old and New Wests, Anglo and ethnic, male and female, real and imagined, etc.), artists (and others) must rend the fabric to let some air in from "outside" and get its circulation going again. As in a complex transfusion, any closed system needs "new blood," any rooted space needs rerouting and opening up, any house must be unhoused.

The Practice of Outside

Robin Blaser, writing of the poet Jack Spicer, identified what he termed "the practice of outside" in which "an other than the reasonable is said to enter the real" that "disturbs our settled relation to language," introducing "some path that you've *never seen on a map before*" (emphasis added).[45] Thus from within and without western studies' conceptual grid, the "outside" becomes a strategy for opening up and scrutinizing established ideologies and languages, canonical practices and texts, resilient and official mythologies. As Elizabeth Grosz writes, "Thought is what confronts us from outside . . . the concepts we already have, from outside the subjectivities we already are, from outside the material reality we already know . . . a wrenching of concepts away from their usual configurations," to constantly challenge and disturb us.[46]

For Foucault, the age of Kant and Hegel formulated "most imperiously" a desire to "interiorize the world, to erase alienation . . . to humanize nature, to naturalize man, and then recover on earth the treasures that had been spent in heaven," and these principles echo the driving forces of Manifest Destiny, defining westward expansion as a divine quest to achieve a new Eden and to produce an American nation whose "interior" absorbed the "world" into its project as it absorbed alienated migrants into the settling and taming of land itself. These assimilations produced an "interiorized" (inward-looking) language of settlement, rootedness, and closure akin to "the old fabric of interiority" that Foucault argues had to be challenged from "outside" by a new (or rediscovered) language that was "directed not toward any inner confirmation—not toward a kind of central, unshakable certitude—but toward an outer bound where it must continually contest itself." Thus in reconsidering the West we might also seek out these "outside" perspectives to contest the "old fabric" and to unravel its existing languages and, thereby, open a space "in which no existence can take root." Foucault refers to this perspective as a mobile "murmuring space" created through "the always undone form of the outside."[47] Foucault's essay was often cited by Deleuze, whose work is also concerned, as we have seen, with "outsideness" that comes before things settle and become fixed, disturbing accepted furrows of thought and practice with alternative ways

of thinking. The "murmuring space" becomes in Deleuze the stammering of minorities and all that resists assimilation, since a "great writer
is always like a foreigner in the language in which he expresses himself,
even if this is his native tongue. . . . He makes the language itself scream,
stutter, stammer, or murmur," placing "language" (and image and ideology) "in perpetual disequilibrium."[48]

Hence in a novel like Canadian Guy Vanderhaeghe's *The Englishman's
Boy* (1997), histories shift and blur across times (1873, 1923, 1953) and
borders (Indian territory, Canada, United States) as scriptwriter/detec-
tive Harry Vincent comes to understand the ways by which Hollywood
constructs its version of the West by traveling beyond its fantasy "grid"—
"make-believe . . . held in quarantine by a ten-foot fence and a gate that
trumpets in black iron scrollwork: Best Chance Pictures." Vincent's encounter with movie mogul Damon Ira Chance exposes him to an ideology of nationhood schooled in the work of D. W. Griffith, that believed
cinema "filled America's spiritual emptiness with a vision of itself," and
desired to produce "an American Odyssey" rooted in a western story of
"poetic fact" that would serve to unite the immigrant population behind
a "single voice."[49] The "American spirit," Chance claims in one of his
polemical sermons, required a form commensurate with "westering . . .
an art form of *forward momentum*. . . . A westering art form. . . . The art
form of *motion*," one provided, for him, through the mythic frame of the
movies. Chance's concept of cinema is, however, monologic and rooted,
a "spiritual Americanism" where "there's no arguing," since "A moving picture is beyond thought" and, for him, the Western is its perfect
form.[50] What the novel reveals, through cowboy Shorty McAdoo's actual
tale told through Canadian Vincent, however, is a complex, messy West
very different from that desired by Chance, but one he is determined to
ignore in order to produce a mythic creation story, "to rewrite history in
lightning . . . rewrite the history of the foreigner, erase completely those
sentimental flowers of memory and light their minds with the glory of
American lightning." Reflecting upon his clash with Chance's fascistic
manipulation of history, Vincent, an outsider to Hollywood, realizes he
has uncovered a valuable lesson, expressed here in familiar language:
"looking at the river, I remind myself the map of the river is not the river
itself. That hidden in it are deep, mysterious, submerged and unpredict-

able currents." Earlier in the novel Chance tells Vincent that "Analysis puts man outside the thing he studies, while intuition puts him inside. Analysis therefore renders partial knowledge while intuition renders absolute knowledge."[51] Perhaps what Vincent learns, as his metaphor of deep, fluid histories reminds us, is that neither position alone is sufficient and that it is only the inside and the outside operating together that ultimately renders the fuller story of the West.

Mikhail Bakhtin theorized this perspective in cultural terms:

> In the realm of culture, outsideness is a most powerful factor in understanding. It is only in the eyes of another culture that foreign culture reveals itself fully and profoundly. . . . A meaning only reveals its depths once it has encountered and come into contact with another, foreign meaning: they engage in a kind of dialogue, which surmounts the closedness and one-sidedness of these particular meanings, these cultures. . . . Such a dialogic encounter of two cultures does not result in merging or mixing. Each retains its own unity and open totality, but they are mutually enriched. (emphasis added)

Preceding Pratt's concept of the contact zone by more than fifty years, Bakhtin proposes a dialogical process in which to be "located outside the object of his or her creative understanding" and to "forget nothing" is the primary critical position. Thus viewing the West differently, from "outside," exercises "creative understanding" providing "new questions for a foreign culture, ones that it did not raise itself," and through our contact with these "we seek answers to our own questions in it," while the "foreign culture responds to us by revealing . . . new aspects and new semantic depths."[52] Bakhtin believes in the reciprocal importance of every individual's "excess of seeing" based on the simple recognition that I can see what you cannot see, and vice versa (your face, behind you, your back, etc.), for "I shall always see and know something that he, from his place outside and against me, cannot see himself. . . . As we gaze at each other, two different worlds are reflected in the pupils of our eyes." Michael Holquist writes of this relational sense succinctly: "my excess is your lack, and vice versa. If we wish to overcome this lack, we try to see what is there together. We must share each other's excess in order to overcome our mutual lack."[53] Similarly, in The Truth of Painting Derrida describes "The parergon [which] inscribes something that comes as an extra, exterior to the proper field . . . but whose transcendent exteriority comes to play, abut onto, brush against, rub, press against the limit itself and intervene in the inside only to the extent that the inside is lacking. It is lacking in something and it is lacking *from itself*. . . . It needs the supplementary work. This additive . . . is threatening. Its use is critical. It involves a risk and exacts a price . . . (*Parergon* also means the exceptional, the strange, the extraordinary)."[54]

Thus, simultaneously, in the acts of sharing our various "excess[es] of seeing," our "supplementary work," we formulate a "collective," negotiated, communal, contested, critical sense of things that by its very nature denies the isolated vision or framed "single," monologic point of view as the only right and "true" one (like that of Ira Chance), providing a dialogical understanding of knowledge developed through the interaction and discussion across and between established boundaries (the deep river metaphor). Hence within western studies, the U.S. western scholar's "essential" knowledge or the established canonical text may appear to be the core knowledge and therefore be central to the framing critical process; however, what is it they don't (or can't) see? What might be supplementary and threatening to it? As Holquist puts it, "An event cannot be wholly known, cannot be seen, from inside its own unfolding as an event"; it needs, in other words, the "parergon."[55] In what follows I wish to sketch out some of this "practice of outside" through the deliberate use of nonwestern examples and suggest how they might intervene productively in the development of western studies.

Koolhaas and Tschumi: The Delirious Outside

If, as I have argued, the western grid system of mapping, land division, and mythic imagining has been so influential in how the region has been constructed, then we might go as far as to call this a form of "architextural" discourse and pursue it through the work of architectural theory. To this end I wish to employ the work of Dutch architect Rem Koolhaas, whose book *Delirious New York* was first published in 1978. It is an astounding and provocative work of history, theory, and urban poetics, interdisciplinary and sweeping in its ideas and approaches to an examination of Manhattan's "culture of congestion." It is useful to this study of the West in two ways: first, because Koolhaas was a European outsider casting his eye over New York, bringing unusual and diverse perspectives to his subject; and second, because his theoretical exploration of the concept and application of the grid system that patterned the streets of New York overlaps with my interest in the grid as a key western motif. In comprehending the grid in New York, his "man-made Wild West, a *frontier of the sky*," Koolhaas unravels a fundamental and recurrent paradox about the United States, between containment and liberation, system and anarchy, the closed and the opened, the inside and the outside, echoing Derrida's "parergon" and our other discussions of excess. Reading from the streets, from the grid, among the "mutations . . . fragments . . . irrational phenomena" and amid the "layers of phantom architecture in the form of past occupancies, aborted projects and popular fantasies," Koolhaas identifies Manhattan as the "20th century's Rosetta Stone" excavating real and psychic space ("Manhattan's unconscious architectural production"). It is a palimpsestic space with Koolhaas as "Manhattan's ghostwriter" picking over its "egocentric . . . inarticulate . . . [and] restless" stories, its "mythical" aura where "the real and natural ceased to exist" and the "discontinuous—even irreconcilable" seemed, so often, its defining features. Through the material architecture of Manhattan he maps an "other" architecture of knowledge, dreams, paradoxes, collisions, and mysteries that cannot be read separately, one that is always inextricably interconnected.[56]

Koolhaas's approach is helpful in my similar journey through the West's complex, multilayered cultural architecture with its constructions, iconographies, and representations "building" its meanings over time.[57] Koolhaas, like Foucault, set out to examine powerful discursive formations through analyzing "the relations between statements" made over time that "refer to the same object" (i.e. the American West) and demonstrating that there was, in truth, no single "object" or mythic coherence, only different disjunctive elements that "constituted" it. Foucault's work, therefore, emphasizes "dispersion," "the interstices," a "series full of gaps, intertwined with one another, interplays of differences, distances, substitutions, transformations," concepts that "differ in structure" and "which cannot enter the unity of a logical architecture" (emphasis added).[58] As this shows, Foucault's exploration of cultural discourse is architectural/architextural, examining one form against another, one framework of expected patterns against a more discontinuous and unexpected "dispersion," where the various lines of construction (images, languages, voices, documents, etc.) trace the outline of the "object" he set out to analyze. In so doing, "one is forced to advance beyond familiar territory, far from the certainties to which one is accustomed, towards an as yet uncharted land and unforeseeable conclusion." In all this Foucault is uncovering "conceptual architectures" ripe for dispersal and interrogation, fully aware of the impossibility of fixing any single, self-contained whole. Koolhaas sees cities this way, especially New York, and his work offers a model applicable also to an investigation of the West.[59]

The Manhattan grid pattern with its "apparent neutrality" was, argues Koolhaas, "an intellectual program" (echoing Fox's "perceptual protocols"), claiming "the superiority of mental construction over reality," ignoring topography in a casual act of "subjugation," superimposing a closed framework, a "gridiron" with a particular and disciplined rectilinear conception of space that had already being unraveled during westward expansion. Koolhaas, however, develops this point, claiming that "The Grid defines a new balance between control and de-control in which the city can be at the same time ordered and fluid, a metropolis of rigid chaos," where from within and without the controlling frame alternative uses of space might emerge demanding ever-inventive architectural creativity straining against the grid, pointing beyond it and challenging its strictures through a "mosaic of episodes."[60]

For Koolhaas, Manhattan was "a man-made Wild West, a *frontier of the sky*" whose paradoxes mirror those of the West, a region similarly mapped by the Jeffersonian grid, within which existed for him the capacity for extraordinarily complex layering. As with Manhattan's 1811 grid, there are curious coherencies between the stories of city and country, East and West, as a collision of the desire for control, organization, fixity, and pattern with the straight lines and rectangles of the western grid, unable to contain what overspills it, bubbling up and outward in ways never imagined in the Jeffersonian dream. As in the West, the urban "new frontier" disciplined space through accepted and designated "efficiencies" or "metropolitan Manifest destiny," only to discover "spectral alternative[s]" that could not be easily or comfortably contained within it. Indeed, as Koolhaas recognized, the grid epitomized a kind of urban "double life" that, although superficially about fixity and control, in reality existed with an "unstated philosophy of the Grid" defined by "mutation" and "latent possibility," awash with spectral alternatives breaking out of its apparent "freeze-frame." Resembling Krauss's "cheerful schizophrenia," the mythic frame encountered tensions, schisms, and splits implicated in the gridded space that could not be contained, which "exceeded" it and leaked out from it, linking to the outside, as in our earlier discussion of outsideness and excess.[61] Koolhaas too named this "schizoid" architecture only a year after Deleuze and Guattari's *Anti-Oedipus: Capitalism and Schizophrenia* was translated into English in 1977.[62] Their "schizophrenia," like Koolhaas's vision of the city, "sets in motion decoded and deterritorialized flows" pushing beyond the grid, with no closed, totalized whole but rather a "process," "a way of thinking a life not governed by any fixed norm or image of self—a self in flux and becoming."[63] Thus "schizoanalysis" finds different perspectives and connections, deterritorializing preformed concepts (like Oedipal theory, conventional urban design, or conventional western studies) by emphasizing the "revolutionary schisis as opposed to the despotic signifier" and fixed structure.[64]

The "despotic signifier" for Koolhaas was the unchallenged, one-dimensional grid and, in my parallel, the metanarratival West as single racial, national, self-contained creation story, as symbolic unifier for the United States, or what Paul Giles calls the "ever-expanding circle" of self-perpetuating myths and beliefs, an idea derived from Adorno's "magic circle that stamps critique with the appearance of absolute knowledge." Such grids and circles defining both material and mental landscapes are "drawn by a thinking that tolerates nothing outside it" and which might, therefore, be challenged by active interference from the "dreaded outside," the "schisis," and other "dispersed" stories.[65] This is made most apparent in Koolhaas's section on Raymond Hood, an architect who saw the grid's contrary dynamics as both functional and liberatory, which begins appropriately with a quotation from F. Scott Fitzgerald's *The Crack-Up*: "The test of a first-rate intelligence is the ability to hold two opposite ideas in the mind at the same time, and still retain the ability to function."[66] Koolhaas is close here to a notion of "thirdspace," the ability to think "between" opposites simultaneously, which introduces his most Deleuzian section, "Schizophrenia," describing how Hood and his colleagues "developed a schizophrenia that allowed them simultaneously to derive energy and inspiration from Manhattan as irrational fantasy *and* to establish its unprecedented theorems in a series of strictly rational steps."[67] In a similar manner, Koolhaas invoked Salvador Dalí's paranoid-critical method, which "through conceptual recycling, the worn, consumed contents of the world can be recharged or enriched like uranium" providing a new vision "to destroy, or at least upset, the definitive catalogue, to short-circuit all existing categorizations, to make a fresh start—as if the world can be reshuffled like a pack of cards whose original sequence is a disappointment."[68] Such dual thought or "doubling" resisted reductionism to a single point of view and allowed for simultaneous and contrary aspects of fantasy and reason to coexist. As we will see, Gilroy later uses W. E. B. Du Bois's notion of "double consciousness" in a similar way, while Giles writes of "looking both ways" as a critical paradigm derived from Adorno's notion of the "double-edged method."[69]

For my purposes, Koolhaas's "frontier of the sky" parallels the West as a space of multiple possibilities with "the simultaneous existence of different programs on a single site"—a schizo-space—at once gridded, rooted, and territorialized (in all senses of the term), while simultaneously ungridded, routed, and deterritorializing, with a capacity for "lines of flight" as well as mythic closure and stasis. However, by seeing differently, from "outside" the systems of thought and expectation (the literal and metaphoric grid), Koolhaas's invocation of Dalí and "schisis" reminds us of the necessity for critical thought that "travels," for reinvention, and for "recycling" as central to a productive cultural space in which established and "taken-for-granted" discourses can be challenged, brought under question, and "surrealized."[70] Koolhaas's outside perspective, his skewed vision of city space, translates into my rethinking of the West as another "grid of specifications" in need of interrogation and expansion.[71] Learning from his "synthetic Wild West of the Skyscrapers" (something many westerners would find repulsive), with its paradoxical grid caught between "rigidity and freedom," reminds us nonetheless of the troublesome space of the West itself with its dialogic tension forging creativity and invention with "something 'implicated in' the gridded space, which it cannot contain, which leaks and spills out from it, linking it to the outside."[72] Like Derrida's discussion of framing in The Truth of Painting, it asserts something implicit about space that cannot be framed and which "may at any point or moment break out of it and cause it to be reframed."[73] In discussing art, Derrida claims that criticism traditionally created oppositions such as meaning/form, inside/outside, and signified/signifier and then set about finding "inner meaning, the invariant . . . the true, full, originary meaning: one, naked." For Derrida this process "circles" and encloses the experience of art and its criticism like a "frame." The "parergon," or that which is extra to the work of art, something at its edge, peripheral, and yet simultaneously revealing and "interlaced" to it (the columns on buildings, the clothing on classical statues, the frames of paintings), functions as an important "excess": "A parergon comes against, beside, and in addition to the ergon, the work done [fait], the fact, the work, but it does not fall to one side, it touches and cooperates within the operation, from a certain outside. Neither simply outside or simply inside. Like an accessory that one is obliged to welcome on the border, on board [au bord, a bord]. It is first of all the on (the) bo(a)rd(er) [Il est d'abord l'a-bord]."[74] In other words, as Rajchman puts it, within all framed space there is "a virtuality," the potential for dynamic "reframing," a form of "excess" latent within the frame and most likely to emerge from "the intervals . . . of the bounded space . . . with a free, smooth, 'rhizomatic' energy that exceeds the framing of site, plan, and program."[75] The invocation of the interstitial spaces of the "border" and the edge, all existing "neither simply outside or simply inside," is why one is reminded again of the relevance of such theories in our consideration of westness as a multifaceted, evolving discursive formation constantly spilling out, reforming, splitting, and connecting.

Many of these ideas are brought together via the work undertaken between Jacques Derrida and architects Bernard Tschumi and Peter Eisenman at the Parc de la Villette, Paris, where Tschumi's "grids of folies" deliberately expressed and utilized this tension between the order of the grid and the unpredictable nature of the folie (a kind of madness).

Like Koolhaas's schizophrenia or paranoia, Eisenman wrote of how grids can become "ambivalent" as a "series of frames that are warped and distorted," providing, not "structural integers," but "traces and imprints" offering "intersections" able "to break out from the . . . bounded space . . . with a smooth 'rhizomatic' energy that exceeds the framing of site, plan, and program."[76] Likewise, Tschumi's *folies* "stress that madness articulates something that is often negated in order to preserve a fragile cultural or social order," and therefore the grid/*folie* deliberately demonstrates the kinds of paradox ("dynamic oppositions") that Koolhaas's Manhattan project explored too: "Such a structure inherently suggests the bars of the asylum or prison, introducing a diagram of order in the disorder of reality" and "both articulates space and activates it" as the *folie* disrupts the grid, extends it, forces its "bars" apart. Out of this disruptive process come what Tschumi calls "grafts of transference" creating or imagining new space from within or beyond the grid, avoiding synthesis, preferring to combine and "superimpose" in order to produce "conflicting logics of the different systems," oppose closure, and stress instead its "potentially infinite field of points of intensity: an incomplete, infinite extension, lacking center or hierarchy."[77] Derrida explained how Tschumi's grid "exposes itself to the outside and spaces itself out in what is not itself," creating a "general dislocation" working against "naturalized architecture . . . bequeathed to us" so that it "animates and disturbs," "effaces or exceeds" such previous frames of reference in a manner that "is valid for other arts and regions of experience as well."[78] Thus from within the grid Tschumi (like Koolhaas before him) articulates an alternative "principle of heterogeneity—of multiple, dissociated, and inherently confrontational elements . . . aimed at disrupting the smooth coherence and reassuring stability of composition, promoting instability and programmatic madness ('a Folie')."[79] Tschumi is interested in "dismantling" cultural architecture, and like Foucault earlier, he invests in "a dispersed and differentiated reality that marks an end to the utopia of unity," but ultimately, as Derrida says, with the intention to "maintain, renew and reinscribe," even to "revive . . . an energy which was infinitely anaesthetized, walled-in, buried in a common grave or sepulchral nostalgia."[80]

The "cultural architecture" of the West with its material, cultural, and ideological gridlike structures can be usefully disrupted and restructured by the application of such radical, outside perspectives drawn from beyond western studies, enabling a rethinking of the West as "a dispersed and differentiated reality that marks an end to the utopia of unity," a way to travel away from essentialist, exceptionalist obsessions with "roots," "place," and nationhood and to reposition the West within a more transnational, global matrix. A new grid maybe, but one of infinite, interconnected "mad" routes derived like Koolhaas's from an expanded field or Tschumi's grid/folie, a "deterritorialized," rhizomatic interpretation of the "West" (or "westness") that looks outward as well as inward, forward as well as back, willing to think of borders as inherent and productive to its construction rather than negative and in need of constant policing. This vision of the West, derived from architectural theory, "leaves opportunity for chance, formal invention, combinatory transformation, wandering."[81] Tschumi sums it up well:

> As with the contemporary city, there are no more boundaries delineating a coherent and homogeneous whole. On the contrary, we inhabit a fractured space, made of accidents, where figures are disintegrated, dis-integrated. From a sensibility developed during centuries around the "appearance of a stable image" ("balance," "equilibrium," "harmony"), today we favor a sensibility of the disappearance of unstable images: first movies . . . then television, then computer-generated images . . . disjunctions, dislocations, deconstructions. . . . Some unexpected consequences, some interesting distortions of long-celebrated icons are to be foreseen.[82]

Circum-Wests: Paul Gilroy

Like the architectural theorists Koolhaas and Tschumi, black Briton Paul Gilroy is interested in the consequences of viewing place and space as "fractured" and "disintegrated," no longer viewing them as separate, identifiable, and stable—*exceptional*, in American terms—but acknowledging that boundaries between places (and identities) have become less clear, blurred by a postmodern, transnational, global age of travel, digital communication, multinational corporations, and various complex mobilities. Spaces (and therefore identities and values) have become more fluid and less fixed, prone to multiple influences and directions with places more porous, overlapping and intersecting as previously "closed" definable locations interfuse and "travel." Thus the desire for "home-place," rootedness, and belonging, for so long linked to a "landscaped" sense of national and local identity, as Stuart Hall terms it, needs to be rethought as well.[83] Viewed from perspectives outside and inside, the West is no longer "epic"—settled, enclosed, and internally coherent, fixed in time and etched in memory—but is seen more "as a meeting place, the location of the intersections of particular bundles of activity spaces, of connections and interrelations, of influences and movements."[84] The region's in- and out-flowing dialogic and diasporic histories and traditions should be given renewed importance in the transnational comprehension of the West as part of a larger global mobility of peoples and ideas—what Clifford terms "intercultural import-export."[85]

Gilroy's postcolonial theory employs "intermediate concepts"—or "thirdspaces"—to move between established parameters and binary definitions, to "break the dogmatic focus on discrete national dynamics" and provide the means of "getting beyond . . . national and nationalistic perspectives."[86] In terms of the West this suggests ways of shifting toward a postwestern perspective where the "post" signifies the "going beyond" and "after" the established and "taken-for-granted" notions of the West as a fixed and settled phenomenon. The cultural insiderism that Gilroy works against is at the heart of my proposition too, opposed to what Jan Pieterse calls the "introverted notion of culture," preferring something more mobile, the "sociology of the in-between, a sociology from the interstices . . . merging endogenous [formed within]/exogenous [growing by successive additions to the outside] understandings of culture . . . to overcome the dualism between the nation-state and international system perspectives."[87] Of course, the West, westness, has flowed in all directions of the compass as a truly rhizomatic presence; however, Gilroy's chronotopes of mobility, contact, and exchange, developed, as he puts it, "in the venturesome spirit of James Clifford," are worth holding on to, applying, and extending here for their highly suggestive reconfigurations of critical thought as we search for new ways to express transnational, "outernational," intercultural experiences.[88] Gilroy's term "outernational" suggests the ways the West, for example, has traveled "outside" the United States and the Americas—back and forth—being appropriated, altered, celebrated, mythicized, performed, and critiqued. In a state of constant "becoming," the idea of the West and certainly any sense of the West as absolute, essential "fact" is put under question, its authenticity interrogated, the more it is performed and "virtualized." Following Gilroy, Joseph Roach's *Cities of the Dead* coined the term "circum-Atlantic" to suggest this dialogic circulation and exchange, drawing heavily on this statement from Renato Rosaldo: "The notion of ritual as a *busy intersection* anticipates the critical assessment of the concept of culture. . . . In contrast with the classic view, which posits culture as a self-contained whole made up of coherent patterns, culture can be arguably conceived as a more *porous array of intersections* where distinct processes crisscross *from within and beyond its borders*" (emphasis added).[89] As I explore the West in this book I have very much in mind a notion of the "circum-West" and its cultures as a "porous array of intersections" crisscrossed "from within and beyond its borders."

Gilroy productively rethinks how essential, racial identities based on static concepts of "roots" and "rootedness" in place can be dialogized (crisscrossed) and hybridized by the exploration of the homonym "routes" as dynamics of encounter and traveling. An inward-looking study of culture and society sees the journey as ending in settlement, in achieving a finished self (or community), in establishing a firm grip on place and, therefore, forming an "invariant identity." In contrast, Gilroy stresses "a process of movement and mediation," or what he terms "routes," preferring an "interplay between these two dimensions" as a more full and sophisticated definition of cultural and identity formation that accepts pluralities and sees them actively engaged in the production of new identities and communities.[90] In order to emphasize this interplay of roots and routes, Gilroy employs the concept of "diaspora" as a "valuable idea [that] . . . points towards a more refined and more worldly sense of culture than the characteristic notions of soil, landscape and rootedness" that are often used to fix national identity.[91] The underpinning idea of dispersal within diaspora allows an alternative perspective upon the West too, as westness located in a "webbed network, between the local and the global, challeng[ing] the coherence of all narrow nationalist perspectives," as decidedly "restless, recombinant."[92] Of course, traditionally the West is identified as the "natural homeland" where America's essential and authentic being was formed with "roots, soil, landscape and natural beauty . . . used so that nation and citizenship appeared to be natural rather than social phenomena—spontaneous expressions of a distinctiveness that was palpable in a deep inner harmony between people and their dwelling-places."

Diaspora theory reassesses this thinking about identity as essential and absolute and "problematizes the cultural and historical mechanics of belonging" by disrupting the mythic, explanatory "links between place, location and consciousness."[93] Diaspora can also challenge primordial concepts of identity rooted in an idealized past where the race was formed, like Wister's Saxon myth-ideal, Turner's frontier, or an Ansel Adams landscape, for under diaspora, identity is constructed as dynamic, interlinked, and hybrid. There is no authentic single "homeplace" in which one's roots are planted, for identity is "spatial" and fluid, formed by the "routes" it travels and the contacts it makes rather than as "a one-way transmission belt; an umbilical cord, which connects us to our culture of origin." The latter produces only a closed, linear version of culture, whereas diaspora redefines it as circular and spatial, "as moving, not in a line but through different circuits."[94] However, someone like Wister lamented a "lost" epic time when the West was unchanged by "Progress," immigration, and movement and where behavior and justice were uncluttered by ambiguity or doubt. This view sees culture as diluted the further it moves away from its "roots" and its origins. Conversely, however, one can see change, as Clifford and Gilroy do, as dynamic and productive, with identity "traveling" and encountering along its complex "routes" of diasporization, with those "identities . . . constantly producing and reproducing themselves anew, through transformation and difference" so "that specific dynamics of dwelling/travelling be understood comparatively," questioning culture as simply "a rooted body that grows, lives, dies, and so on." Their work values and emphasizes dialogically "tangled cultural experiences" challenging us to see a phenomenon like the West as a complex diasporic contact zone of "intersecting histories—discrepant detours and returns," where diaspora "involves dwelling, maintaining communities . . . [and] articulates, or bends together, both roots and routes to construct . . . alternate

people are not rooted but routed.

public spheres, forms of community consciousness and solidarity that maintain identifications outside the national time/space in order to live inside, with a difference."⁹⁵ As Bharati Mukherjee puts it in her diasporic novel *Jasmine*, as her central character explains her new life in the West, based on "read[ing] only *Shane*, and [having] seen only one movie," "Jyoti, Jasmine: I shuttle between identities."⁹⁶

To see the West as such an unfinished mobile process is to reimagine both identity and community in ways that shift the emphasis from the inside only, or what Gilroy terms the "one-way flow," toward the "global dimensions of diaspora dialogue" so that one might "live inside, with a difference." Like Gilroy in his analysis of black musical cultures, I would see the West as full of "histories of borrowing, displacement, transformation, and continual reinscription" that "should not be reified in the primary symbol of the diaspora and then employed as an alternative to the recurrent appeal of fixity and rootedness," but rather be viewed as a space where identity is "neither fixed essence or . . . a vague and utterly contingent construction reinvented by the will and whim of aesthetes, symbolists and language gamers." From this critical "thirdspace" Gilroy reimagines the black Atlantic (as I will the West) as a "non-traditional tradition, an irreducibly modern, ex-centric, unstable, and asymmetrical cultural ensemble that cannot be apprehended through the manichean logic of binary coding," a tradition redefined as "the living memory of the changing same." Through this revision of terms he stresses that tradition is no longer about "a lost past" or a "culture of compensation" that might retrieve it, but about "circulation and mutation," a "two-way traffic" that shifts us from the "chronotope of the road to the chronotope of the crossroads" to demonstrate the nature of this intercultural process of exchange. The straight line (road, frontier, grid, linear history and narrative, monologue) is disrupted by the trope of crossing (dialogue, diaspora, rhizome, the fold) in a revisionary process full of "untidy elements in a story of hybridisation and intermixture that inevitably disappoints the desire for cultural and therefore racial purity."⁹⁷

Virtual Wests: Paul Giles

British Americanist Paul Giles's *Virtual Americas* (2002) is also concerned with examining "points of intersection" between cultures and recognizing and using critically a "position of reflection and estrangement" that comes from looking at the United States "from the outside." Giles argues for what he terms a "virtualization" process that represents "native landscapes refracted or inverted in a foreign mirror" so that "it becomes easier to appreciate the assumptions *framing* these narratives and the ways they are intertwined with the construction and reproduction of national mythologies." He investigates how from this "position of estrangement" America's unconscious is illuminated through its "assumptions, boundaries, and proscribed areas" which "remain latent or unexamined in studies of a national culture that are generated wholly from the inside or that lack a comparative dimension." Apparently familiar, "natural" assumptions and narratives solidified into the myths of cultural identity, such as those abundant in the images and representations of the American West, need to be "denaturalized" and "deframed," a task Giles believes is served best by the critical role of the "outside." Of course, the aim is not to replace the "inside" view with the "outside" but to register the importance of both in the construction, comprehension, and interrogation of cultural definitions—of nationhood (for Giles) or the West (for me)—in a "dialectic of familiarity and alterity," an "ideology of exchange."[98] His aim is to find a critical perspective to "engender double-edged discourses liable to destabilize traditional hierarchies and power relations, thereby illuminating the epistemological boundaries of both national cultures." His approach hinges on the point that "national histories . . . cannot be written simply from the inside," where the narrative often involves "the incorporation of multiple or discordant voices in a certain preestablished framework of unity," an "ever-expanding circle of a national narrative."[99] Instead, it requires "external points of reference that serve to relativize the whole conceptual field, pulling the circumference of national identity itself into strange, 'elliptical' shapes."[100]

Thus, according to Giles's argument, the assimilation of multicultural voices into an expanded, gridlike definition of what constitutes western studies would not be sufficient, for it would merely recirculate a particular model of American studies (and American culture) as consensual and unified. His preferred model allows for immense tension and movement, "pulling the circumference" (of the circle/grid) centrifugally in differing directions rather than centripetally toward a singular whole.

The goal of Giles's work is to "locate an alternative kind of American studies, one predicated on division, disjuncture, and dispersion rather than a mythic integrity and interdisciplinary synthesis that gave the subject its methodological rationale during its nationalist heyday of the 1950s and 1960s."[101]

My lengthy use of Giles's work is to align this study, in part, with his aims, and to turn his critical position to a particularly influential version of American studies whose "narratives of cohesion" are identified with the West: Henry Nash Smith's *Virgin Land* , Leo Marx's *The Machine in the Garden*, R. W. B. Lewis's *The American Adam*, and Roderick Nash's *Wilderness and the American Mind*. The West—"America only more so"—epitomized by Turner's "The Significance of the Frontier in American History" emerged at the very same moment that Giles argues this sense of a unified American nation does, at the Columbian Exposition, Chicago, 1893. While Henry Adams stated that "Chicago was the first expression of American thought as a unity," Turner articulated his thesis on the frontier as the unifying principle of Americanness, the space in which national "traits" emerged out of contact with the rigors of the western frontier life to forge the nation as distinct from Europe. To counter such "universalist, integrationist concepts" defining the national imaginary from within, Giles argues that "the subject must play off what is inside a framework defined as 'American' [or 'western'] against what is outside it, thereby illuminating the ways specific local conditions and cultural landscapes reconstitute transnational networks in different ways." Giles's notion of the "virtual" suggests all those supplementary elements "implicit" within America but which are suppressed by its mythic narratives and which, if revealed, would "illuminate the fictional, contingent condition of such national mythographies." These are the equivalent to those rhizomatic forces within Koolhaas's grid or Derrida's frame. As Giles puts it, "A virtual America, therefore, would be a mythic America turned inside out." In their efforts to present an integrated vision of rooted nationhood, earlier "myth and symbol" writers firmly working from "within" the mainstream, "unconsciously" suppressed boundaries, borders, and tensions, but subsequently, if one rethinks American culture as a virtual construction one is positioned "on these boundaries and, by looking both ways, to render the mythological circumference of the nation translucent" (emphasis added). In this Giles echoes Chicana Gloria Anzaldúa, as we will discuss later, who has written that "Living between cultures results in 'seeing' double, first from the perspective of one culture, then from the perspective of another. Seeing from two or more perspectives simultaneously renders those cultures transparent."[102]

To "look both ways," inside and outside, as we have seen throughout this introduction, is to crave an "in-between," a form of "thirdspace" not associated with liberalism or taking no position but rather a dynamic and critical "border," a "middle" (as Deleuze and Guattari would term it) that acts as Giles's virtual reflecting "mirror" not simply reinscribing antithesis or asserting synthesis, but negotiating spaces between, presenting the virtual as a "hybrid form," a "tantalizing position in between the material event and its shadow."[103] Thus the virtual, as a name for Giles's rethinking of a critical space, conforms to Rob Shields's definition of it as "a crisis of boundaries . . . between time zones and between spaces, near and distant."[104] In fact, Shields develops and extends this point in The Virtual connecting back to Giles's earlier point of "looking both ways," associating virtuality with liminality: "In between is a 'time out of time' on the 'limen' (threshold) of membership or a new status. In this space, initiates are instructed in their new identity and responsibilities." Such liminal "third" spaces (like the borderlands in Chicano/Chicana studies—see chapter 2) "face both inward and outward, creating an equivocal, ambiguous zone . . . a strongly marked, interstitial space. 'Limen' are thus 'threshold' spaces in which one is neither 'in' nor 'out.'" Indeed, Shields indirectly explains why Giles's "metaphor" of virtual America is such a useful critical tool: "The virtual infects the actual as a metaphor . . . [and] shifts the commonsense notions of the real away from the material," and breaks apart simple dualisms "of here and there, inside and outside . . . concrete and abstract, ideal and actual, real and fake, transcendent and immanent" so that the "either-or model" is shifted "into a system of hybrids of the old dualisms which are best understood as intensities and flows."[105] This critical "in-between" or "thirdspace" exists between accepted oppositions such as real/imagined, East/West, or inside/outside, offering a means to rethink and restructure normalized patterns of order and thought.

Giles relates this "spatial turn" to his ongoing project to "virtualize"

American studies: "To problematize the geographical integrity of the United States"—and, I would add, a region like the West—"is, inevitably, also to problematize the 'natural' affiliation of certain values with a territory that can no longer be regarded as organically complete or self-contained."[106] Giles questions critics whose definition of America is based upon the "addition" of previously marginalized peoples, for this perpetuates the idea of an "ever-increasing circle" of inclusion without looking beyond it, and therefore inadvertently contributes to an exceptionalist, imperial ideology.[107] He often refers in this regard to "western" critics like Annette Kolodny or José David Saldívar, whose work, he claims, although innovative, fails to engage with "the interlocking, multifaceted global culture of today."[108] In this Giles is too dismissive of works that are clearly directional and part of "a new intellectual regionalism" pointing toward approaches and theories that contribute to this rupture of the critical grid, directions that have, in many ways, provided signposts for this book.[109]

Ultimately, however, Giles calls for a "critical transnationalism" to "probe the significance of cultural jagged edges, structural paradoxes, or other forms of apparent incoherence and illuminate our understanding of where the culture of the United States is positioned within a framework of broader global affairs." Indeed, his argument hinges on the fact that such transnational perspectives exist precisely to "disturb any idea of it [American literature] as a homogenous or inclusive cultural field."[110] "Is the case," he asks, as I do about the West, "in the migrant and digital conditions of the twenty-first century, that American narratives are the exclusive preserve or prerogative of those who 'live' there?"[111]

Deleuze and Guattari Go West: The Rhizome and the Fold

America, and the West in particular, figures frequently in Deleuze and Guattari's work, in part because of its countercultural associations, but also because of the tensions between the apparent openness of its space and the constant efforts to control and order it. Deleuze commented that his coauthor had a "sort of wild rodeo" and "desert" within him and said of himself, "I am a poor lonesome cowboy."[112] They are fascinated by the West as a "line of flight," "combining travel, hallucination, madness, the Indians, perceptive and mental experimentation, the shifting of frontiers, the rhizome (Ken Kesey and his 'fog machine,' the beat generation etc.)."[113] One quotation helps link this fascination with the ideas already developed in this introduction: "States of things are neither unities nor totalities, but multiplicities . . . a set of lines or dimensions which are irreducible to one another. . . . In a multiplicity what counts are not the terms or the elements, but what there is 'between,' the between, a set of relations which are not separable from each other. Every multiplicity grows from the middle, like the blade of grass or the rhizome . . . A line does not go from one point to another, but passes between the points ceaselessly bifurcating and diverging, like one of Pollock's lines."[114] Deleuze's American example is a "westerner," Jackson Pollock, born in Cody, Wyoming, living in Arizona and California, influenced by Native American sand paintings and obsessed with notions of space derived (in part) from experience of the West, and one of whose earliest paintings, Going West (1934–38), depicts a swirling western landscape with wagon train and cowboy. For Deleuze, Pollock's extraordinary "multidirectional," deframing line, which "the eye has difficulty following" and pinning down because it refuses to "form a contour," was inherently "western," since it "delimits nothing, neither inside nor outside," and "does not go from one point to another, but passes between points, continually changing direction, and attains a power greater than 1, becoming adequate to the entire surface."[115]

Pollock epitomized the restless, rhizomatic principle growing from the "middle" and always breaking across established gridded spaces, echoing the approach to revising the cultures of the American West explored in this introduction. Discontented with the "compartmentalization of knowledge" of overarching, single dominant narrative approaches, Deleuze and Guattari preferred juxtaposing or superimposing different layers in montage, forming a complex of overlapping "routes" in which "established strata start to shift, opening up new fault lines and possibilities, [and] through which older conceptual personae mutate and reappear in new guises as in what Foucault called Deleuze's 'philosophical theatre.'"[116] These ideas, as we have seen, find a focus in the concept of the rhizome, articulating principles of multiplicity, signifying "diverse form," "the best and the worst," "a throng of dialects," "connection and heterogeneity . . . [with] any point . . . connected to anything other."[117] The rhizome is the "weed" or the grass that "overflows ... grows between. It is the path itself," located most often for Deleuze and Guattari in American art—in Pollock, Melville, Fitzgerald, Thomas Wolfe, Henry Miller, Jack Kerouac, Allen Ginsberg, William Burroughs, Leslie Fiedler, and Carlos Castaneda, for "In them everything is departure, becoming, passage, leap, daemon, relationship with the outside. They create a new Earth."[118]

Most of these artists understood the West's geography and symbolism within American culture—that "the true East is in the West"—and their experimental styles demonstrated that "frontiers [were] something to cross, to push back, to go beyond . . . [that] becoming is geographical." For geography, as Deleuze argues, is "no less mental and corporeal than physical in movement," since space, as Henri Lefebvre would say, is both conceived and perceived, real and imagined—and always ideological.[119] This "geography of becoming" is rhizomatic, like the grass in Walt Whitman's poem, "the uncut hair of graves" in our heads, for "what thinking signifies is what the brain is, a 'particular nervous system' of grass"—as unruly and incomplete as any "voyages of exploration."[120] These American writers "know how to leave, to scramble the codes, to cause flows to circulate, to traverse the desert of the body without organs. They overcome a limit, they shatter a wall, the capitalist barrier. And of course they fail to complete the process, they never cease failing to do so."[121] These writers cry, "Go across, get out, break through, make a beeline, don't get stuck on a point. Find the line of separation, follow it or create it, to the point of treachery"—and in so doing, offer an alternative to essentialized, inward-looking, and rooted containment.[122]

For set against the rhizome, as we discussed earlier, is the rooted metaphor of the "tree," "an image of thought, a functioning, a whole apparatus that is planted in thought in order to make it go in a straight line and produce the famous correct ideas." The "arborial" has a "point of origin, seed, or centre; it is a *binary machine* or principle of dichotomy . . . an axis of rotation which *organizes things in a circle*, and the circles around the centre . . . a system of points and positions that fix all of the possible *within a grid*, a hierarchical system or transmission of orders . . . a future and a past, roots and a peak, a whole history, an evolution, a development . . . trees are planted in our heads: the tree of life, the tree

34

of knowledge, etc. *The whole world demands roots.* Power is always arborescent" (emphasis added).[123] It is, however, the rhizomatic "multiplicities"
whose "lines" resist the "binary machine" by overflowing its system,
center, and order, breaking the "grid" and upsetting the notion of identifiable "roots," that interest Deleuze and Guattari and that also form the
basis for this study of the West. It is the rhizome and fold, not the root
or tree, that produces the unruly line and not the point (of origin). The
madness or schizophrenia inherent in this approach links back to our
discussion of architecture in which Koolhaas and Tschumi invoke the
schizoid as an innovative approach that refutes, like the rhizome, "reassurance in any solidity: not in ground or tree, horizontality or verticality,
nature or culture, form or foundation or finality."[124]

For me, this is a way of comprehending the circum-West too, less solely
about "roots" than about rhizomes (or "routes"), since the search back to
find origins and essences is only one approach in a complex space of migratory, hybrid cultures that extends both within and without the region.
For Deleuze and Guattari there is "a model . . . perpetually in construction
or collapsing . . . a process . . . perpetually prolonging itself, breaking off
and starting up again," specifically the "rhizomatic West, with its Indians
without ancestry, its ever-receding limit, its shifting and displaced frontiers," and contrary to the Turner thesis's view that "The United States lies
like a huge page in the history of society" to be read "line by line from east
to west" in an orderly and coherent manner, they reject "the book as an
image of the world" as "vapid," since "the multiple must be made" in a
"book all the more total for being fragmented." In the West they see not
the sedentary but the rhizomatic in all its forms, as "reducible neither to
the One nor the multiple . . . composed not of units but of dimensions, or
rather directions in motion. It has neither a beginning nor end, but always
a middle (milieu) from which it grows and which it overspills. . . . [It] operates by variation, expansion, conquest, capture, offshoots . . . a map that
is detachable, connectable, reversible, modifiable, and has multiple entry-
ways and exits and its own lines of flight." In parallel with the idea of the
hybrid, dialogical, and diasporic, as a means of understanding the West's
diverse communities and voices, and its global overspill, the rhizome has
no beginning or end, "it is always in the middle, between things, interbeing, *intermezzo* . . . alliance . . . conjunction."[125]

This is further conceptualized through Deleuze's notion of the fold, of a world full of curves and textures, folding and unfolding so that the inside and the outside become inseparable and interconnected into an infinity of possibilities as the folds interact and multiply in a similar manner to that traced earlier in Pollock's art. In describing this metaphor Deleuze provides another conceptualization of how the West-as-discourse functions, for "the multiple is not only what has many parts but also what is folded in many ways . . . a continuous labyrinth is not a line dissolving into independent points, as flowing sand might dissolve into grains, but resembles a sheet of paper divided into infinite folds or separated into bending movements, each one determined by the consistent or conspiring surroundings." The fold, with its "inflections" and curves, can be contrasted both to the straight line and patterned grids, since there can never be "a straight line without curves intermingled" or a "curve of a certain finite nature unmixed with some other," for there is always "turbulence" contributing to the "erasure of contour" producing a "detour" that breaks apart any semblance of closed pattern, shape, and order and displaces any "essential form" producing "a line emanating from lines." Thus the fold "moves between" established oppositions (matter and soul, the facade and closed room, outside and inside)—"a virtuality that never stops dividing itself."

The fold, like the rhizome, becomes a way of rethinking westness as a series of discourses "tucked inside" the United States as local color, regional interest, and mythic wonderland that "spills onto the outside," overflowing beyond these limits in multiple ways. From within the Americas westness is folded into the lives and cultural politics of "people in motion": races, migrants, minorities who traverse its establish "surface" and inscribe alternative stories upon it, enfolding them within the existing folds: "It radiates everywhere, at all times, in the thousand folds of garments that tend to become one with their respective wearers, to exceed their attitudes, to overcome their bodily contradictions," "flow *out of the frame* . . . it does not suffice to contain the mass that *spills over* and passes up above" (emphasis added).[126]

The rhizomatic, folded West I explore here is just such a "multiple fabric" whose many voices and "lines" cannot be framed or contained in a single uniformity or "point," for the rhizomatic, folded critical process

actively dismantles such processes in favor of dispersion and differen-
tial relations. Thus the West is less a distinct and definable location, a
region or geographic space, than "an itinerary . . . a series of encounters
and translations," and in exploring its many rhizomatic traces I will be
drawn toward metaphors of mobility—travel, diaspora, migration, flow,
borderlands, hybridity, and transnationalism—all of which are problematic for the reasons I have started to indicate above.[127] This book,
therefore, is transmotional "route work" following connections, trails,
traces, pathways, and echoes, peeling back the layers of a complex, un-
ending palimpsest, following glints and glances, joining and departing
from dialogues, but above all, attempting to reflect upon and examine
the presence of westness in its various, complex forms of mobility as it
has traveled globally resting in certain forms, mutating into others, and
disrupting still more.[128]

Global West: A New Architecture for Area Studies?

Doreen Massey's essay "A Global Sense of Place," written in Mexico City
in 1991, offers an important rethinking of "locality" (or region) in which
Massey argues for a "progressive" rather than reactionary and containing definition. Similar to Gerald Vizenor's plea for "transmotion" in
Fugitive Poses and Deleuze's interest in rhizomatic space, Massey argues
that places such as the West should not be "gridded" off and defined
by "boundaries" ("divisions which frame simple enclosures") creating
something "stable, coherent, uncontradictory," distinguishing "between an inside and an outside," "us" and "them," but instead should
be viewed as "processes" constructed out of "the juxtaposition, the intersection, the articulation, of multiple social relations [and] . . . riven
with internal tensions and conflicts." Place is not defined by its boundaries, its "long internalized history," and its stability, but is rather "constructed out of a particular constellation of social relations, meeting and
weaving together at a particular locus . . . articulated moments in networks of social relations and understandings . . . constructed on a far
larger scale than what we happen to define for that moment as the place
itself. . . . And this in turn allows a sense of place which is extroverted,
which includes a consciousness of its links with the wider world, which
integrates in a positive way the global and the local." Rejecting the root-

edness of "some long, internalized history," Massey favors a progressive "extroverted" sense of place unthreatened by its connections beyond itself, what she terms "a global sense of the local, a global sense of place." Indeed, in her latest book she sounds increasingly Deleuzian, stating that space is "the sphere of possibility of the existence of multiplicity in the sense of contemporaneous plurality . . . in which distinct trajectories coexist . . . the sphere . . . of coexisting heterogeneity."[129]

Arjun Appadurai takes up this argument, making the distinction between "trait" and "process" geographies, defining the former as a way of seeing "areas" based on "geographical, civilisational, and cultural coherence" using an agreed-upon and normalized list of "traits" (values, languages, material practices, ecological adaptations, marriage patterns etc.), which tend, therefore, "to see 'areas' as relatively immobile aggregates of traits, with more or less durable historical boundaries and with a unity composed of more or less enduring properties."[130] In terms of the American West, it is noticeable that Turner embodies in the final section of his frontier thesis just such a list of "traits" that together forged "the American intellect" from which the American people have "taken their tone": "coarseness and strength . . . a cuteness and inquisitiveness . . . practical, inventive turn of mind . . . masterful grasp of material things . . . restless, nervous energy . . . dominant individualism."[131] In contrast, Appadurai suggests an alternative "architecture for area studies" based on "process geographies" and determined by "large scale and shifting" forces of "action, interaction, and motion—trade, travel, pilgrimage, warfare, proselytisation, colonisation, exile, and the like." So, rather than seeing the West as a fixed, permanent geographical and ideological fact, constructed of "apparent stabilities," we see it always as problematic, variable, and processive. In other words, the gridlike literal and metaphoric patterns of mapping, perceiving, and representing are in need of constant rearrangement and dismantling to examine how in a changing, globalized world an "area" (such as the West) has been reimagined by disjunctive activities and "processes" of "migrants, media, capital, tourism" and other "imagineers" of contemporary culture. Given the rhizomatic "flows" of media discourses across national boundaries, my contention here is, like Appadurai's and Massey's, that "areal worlds [like the West] are globally produced," consumed, exchanged, and circulated, and so it is vital to examine alternative, "outside" perspectives in order to create "a critical dialogue between world pictures" that allows for such foldings.[132] As the philosophy and architectural and art theory used earlier reminds us, any grid or frame "only exists within a larger virtual complexity that exceeds it" and always has, and therefore there is the potential for "reframing" as the grid is reformed in its relations with the "virtual" that exists beyond it.[133] In this sense, as Grosz writes, "the outside is a *virtual* condition of the inside," folded together as the thought/seen and the unthought/unseen, one stretching and interconnecting with the other in a dialogic, interposed relationship.[134]

As I will discuss more later, Anzaldúa's notion of "nepantla" draws many of this introduction's points together, coming as it does "from outside as well as within the system" and representing an "overlapping space between different perceptions and belief systems . . . rendering the conventional labelings obsolete" because within it one is in a "liminal, transitional space, suspended between shifts, you're two people . . . where the outer boundaries of the mind's inner life meet the outer world of reality . . . a zone of possibility." Nepantla is a form of "virtuality," in the sense suggested above, on the edge of the grid where, she argues, "you are exposed, open to other perspectives, more readily able to access knowledge derived from inner feelings, imaginal states, and outer events, and to 'see through' them with a mindful, holistic awareness." Despite Anzaldúa's spiritual tone, her notion of nepantla demands and facilitates critical reflection because it is always a "site of transformation . . . where different perspectives come into conflict and where you question the basic ideas, tenets, and identities inherited from your family, your education, and your different cultures." Thus, in a comment that relates her work back to the "schisis" of Koolhaas and Deleuze and to the doubling of Gilroy and Giles, she claims that "Living between cultures results in 'seeing' double, first from the perspective of one culture, then from the perspective of another. Seeing from two or more perspectives simultaneously renders those cultures transparent. Removed from that culture's center, you glimpse the sea in which you've been immersed but to which you were oblivious, no longer seeing the world the way you were enculturated to see it." In these words, from her own position both "inside" and "outside" the West (as Chicana, feminist, lesbian), Anzaldúa restates the purpose of this book: to see "double" by using texts that remove us from the dominant center so that we might glimpse alternative, critical, transformative, "virtual" (unthought/unseen) perspectives that help reshape and question persistent grids of representation. As she says, "yesterday's mode of consciousness pinches like an outgrown shoe," so surely it must be time to resize and move on.[135]

1. TOWARD AN EXPANDED CRITICAL REGIONALISM
Contact and Interchange

Region is a mental act
and region is real, at one and the same time.
Patricia Nelson Limerick

The best place to find new landscapes is in the West.
John Brinckerhoff Jackson

Regional Worlds

As discussed in the introduction, a central concern of this book is how to think differently about the American West, to decentralize and dislocate the ways it has so often been considered, even among so-called revisionist writers and scholars, so that we might see westness as part of a larger system of discourse, beyond the national imaginary, pointing in many directions at once. As I have written elsewhere, "The American West is more than geography, it is a complex, unstable signifier that has been given meaning by those who have lived within it, passed through it, conquered it, settled, farmed, militarized, urbanized, and dreamed it," but beyond even this, it is clearly a global presence too.[1] At the end of an essay in which he seeks to explain western regionalism as changing and "layered," Clyde Milner claims that "the best sustained understanding of western selfhood will start at bedrock, in a local context," as if to reiterate and promote traditional ideas of "insider" knowledge and "roots" critiqued by the likes of Paul Gilroy and Paul Giles (see introduction).[2] However, what of the stories from elsewhere, from beyond the bedrock? In fact, what could this actually mean in the context of the West with its patterns of migration, change, and discontinuity, and of westness as a series of iconographies, discourses, and ideas? Although there might be a "mappable," gridded West defined by state and national borders that one could label as region, one often feels that such a process is too narrow and restrictive, excluding vital aspects of all that exceeded such contained definitions: the West "traveled" beyond the grids and maps of regionalism, state and nation, existing as real and imagined in the lives of many communities inside and outside the United States who had particular relationships to something they referred to as "western." A theme park, a tourist trip, a migrant plan, a movie, a song, an interior design, an architectural blueprint, a fashion statement, an advertising image, a novel, a painting, a photograph—any one of which might refer, in many differing ways, to the West's iconographies and ideologies. In all these western "exchanges" one can trace the mobilities of a transnationalism within which we have to examine and situate the regionalism of the West as it moves and transgresses its traditional boundaries. Traditional grids of representation that have so often defined and fixed the West, in Arjun Appadurai's words, "as relatively immobile aggregates of traits, with more or less durable historical boundaries and with a unity composed of more or less enduring properties," are tested, expanded, and even disrupted by such rhizomatic, traveling approaches to westness whereby ideas and concepts spill out and spread, making connections and disconnections, hinting and interrupting as much as concluding and closing.[3] Thus the texts considered in this book are in their different ways "border discourses," to borrow a phrase used and defined by German critic Gunter H. Lenz: "Conceived from both an intracultural and an intercultural perspective" and able to "address in a self-critical, self-reflexive manner the question of 'authoring,' and of 'authorizing' cultural critique; the problem of 'speaking for others' or of your own 'group'; the logic of multiple subjects; and the dialogics of competing critical discourses."[4]

The border discourses in this book relate, of course, to a particular region—the West—and so, to an extent, this project is about regionalism and about how considerations of region might be mobilized in different ways in the postmodern, global age. The West, however, has never been simply a geographical region contained by traditions and customs; it is instead a complex construction, an architecture, designed and built by the intersection of discourses from many interested parties, refracted through time, space, and nations. For example, Rob Wilson argues that if one reimagines the American Pacific outside the "historical project of Manifest Destiny," then one dissociates the American West from projections of utopian desire and sees it instead as a "switching point between the mobile discourses of migration from Asia and the Americas where, according to perspective, east can become west and vice versa."[5] The West—as westness—exists in multiple, international spaces and texts, and is commented upon, used, and interpreted in all manner of different ways that challenge any simple gridded notion of regionalism. As Stephanie Foote writes of literary regionalism, "focusing on the shifting historically contingent category of the local can help us find in regional writing an important, still-vital model for understanding cultural difference in the early twentieth-first century." She goes on to argue that rather than simply "shoring up or abetting" the nostalgic and sentimental associations of regionalism, regional writing (or, I would argue, other forms of representation) "radically reconfigures it, making it as contentious as 'the real' or 'the natural.'" Regionalism, in other words, could always function from the "outside," representing "non-normative communities or cultures" and mediating between the fascination with lost, rural, "residual" culture and the simultaneous interest in emergent ones. On first impressions this process, according to Foote, became symptomatic of much regional writing, reconciling such tensions and, therefore, appearing conservative, as though balancing out these different worlds. Of course, as we will see, a reconfigured regionalism might indeed articulate these tensions as contested, productive, and unfinished, placing more emphasis on the borders between the emergent and residual than on the quest for reconciliation or the refuge in the one over the other. Thus mediation is not the same as negotiation, and a more critically aware version of regionalist sensibility is as much concerned with negotiations amid complex spaces as it is with any absolute point of coherence within a national narrative framework or grid. As many have recognized, "Regional writing is therefore one of the first genres that tried to understand the nation itself as an ideologically inflected cultural construct, and that tried to supplement the official story of what counted as American by providing 'unofficial' histories of the nation's inhabitants."[6]

New Western history represented a clear exercise in aspects of regionalism. As Patricia Nelson Limerick puts it, "region permitted one to adjust and train one's vision in a way that uncovered connections, ties, and relations." In the effort to make these broader relationships, however, she admits that any region is more the creation of "human thought and behavior" than of nature, and in the West this results in a constant struggle with "myths, dreams and stereotypes" that have provided its core meanings for generations. Her hope was that regional history framed in this way might rekindle an "inclusiveness," a "common ground" that had always been part of the western experience for her but had been lost in the push to nationhood and the perceived unity around certain values, traditions, and assumptions. She adds, most significantly, "With particular people in particular places brought into focus, one could build one's units of generalization outward, from place to subregion to region to nation to hemisphere to planet." Crucially, Limerick knows that region is not contained by the boundaries of place, but its study can relate directly and vitally to the comprehension of a wider world. Although she has intimated the international ("hemispheric") significance of the West, she only concludes that "The word *West* . . . is finally a piece of national common property" rather than developing the process in which it rolls "outward," becoming, as I would claim, "international" property.[7]

The reframed region/regionalism I intend to extend here is an international, living mix of voices, uncontained, problematic, contradictory—a series of "border discourses" that articulates the contemporary West as it "works" inward and outward. This is a redefinition of regionalism that refuses to get to the border (of region or nation) and turn back, to simply close up on itself in some homely and familiar act of territorialization, as if protecting itself from the wider world beyond, but one that also deterritorializes and directs us simultaneously outside itself to the postregional and the postwestern. The capacity I envisage here is for regionalism (westness) to disrupt its oft-discussed, conventional sheltering role and to fold outward, engaging with its own assumptions and defining principles, becoming a reinvigorated "critical (cultural) regionalism" that enables us to comprehend the West as a complex process, akin to Massey's or Appadurai's sense of the global local, continually being constructed, deconstructed, and reconstructed in multiple spaces.

Appadurai's Regional Worlds Project suggests this productive tension between "region" and "world" in its determination to create a new approach to area studies deemphasizing the durable "traits" of coherence and stability while stressing "process geographies" defined by travel, trade, diaspora, pilgrimage, warfare, colonization, and exile.[8] Appadurai's work interconnects with the aims of this project, arguing that we live in a "world of flows" characterized by "objects in motion . . . ideas and ideologies, people and goods, images and messages, technologies and techniques," while apparently stable objects, at closer inspection, are merely "our devices for handling" the flux. The nation-state is the example of such a "handling device" providing a sense of stability to set against a globalizing world where all the flows are "not coeval, convergent, isomorphic, or spatially consistent" but rather characterized by their "relations of disjuncture"—that is, they have "different speeds, axes, points of origin and termination, and varied relationships to institutional structures in different regions, nations, or societies."[9] My own sense of westness is that it flows in this disjunctive manner in and out of different structures and communities, being used, adjusted, celebrated, and critiqued in diverse ways across what Appadurai elsewhere terms "ethnoscapes . . . mediascapes . . . technoscapes . . . finanscapes . . . and ideoscapes."[10] Appadurai's "new architecture for area studies" rejects "rooted" notions of nationhood and region, preferring instead "process geographies" that are "routed," contingent, and mobile, formulating an alternative regionalism "viewed as initial contexts for themes that generate variable geographies, rather than as fixed geographies marked by pregiven themes." Central to his altered regionalism, and something missing in Limerick's comments above, is the recognition that "the capability to imagine regions and worlds [via migrants, media, capital, tourism, etc.] is now itself a globalized phenomenon."[11] As the Regional Worlds Project puts it, such process geographies allow a conceptualization of the world "not as an aggregation of fixed, historically stable, geographically bounded civilizations, but rather as a cross-cutting map of diasporic identities, translocal interactions and large-scale resource flows."[12] Thus new "regions" are created with different boundaries that include, but are not limited to, geographical space, for they overlap and contradict one another as multilayered webs of power, interaction, and imagination (like Appadurai's multiple "scapes"), constantly mobile and changing. Seen in these terms, the American West can be reconceived within a "new cultural architecture of area studies" proposed in this book: fluid, imaginative, transnational, global, regional—but regional in the critical mode that Appadurai touches on here and which I will define further in the next section.

45

Toward Critical Regionalism

Architecture once again provides a way of examining some of these ideas through Kenneth Frampton's influential essay "Towards a Critical Regionalism" (1983), which gave a focus to these debates about regionalism and offers a potentially productive framework for this study of westness. At the heart of Frampton's piece on architecture is a discussion of a tension between "universalization" (closely allied to what we might now term globalization) and the "local/regional," beginning with a long quotation from Paul Ricoeur in which a "universalized" world is spelled out: "the same bad movie, the same slot machines, the same plastic or aluminum atrocities." Ricoeur traces a "paradox" by which a nation wants to "root" itself in "the soil of its past" against colonialism, and yet, at the same time, it is expected to embrace a "scientific, technical, and political rationality" that seems to require the abandonment of "a whole cultural past." We have seen this dilemma at work in the American West's attachment to authenticity and the past (myths and all), rooted deep in the landscape itself, and paradoxically the rejection of those mythic imaginings in favor of the "real" and the "new." This desire for rootedness in some essential tradition and authentic, communal narrative, such as the frontier or the Wild West, is, after all, so often seemingly at odds with another desire to articulate a "routed" history of contact, cultural collision, and mobility. As Ricoeur defines the paradox, it is all about "how to become modern and to return to sources; how to revive an old, dormant civilization and take part in universal civilization." Although Ricoeur never directly discusses the West, these tensions seem apposite to a region whose relation to the nation and the world beyond has always been complex and difficult, torn between visions of authenticity (usually clouded by myth) and the rapidly changing present. The development of Frampton's ideas and their original location in the writings of Liane Lefaivre and Alexander Tzonis can be helpful in the further discussion of the West's position as a critical region in an era of globalized transnationalism.[13]

Frampton's essay became well known as part of Hal Foster's landmark book of essays *Postmodern Culture*, first published in 1983. In this context it argues that architecture is dominated by universalized, imposed styles

46

and a climate of spatial restriction, limited scope, and social control whereby assumptions about modern architecture and liberation are no longer tenable. Instead, Frampton claims, architecture "has to remove itself from both the optimisation of advanced technology and the ever-present tendency to regress into nostalgic historicism or the glibly decorative" and in this way forge "a resistant, identity-giving culture while at the same time having discreet recourse to universal technique." His project, critical regionalism, refutes conservative populism and sentimental regionalism and asserts "the hallmark of ambiguity" as a means of mediating the impact of "universal civilization with elements derived *indirectly* from the peculiarities of a particular place." This latter idea, like the phrase "critical regionalism" itself, is borrowed from Lefaivre and Tzonis, who first coined it in 1981. Imbued with "critical self-consciousness," their approach is not interested in reviving "a lost vernacular" with its echoes of compensatory idealism; rather, it functions through what Frampton calls "double mediation": "to 'deconstruct' the overall spectrum of world culture which it inevitably inherits" and "to achieve through synthetic contradiction, a manifest critique of universal civilization." Frampton's architectural examples, such as Utzon's Bagsvaerd Church, shift or "mediate" between styles, forming "conjunctions" of "rationality" and "arationality," the "regular grid" and "idiosyncratic form," standardized concrete and extravagant "patent glazing," and most clearly between the inside and the outside. The architecture exudes "multiple cross-cultural references" and, as with all these elements, constitutes a form of new regionalism that might indeed be "potentially liberative in and of itself since it opens the user to manifold *experiences*" (emphasis in original).[14] In a later version of the original essay, Frampton refers to this process as a dialogue across an "antithesis between rooted culture and universal civilization," suggesting a productive space in which the sentimental and nostalgic attachment to the region-as-authentic-past is interrupted by other forms from "outside."[15]

In their later work *Critical Regionalism: Architecture and Identity in a Globalized World* (2003), Lefaivre and Tzonis explain their choice of the term "regionalism" as a "tool of analysis" combined with the interrogative use of "critical" as a determined effort to ensure "the responsibility to define the origins and constraints of the tools of the thinking that one uses." However, they felt the older use of "regionalism" as "sentimental, prejudiced and irrational" too often resurfaced, and as a result their term was "misused" and "rather than being used critically . . . was being transported back to its obsolete, chauvinistic outlook." At this point in their text the footnote refers the reader to Frampton's essay, suggesting their doubts about his use of their term and his tendency (despite his intentions, I believe) to see modernism as beyond control and instead yearning for some premodern whole.[16] They might have also had in mind Catherine Slessor's book *Concrete Regionalism* (2000), which follows Frampton closely, asserting at one point that regionalism "is immutably rooted in the tangible realities of its situation," and elsewhere that "the truest and most seminal invention [in architecture] had regional roots."[17] Lefaivre and Tzonis constantly assert the need for critical approaches to regionalism, seeing its architectural forms (as its theories themselves), as does Foote, as selfreflexive and unsettling rather than reassuring or sentimental.

Frampton's attachment to authenticity is most evident in his attack on the "rapacity" of "apocalyptic . . . modernization" for eroding "the ground in which the mytho-ethical nucleus of a society might take root."[18] Fredric Jameson also critiques Frampton's "neoregionalism" as a "flight from the realities of late capitalism," which has destroyed regions through standardization, commodification, and rationalization. The vernacular regional then appears as a mere assertion of a lost world, a refuge from these forces instead of an engagement or dialogue with them (Frampton's stated intention). Jameson's major problem with Frampton's work is its reliance upon and elevation of (as Jameson sees it) pluralism and difference, concepts that Jameson, with his interest in a renewed totalization, ultimately sees as part of the "internal dynamics" of late capitalism rather than a bulwark against it. The post-Fordist economy with its tailored, postmodern marketing seems to fit perfectly into a "regionalist" model of plural and differentiated markets "adapting its various goods to suit those vernacular languages and practices," thus inserting the corporation into the very heart of the local and regional rather than in some way resisting it. For Jameson, therefore, the regional becomes the business of "global American Disneyland-related corporations, who will redo your own native architecture for you more exactly than you can do it yourself."

48

However, Jameson does concede that critical regionalism also presents the "possibility of inventing some new relationship to the technological beyond nostalgic repudiation or mindless corporate celebration."
And through such invention it has the "capacity to 'enclose' or to *reopen
and transfigure* the burden of the modern," and potentially "to fashion a
progressive strategy out of what are necessarily the materials of tradition
and nostalgia" (emphasis added). At the end of his essay Jameson does
remind the reader of the word "critical" in Frampton's critical regionalism, as if to resurrect some of the "invention" and "possibility" inherent in the work.[19] The idea that Frampton was defining a "distinctive regional culture," as Jameson suggests, misreads his work and loses sight
of its "anti-centrism" and its interest in "dialogically opposed values."[20]
Rather like Lefaivre and Tzonis's criticism of his "chauvinistic outlook,"
it may be that Frampton's essay simply loses sight of the "critical" in his
use of their terms, as Jameson suggests. Although uneven in its expression, Frampton's essay desires "the dialectical interplay between [uni-
versal] civilization and [local] culture" and does assert that this might
happen through "double mediation" and "interaction" whereby modern universalization is constantly interrupted and unsettled by what, in
one example, he usefully terms "a revealed conjunction between."[21] The
"conjunctural" denies the assertion of hierarchical order, of the dominant, universal form over the regional, and instead finds effective ways
to "mediate" (or "cross-fertilize," as Wilson calls it) between and across
forms—for example, by rejecting the "tabula rasa" of modernist sites
and instead working with the region and its history so that both become
"inscribed into the form and realization of the work."[22] This conjunctural process (referred to by Lefaivre and Tzonis as the "bridge") Frampton calls "in-laying" or "layering," whereby the site "has many levels of
significance . . . the prehistory of the place, its archeological past and its
subsequent cultivation and transformation across time," displaying all
the "idiosyncrasies of place . . . without falling into sentimentality."[23]
In these final points, despite his many critics, Frampton does present a
radical vision of critical regional space as a complex, layered, multiple,
and mobile concept comprising past, present, and future that opposes
any effort to reduce or limit its capacity through narrow definition or
"rootedness." In so doing his architectural ideas relate back to the intro-

duction's discussion of Koolhaas and Tschumi and their rejection of the grid as absolutely containing.

In fact, it is in Lefaivre and Tzonis's latest work that the possibilities of critical regionalism find their most helpful form and might be applied to this study of the American West. This is most noticeable in Lefaivre's "Critical Regionalism: A Facet of Modern Architecture since 1945," in which she very consciously constructs a history of the term beyond that already set out in Tzonis's "Introducing an Architecture of the Present: Critical Regionalism and the Design of Identity" (both in 2003). Tzonis's brief preface states the "potential" of a critical regionalist "method" to "fully understand the *limits and promise* of regional constraints" (emphasis added) and that this is reliant upon a rejection of any sentimental definition of regionalism and an equally assertive use of the "critical." The latter, says Tzonis, was a "Kantian concept," the "test of criticism," meaning here "a baring, exposing and evaluation of the implicit presuppositions of an argument, or a way of thinking." The marked emphasis of the critical is vital, and yet it is often overlooked, as we have seen, in discussions of what the terms and method of critical regionalism might mean. In effect, the implication here is that Frampton's more famous rendition of their idea was not true to this critical testing process and too often resorted to a sentimentalized version of "rooted" place as opposed to the "international/universal."[24]

In order to interrupt this tendency, Tzonis and Lefaivre want to "*reframe* regionalism," breaking down this sentimental, gridlike vision to reassert its more radical potential, by invoking the work of two Americans, Lewis Mumford and John Brinckerhoff Jackson (whose work I will consider later).[25] At the heart of this reframed regionalism is the desire to oppose "mindlessly adopting the narcissistic dogmas in the name of universality," to "value the singular," and to aim "at sustaining diversity while benefiting from universality." Through examining these American writers, these ideas of a reframed regionalism move closer to a western focus. Mumford, writing in 1947, opposed the International Style of architecture with "regional" alternatives from the San Francisco Bay Region School of Architecture and spoke of their "from the ground up" approach, rather than an elitist "top-down," imposed one. In one phrase, Mumford suggests another link to Jackson and others we will

consider when he attacks the gridlike hold of modernism, with its regularized patterns and striated space, and praises instead reframed regionalism's ability to "liberate us from the tyranny of the rectangular form."
Even earlier in his career, Mumford, in a similar vein, had written of the
"imperial façade" of the Beaux-Arts tradition as the "very cloak and cos-
tume" of an "imperialist approach to the environment" still lingering
in the United States. The "imperial" here is the imposition of a dominant style, a kind of "gridded" pattern that took no notice of site, local
conditions, or human use. Traditional regionalism for Mumford was a
"blind reaction" to modernism and technology, an "aversion from what
is" rather than "an impulse toward what may be."[26] Mumford's essays,
according to Lefaivre, were critical not only of this imposed, "imperial,"
or later International Style but also of traditions of romantic regionalism itself, refusing to entirely reject universal, global connections and
instead "infus[ing] [regionalism] with a notion of relativity," regarding
it as "engagement with the global, universalising world rather than by
an attitude of resistance," becoming "a constant process of negotiation between the local and the global on the many different issues that
traditionally made up regionalism."[27] His preference is for reciprocity,
seeing culture as a contact zone, where the "regional" "has contributed
something of value to the universal movement . . . without forfeiting its
. . . characteristics [and] can absorb something in return . . . a continuous give and take."[28] In this Mumford goes back to the origins of critical philosophy in Kant and the Frankfurt school, their refusal to accept
received truths, and their "constant self-criticism and rethinking of its
own categories of cognition," representing (like Jackson) a true critical
regionalist whose regionalism "evolved from an internal, self-directed
criticism."[29] However, as I will argue throughout this book in relation to
my rethinking of the American West, a further, extended form of critical
regionalism must also evolve from an "external" criticism and encounter—so that an outside perspective supplements the best traditions established by the likes of Mumford and Jackson.

In *The South in Architecture* (1941), Mumford wrote: "It would be useful
if we formed the habit of never using the word regional without mentally
adding to it the idea of the universal—remembering the *constant contact
and interchange* between the local scene and the wide world that lies be-

yond it" (emphasis added).[30] Thus, more than forty years before Mary Louise Pratt wrote of the contact zone, Mumford articulated regions as complex contact zones whose many overlapping elements were all to be considered crucial to the dynamic formations of space and place. However, he rejects attempts to duplicate and imitate the past, "equating the search for authenticity and the return to one's roots as an exercise in anachronism," and wrote that "Our task is not to imitate the past, but to understand it, so that we may face the opportunity of our own day and deal with them in an equally creative spirit." In addition, sounding very much like Paul Gilroy, Mumford was uneasy with regionalism's idea of community as "mono-cultural, based on tribal associations, blood ties and an attachment to a soil that was exclusively native." Instead, he "espoused the view that community could be something multicultural," like that he envisioned for Honolulu: "a significant experiment in the hybridisation of cultures which perhaps will mark the future of human society; it is a miniature experimental station."[31] Ultimately, Mumford saw regionalism as critically engaged with the wider world:

> [E]very regional culture necessarily has a universal side to it. It is steadily open to influences that come from other parts of the world, and from other cultures, separated from the local region in space or time or both together. . . . To make the best use of local resources, we must often seek help from people or ideas or technical methods that originate elsewhere. . . . As with a human being, every culture must both be itself and transcend itself; it must make most of its limitations and must pass beyond them; it must be open to fresh experience and yet it must maintain its integrity.[32]

Lefaivre is quick to see the significance of this position, as Mumford appreciated the need for "mutually beneficial negotiating" between region and globe rather than an "adversarial stance" that had long been the tradition in regionalist thought. Lefaivre argues that Mumford's preferred approach is one of "engagement and inbetweening," bringing together ideas, traditions, and styles in negotiated dialogue to create a "multidimensional, multi-functional, interdisciplinary approach . . . involving identity, sustainability, memory, community in a globalizing, post-colonial and fragmented world" better suited to the postwar experience.

Of course, Lefaivre goes on to demonstrate how many of Mumford's groundbreaking ideas have since been echoed and developed by contemporary critical regionalists within architecture, such as Richard Neutra, Alvar Aalto, and Paul Rudolph, but all the time her approach (like Mumford's) is to see building and design as part of a wider response to global issues and tensions.[33] In fact, as Cheryl Temple Herr puts it, "critical regionalism refers less to a specific kind of building than it does to the resistances that architecture can offer to a totalising environment."[34]

In a project similar to that of Lefaivre and Tzonis, Catherine Slessor's *Concrete Regionalism*, despite its occasional lapses into overstated nostalgia for regional authenticity and roots, expresses what Slessor terms "resonant regionalism." This is best defined as closer to Lefaivre's work and to the idea of a constantly developing critical regionalism concerned with both roots and routes, or what Lefaivre calls "engagement and in-betweening." To modify a quotation from Slessor, critical regionalism might be usefully redefined as drawing "upon indigenous wisdom without resorting to pastiche, penetrating beyond the superficial features of regional style to explore a more resonant architecture rooted [and, I would add, routed] in immemorial responses to landscape and climate."[35] Or as Lucy Lippard puts it in *The Lure of the Local*, "Good regional art has both roots and reach."[36]

Thus the regional travels outward and inward, from what Frampton calls "cultural interstices," between the universal and the local, echoing ideas discussed in the introduction that emphasize the significance of "looking both ways" and appreciating the special angle of critique that emerges from such a "third space." Temple Herr terms it "a bifocal viewpoint" created from "the space-between, interbeing, dialogism, nomadic space, intertextuality, hybridity, the assemblage," defining zones "where unexpected and unmapped things can occur." Invoking postcolonialist theory and Deleuze and Guattari, she correctly claims that "individual regions encompass multi-layers that host indigenous meanings, imported materials, and varieties of interconnection," existing as "smooth spaces" amid "striated" or bureaucratized zones. It is in this complex "reframed regionalism," this "layering and thresholding of cultures," that we find, she argues, "the existence of a dialogue with other regions outside our own" that may provide a "foothold for our collective entrance into the future."[37] It is from these histories of new regionalist thought that we might continue to reimagine the West as part of a wider, interlocking discursive system.

Critical Regionalism, Western Studies, and Beyond

My intention in examining at length the genealogy of critical regionalism as an architectural concept is to borrow it, apply it, and develop it as a further gesture toward Appadurai's "new architecture for area studies" discussed in the introduction—that is, to be critical with and of regionalism (the normative mode used to define texts of the West) and to employ and extend this concept as a means of interrogating how and why westness is used regionally, nationally, and internationally. Edward Soja suggested in his 1989 *Postmodern Geographies* that critical regional studies had the potential to open up whole new knowledges because it was flexible and willing to "try new combinations of ideas rather than fall back to old categorical dualities."[38] He explored this via the West in his own work, examining the city of Los Angeles, the epitome of what he has termed the "regionality of cityspace."[39] Krista Comer took up the challenge of "new regionalism" in her *Landscapes of the New West* (1999), seeing it as engaged with modernism and postmodernism in a variety of critical dialogues, and has developed this in her later work. She writes that regionalist practices such as literature perform the "role as a kind of 'under' literature—under the sign of the nation, subsumed within or by 'larger,' more central, or seemingly efficacious discursive fields." Comer too wants to innovate "the category and analytic practice of regionalism" so that it does not simply reinforce the nation-state's values but may, indeed, open up "more postnational and transnational" perspectives. In order to do this, she believes it is vital that American regional studies "goes global" and reckons with and displaces "the centrality of the nation-state in accounts of US cultural production."[40] At this point it is worth recalling Mumford's statement that "it would be useful if we formed the habit of never using the word regional without mentally adding to it the idea of the universal—remembering the *constant contact and interchange* between the local scene and the wide world that lies beyond it."[41] In her latest work, Comer begins to chart an updated version of critical regionalism applied to the field of cultural studies whereby the radical potential of region is employed to interrogate universalized norms and assumptions through asserting "constant contact and interchange between the local scene and the wide world that lies beyond it." As she asks specifically about western studies, echoing the ideas of Paul Giles discussed earlier, "what if 'the West' were *not* about America"—that is, if its narratives were not always telling the nation's story (Manifest Destiny, progress, rugged individualism, frontier, entrepreneurialism, etc.), imbued with what Alison Calder calls "inside knowledge," and endlessly refetishizing the national imaginary as exceptionalist, but were read differently, across traditions, to tell complex, multiple stories and to redraw that region's political maps?[42] Again, as Comer puts it, echoing Lefaivre and Tzonis, "suppose that critics *reframed regionalism*," and her example is to think of the American Southwest as signifying Greater Mexico, therefore undermining established "national" boundaries with "transnational" gestures and connections.[43]

Thus reading the West does not simply sustain established myths or conform to regional or intranational debates but rather spills over and beyond those boundaries, moving off in different, multiple directions from this distinct regional space. Picking up on Calder's phrase, I see this new critical regionalism as having to assert "outside knowledge" too, defining "westness" as rhizomatic once freed from the "normalized" interpretative use that dictates the West as only about the United States—"America only more so." Indeed, what Comer reminds us about the nature of the regional (following Limerick) is that it was always already the site of encounters, a mixed economy of histories and traditions, a multilayered and complex space. As Lippard puts it, "Each time we enter a new place, we become one of the ingredients of an existing hybridity, which is really what all 'local places' consist of. By entering that hybrid, we change it; and in each situation we may play a different role."[44]

Following in a similar-vein to Appadurai's Regional Worlds Project discussed earlier, "region" (or "area") has to be revised as a "process geography" rather than a cluster of cartographic materials so that "roots" (of the local, the placed, the regional as conventionally drawn) become more intimately connected to "routes" (of mobility, encounter, and travel). Indeed, it is in the tensions between these processes that we might understand a *reframed* critical regionalism and employ it productively to examine how and why the West (as region *and* more-than-region) functions as real and imagined space, crisscrossing cultural boundaries. This shift within western studies might be paralleled to another course being undertaken (or debated) in American studies over the last ten years, variously referred to as "worlding," "dislocating," "globalizing," "critical internationalism," and "critical transnationalism." Critical internationalism, for example, has been defined as "a conceptual orientation that resituates the United States in a global context on a number of terrains simultaneously," and it has most often produced work focusing "on difference, multiculturalism, and transnational flows of people, products, capital, and ideas." Despite this intention, as Jane Desmond and Virginia Dominguez point out, the tendency has been for there to remain an "inward orientation," avoiding comparative, cosmopolitan studies from "outside," and therefore unwilling to create the necessary "critical interface."[45] John Carlos Rowe took up this argument in his collection *Post-Nationalist American Studies* (2000), claiming that a viable approach would be not just to encourage "outside" perspectives but to define American studies as a "negotiation among local, national, and global frames of analysis that seeks its justification neither in objective and progressive historical processes of globalization nor in implicit celebrations of the local and the national."[46] Once again, it is noticeable how much Rowe's comments echo Lefaivre and Tzonis's definition of Mumford's reframed regionalism as "a constant process of negotiation between the local and the global on the many different issues" and, as with the latter, reject any neat either/or choice between global and local.[47] In both critical positions, what is emphasized are nuanced readings of how the local and the global interconnect and deviate under conditions of difference and different conditions, thus reformulating regionalism as a contact zone where "disparate cultures meet, clash, and grapple with each other often in highly asymmetrical relations of domination and subordination . . . as they are lived out across the globe today." Thus even where the relations of power are asymmetrical, contact takes many complex forms, such as transculturation and hybridity that emerge from the "interactive, improvisational" nature of encounter.[48] With such a layered reconfiguration of what regionalism might be and do, one can see how it might become (as

Comer hopes) a more radical tool for reassessing postnational identities. Indeed, to return to Rowe's work, it is from this use of the contact zone that he is able to move toward a description of what he terms "new intellectual regionalism" (based for him in universities), which pays close attention to local issues and community differences and comes out of and is aligned with other "new regionalisms established by different demographics, ethnicities, and global economic and cultural affiliations."[49] These definitions point toward this new regionalism as occupying an important critical space between established frameworks, a "curious liminality" for Comer, an "intersection point for deconstructions of any assumed universalism" for Dick Ellis, well placed to intervene in debates over globalization.[50] Thus, out of such a close, sensitive, and open understanding of the regional/local, with all its contact zone complexities, Rowe, like Comer and Ellis, sees the possibility of a greater "internationalization" of American (or western) studies that would "avoid the one-sided, often neo-imperialist cosmopolitanism of an earlier American Studies."[51]

Such a shift must, of course, be vigilant about thinking only in terms of the influence and impact of America on global events, that is, of thinking about a one-way Americanization process as the key to a widening of American studies. Similarly, one should guard against seeing America and the West only from within—a kind of "interior regionalism," as David Wrobel has termed it—and ensure that the "exterior" perspective is also considered.[52] I would agree with Gunter Lenz, who demands instead a "dialogic notion of cultural critique and of inter-and post-national American Culture Studies" that would be comparative, placing emphasis upon the multiple exchanges among and across cultures and how these work to alter and disturb existing definitions.[53] In this manner, regions like the West are viewed as formed by a network of discourses perpetually constituted and reconstituted not only regionally or nationally but also internationally and transnationally. Martin Heidegger uses the idea of region in ways that might be useful to this proposed expanded critical regionalism, for in trying to comprehend the complexities of thought, his essay "Conversation on a Country Path about Thinking" defines "region" and "regioning" as "an abiding expanse which, gathering all, opens itself, so that in it openness is halted and held, letting everything merge in its own resting," where "rest is the seat and reign of all movement." In these contradictory, challenging processes and op-positions—abiding/expanse, gathering/opening, openness/halt, rest/movement—Heidegger suggests the selfsame possibilities of critical regionalism as a conceptualization of tensions that constantly challenge us to think differently about the relations *between*.[54]

Thirdspace and John Brinckerhoff Jackson's Critical Regionalism

Near the end of *Postmodern Geographies*, Edward Soja argues for the ben-efits of critical regional studies as an approach to the changing relations among the urban, the national, and the global, claiming it operates with openness, flexibility, and an "inclination to try new combinations of ideas rather than fall back to old categorical dualities."[55] In the remain-ing two chapters of that book he develops a critical regional approach to the analysis of Los Angeles that he later extends in both *Thirdspace* (1996) and *Postmetropolis* (2000). My purpose in this section is to examine how Soja's theory of thirdspace might help to uncover the critical regionalist credentials of an earlier, largely unrecognized figure, John Brinckerhoff Jackson. Recall that in their groundbreaking discussion of critical re-gionalism, Lefaivre and Tzonis selected Jackson and Lewis Mumford as their "pioneers." The concept of thirdspace has different histories, but it is most notably explicated in *Thirdspace: Journeys to Los Angeles and Other Real and Imagined Places*, where Soja traces the term's various uses across cultural and social studies.[56] His aim was to make the reader "think dif-ferently about the meanings and significances of space and those related concepts . . . place, location, locality, landscape, environment, home, city, region, territory, and geography."[57] This has always been a central concern of western studies too: rethinking western "spatiality" as na-ture and human nature in interaction and dialogue—always a complex, "real-and-imagined" spatiality, as Soja is quick to remind us.

As we began to examine in the introduction, thirdspace is a means of rethinking space in a transdisciplinary manner demonstrating "a grow-ing awareness of the simultaneity and interwoven complexity of the so-cial, the historical, and the spatial, their inseparability and interdepen-dence." Soja's radical postmodernism rejects the either/or perspective and recognizes instead a both/and logic that encourages new combinations alongside the mixing and hybridizing of thought and idea. It becomes an "invitation to enter a space of extraordinary openness, a place of *critical exchange* where the geographical imagination can be expanded to encompass a multiplicity of perspectives" (emphasis added). Thus the "spatial imaginary" (such as that of the West) is opened up by this process of critical exchange and interrogation, unfixed from its binary position through the intervention of a third perspective—"interjecting an-Other set of choices."[58] Soja calls this "critical thirding" whereby the two original positions are not dismissed but subjected to a creative and critical process of restructuring that allows for a more sensitive and complicated understanding of "expanded" space. Hence the assumed binary that space can only be categorized as either real or imagined, local or global, is interrupted, restructured by the concept of a thirdspace that is both real *and* imagined, local *and* global. Our experience of space, as in the American West, is a combination and mixture of these effects, an elaborate and perpetual crossing or dialogue between positions, as in the architectural theories of Lefaivre and Tzonis and Frampton discussed above. Borrowing heavily from Henri Lefebvre's *The Production of Space* (1974) and Michel Foucault's "Of Other Spaces" (1985–86), Soja is concerned with what he terms a "trialectics"—perceived, conceived, and lived space—which equates to spatial practice (material expression of social relations within a space), representations of space (conceptual abstractions that inform the configurations of space, such as geometry or the grid), and representational space (as imagined).[59] For Lefebvre such divisions were not separable but rather an "interweaving incantation" through which to comprehend the complex uses of space and to recognize their overlapping status.[60] It was a spatial response to the late 1960s, according to Soja, as people searched for alternative models for understanding society and saw spatial interaction as a relatively unexamined concept. Precisely because of this attention to multiplicity, to other spaces, and to their complex interrelations, thirdspace has also emerged as a concept useful to postcolonial critics like Homi Bhabha who seek a means to express hybridity as a process of identity and nation formation. In his 1990 interview "The Third Space," for example, Bhabha speaks of hybridity as "the 'third space' which enables other positions to emerge. . . . [It] displaces the histories that constitute it, and sets up new structures of authority, new political initiatives, which are inadequately understood through received wisdom." Importantly for Bhabha, such hybridity "bears the traces of those feelings and practices which inform it, just like a translation," and gives rise to "a new area of negotiation of meaning and representation."[61] Echoing Appadurai, Massey, and Gilroy, such definitions view cultural space as dynamic and processive, a complex mix of traces, translations, and negotiations that resists any simplistic conceptualization of how we relate to, organize, imagine, and use space. Out of these clusters of ideas and possibilities Soja formed his concept of thirdspace.

Although the American West is an immensely complicated and multiple cultural space, it has too often been defined by similar binary and reductionist grids of thought and image, expressing the region uncritically as myth and reality, true and false, utopia and dystopia, rural and urban, local and global, when, in fact, it has always existed as a blurred, contested zone, both region and more than region, national and international, imagined dreamspace as well as real, material space. Western studies have long sought to challenge such binary approaches by questioning defining texts like Frederick Jackson Turner's frontier thesis, by taking popular culture seriously, by exploring the "hidden histories" of race and gender, and by engaging with the complexities of border studies. Without doubt Soja's thirdspace as a tool of critical regionalism helps us to theorize these developments, linking western studies with many key movements in critical cultural studies but also, and in some ways even more importantly, linking these concepts back to earlier American predecessors.

In his history of thirdspace, Soja fails, unlike Lefaivre and Tzonis, to look closer to home and to go back beyond the late 1960s to the work of another cultural geographer, John Brinckerhoff Jackson, who, although born in France in 1909 and influenced by French geographers Deffontaines, de la Blache, Demangeon, and le Lannou, was an American who lived and worked for much of his life in the American West—New Mexico and California, specifically.[62] By working with and through critical regionalism and the concept of thirdspace, I will reassess the significance of Jackson to western studies in three ways relevant to the approaches adopted and developed throughout this book: first, as a trailblazer of new critical thought and transdisciplinary approaches, whose definition of culture opened up academic thought and practice before British cultural studies;[63] second, as a writer whose work within (primarily) western cultural geography prefigures the more fashionable theoretical ideas made famous by Soja's book;[64] and third, as a self-professed outsider whose perspectives (his "practice of the outside" as defined in the introduction) foreground later, more globalized and transnational concepts of western studies developing in the twenty-first century.

Jackson was a deliberately provocative and opinionated man whose essays range in tone from questioning and confrontational to ironic and deliberately obscure. In his first editorial for his journal *Landscape* (1951) he wrote: "Beyond the last street light, out where the familiar asphalt ends, a whole country waits to be discovered. . . . A rich and beautiful book is always open before us. We have but to learn to read it."[65] His attentiveness to local, everyday detail and his unwillingness to engage in academic jargon might make his work unfashionable today, but they should in no way detract from its significance and value. Jackson always understood that space was ideological and that in analyzing its uses, meanings, and designs one could understand the wider political climate of the age. Through the semiotics of the highway, the small town, the trailer park, and overlooked "everyday regionalisms," Jackson began to construct a very different and revealing commentary on America, and most often on the West, focusing on a vernacular landscape defined as "temporary, utilitarian, unorthodox" with no desire to "express universal principles," but rather as "contingent; it responds to environmental influences—social as well as natural—and alters as those influences alter."[66] Jackson's work engages constantly in a Soja-like restructuring of established thought and principle, interjecting some "Other" into fixed, universalized, and "binary" landscapes, and above all, I would suggest, through launching revisionist approaches to definitions of the American West from "outside" perspectives. This vernacular landscape of "in-between" is, in part, a practical exploration of thirdspace—or what Jackson termed "Landscape Three."

By deliberately selecting "spaces that have no documentation," Jackson undertook a radically alternative approach to cultural analysis that contrasted established, official, and dominant geographical views with the "other spaces of a humbler, less permanent, less conspicuous sort," or what he also called "minor and local episodes."[67] Jackson excavated a secret history of the West from the 1950s onward, looking at the overlooked in the manner of Foucault's genealogical history, while New Western history only began to adopt some of these approaches for its own purposes in the late 1980s.[68] Donald Worster has defined New Western history as putting the West "back into the world community, with no illusions of moral uniqueness," and "restor[ing] to memory all those unsmiling aspects that Turner wanted to leave out . . . a history beyond myth."[69] Indeed, just as New Western history took the Turner thesis as its starting point for a revision of a subtler and more complex reading of the West, Jackson looked beyond and behind the simplified overlays of cultural landscape, such as the grid system, to produce a richer and fuller comprehension of western space and its variant layers of meaning. To this end, Jackson's invocation of the "minor and local" relates his project in some respects with that of Deleuze and Guattari, who defined "minor literature" as "deterritorializing" because it used its language to displace or question dominant, normalized, and official "territory." Their spatial, geopolitical metaphors lend themselves to parallels with the scope and purpose of Jackson's efforts to rethink how cultural landscapes are perceived and used in the contemporary world. Inside the dominant "language" of landscape studies (in Jackson's case) there exists another "minor" (or local, regional, vernacular) one "within the heart of what is called great (or established) literature," which is articulated through "[w]riting like a dog digging a hole, a rat digging its burrow . . . finding . . . his own patois, his own third world, his own desert" in opposition to the dominant/official language that, sounding rather like the rhetoric of westward expansionism, colonizes a territory "along river valleys or train tracks; it spreads like a patch of oil."[70] In their most repeated example, Deleuze and Guattari cite Marcel Proust, who believed that writers "invent a new language within language, a foreign language, as it were. They bring to light new grammatical or syntactic powers. They force language outside its customary furrows, they make it delirious."

As we saw in the introduction, this "delirious outside" can be conjured through different disruptive energies, bringing a foreign "language" (which is always more than mere words) that "communicates with its own outside" and so gets "beyond" all the "furrows" of accepted and "taken-for-granted" cultural frameworks, becoming "the outside of [established, normative] language."[71] As the upper-class, Europe-educated American whose ideas seem to "shadow" the fashionable theories of the academy, Jackson saw himself as a kind of outsider, as Grady Clay has written: "Buried as he forced himself to become in his Western-Pioneer-Frontier explorations, he seemed always to carry with him the judgemental baggage of the Outsider."[72] From the "outside" of accepted academic frameworks, traditions, and language, Jackson created his own "minor" literature of cultural landscape studies, a story from below, from the roadside, from the small town and urban center that assembled an alternative iconography of the West resembling Deleuze and Guattari's own project, one that "brings together extracts . . . presents samples from all ages, all lands, and all nations . . . a collection of heterogeneous parts: an infinite patchwork, or an endless wall of dry stones (a cemented wall, or pieces of a puzzle, would reconstitute a totality). The world as a *sampling*: the samples ('specimens') are singularities, remarkable and nontotalizable parts extracted from a series of ordinary parts." Here is a "proto-postmodern" vision of the West without metanarratives of the frontier, Anglo-Saxon authority, nationhood, the geographical grid—a vision at whose heart lie "singularities" and "minor scenes . . . more important than any consideration of the whole."[73] Thus Jackson's writing about the roadside, for example, celebrates, in language reminiscent of postmodernism, its singular and transient styles as "conspicuous . . . exotic . . . lavish . . . [with] an indiscriminate borrowing and imitating" understanding its "festive purpose" to intervene and unsettle the conformist strictures of overblown modernism.[74] Predating the work of the *New Topographics* photographers (see chapter 5), Jackson's large collection of photographs charts his effort to record this alternative vision of the West and demonstrates his awareness of the liminal quality of landscape as a thirdspace where the local and global, urban and rural, real and imagined, blur into a dynamic and mobile spatiality. For example, in figure 2 see how Jackson captures the western landscape as a contact zone of nature and culture, speed and vision, a simultaneous glance forward and backward. The multilayered frame is typical of both

2. John Brinckerhoff Jackson, untitled (date unknown) (original in color).
Used courtesy of Paul Groth.

his written work and his illustrative images that challenge the eye, pushing it beyond, deterritorializing preconceived notions of region through
the interjection of "other" discordant, adjunctional spaces.

Predating Foucault's work of the 1970s on alternative histories, genealogy, and "subjugated knowledges," Jackson's new geohistory is precisely
"a complex system of distinct and multiple elements, unable to be mas-
tered by the powers of synthesis," consciously working at the margins of
accepted practice, giving voice to everyday artifacts and the structures of
a dynamic and changing social landscape with "a history of its own."[75]
Jackson defined his methodology, appropriately for someone working in
both words and photographs, as seeing "out of the corner of my eye," recording a mobile and evolutionary world to set against the "forces of stability" that constituted what he terms the rigidified "political landscape"
epitomized ultimately by the trope of the grid.[76] Jackson's work, like many
others I consider in this book, sees beyond the grid, "burrows" below its
dominant patterns of control and regulation, and confronts us with alternative, contradictory, and challenging perspectives that—to borrow an
image from one of his own essays—navigate a kind of "stranger's path"
into unexpected, unrecorded spaces "beneath the surface," bringing in
"new life" through being in "touch with the outside world."[77]

The Jeffersonian grid system, as I discussed in the introduction, forms a material and mental iconography in the West, representing what fellow geographer Wilbur Zelinsky called a "remorseless rectangularity," a material manifestation of spatial discipline, territorial control, and a metaphoric conceptualization of a particular way of thinking within boundaries.[78] Jackson's work opposes and challenges such impositions, both on the land and psychically, seeing them as "too rigid," "a web of inefficient, arbitrary boundary lines which handicap social or economic action" and "strangle" and "impoverish" the lives of those contained and defined by it (see figure 1).[79] Jackson points out with typical humor and irony that the grid was also an organizing principle whose deadly grip became the norm even for cemetery design.[80] Before Koolhaas, Jackson understood the grid's effects as political and ideological as well as geographical, "imprinted at the moment of conception on every American child" and constructing a spatial, national narrative: "It is this grid, not the eagle or the stars and stripes, which is our true national emblem," representing an "over-powering," "all-pervading sameness" and "ignoring all inherent differences."[81] It was an apparently innocent method of land division that Jackson defined ideologically as a metaphor for territoriality, social control, imaginative reduction, and standardization.[82] One of his students, John Stilgoe, wrote that "the grid objectified national, not regional order," an order that Jackson defined in terms redolent of Foucault and Deleuze and Guattari: "we had to discipline those meandering, unpredictable roads and paths and alleys and trails which had proliferated since the beginning of history and which, like a web of roots [rhizomes?], always threatened to heave up and ruin even the most carefully planned landscape of spaces." The "anarchic instinct" that Jackson celebrated opposed the dominant spatial narrative epitomized by the grid's "disciplining" of the land with "monotony," a process Jackson recognized mirrored in America's cold war cultural politics itself threatening a more mobile, differentiated, and democratic national identity.[83] In A Thousand Plateaus, published in French in 1980 (the year Jackson published The Necessity for Ruins), Deleuze and Guattari distinguish between "smooth space" and "striated space," defining the former as "vectorial, projective, or topological . . . occupied without being counted" and the latter as "State space" "counted in order to be occupied." The striated State space is "gridded" and movement within it is confined and limited by preset patterns, whereas "smooth space" is nomadic and open-ended, rich with connections and offshoots that intervene and traverse controlled spaces.[84] Very much in the spirit of postwar radicalism, Jackson's critique of a gridded western landscape, or "territorial space," rapidly emerging in the Sun Belt was linked to a rampant Taylorism/Fordism in which industrialization was defined by "standardization . . . training, supervision, and production planning," producing spatial values that translated into a wider, ideological framework Jackson saw mapped most clearly (and also potentially countered) in the West.[85]

To counter such "official" (gridded/striated) space, Jackson reinscribes it with the unrecorded and overlooked local and vernacular, with "in-between" thirdspaces that bring into the grid those excluded, hybrid elements to "reframe" or break out from its "inflexibility," altering perceptions by acknowledging the "imperceptible" and challenging the logic of regular, "linear" landscapes with irregular, folded, and rhizomatic spaces of "affect" and "sensation" (to borrow terms from Deleuze). Like Deleuze, who wrote his book on the baroque in 1988, Jackson often commented on his admiration for baroque forms over modernist geometry and shared some of his fascination with its "folds": "the Baroque trait twists and turns its folds, pushing them to infinity, fold over fold, one upon the other," wrote Deleuze.[86] Jackson compares the "real vitality" of roadside architecture and everyday experience in the West, "creating a dream environment" out of extravagant forms of lights and signs, to the baroque and its "capacity to transform."[87] As John Rajchman puts it, "the fold creates a different kind of 'flow'—the flow of an energy that the bounded spaces [like the grid] seems to be impeding, that is spilling over into its surroundings, interrupting the calm narrative of its context and so opening new readings in it."[88] In Jackson's essays and photographs there is often this precise sense of overspill, of both land and experience as a grid undergoing constant transformation as they engage with all that exists "outside."

Jackson's "interruptive" mappings of "baroque" western spaces transform perceptions of "normal," accepted landscapes and interfere with the "calm narratives" of official history and the boosterist mythmaking of State space that he termed in 1954 "the old reliable line of goods: Billy the Kid and Pioneer Day beards . . . Tombstone . . . and chuck-wagon suppers."[89] As Kathleen Stewart puts it powerfully, such "cultural productions that constitute an 'America' of sorts are frozen into essentialized 'objects' with fixed identities; a prefab landscape of abstract 'values' puts an end to the story of 'America' before it begins." Stewart's book (about southwestern West Virginia) uses an approach similar to that of Jackson's work (although she does not refer to Jackson at all) by claiming a new narrative space, another thirdspace—"a space on the side of the road" (her book's title)—through which to create "the site of an opening or reopening into the story of America." As in Jackson's work, this constitutes a reframing process, assaulting the material and metaphoric grid containing and constraining the landscape stories told and represented in the national imaginary, refiguring space (always mental and material) as open, dynamic, and "becoming" rather than fixed and closed.[90] Her concerns, like Jackson's, are to explore "minoritized spaces" and to provide "a kind of back talk to 'America's' mythic claims to realism, progress, and order," demonstrating and utilizing "a gap in the order of myth itself."[91] For Jackson, western cultural landscapes included truck stops, highway strips, and trailer parks as much as any mythic Ansel Adams landscape ("That school of 'timeless' photography," he called it) or grand historical monument, for in his reframed critical regionalism these coexisted dialogically within what he termed "cultural landscape"—the "living, pulsating, infinitely complicated organisms which man has made over and over again."[92]

Some thirty years before postcolonial critic Homi Bhabha's work on thirdspace as hybridity, Jackson recognized the hybrid potentiality (or "anarchic instinct") of the haphazard western roadside breaking up the dominant gridded forms, the metanarratives of the West, and with it the need for a "critical thirding" to unsettle such a dominant spatial imaginary. As Bhabha put it, with particular parallels to the significance of the West within the American cultural imagination, "Such an intervention quite properly challenges our sense of the historical identity of culture as a homogenizing, unifying force, authenticated by the originary Past, kept alive in the national tradition of the People."[93] In a 1980 essay, "Learning about Landscapes," Jackson prefigures the ideas already discussed of Appadurai, Gilroy, and Massey, arguing against seeing landscapes as essential, a habit too common to the American western tradition, refusing to see them "as profound expressions of ethnic or racial traits . . . [which] created a special breed of men and women with common psychological and physical characteristics . . . *rooted* in the land . . . [and providing] a cultural heritage that must at all costs be preserved intact."[94] Such a narrow and simplistic link between roots, land, and national identity, a dangerous "regional nationalism," reminded Jackson of the fascist ideology he had experienced during World War II, with its call to an "ancestral landscape" which he felt "did enormous damage."[95] In breaking this link between rootedness and exceptionalist, imperial identity, Jackson asserted instead an alternative multilayered, folded landscape and cultural identity of mobility, ambivalence, and hybridity—a complex thirdspace constantly capable of appropriating, translating, recombining, and creating things anew "in-between" fixed states.

Prefiguring the postcolonial and poststructuralist theories of Deleuze and Guattari, Clifford, Bhabha, Gilroy, Hall, Massey, and others, Jackson sought the "balance between the forces of stability and those of mobility," between roots and routes (or striated and smooth space), and in so doing created an early form of critical regionalism.[96] As stated earlier, Lefaivre and Tzonis invoked Mumford and Jackson, whose writings, they claim, "value the singular" and aim "at sustaining diversity while benefiting from universality."[97] Jackson had first read and been influenced by Mumford around 1928 at the University of Wisconsin, and later he contributed to *Landscape* magazine. Like Jackson, Mumford disliked the International Style of architecture, preferring more "regional" forms from the West Coast. Certainly, Mumford's notion of reframed regionalism "remembering the constant contact and interchange between the local scene and the wide world that lies beyond it" and able to "both be itself and transcend itself . . . [to] make most of its limitations and . . . pass beyond them . . . be open to fresh experience and yet . . . maintain its integrity" had a genuine impact on Jackson's thinking.[98] Jackson wrote, "the values we stress are stability and permanence and the putting down of roots and holding on," but there is another "tradition of mobility and short-term occupancy" that is equally powerful, particularly in the West. In between extreme opposite positions—of "roots" and "routes"—Jackson sought out an alternative space of "constant contact and interchange between the local scene and the wide world," or what he called "Landscape Three," created in dialogue with earlier versions of a static, rooted community ("homogenous and dedicated to a single purpose") and a vernacular, local one ("mixing all kinds of spaces and uses together").[99] Like Mumford (and Deleuze and Guattari), Jackson knew that "the two spaces in fact exist only in mixture: smooth space is constantly being translated, transversed into a striated space; striated space is constantly being reversed, returned to a smooth space."[100] Jackson saw a "danger" in "having two distinct sublandscapes, one dedicated to stability and place, the other dedicated to mobility," for as I have argued throughout, he saw the necessity of both folded into the creation of a dynamic, contested, living community. Rather than a simple regionalism "clinging to obsolete forms and attitudes" as a denial of process and history, Jackson's West had to be a reframed, critical regionalism, a third landscape "creating a new nature, a new beauty" out of the hybridized, diasporic space of crossing between the two, where there exists, according to Victor Burgin, a thirdspace, "neither within nor without; it was an experience of being between the two, a 'between' formed only in the simultaneous presence of the two."[101]

This "space between," echoing Stewart's "space on the side of the road," was most evident for Jackson in postwar western roadscapes like those often figured in his photographs, where messy contradictions— what he called "ambidexterity"—combined private and public, work and play, in a carnival of creativity and contact that expressed a hybrid spatiality mirroring his own hope for an America of "shared interests and mutual help" with an infinite capacity for regenerative energy and for "a new kind of history, a new, more responsive social order, and ultimately a new landscape."[102] Against the increasing standardization, corporatization, and McDonaldization of the highway "strip"—"being conveyed through a complex, well-ordered, admirable world" at "uniform speed"—Jackson saw the "immense potential" and "vitality" of a "mixed public" interacting in transient, heteroglossic, "new centers of sociability": "a jumbled reminder of all current enthusiasms—atomic energy, space travel, Acapulco, folksinging, computers, Danish contemporary, health foods, hot-rod racing, and so on."[103] This utopian hybrid roadscape is a powerful agent in Jackson's sense of and hope for (western) cultural identity, for it "prescribes no traditional behavior" but, along with the automobile, suggests a potential diasporic "meeting place" of "almost complete freedom" where the New West's "self-definition" is as plural as its varied landforms.[104]

This mobile thirdspace (what Deleuze calls "becoming") confronts the essentialist tendencies of a rooted sense of place where "land was the object men could best use in their search for identity" with an "existential" perspective "without absolutes, without prototypes, devoted to change and mobility." Emphasizing this as early as 1957, Jackson's work is scattered with words like "exchange," "trans-shipment," and "contact," emphasizing the West as a space of interaction and encounter where the "uniformity of taste and income and interests" is countered by "this ceaseless influx of new wants, new ideas, new manners, new strength." Jackson's vernacular, unofficial, anarchic roadscapes test and expand the monotonous grid (and its inherent ideology), spilling out in real and imagined directions denying all notions of metanarratival discipline and control and favoring "fragments of the whole—studies of micro-ecosystems, isolated structures and spaces of little significance."[105] These are deeply political ideas about class, control, and social organization sited in the various struggles over the use and representation of land.[106] Jackson wrote that by "political" he meant "those spaces and structures [like the grid] designed *to impose or preserve a unity and order on the land, or in keeping with a long-range, large-scale plan*" (emphasis added).[107] His work continually argues against such essentialist absolutism in favor of what Michel De Certeau would later call "making do" or practice—that is, how people use and affect space at close range.[108]

In his contribution to Michael Conzen's *The Making of the American Landscape* (1990), Jackson asserted that vernacular space "has no inherent [fixed] identity, it is simply defined by the way it is used," as distinct from "the middle-class or established concept," in which "each space is unique and can in fact affect the activity taking place within it."[109] Jackson contrasted "planned, specialized organization," defined by "inertia" and an inclination toward the "sterilizing of our roadsides" and the containment of both individual and community, with "fluid, undifferentiated spaces" and renewed, dynamic public spaces through which alternative values could be expressed and exchanged in an atmosphere of "gaiety and brilliance," in a "community where the streets are still common property, still part of the living space of every citizen."[110] Unsurprisingly, his idealized example of a kind of hybrid, democratic thirdspace was a western one, Santa Fe in 1954: "gregarious . . . hostile to . . . regulation," and full of "color and vitality." Such utopian spaces, Jackson believed, opposed the sterility of the grid and of more "regulated" communities and landscapes and made possible an "existential landscape, without absolutes, without prototypes, devoted to change and mobility and the free confrontation of men." In this vein, Jackson described landscape as a growing, evolving language, with "obscure and undecipherable origins . . . the slow creation of all elements in society . . . clinging to obsolescent forms, inventing new ones . . . the field of perpetual conflict and compromise between what is established by authority and what the vernacular insists upon preferring."[111]

Always ahead of his time, Jackson understood the global and the transnational relations inherent in the West, writing, for example, in 1954 of how the "Great social and economic forces, as remote in origin and as irresistible as the wind that blows incessantly from the west, helped form the human landscape of the region." This desire to bring the outside into the frame, in every sense, locates Jackson's work as both critical regionalist and decidedly postwestern, seeing the "shared [third] spaces" of the region as constructed by a set of complex discourses interrelated with global, transnational issues and representations.[112] His work is not, to borrow a phrase from Deleuze and Guattari, about "the revival of regionalisms," for how would that "serve a worldwide, transnational technocracy," since a minor language and literature must "travel," become "vehicular," and follow "creative lines of escape." The "regionalizing or ghettoizing" of a minor language has a limited political purpose, as in the tradition of the "local" within the American West, since it should always relate, at some level, with the global. The goal is, as Deleuze and Guattari put it, "to make use of the polylingualism of one's own language, to make a minor or intensive use of it, to oppose the oppressed quality of this language to its oppressive quality." Hence, the minoritarian (or regionalist-vernacular) impulse in this sense opposes reductionism or the "one single dream" and its "state . . . official

71

language" that "masters the signifier" and instead "create[s] the opposite dream . . . a becoming-minor."[113] This vital process of turning the "inside" and the "local" outward is not nationally defined but is rather transnational in the same way that the West is not only consumed and produced by westerners but also a globalized "language" whose "polylingualism" extends outside the United States through its various rhizomatic sproutings in other places, texts, and cultures. Thus the rupturing minor language of a critical regionalist like Jackson is always, by implication, transnational, intervening in the closed "single dream" of a particular, nostalgic, or official version of the West, interrogating and opening it up in new and challenging ways. This enacts Deleuze and Guattari's "method of the rhizome," "decentering [language] onto other dimensions and other registers" so as to keep it open, with "the idea perhaps com[ing] first from outside" as a kind of "stammering": "To be a foreigner, but in one's own tongue, not only when speaking in a language other than one's own. To be bilingual, multilingual, but in one and the same language, without even a dialect or patois. To be a bastard, a half-breed." Jackson's "stammering" disrupts the accepted norms of critical "language" about cultural landscape, "illegitimizing" the official, sanctioned stories and myths about western life and history, "uprooting them from their state as constants," providing the "cutting edge of deterritorialization," pushing language "toward the limit of its elements, forms, or notions, toward a near side or a beyond of language."[114] In deliberately and consistently unsettling established thinking and countering it with an askance view of cultural landscape, Jackson always looked "beyond" a defined West, both as local, vernacular culture and as national narrative, seeing its place within a wider transnational economy and an increasingly global world system.

Denise Scott Brown, whose work with Robert Venturi was directly and dramatically influenced by Jackson, certainly recognized this, believing that "cross-cultural crossfires" in Jackson's work were not to be "solved" but "lived with," "using its tension to foster creativity. . . . This . . . is what Brinck did. The skewed view—the view from the marginal position—can produce useful insights and an unusual vision."[115] Jackson's influence is clear in Robert Venturi, Denise Scott Brown, and Steven Izenour's Learning from Las Vegas, a work that takes seriously a western vernacular landscape and its relations with wider economic and cultural forces. From Jackson's "stammering" or "skewed" cultural architecture of the West we follow the "stranger's path," finding new ways of looking at accepted narratives, spatial or otherwise, differently, to question and challenge received wisdom, and to disrupt overly rigid systems of order (the inflexible grid).

The "practice of outside" cultivated by Jackson is a tool to get at the inside and alter it, to open up the discursive West and look into its spaces differently, enabling reflexiveness, greater understanding of its relationships to others and of its role—both real and imagined—within a wider global community. The grid, in other words, spills out further than the West, further than America. In rethinking this architecture one might pay more attention, as Jackson did, to the "in-between space" (thirdspace) as a mobile space of contact, translation, and negotiation in order to, as Bhabha put it, "open the way to conceptualising an international culture, based not on the exoticism of multiculturalism or the diversity of cultures, but on the inscription and articulation of culture's hybridity."[116] In his early rejection of essentialism and rooted identity and in his insistent excavation of the mobile, the marginalized, and the everyday, Jackson demonstrated a refreshingly open and outward-looking perspective that folded the local/vernacular West into a globalizing outside space. For living is ultimately, he wrote, "a dialog, not a monolog. . . . Existence means shared existence. We are all increasingly dependent on the presence of our fellow men—not necessarily on their approval."[117] It is only in mapping and "exploring this Third Space," as Bhabha says, and as Jackson's work consistently shows in his rethinking of western cultural landscapes, that "we may elude the politics of polarity and emerge as others of our selves."[118] In one startlingly Deleuzian description based on his favorite pastime of motorbiking, Jackson conveys an ideal, experiential relationship that tells us much, finally, about his critical method and its aim of transformation: "In short, the traditional perspective, the traditional way of seeing and experiencing the world is abandoned; in its stead we become active participants, the shifting focus of a moving, abstract world; our nerves and muscles are all of them brought into play. To the perceptive individual, there can be an almost mystical quality to the experience; his identity seems for the moment to be transmuted."[119]

As he imagines a perfect mobile space, Jackson articulates a sense of "becoming" through which individual, place, and idea are caught in the process of transformation, of being shifted away from the fixed, traditional perspective toward something else, something "outside" bound up intimately, almost mystically, with the "inside." From this vision—which is clearly, as so often in Jackson's work, an idealized one—he reaches for what others would, in very different ways, continue to chart and explore as variant, promiscuous forms and mutations of critical regionalism. He knew, as he wrote in 1976, that "A sense of the stream of time is more valuable and more poignant and engaging than a formal knowledge of remote periods. New things must be created, and others allowed to be forgotten." For in this dynamic flow he defined his vision both of the West and of "our common humanity: hard work, stubborn hope, and mutual forbearance striving to be love . . . [and] a landscape which makes these qualities manifest is one that can be called beautiful."[120] I, for one, see in his experiments with "minor" cultural landscapes something of the directions critical regionalism would take in the future, summarized by Comer's belief that the "regional" could be "recuperated . . . as not inevitably productive of conservative nationalisms, masculine or white authority, or essentialist/authentic definitions of place."[121] Jackson's ideal critical regionalism, formulated in the 1950s, rejects notions of the West as a "static utopia" while dreaming of an "environment where permanence and change have struck a balance" and comprehending "a new and challenging field" constantly forming and adapting that would provide a crucial history for "new" western studies, since, as he once wrote, "the value of history is what it teaches us about the future."[122]

2. FEASTS OF WIRE

Rubén Martinez and the Transfrontera Contact Zone

Our psyches resemble the bordertowns.
Gloria Anzaldúa

But to cross over, to be a wetback, is itself a baptism into a new life.
Rubén Martinez

"Everyone Has His South": Border Theory

To examine one specific type of critical regionalism I wish to turn to José David Saldívar's *Border Matters: Remapping American Cultural Studies* (1997), a work influenced by the theoretical syncretism of Stuart Hall's and Paul Gilroy's British cultural studies and seeking to present "the U.S.-Mexico border zone as a paradigm of crossings, intercultural exchanges, circulations, resistances, and negotiations as well as of militarised 'low-intensity' conflict." Saldívar argues that the border represents "a model for a new kind of U.S. cultural studies . . . that challenges the homogeneity of U.S. nationalism and popular culture," with the nation "re-imagined . . . as a site within many 'cognitive maps,'" a new transnational "field-Imaginary" in which migration and immigration challenge and reconfigure established, preconceived definitions and assumptions.[1] The term "field-Imaginary" refers to Donald Pease's definition of a disciplinary field's "unconscious," its "fundamental syntax . . . tacit assumptions, convictions, primal words, and the charged relations that bind them together."[2] Therefore, the "diasporic" dynamics of the borderlands (as defined by Hall and Gilroy—but *not* directly by Saldívar) link this model to still wider concerns, to crossings beyond the U.S.-Mexico geocultural space, and to "the study of international relations and empire." Hence Saldívar's paradigm of crossing, mixing, resistance, and circulation points beyond its own concerns for Chicano/ Chicana studies, toward "the 'worlding' of American studies and further . . . to instil a new transnational literacy."[3] Thus as Chicano/Chicana studies addresses questions of assimilation, immigration, nationalism, and cultural identity around the instability and possibility of the border zone, it articulates a series of complex theories and imaginings that have a wider domain for an understanding and rethinking of the West as a "traveling" term, part of this transnational imaginary. The deterritorialization of the borderlands, neither purely Mexican nor purely American, gives them a particularly resonant force in cultural studies and explains why the whole metaphor of "borders" has become so bound up with postmodern critical writing. Also, the "traveling" implied by migration has a precise meaning for legal and illegal border crossers of the "*transfrontera* contact zone*,*" creating a "social space of subaltern encounters . . . [where] new relations, hybrid cultures, and multiple-voiced aesthetics [emerge]." In exploring these "voices," Saldívar wants to challenge, like Gilroy, accepted definitions of American "nationhood" and show how the "absolutism" so often associated with pure visions of national or regional identity is "disrupted and customized" by the intervention of other (forgotten, minor, or marginalized) histories and narratives.[4] The Chicano/Chicana critical presence, led by writers such as Américo Paredes and Gloria Anzaldúa, has been vital to this disruption of the American national narrative and its canon, and its western/southwestern geography lends it to the particular focus of this book, for it reminds us of the need to stretch and break the grids drawn around representations, to cut across them and beyond them to other visions and relations often relegated to minor roles and given limited weight. For the real and imagined West and its centrality to definitions of Americanism to be reenvisioned from south of the border has given western studies a massive jolt and forced it to reexamine its premises and its groundings—to "remap" itself, as Saldívar would term it. Deleuze coincidentally uses the term "south" in a similar manner to suggest the disruptive presence and the unsettling of established binary codings, such as East/West. He writes, "there will always be someone to rise up to the south . . . a direction which is different from that of the line of segments. But everyone has his south—it doesn't matter where it is—that is, his line of slope or flight. Nations, classes, sexes have their south." For Deleuze, this is the "frontier, through which everything passes and shoots on a broken molecular line of a different orientation," a "border or a frontier," he goes on, with the capacity to "turn the set [binaries] into a multiplicity," or a new "assemblage."[5]

Saldívar creates just such an assemblage of voices from his border zone through writers like Renato Rosaldo examining "people between cultures" through which a "crucial research agenda for U.S. and global cultural studies opens up." Or via the work of Néstor Garcia Canclini, whose vision of a playful, postmodern Tijuana provides an interesting touristic focus for Saldívar's arguments, seeing in the billboards and heteroglossic popular forms a thematization of "the hybrid, polyglot culture . . . of the . . . borderlands" where simulation and "authenticity" have become interfused and blurred. In the strange, diasporic mix of the border as an expanded West, Saldívar witnesses relations between the local and the global where displacement, interculturalism, and transnationalism are emergent forms. Within the borderlands, both "shifting and shifty," is glimpsed a globalizing transnationalism presenting the direction (if not the actual practice) of Saldívar's book.[6] This is a road Saldívar will not travel fully in *Border Matters* but whose implications I trace in other ways in this book. Indeed, Paul Giles criticizes Saldívar for "valorizing" Chicano writers to the extent that he practices a kind of "pure" identity politics "whereby marginal figures are incorporated into the ever-expanding circle of a national narrative . . . enfolding oppressed or minority cultures in a Neoplatonic embrace. . . . [Thus] to displace a cultural heritage from one side of the border to the other is to shuffle the critical pack without necessarily changing the rules of the game." Giles's objective, as we discussed earlier, is to see the "field-Imaginary" of American studies not as an ever-expanding circle of "self-fulfilling definitions" incorporating and including diversity, but rather redefining it as a "site of perennial struggle and rupture" full of "lines of tension" to be explicated and complicated. For Giles this is the heart of what he calls "critical transnationalism," capable of probing the "significance of cultural jagged edges, structural paradoxes, or other forms of apparent incoherence" so as to "illuminate our understanding of where the culture of the United States is positioned within a framework of broader global affairs." Accordingly, "critical transnationalism" seeks out and examines "points of intersection, whether actual border territories [like those in Chicano/Chicana writings] or other kinds of disputed domain, where cultural conflict is lived out experientially."[7]

For my purposes in this book, the American West provides the "disputed domain," a prism through which to reflect upon types of conflict, intersection, dialogue, encounter, and exchange through texts that serve to "trouble" certain established "self-fulfilling definitions." As the West travels between cultures and "uses" it reveals similarities and differences, cultural overlaps, and misunderstandings, and therefore to rethink the West transnationally disturbs any idea of homogeneity or of an "inclusive cultural field," displacing it from the center of American consciousness and replacing it within a wider, global domain.[8] Gilroy's work, as we saw in the introduction, examining the "intercultural and transnational formation" he terms the "black Atlantic" with its capacity to unsettle "nationalist paradigms," ideas of racial purity, and authenticity by arguing *for* "the inescapable hybridity and intermixture of ideas" and *against* any "closure of the categories with which we conduct our political lives," is important to Saldívar, as it is to Giles, and offers some helpful pointers for our study of the shifting West along the border. Gilroy charts, like Saldívar, "the instability and mutability of identities which are always unfinished, always being remade." Utilizing "double consciousness" as a model, Gilroy examines alternatives to the "absolutist discourses" that insist upon divisions, lines of demarcation, and oppositional structures ("immutable, ethnic differences") as the way to define identity, presenting instead "the space between" these various entrenched positions and examining the benefits of new perspectives, allowing for mutation and change as inevitable parts of the process, and developing a critical position that sees both ways.[9]

Sharing a view of colonialism also articulated by writers like De Certeau, Rosaldo, and Pratt, Gilroy maintains that groups were not "sealed off hermetically from each other" but had a variety of complex relations within this "in-between" or "thirdspace." Gilroy is concerned with those elements that "exceed racial discourse," spilling over neat grids and categories used to restrain definitions and curtail innovation. It is the excess that cannot be contained within the grids of traditional discourse, that links Gilroy to Bakhtin's concept of the "excess of seeing," to a critical outsideness discussed in the introduction and chapter 5, and that may be applied here as we explore alternative ways of seeing westness as an excessive and global signifier. So Gilroy's aim is to project "the stereophonic, bilingual, or bifocal cultural forms" that have emerged out of "dispersed" or diasporic black cultures and to show how such forces are "rooted in and routed through the special stress that grows with the effort involved in trying to face (at least) two ways at once." Thus his project, like mine, is syncretic, demonstrating how forms and texts are reworked and reinscribed as they travel between cultures.[10]

Finding "non-national" counterpoints to "cultural insiderism," nationalism, and authenticity has become something of a new tradition in the so-called New American studies (Pease, Kaplan, Rowe, et al.). To borrow from Gilroy and Giles, perhaps it is precisely "outsiderism" that is needed, not to replace but to supplement "insiderism" and to set up more complex and multi-accented, disruptive dialogues across these lines.[11] As Giles says, Gilroy's work brought an "internationalist slant on the study of the United States" and was "frankly hostile to the nostalgia for national, regional, and ethnic particularisms that still lingers in many aspects of the American studies movement."[12] Fundamentally, Gilroy is concerned with "that narrowness of vision which is content with the merely national," so this means renouncing "exceptionalism" from within the black community (emphasizing race purity, local, family, authentic, rootedness, etc.) and opening it up to "global, coalitional politics in which anti-imperialism and anti-racism might be seen to interact if not to fuse." Through the assemblage of border voices suggested by Saldívar, one might imagine how such "outside westerners," from the south, can contribute to just such a disruptive rethinking, providing something as dynamic as Gilroy's "rhizomorphic, fractal structure of the transcultural, international formation" called the "black Atlantic," enabling Saldívar to argue that "the culture of the U.S. borderlands, like the black Atlantic diaspora culture, cannot be reduced to any nationally based 'tradition,'" and by extension to expand and interrogate more general notions of westness.[13] In the words of Rubén Martinez, who will be the focus of much of this chapter, "The border—be it between San Diego and Tijuana, or between North Africa and Europe—is a historical space of flux, a zone of gestation, an identity bazaar, where the Line becomes Lines. Tijuana was 'global' and 'postmodern' long before these became the terms *du jour*."[14]

"Where the Line Becomes Lines": Border Stories

In Gloria Anzaldúa's *Borderlands/La Frontera* (1987), the space between the United States and Mexico is mapped as both real, geopolitical territory and as an increasingly contested psychological, sexual, and spiritual domain, "an intricately refractory zone where different cultures meet and clash."[15] Writing from a radical lesbian-feminist Chicana position, Anzaldúa connects the various struggles of her own life to the multidimensional experience of the southwestern borderlands, constantly shifting across the boundaries of the personal and the political in pursuit of some new perspective, comparable to "trying to swim in a new element, an 'alien' element." Her narrative perspective is itself alien, "caught between *los intersticios*, the spaces between the different worlds she inhabits," an outsider to the many cultures that collide on the border, belonging to no single community, but trying to comprehend them, "to carve and chisel my own face . . . to stand and claim my space, making a new culture."[16] Earlier she wrote of being a "wind-swayed bridge, a crossroads inhabited by whirlwinds," split by cultural labels, torn between "what is and what should be," and yet engaged in a process she termed "traveling El Mundo Zurdo path," a passage into the self and outward to the world.[17] The imagery evokes the process of crossing (the border, the bridge, the crossroads, the river, the fence, etc.) as central to the deterritorialization of the self as it eludes the grids and frames that define and contain it to explore new territories emerging at the edge.[18] As Anzaldúa puts it, "she has to 'cross over,' kicking a hole out of the old boundaries of the self and slipping under or over, dragging the old skin along, stumbling over it . . . dragging the ghost of the past with her." Her new mestiza (mixed ancestry) consciousness is forged from such a process of "conscious rupture"; the "shift out of habitual formations . . . to divergent thinking . . . [a] movement away from set patterns," the "breaking down of paradigms . . . the straddling of two or more cultures," and the "continual creative motion" toward inclusion not exclusion, toward a "new perspective." All these migratory images demand an often painful willingness to step outside the frames of reference called "home" or "nation" and, as she writes in one of her most telling lines, "to make herself vulnerable to foreign ways of seeing and thinking." Once again, it is this position from "outside," following the stranger's path, that permits, indeed demands, the rigorous critique of the "what is" by the "what should be," employing "*Coatlicue* states which disrupt the smooth flow (complacency) of life."[19] Learning to live in and through the borderlands might enable Chicanas/Chicanos to lead the way toward some new consciousness, to Saldívar's "remapping," since as Rosaldo put it, "the rear guard will become the vanguard."[20] Anzaldúa sums up this process as "Deconstruct, construct."[21] Making a similar point, Iain Chambers writes that it is indeed the stranger's perspective that leads the way, since "To come from elsewhere, from 'there' and not 'here,' and hence to be simultaneously 'inside' and 'outside' the situation at hand, is to live at the intersections of histories and memories, experiencing both their preliminary dispersal and their subsequent translation into new, more extensive, arrangements along emerging routes."[22]

Although Anzaldúa's perspective developed markedly over her lifetime, her emphases upon the processes of fragmentation and crossing, of home and deterritorialization, and the desire for a "new birth" dialogue well with other border narratives. Her radical Chicana feminism provides a direction and purpose, a means of cutting through cultural grids in a "left-handed" manner that, I believe, demonstrates approaches useful in the discussion of other cultural critics, such as Rubén Martinez and Luis Alberto Urrea, whose own works, though very different, search equally for the "outside," an "interface" allowing them to see both ways.[23] The philosophical mysticism of Anzaldúa, although anchored in her own experience, is materialized in the ethnographic-inflected writings of Martinez and Urrea charting the everyday lives "across the wire" of the borderlands, capturing the "dynamic and iniquitous relationships" and recording the "migrant culture" they witness "springing up with narratives running contrary to the Official Story."[24]

Urrea has produced a series of books shifting among fiction, political documentary, and personal memoir examining life on the border. As a mixed-blood Mexican American, he deliberately incorporates his own perspective, family history, and transient lifestyle into his tales, providing a multiple and often uncertain narrative focus that fluctuates between connection and disconnection, tragedy and comedy, the inside and the outside.[25] As he states in *Nobody's Son: Notes from an American Life* (1998), whose very title testifies to his own "traveling" identity and sense of rootlessness, "We are sons and daughters of the middle region, nobody's children, marching under a starless flag. . . . My life isn't so different from yours. My life is utterly alien compared to yours.

You and I have nothing to say to each other. You and I share the same story. I am Other. I am you."[26] These contradictions are, as with almost all border writing, its key, creating the ambivalent tension from which springs new perspectives emerging out of what Gilroy terms the "instability and mutability of identities which are always unfinished, always being remade."[27] Urrea comments on growing up in the "Haunted City" of Tijuana, a "no-man's land," as a "son of the border" with "a barbed-wire fence neatly bisecting my heart," the product of a white American mother and a Mexican father, a family always at the very center of his writing.[28] Indicative of this, his work is rarely far from an analysis of "home": "But where is home? Home isn't just a place, I have learned. It is also a language," a language, however, as mixed and hybridized as the border culture in which he grew up. As he writes, "America is home. It's the only home I have. Both Americas. All three Americas, from the Arctic circle to Tierra del Fuego."[29] The unstable concept "home" is, for Urrea, similar to Guillermo Gómez-Pena's definition of it as "a sort of moving Bermuda Triangle inhabited by a floating community."[30] There can, in other words, be no essentialized "home"; it is just another trace, a ghostly, layered presence in the complex mix of the borderlands that has to be exorcised, summoned up through writing, whether fiction or nonfiction, new journalism or poetic memoir—"sweating out the demons of the border."[31] Urrea's work is about traveling and questing, as his book titles demonstrate: In Search of Snow, Wandering Time, Across the Wire, The Devil's Highway—writings about the inner and outer migrations that map the "routes" and "roots" inherent in his expanded version of westness. Unsettled and unsettling, his work reflects rhizomatically "an early fascination with escape, then deals with returning, then staying put and dealing with it, whatever it is," always juggling the positions of "insider" and "outsider."[32] This latter position, as in Martinez's work, allows Urrea to see the world from different perspectives, a point that comes across most powerfully in an exchange between two characters (one Mexican, one Anglo) in his novel In Search of Snow:

> "I likey inside, inside okay, but no too much. Es mucho mejor outside. I like pooty good!"
> Mike nodded.
> "Yes," he said, "I like outside too."[33]

Again and again Urrea's writing explores these issues, drawing out the ghosts of cultural memory from both sides of the border, searching for finished stories in a world that denies them, and seeking reasons in an irrational universe. At the end of Nobody's Son, "The ghosts and I pile into the Jeep. . . . I drive out of town. . . . Father Escalante and his men wandered in these unforgiving hills. . . . I sit here staring at their bewildering landscape, can feel them wondering what to do now. . . . I don't know where I'm going."[34] His identification with the ghosts of the borderlands, los muertos (the dead), with other migrants, adventurers, conquistadores, and wetbacks is typical of his endless literary motion—"escape, returning, staying put"—a recurrent position that is reemployed in his Pulitzer Prize–nominated The Devil's Highway, where contemporary migrants link across time to 1541 and Melchior Díaz on the Coronado expedition, trying to reach the Sea of Cortés, but dying in the scorching desert. Yet even in 1541, as Urrea says, "the land had been haunted before Melchior died, and it remained haunted afterward" by the ghosts in the earth now dispersed and vanished, "the ancient Hohokam . . . the Anasazi. . . . Their etchings and ruins still dot the ground; unexplained radiating lines lead away from the center like ghost roads in the shape of a great star." Everywhere in the liminal geography of the borderlands remain the rhizomatic traces, "Footprints of long-dead cowboys . . . wagon ruts and mule scuffs. And beneath these, the prints of the phantom Hohokam themselves," reminiscent of Charles Bowden's sense of the border as a space of "Tracks, everywhere tracks, marks racing up the arm, footprints pasted against the desert soil, tongues of air moving overhead rich with pollutants . . . spore floating, seeds moving at will in the bellies of birds, everywhere tracks making their imprint and being ignored."[35]

Indeed, Urrea's collected works seem to search out these traces, attempt to follow the "ghost roads" and diasporic tracks of the expanded circum-West, of Greater Mexico, to gather its fragments and stories, like those people he writes so much of sifting the trash on the Tijuana garbage dumps. Amid the seams of stories, the archaeology of voices, Urrea constructs an archive from a landscape "no tourist will ever see," full of horror, violence, resilience, and beauty, echoing Malaquias Montoya's powerful silkscreen image Undocumented (1981), of a stark, border "crucifixion."[36]

3. Malaquias Montoya, Undocumented (1981) (original in color).
Used by permission of the artist.

The danger here, as Saldívar has pointed out, is that Urrea becomes the gringo-looking ethnographer telling exotic and tragic tales of others, acting out the role of traveler/missionary/anthropologist whose linked desires are for "encountering and incorporating others, whether by conversion or comprehension."[37] Saldívar argues that Urrea is not reflexive enough, is not sufficiently interrogating his own social and political position in relation to the "Others" he writes about, but this is a view based on only Urrea's first book, *Across the Wire*, when, in fact, his work has increasingly commented, like Martinez's, on his own history and the psycho-geography of border culture. Even in *Across the Wire* this surfaces in chapter 10, "Father's Day," dealing with his own Mexican father's death, a constant theme in his later work, appearing as prose and poetry, signaling, I would suggest, his own unease about his cultural position and in particular his relationship with the "fatherland." His father, Alberto, is the ghostly presence of Mexico, the "ghost sickness" that Urrea's writing is trying to heal: "My father, dead / Now for interminable years, won't leave me / In peace: doesn't want to go: I see him / Every day." His father represents the "strange landscape" of home with which Urrea struggles, providing an ambivalent perspective toward the "subjects" in his writing: "My father, planted / In his Mexican soil, laying roots / Into the dark meadow of forget, shines . . . / I see him without seeing."[38] The nation of Mexico, the village of Rosario from where his father came, the earth, and the "roots" deep in these places exercise a strong pull to the past, haunting Urrea's memory and simultaneously transforming him into a migrant *from* his own past, his father, his homeland. The writer migrates literally and metaphorically—literally as he travels endlessly from place to place, job to job "across ghost-heavy night" on his quest ("I love travel . . . I like to keep moving. Running streams can't get stagnant. I hope"), and metaphorically through words, since "walking is writing" and every sentence is a displaced migrant activity. These ideas come together most tellingly in a passage from *Wandering Time*: "On the surface, I smile. I'm Mr. Blonde Mexicano. . . . Inside me though, there is another landscape. If you look into my heart, you would find a sparkling obsidian chip, you would see reflected a desert plain. . . . I walk in a world of ghosts."[39] The tensions of a hybrid cultural identity, of the pull between roots *and* routes, come through starkly here as Urrea's split self merges with the history of his family and the border itself. As he terms it elsewhere, it is as if he is reaching for "The Understory"—"the dark stirrings in the basement of the story . . . the boiler room . . . the engine room . . . where it's cobwebby and dusty, oily and stinky, weird and a little frightening. . . . Rosario . . . was certainly imbued with understory."[40] His work constantly reaches back to the metaphoric "Rosario" and his real and symbolic father, to its hidden histories and silenced voices, allowing Urrea's personal journey to overlap with the stark experiences of the *alambristas* (wire crossers) his work records, ultimately contributing to a more complex and inclusive narrative of Greater Mexico's circular contribution to an evolving circum-West.

"The Other Outside": Rubén Martinez

To explore some of these ideas further, I wish to turn to the writings of Rubén Martinez, whose first major work, The Other Side, was published in 1992, beginning a trilogy that continued with Crossing Over (2001) and The New Americans (2004).[41] As a middle-class, American-born Mexican American, Martinez sees himself as "an ethnic rebel attempting to foil the melting pot," an "outsider" who can travel by choice rather than necessity, using this "inside/outside" perspective to carry back and interrogate messages from the cultural "fault lines."[42] The political drive of his work comes from his sense that "truly American ideals . . . have been betrayed" and tracing the consequences of this betrayal in the lives of migrants.[43] The opening essay of The Other Side begins with Martinez's dominant tropes—fragmentation and splitting—recalling how the 1960s began to break up the consensus of supposed national unity, providing the "explosions that shook my childhood awake," the "years of snapping in two": "I have lived both in the North and the South . . . trying to be South in the South, North in the North, South in the North and North in the South. Now I stand at the center—watching history whirl around me as my own history fissures: my love shatters, North and South, and a rage arises from within as the ideal of existential unity crumbles."[44] Martinez has often commented that Mexicans were the first postmodernists, dating back to the conquest: "it's that split consciousness that creates a world view that's a priori fragmented, occupying several spaces at the same time . . . a mixed mutt of traditions."[45] He shares views about the significance of the border with performance artist Guillermo Gómez-Pena, with whom he worked and whom he acknowledges in The Other Side and Crossing Over.[46] Although less well known for performance art and poetry, Martinez has been aligned with them throughout his career. He is also known for his musical collaborations with The Roches, Concrete Blonde, and Ruben Guevara's Mexamérica project. There are, in fact, many helpful parallels between Martinez and Gómez-Pena. For example, Gómez-Pena claims his own work is a "crisscross from the past to the present, from the fictional to the biographical . . .

fus[ing] prose and poetry, sound and text, art and literature, political activism and art experimentation," and as a result he creates, like Martinez, hybrid texts that deliberately stretch and break boundaries.[47] He writes of how his identity is a "kaleidoscope" that "possesses multiple repertoires," allowing him to become "a cultural topographer" charting the "intersection . . . the intermediate stage . . . [the] in between" of the borderlands of "weary travellers, the dislocated, those of us who left because we didn't fit anymore, those of us who still haven't arrived because we don't know where to arrive at, or because we can't go back anymore." Like Gómez-Pena, Martinez reflects the border's ambiguity, "full of uncertainty and vitality," "attending the funeral of modernity and the birth of a new culture."[48] Gómez-Pena's humorous, ironic, and satirical style uses performance art and language to bombard the viewer/reader with a blitz of ideas and impressions that engage the mind and stir the feelings. Gómez-Pena describes himself as "a migrant provocateur, an intercultural pirate, a 'border brujo,' a conceptual coyote (smuggler). . . . I am, therefore, I travel, and vice versa. . . . I travel in search of many Mexicos, my other selves, and the many communities to which I belong. . . . I travel from myth to social reality, always returning to my origins (by now mythical as well), retracing the footprints of my biological family and revisiting the many overlapping communities of which I am a part."[49] His interdisciplinary, promiscuous forms (performance, prose, poetry, video, interview, CD-ROM, internet, etc.) are themselves rhizomatic, especially when defined by the artist as "multidirectional links that connect throughout the book, emulating the endless journeys and border crossings which are at the core of my experience, and therefore my art. In fact, I encourage readers to create their own order for the material."[50]

Martinez's outputs have been similarly varied and "experimental," aimed at a diverse audience and "emulating the endless journeys and border crossings" that his writings describe.[51] Though his work is less extreme in approach than Gómez-Pena's, some of the underlying concepts are similar: Martinez questions the effects of the North American Free Trade Agreement (NAFTA), state power, oppressive regimes of border control and surveillance, and mixed and fragmented identities, and he muses on the possibility of emergent new cultures from the "shattered puzzle" of the transnational borderlands. As he has said, Gómez-

Pena was key to "propagating the idea of the border as both wall and sieve, both an experience and a metaphor of the global."[52] Saldívar claims that Urrea and Martinez employ, in contrast to the flamboyant style of Goméz-Pena, "autoethnography," weaving together their personal lives and the experience of living between the United States and Mexico, recognizing a quest for a "true center" or a "romantic home" as examples of a "unity" no longer available to them.[53] "My own identity," Martinez writes, echoing Urrea, "is the product of this kind of movement. . . . I have shuttled between my parents' Old Countries and my life in the 'New World': California, land of perpetual immigrant hopes and dreams. . . . I am who I am today because of the interplay between history and momentous decisions based on individual will." In Gilroy's terms, the "roots" of self and community cannot be assumed in a world of mobility and flux, for what one has instead is "many selves" and many "routes," and despite the urge to overcome such fragmentation, we have to learn "to live so many realities at once."[54] Indeed, Martinez's existence is like a "crucifixion . . . a contradiction, a cross," and The Other Side, rather like Urrea's work, becomes his account of a series of crossings, "a search for a home I've lost and found countless times . . . a search for a one that is much more than two. Because wherever I am now, I must be much more than two. I must be North and South in the North and in the South."[55] As Anzaldúa writes, as if to speak for all these border writers, "Living between cultures results in 'seeing' double, first from the perspective of one culture, then from the perspective of another. Seeing from two or more perspectives simultaneously renders those cultures transparent."[56] Indeed, Gómez-Pena commented that the mestizo experience provided a vital syncretic perspective: "It is only until we cross the border that we face 'the other outside,' thus becoming the outside other for Anglo culture. When we cross the border our art becomes the double mirror that reflects this painful dynamic" (emphasis added).[57]

Martinez's earliest work is characterized by a similar "painful," troubled, and "doubled" narrative voice. Uncertain and doubtful of his own position, Martinez continually reflects upon his role as participant-observer and outside-insider in the "whirl" of border culture. In The New Americans, for example, he comments upon Crossing Over and his "ethnographer's typical reflexive path" in which he tried to "create a dialogue of subjectivities" and yet still had "nagging doubts as to how I ultimately portrayed my subjects."[58] His collaboration with photographer Joseph Rodriquez in *East Side Stories: Gang Life in L.A.* and *The New Americans* is a further clue to his position. Martinez comments that what he admired in Rodriquez was that he was not a "simple documentarian: he is participant-observer," a "subject behind the lens as well as in front of it" whose "honest representation" sought to "foreground one's experience, one's place in the world, and draw in the Other through its lens."[59] This examination of participant observation relates to Deena González's definition of "outside-insiders" as those whose "critical vantage points" are derived from having "special relationships with their topics," expressing knowledge "primarily as feelings or as images . . . [whose] evidence serves as verification of these expressions."[60] It is then no surprise to learn that *The New Americans* project owes its name and much more to another outsider, Robert Frank, whose mid-1950s journey around the United States became the photographic collection *The Americans* (introduction by Jack Kerouac). Rodriguez gave the book to Martinez as a gift with the inscription, "To Rubén: An important time to look at America again." Indeed, reminiscent of Frank's setting off around the postwar United States to gauge and record its sociopolitical climate, Martinez has written that "Joe and I went out on the road looking to see the country at this new crossroads"—a crossroads born, in their case, of cultural change in a post-NAFTA world of economic and identity crisis—seeking to "reveal an 'invisible America'—an America that had been ignored—much like Frank had."[61] Thus, like Frank and Urrea, Martinez is clearly sensitive throughout his work about being seen as a voyeur, a trauma tourist visiting other people's worlds and merely translating such subjects into objects for the tourist's gaze. He can, of course, never fully overcome this, but he guards against it through self-awareness of himself as an "outsider" and by determined efforts never to romanticize the figures in his books or to present them as stereotyped victims or stoic heroes.

To this end, the works of Martinez and Urrea share something with the urgent political genre of "testimonio," defined variously as produced by a "narrator who is a real protagonist or witness . . . whose unit of narration is usually a 'life' or a significant life experience" and containing elements of "autobiography, autobiographical novel, oral history,

memoir, confession, diary, interview, eyewitness report, life history,"
but fundamentally remaining an "uncanny" genre with no fixed home
or simple definition.[62] Shoshana Felman defines it in ways that relate
closely to the imperatives of Martinez and Urrea's writings: "[Testimo-
nio] seems to be composed of bits and pieces of a memory that has been
overwhelmed by occurrences that have not settled into understanding
or remembrance, acts that cannot be constructed as knowledge nor as-
similated into full cognition, events in excess of our frames of reference.
. . . Texts that testify do not simply report facts but, in different ways,
encounter—and make us encounter—strangeness."[63] In his efforts to
encounter strangeness from the cutting edge of the borderlands, Martinez develops writing that crosses borders and blurs distinct, gridded
forms, creating something unnameable, doubtful, provocative, and
hybrid—a "mestizo/mestiza" form "in excess of our frames [or grids]
of reference," intended to unsettle and challenge assumptions in both
form and content. At one point in *Crossing Over* this style finds a parallel
in the border crossers themselves with the "grids of beams" from lasers
that seek to contain, surveil, and define the migrant, simultaneously opposed by the resistance from those who "made [their] way around the
grid," refusing to be curtailed.[64]

Just as Rosaldo called for a "remaking of social analysis" in his *Culture and Truth* in 1989, it is as if Martinez has taken up the cause in his
writing, appreciating that "A renewed sense of culture thus refers less
to a unified entity . . . than to the mundane practices of everyday life,"
looking "less for homogenous communities than for the border zones
within and between them . . . always in motion, not frozen for inspection." Martinez recognizes the "longing for the time before the fall into
the chaos of the global era," for a rooted and "pure" life, yet he simultaneously knows, like Rosaldo, that in "the present postcolonial world"
the "notion of an authentic culture as an autonomous internally coherent universe no longer seems tenable, except perhaps as a 'useful fiction' or a revealing distortion."[65] Rosaldo compares the old "rhetoric of
ethnography," which valorized stability, order, and equilibrium, with
viewing culture as a museum, whereas he favors, as Martinez does, a
version of culture akin to a "garage sale" (or "identity bazaar") where
"cultural artifacts flow between unlikely places, and nothing is sacred,

permanent, or sealed off."[66] Rosaldo's work, like Gilroy's, owes much to James Clifford's notions of traveling cultures and to the deliberate unsettling of traditional objective ethnographic approaches through tactically "shifting insides and outsides, affiliations and distances" and therefore providing a "critical intervention against [the] disembodied, neutral authority" of the authoritative voice of the ethnographer.[67] Indeed, one of Rosaldo's chapters, "Putting Culture in Motion," represents this urge to reconfigure how cultures are examined as being about both routes *and* roots, traveling *and* dwelling, while rethinking the tired binaries that have so often dominated cultural analysis. In one of his most famous statements, Rosaldo summarizes a version of culture as "a busy intersection" that announces perfectly the relationship I see between his work and that of Martinez and, to a lesser degree, Urrea: "In contrast with the classic view, which posits culture as a self-contained whole made up of coherent patterns, culture can be arguably be conceived as a more porous array of intersections where distinct processes crisscross from within and beyond its borders."[68] By working across this "porous array of intersections," or what Martinez calls "a nexus where myriad forces intersect," his self-conscious and troubled narrative voice is able to represent reflexively the almost surreal world of the global-local West that shifts and flows rhizomatically in all directions in a manner that echoes what Anzaldúa has called "autohistoria": "I call it 'auto' for self-writing and 'historia' for history—as in collective, personal, cultural, and racial history—as well as for fiction, a story you make up."[69]

Indeed, *The Other Side* often reads like a form of testimonio fiction, especially in "The Winds of October," which records the earthquake in El Salvador as a parallel to Martinez's own identity fragmentation, an image Anzaldúa has used in her own work as a metaphor for impending change: "Este arrebato, the earthquake, jerks you from the familiar and safe terrain and catapults you into nepantla, the second stage."[70] As in Anzaldúa's quasi-mystical images of emergence, Martinez himself undergoes journeys of despair full of "doubts . . . [and] dread" as he migrates physically and psychologically across borders where conventional, rooted support systems, like home and family, are disrupted and breached (*arrebato*).[71] One is reminded of Anzaldúa's key term "nepantla" (discussed in the introduction), "the birthing stage where you feel like you're reconfiguring your identity and don't know where you are. . . . You're changing worlds and cultures . . . el lugar en medio, the space in between, the middle ground." The cultural borderlands that gave rise to nepantla resonate with Rosaldo's "porous array of intersections," crisscrossed with real migrations while suggesting the epistemological shifts taking place in notions of self, identity, nation, and culture. For Anzaldúa, identity is a "kind of stacking or layering of selves, horizontal and vertical layers, the geography of selves made up of the different communities you inhabit. . . . Where these spaces overlap is nepantla, the Borderlands. Identity is a process-in-the-making. This in-between space is nepantla, the liminal stage. You're confused, you don't know who you are."[72] This also recalls Urrea's similar sense of identity in "the middle region" (the literal meaning of "nepantla") as "nobody's children . . . I am Other. I am you."[73] As Martinez charts his and others' way through the various "ruins" of a globalized world he is simultaneously in nepantla, undergoing a complex process of change and discovery, something that becomes apparent, as we have seen, in his own use of tropes of crossing—hence the crucifixion image discussed earlier, his migratory shifts between North and South, his constant feelings of doubleness, and his developing sense that "significant" things "happened in-between."[74] Thus, Martinez's early work reads like a struggle between the disruption of some dream of tradition and coherence and the growing knowledge of fragmentation and multiplicity, as well as the recognition that to live in a postmodern, "postwestern" society one has to learn to negotiate this "liminal" or "borderlands" space. Just as the migrant lives at no single point but rather moves between many, where "neither the points of departure nor those of arrival are immutable or certain," so the narrator of The Other Side gradually comprehends his own position as similarly complex—not one identity but rather a "geography of selves," as Anzaldúa put it, living at the "interface."[75] In Anzaldúa's work this latter term is derived from needlework and means "sewing a piece of material between two pieces of fabric to provide support," but it clearly relates to the experience of the borderlands, of inhabiting different realities simultaneously.[76] In The Other Side this is nowhere clearer than in one of its key sections, "A Festival of Moments," where the dream of the edenic West, now distilled as the Pacific Rim paradise of Los Angeles and the singular ideal subject that inhabits its space, is for Martínez in need of careful, critical revision through an assertion of the processes that happen "in-between" the regularized and official stories and ideological myths of the dominant culture.

In this section, Martínez's *testimonio* recalls the Los Angeles Festival in 1990, and in keeping with the developing position of much of his work outlined above, its focus is not the organized, ideological event—the celebration of Los Angeles as coherent urban center where "everything comes together" as a new "world community"—but what happened "in-between" these strategic points. In the interstices, between the marketing of the city, its slogans, and its surface diversity, Martínez, "as participant and observer . . . cynical as hell . . . suspicious," intervenes in the mythmaking project of multiculturalism to assert a more impure version of the new urban West.[77] And yet he is always simultaneously struggling in the text with his own desire for order and unity ("I need my cities, my families to be one"), "yearning for the time before the Fall into the cynicism that paralyzes me," for a dream of social and psychical coherence that he associates with "trips south to Mexico" and a fantasy of "home." Like Urrea's literary coming-to-terms with his father's Mexico, Martínez's narrative is a "troubling" of this "sublime nostalgia" and "idyllic" vision, presenting an alternative Los Angeles "fragmented, schizophrenic and contradictory," with "class and race divisions," economic inequalities, and vast differences in power and authority. Rather than "covering up the tensions with a Disneylike It's a Small World After All theme," Martínez's goal is, like Anzaldúa's and Gómez-Peña's, to expose these "breaches" and lay bare the divisions and fragments in himself and in the city, a process best encapsulated in the vital and telling parallel with conceptual artist Sabura Teshigara's *Blue Meteorite*: "a dance over a long rectangle of broken glass before an ethereal blue panel—those shards and bodies terrify me as much as they overwhelm me with their beauty. Shards of Los Angeles's identity, compacted into a two-week time frame." Here the fragments, "shards of time and space," coexist without the absolute scramble for unity and the need to transform the city (and the self) into a single definable object, coexist as Martínez's "Festival of Moments" that come together and fall apart as an incomplete and asymmetrical "process" of becoming.[78]

Earlier, in his essay on Tijuana, Martinez defines it as "the city without which L.A. would not be L.A.," a space for the "clashing, the melding, the hybridisation of culture" where graffiti artist Hugo Sanchez responds with a "propuesta" (manifesto), "a new aesthetic, a new identity" of "splashes and sprayings and scratches . . . all a crazy dance . . . a crossroads, a cross-commerce, a cross-culture."[79] Here the cultural shards resemble the *Blue Meteorite* image of Los Angeles, a borderlands "rasquachismo," as Hugo Sanchez calls it, a term defined by Tomás Ybarra-Frausto as "the utilisation of the available resources for syncretism, juxtaposition, and integration . . . a sensibility attuned to mixtures and confluence . . . self-conscious manipulation of materials or iconography . . . of *rasquache* artifacts, code and sensibilities from both sides of the border." Its subversive potential turns "ruling paradigms upside down . . . [through] witty, irreverent and impertinent posture that re-codes and moves outside established boundaries."[80] In Tijuana, as in his alternative Los Angeles, Martinez maps his version of nepantla, a complex, layered, fragmented space where things break up into elements of change and reinvention, a deeply ambivalent vision to put alongside Urrea's Haunted City *and* Wonderland, and the more mystical but related philosophy of Anzaldúa. In Martinez's "notes," his own literary and photographic fragments and "moments" that shift readily between autobiography and journalism, poetry and documentary, testimonio and polemic, he creates his own "rasquachismo," and out of his troubled and cynical journey emerges an incomplete "Manifesto" that culminates with several moments of revelation:

> History is on fast forward
> it's the age of synthesis
> which is not to say
> that the Rainbow Coalition is
> heaven on earth and let's party.
> This is neither a rehash of
> the summer of love or
> Fidel and Che.
> All kinds of battles are yet to come
> (race and class rage bullets and blood);

choose your weapons . . .
just know that everyone is everywhere now
so careful how you shoot.[81]

Identifying the global nature of the new, transnational West where "everyone is everywhere," he acknowledges the complexity of contemporary culture in ways that cannot be simply divided or unified, preferring instead an indeterminate, rhizomatic vision of interconnection and negotiation across borders.

In "L.A. Journal (VIII)" Martinez applies this critical process to his own contradictory desires for essential stability in place and family ("one pure thing") and for the simultaneous comprehension of a mobile, differentiated identity. Again he returns to familiar metaphors to deal with this, to a personal story of how he "smashed the framed image of Jesus I've kept since early childhood" and in looking upon the fragments saw a distorted vision of himself that sparked the following: "We must be stripped of whatever certainty we have—pride, ego, and concrete sense of self—in order to move on to what may be the true moment of pure will." But this is not the answer, for again it has to be broken down: "Somebody get me a sledgehammer for Christmas. I want to take it to the reflection of myself in those bloody shards of glass lying on Jesus's image and to do away with myself spectacularly well. To be truly new, to move finally toward something/someone." Christ, like all other essences eschewed throughout the book, is no "pure thing" to save the author but reiterates the powerful metaphor of the cross, of man torn in all directions, stripped and broken down. The final section of this self-interrogation, "L.A. Journal (IX)," places us before his personal "altar" containing "objects from the living and the dead . . . shards of my identity" echoing all the parts of his journey through the book, and forcing him to a point of recognition that this "jumble of objects is as close as I get to 'home.'" His home is L.A., and, as he puts it, "L.A. is an anti-home," an uncanny space that forbids the easy rootedness for which he longs but which he knows is unrealistic in a world characterized by incessant motion and displacement. "Taking to the road, I've crossed and recrossed the border heading south and north," he writes in perplexity, "trying to put things back into place the way they were before . . . before what?" As he gazes across the altar, the jumbled, reflective "shards" become all he is, his "history," in all its chaotic, contradictory, "not-so-neat little piles," while hearing all the "ghost voices of the dead, next to my omnipresent moving boxes . . . as if there were cities strewn across my living-room floor: a history aglow in the wavering candle flame." At this moment the persistent imagery of ghosts, traced earlier in Urrea's work, finds expression as Martinez struggles to place himself in the fragmented landscape of the border, suggesting that both writers are haunted, to different degrees, by the past and by their desire to exorcise it for the present and future.[82]

In Martinez's next book, *Crossing Over* (2001), one is reminded of this ending in two particular ways. First, its starting point is the death in 1996 of the Chávez brothers as they crossed over to labor in the North; like Martinez's living room, their deaths are marked by the debris and fragments scattered across the road where their coyote-bus flipped off the highway: "I find a screen from the window of the truck's camper shell and a blue piece of plastic from the shell itself. . . . And another piece of black plastic: a fragment of the truck's running board. I pick up and examine a faded, crumpled tube of Colgate toothpaste, its ingredients listed in Spanish. There is an equally faded and torn McDonald's medium-size Coca-Cola cup."[83] These fragments resonate with the "ghost voices of the dead" that drive Martinez on to uncover the entangled histories of the border crossers and a version of westness that helps redefine the contours of nations in a globalized world. Second, *Crossing Over* reinvokes the metaphor of cities used at the end of *The Other Side* to articulate feelings about the endless transit of Mexicans from South to North and back again along the "migrant trail." In this section, "Fiesta," he writes of the circum-border cultures of Mex-America, spaces of crossing in which both human beings and their "commodities and cultural practices changed hands many times."[84] As discussed in the introduction, the term "circum," derived from Joseph Roach's work, suggests the movements back and forth, and around, like a "vortex" in which cultures are exchanged, translated, remembered and forgotten, performed and "surrogated."[85] Indeed, Martinez's *Crossing Over* employs many images of circularity to suggest the complex routes of return (arrival and leaving, as Tomás Rivera calls it) pursued by migrants—"It's a chain looped over many gears," a "loop not only in space but in time," an "incredibly complex web," "the great wheel," where "the movement is circular: you meet the future by moving out, render tribute to the past by coming back home."[86] In Roach's work, influenced by both Clifford and Gilroy, there is a determined effort to render "the insufficiently acknowledged cocreation of an oceanic interculture" and not just see the two sides of the "transatlantic" binary or to rest upon the notion of "a fixed and unified culture," which he views (as I have stated elsewhere) as "a convenient and dangerous fiction." Thus, for Roach, as for Martinez, it is vital to capture everything produced and "performed" "*between* the participating cultures" as the migrant "shuttles between the two" worlds, across Rosaldo's "porous array of intersections" where cultures collide in diasporic contact zones.[87] Such directions "from within and beyond [western] borders," as Rosaldo puts it, might enable a reorganization of how to think critically about the West as a more open, conflictual discursive territory defined as much from without as from within. Indeed, Roach, under the influence of Clifford once again, discussing the adaptation and ingenuity of Native American survival, argues against the "mirage of monocultural continuity or its related hallucination, the binary of two impermeable races opposed [across a border]," in favor of "culture reconceived as inventive process or creolised 'interculture.'"[88]

In Martinez's "Fiesta," the metaphoric "cities strewn across my living-room floor: a history aglow in the wavering candle flame" resurface as a means to define the "interculture" along the migrant trail where "Home is no longer located in a single geographical point" and all the towns, south and north, are "joined" to "create a city space of the mind" and "migration has forged a line of communication between and among these spaces."[89] This "city space of the mind" mirrors the cities analyzed by Roach, "occasions for memory and invention," full of death and life, hope and despair, where forgetting and remembrance are in constant tension. For Martinez, the task is simple: "I followed their ghost steps across the border. And then, across the United States," paralleling Urrea's "ghost-heavy night," recalling Anzaldúa "dragging the ghost of the past with her," and, for all of these border writers, as Roach points out, the narrative purpose is equally clear, since "the voices of the dead may speak freely now only through the bodies of the living."[90]

This is the writer's imperative—to give voice to the unvoiced—for, as Urrea puts it, "Sometimes the dead speak to you."[91] It is no surprise then that both Martinez and Urrea chose to write books about Los Muertos, the "dead"—*Crossing Over* and *The Devil's Highway*—literally reincarnating through language the stories of two sets of migrants, the Chávez family and the so-called Yuma 14, and in so doing returning the culturally repressed to mainstream culture. Not content with the process of forgetting, of "burying" death and its stories in the "strict silence of the tomb," Martinez and Urrea deliberately reverse this cultural strategy of repression and forgetting to answer Roach's question: "If the dead are forever segregated, how are the living supposed to remember who they are?"[92]

The recognition of the "cultural and material space of and between" (north/south, living/dead) is critical to Martinez's developing ideas as a writer in *Crossing Over*, relating back to Anzaldúa's concept of nepantla, but here drawing upon the everyday experiences of migrants whose lives constantly perform transnationalism. Charting the cultural import-export of the "borderscape," the "migrants carry back other kinds of goods, ones that reside in the head and the heart, comprised of language and myths and rituals" as they move between Cherán in the South to various points north, "in between the Old World (Virgin of Guadelupe votives always aglow at my grandparents' house) and the New (the tube flashing with The Brady Bunch at my parents')."[93] This is the mestizo/hybrid culture, the "cultural swirl" that mixes "pre-Columbian times" and MTV in a single town like Cherán where one-third of the population travels north for work each spring, returning again for fiesta in October. The Purépechas who live in Cherán have a name that translates as "a people who travel," linking them into a long history of migrations in the Americas, to the pioneers of Manifest Destiny, to Native Americans, and to immigrants to the New World, and who, like many other migrants, survive "cultural vertigo" through complex acts of adaptation.[94] As Martinez puts it in *The New Americans*, "The in-between space is dynamic and ever shifting," space where people are not transformed, as in the old "melting pot" ideology, but "acculturated" or adapted to their changing conditions, involved in a "constant negotiation of influences."[95]

Part of Martinez's purpose in *Crossing Over* and in the trilogy as a whole is to reclaim Mexican migrants for the literature of the Americas and the literature of the West, because "their travels are not mythologized in American literature," and to this end he parallels their journeys with that of the Joads in John Steinbeck's *The Grapes of Wrath* and of Jack Kerouac's heroes in *On the Road*. To achieve this he invokes other Mexican traditions with similar credentials; the border ballads ("corridos"), the epic, subjective histories ("relaciones"), Anzaldúa's *Borderlands/La Frontera*, and Rivera's . . . *And the Earth Did Not Devour Him*, which was in turn itself influenced by Steinbeck and *The Grapes of Wrath* in particular.[96] This interconnection and circularity further suggests, as in Martinez's work as a whole, a blending of forms and traditions, "creating a surreal hybrid in the process: in essence, Chicano culture."[97] His attention to border stories, to "ruptures . . . departure, becoming, passage, leap, daemon, relationship with the outside" brings his work closer to Deleuze's definition of all he admired in American literature—"the sense of the frontiers as something to cross, to push back, to go beyond," and the sense that "Becoming is geographical," "formed on lines of flight." In fact, this kind of mobile, mestizo writing can itself be seen as rhizomatic, proceeding "by intersections, crossings of lines, points of encounter in the middle."[98]

Rivera's . . . *And the Earth Did Not Devour Him*, which Hector Calderón terms a "novel-in-pieces," weaves a tale from the voices of border crossers and migrants, a tale of loss, violence, shame, and survival where ghosts again emerge through glimpses and fragments to reveal a secret history: "It's like I can hear all the dead people buried there saying these words and then the sounds of these words stays in my mind and sometimes even if I don't look up when I pass through the gate, I still see them."[99] Rivera's book literally builds a migrant history from the "minor" literature of forgotten migrants—their memories, stories, and testimonio—a history gathered as a means of understanding and discovering diasporic Mexican American culture from different points of entry, and presenting questions like those when one of narrative voices asked, "How come we're like this, like we're buried alive? . . . Why us, burrowed in the dirt like animals with no hope for anything?"[100] The "burrowing" narratives of Rivera's text are rhizomes with various entrances and exits, breaking out where one least expects them, forming an assemblage, a collage of voices and images that constitute the diaspora, but above all they represent a refusal to be "devoured" by the earth, to remain dead and buried. The ghost voices, as in Martinez and Urrea, rise up and, "since the [dominant] language is arid, make it vibrate with a new intensity."[101] A section like "When we arrive" is typical, beginning with an interrupted migrant journey through which Rivera expresses the routinized thoughts and worries of the travelers as they mull over their lives and dream of their eventual arrival in the North. The harsh conditions of the journey, its irritations, and exploitations are mixed with its momentary beauties and its desperate hopes—"Why couldn't it always be early dawn like this?" Yet in the "understory" of these diasporic voices bubbles a deeper, more painful consequence of the endless crossings that the whole book charts: "Arriving and leaving, it's the same thing because we no sooner arrive and . . . the real truth of the matter . . . I'm tired of arriving. I really should say when we don't arrive because that's the real truth. We never arrive."[102]

Rivera captures here the cycles of transit that promise "arrival" and the dream of some settled, better, rooted life on the other side, but one which in reality is much more about the endless motion of migrancy and the space *between* leaving and arrival. And it is precisely in this space that Rivera's mix of hope and horror exists and where, as José Aranda has said, lives are shaped.[103] Echoing Rivera, Martinez in *The New Americans* comments that "The migrant life is an emotional rollercoaster, an endless series of arrivals and departures, dictated by invisible forces that have such visible, visceral impact on our lives."[104] In the nomadic space of migration, Rivera connects Mexicans with other groups, as Martinez does more directly, with those "fleeing Egypt for the Canaan just across the Rio Grande," the "American migrants who rode the wagon trains westward," Coronado's men searching for Cibola, or religious penitents reenacting the Passion. In a key moment in *Crossing Over*, at the symbolic Gateway Arch in St. Louis, Martinez describes the Mexican experience in terms of the westward expansions of the nineteenth century, comparing and contrasting the "pioneers" who "gazed westward across the river" to an open prairie "promising another coast, another world" with those new migrants following in this great American migrant tradition, "the great rite of passage . . . the symbol of America," and yet who are persecuted, exploited, and "invisible, pinpoints of brown on a field of white." Despite these ironies of how migrancy is viewed culturally, Martinez, like Rivera before him, remains optimistic, recording the resilience and fortitude of those who may never fully "arrive" into the host nation.[105]

As Rivera's narrator lies symbolically "under the house" in a space apart where he can think and imagine "all the people together," he imagines a community that unites the past and the present and the future and steadfastly refuses to be "devoured" by loss or nostalgic longing, but instead recognizes a significant process: "To discover and rediscover and piece things together. This to this, that to that, all with all. That was it. That was everything. . . . When he got home he went straight to the tree. . . . He climbed it. He saw a palm tree on the horizon. He imagined someone perched on top, gazing across at him. He even raised one arm and waved it back and forth so that the other could see that he knew he was there." The future and the past are linked here, as are the North and the South, life and death, and the narrator and his "other," all linked by a border that in this last moment of the book has become rendered almost invisible, erased by movement and by imagination.[106]

In Martinez's twenty-first-century text, *Crossing Over*, Rivera's migrants look even farther than the immediate horizon for their "arrival," engaged in elaborate circular journeys into and out of the United States, north, east, south, and west. The migrant trail embodies the new global economy that moves workers like commodities across borders, both legally and illegally. The experience of the borderlands, of exchange and motion, has become the currency of globalization: "everywhere at once." "But the biggest draw," for the people of Cherán, "is the world. . . . To move is to live. To move is to head toward the future. Working in the States not only elevates Cherán's economic status but also connects it, culturally, to the whirlwind of globalization," making it an example of what Mike Davis calls a "transnationalized" community.[107] Through circumstance, tradition, and the inevitable presence of the rich neighbors to the north, towns like Cherán are emblematic communities, "turbulently transcultural," blending the cultures of tradition with those of the future and reminding Martinez that "The border is indeed everywhere now, has moved northward from the Rio Grande clear across the country."[108] Martinez refuses nostalgia for some lost time and sees in this migrant community, as Rivera had in the 1940s, a strong will to adapt via the various routes they experience: geographical passage, return, and escape, as well as those other routes of imagination, rumor, story, and hybridization. Along such multiple routes Martinez charts changing identities, a global mestizo/mestiza, in keeping with a long-held tradition of what Davis calls "adaptive mutation," best epitomized by the youth cultures of Cherán wearing African American gangsta clothing, U.S. basketball affiliations, and whose "banda" music spells out the various traditions that collide there, as in the figure of Dante Cerano, a local disc jockey.[109] Martinez calls him the "embodiment of the clashing and melding that define Purépecha identity in the twenty-first century," "bilingual" and aware of community values such as "collectivism and solidarity" played out in the many rituals but also aware of the need to meet economic demands through migration. For him this double process means the Purépechans "create their identity . . . tell their own stories" by "sorting through what remains of pre-Conquest history . . . and by taking stock of what the conqueror offers." For Cerano, these migrants "can have their cake and eat it, too: they can partake in—indeed, be protagonists of—transnational or 'global' culture even as they nurture the vestiges of their roots. In this context, the regional is global and vice-versa." In practice, this is the exercise of what Davis terms "strategic mitosis, dividing themselves into two parts to sustain a single heredity."[110] Almost invoking the language of Gilroy and Clifford, Ceran explains the concept of routes/roots and how, in the global, transnational circuits of the "circum-West," one can form an identity through both.

Rivera's narrator gazing across the border to the "Other" beyond is here amplified to a global scale, along both real and virtual routes of connection that form coherent if fluid new communities. Whatever globalization is, it is far from simple in its consequences, and indeed, for many, as here, it seems contradictory, forcing us to rethink notions of identity, nation, and culture. Echoing Doreen Massey's sense of place, discussed earlier, "as a meeting place, the location of the intersections of particular bundles of activity spaces, of connections and interrelations, of influences and movements," borderlands space is a complex contact zone formed from "some never-completed, complex process of combining elements from different cultural repertoires to form 'new' cultures

which are related to but which are not exactly like any of the originals
. . . this process of transculturation is sometimes referred to as hybridisation."[111] This is precisely what is being uncovered through the actual
participant observation of Martinez's work alongside his "informants,"
like Ceran or Wense, whose lives, as lines of flight, are being shaped by
diasporic processes. As another informant, Jordán, puts it, "The roots
always lead me back . . . and then I start to miss the life that I'm used to.
I guess I've got roots in both places now" (emphasis added). Ceran's lived experience of "transculturation" defines transnationalism (and perhaps
points toward a form of postnationalism) where his social relations
and networks have become stretched over space and memory, across
the border, across nations, to the point that his own sense of locality
and belonging (of "roots") has been altered by his participation in globalization.[112] Yet the older traditions survive too under new conditions,
often despite them, as Martinez explains: "In the end the joke will be
on the gringo and Mexican guardians of reified notions of culture. The
kids will be neither Mexican nor gringo but both, and more than both,
they will be the New Americans, imbibing cultures from all over the
globe."[113]

It is this position that Martinez himself also identifies with, an "in-between": "we are neither, we are both . . . painful and exhilarating . . . we
cannot be one, must always be two and more than two: the sum of our
parts will always be greater than the whole," a human equivalent of the
border radio where "signals cross" mixing Pedro Infante with Johnny
Cash and where "Vicky Carr's purr hovers like a ghostly harmony over
Elvis Presley's croon."[114] As Hall and Gilroy have explored, this is a form
of diasporic identity: "people who belong to more than one world, speak
more than one language (literally and metaphorically), inhabit more than
one identity, have more than one home; who have learned to negotiate
and translate *between cultures*, and who because they are irrevocably the
product of several interlocking histories and cultures, have learned to
live with, and indeed to speak from, *difference*." This position "between"
is "always unsettling the assumptions of one culture from the perspective of another," providing an "alternative framework" that "cuts across
the traditional boundaries of the nation-state, provides linkages across
the borders of national communities," forcing us to rethink notions of

identity, culture, and place.[115] These theories, materialized in the lives and stories of Martinez's migrants, clearly contest simplistic readings of culture, place, and identity as static, rooted, and linear, seeing instead how cultures, in reality, move along various routes, like those defined by Gilroy as "striking the important balance between inside and outside activity—the different practices, cognitive, habitual, and performative, that are required to invent, maintain, and renew identity. These have constituted the black Atlantic [or circum/rhizomatic West] as a non-traditional tradition, an irreducibly modern, ex-centric, unstable, and asymmetrical cultural ensemble that cannot be apprehended through the manichean logic of binary coding."[116]

In all these complex circuits of identity, Martinez is self-consciously looping his text to provide an ironic, folded vision of the West as an "ex-centric, unstable, and asymmetrical cultural ensemble" stretched by globalization, rewritten by migration, and reinvented through its hybrid cultures. Any nostalgia for a simple, clear-cut vision of culture, place, and identity is as remote as Urrea's dream of being a western gunfighter who could "rob a bank . . . wield a six-gun and make it all better . . . ride into my past and shoot the daylights out of everything, grab everybody and ride into the sunset." The reality is always more messy and complex; as he puts it, "Man, you can't shoot a ghost."[117] Similarly, Martinez's iconic memories of the Hollywood Westerns he watched as a child stereotyping Mexico, migrant children "enraptured at the sight of cowboys on horses thundering over the red dirt of Monument Valley," his father's ability to juggle John Wayne, the Lone Ranger, and Old Mexico, and even in his own admission that "I wanted to be a cowboy, just as my father had sided with the cowboys against the Indians in the Western flicks," all signify a unproblematic reading of culture rooted in supposedly stable, unquestioned myths.[118]

In Crossing Over, where cultural lines are blurred and identities often fuzzy, these myths resurface as a more layered vision of the present, where "the migrants, the new cowboys of Watsonville" mix with their "original" counterparts on the dance floor on Saturday nights so that "the cowboys, the Indians, the cowboy Indians dance" as if in some elaborate "Cowboy drag." As he asks, "So if They've Become Us, then Who are We?"[119] In the swirl of global economic movement and migration, the western "dance" is perhaps a fitting metaphor for Martinez's circulated and mutated West, a semi-patterned "contact zone" where improvisation is encouraged and where different people mix and interrelate, move in and out, arrive and depart, stop and start, argue and love. It simultaneously recalls earlier uses of the metaphor to describe both Teshigara's *Blue Meteorite*, "a dance over a long rectangle of broken glass," and Sanchez's urban art "all a crazy dance . . . a crossroads, a cross-*commerce*, a cross-*culture*," as well as, most significantly, Anzaldúa's description of her work as "a crazy dance" "barely contained . . . to spill over the boundaries of the object it represents and into other 'objects' and over the borders of the frame."[120] Even Bowden employs the image to suggest the edgy cultural shifts of Chihuahua opposed to the official strictures of the border: "It is the reality jerking our limbs, moving our feet, lifting us from our slumbers, and causing us to dance."[121] This intertextual image cluster represents the complexity of contemporary culture, a borderlands "dance" that spills still further outward, across the United States and beyond, presenting a vision of hybrid, transnational flows that conjures up a sense of the circum-West in all its rhizomatic intensity where "We all dance to a World Beat."[122] Like the dance, these writings formulate complex new "corridos" for a global age, and, as Bowden puts it, "The songs will cross all known borders. But they will have an edge. Believe it, *companero*."[123]

Conclusion: The Alchemy of Connection

With this in mind I wish to turn again to Gloria Anzaldúa, whose work, though more mystical and poetic than Martinez's, has, as I indicated earlier, interesting points of intersection, developing from radical Chicana lesbian feminism toward a wider cultural politics. In her later writings, Anzaldúa mused on the ideas of "conocimiento," "nos/otras" and "new tribalism," which I believe have relevance to this discussion of Martinez's work in particular. In her efforts to be more inclusive (with men and whites) and to break the habits of defining by exclusion, Anzaldúa called for a "new tribalism" to create "bridges" between groups, since "To bridge means loosening our borders, not closing off to others. Bridging is the work of opening the gate to the stranger, within and without . . . into unfamiliar territory." Once again, there are points of connection between Anzaldúa and Gómez-Pena, who has also written of how the "hybrid" perspective allows the "outside" into the frame, being "at the same time an insider and an outsider, an expert in border crossings, a temporary member of multiple communities. . . . His/her job to trespass, bridge, interconnect, reinterpret, remap, and redefine; to find the outer limits of his/her culture and cross them."[124] Like Martinez in *The New Americans*, Anzaldúa writes in the awareness of globalization, of "hierarchies of commerce and power—a collusion of government, transnational industry, business, and the military," and argues that a "new paradigm must come from outside as well as within the system." For Anzaldúa, as we have seen, this means an "inner exploration" and a rupture from "current categories, classifications, and contents," or what Chela Sandoval calls "the grids of domination and subordination," into "nepantla" ("the zone between changes"), and the creation of "conocimiento" with "new stories [which] must partially come from outside the system of ruling powers."[125]

Martinez is often rightly skeptical about how the idea of the border has become a source of "appropriative fascination" for academic theorists and has been employed to articulate imprecise, apolitical theories, and he believes that what must always be remembered are "the critiques of power relations that had spawned it": the realpolitik of NAFTA, the maquiladoras, the violent oppression, and "the fabled New World Order, in which capital moves easily and labor is trapped by borders."[126] His writings, like Urrea's, aim to remind us of these imbalances of power through capturing the everyday, lived experiences of those for whom the promise of migration is as real and terrifying now as it was for Rivera's characters, or those in Gregory Nava's films *El Norte* and *My Family* or Robert M. Young's *Alambrista*—people for whom the reality of border-crossing is a "constant negotiation of influences from both North and South," experiencing "globalisation from below," however painful and dangerous.[127] Yet, despite its often philosophical and mystical resonance that seems to distance it from such material concerns, Anzaldúa's work has always been informed by the painful cultural politics of the border's "*herida abierta* [open wound] where the Third World grates against the first and bleeds":

1,950 mile-long wound
   dividing a pueblo, a culture,
    running down the length of my body,
       staking fence rods in my flesh,
       splits me splits me . . .
  This is my home
  This thin edge of
     barbwire.[128]

Indeed, her later preface to *This Bridge We Call Home*, like Martinez's con-clusion to *The New Americans*, was written after the 9/11 attacks on New York and Washington DC and in the light of calls for a "war on terror" and the securing of national borders, and yet Anzaldúa argues that one needs even more to "reflect on this arrebato" (breach) and use "conflict" to "trigger transformation" and lead to "conocimiento" (understand-ing). For those attempting this inclusive healing process are "nepant-leras" forging bridges and links, seeking conciliation and understand-ing out of these moments of nepantla enabling "us to reimagine our lives, rewrite the self, and create guiding myths for our times." Such a process emerges, as in Martinez, from "outside," from "living between cultures," forging a "double" vision, estranged from the centers of both cultures so that one no longer sees the world "the way you were encul-turated to see it . . . you see the fiction of the monoculture."[129]

In a brave call for "new tribalism," like a spiritualized extension of Martinez's "New Americans," Anzaldúa demands, as does Gilroy, the abandonment of narrow essentialism and nationalism in the search for common ground: "How can you step outside ethnic and other labels while cleaving to your root identity? Your identity has roots you share with all people and other things—spirit, feeling, and body make up a greater iden-tity category . . . the new tribalism . . . propagating other worldviews, spiri-tual traditions and cultures. . . . Your resistance to identity boxes leads you to a different tribe, a different story (of mestizaje) enabling you to rethink yourself in more global-spiritual terms instead of conventional categories of color, class, career." Anzaldúa's call is to "an emerging planetary cul-ture" to bridge nation-states and defined, gridded identities, for in this "the narrative national boundaries dividing us from the 'others' (nos/

otras) are porous and the cracks between worlds serve as gateways." She explains this latter concept as follows: "In nos/otras, the 'us' is divided in two, the slash in the middle representing the bridge—the best mutuality we can hope for at the moment. Las nepantleras envision a time when the bridge will no longer be needed—we'll have shifted to a seamless noso-tras." New tribalism, emerging from the borderlands experience, stresses interconnectivity over division, new forms of community that cut across dominant modes of power and organization: "You look beyond the illu-sion of separate interests to a shared interest—you're in this together, no one's an isolated unit." Although there is a strong spiritual and internal aspect to Anzaldúa's commitment to change, she knows this has to be wedded to the "struggle for social transformation," from the self outward to the world. Importantly, she links this to the "archetypal journey home to the self," recalling the work of both Martinez and Urrea, and recog-nizing there is no essential home but only "that bridge, the in-between place of nepantla and constant transition, the most unsafe of all spaces," since "you don't build bridges to safe and familiar territories, you have to risk making nuevo mundo, have to risk the uncertainty of change. And nepantla is the only space where changes happens." The "nuevo mundo" refers back to Martinez's and Urrea's circuits of migration searching out the promise of new and better lives, bridging between worlds, bearing the pain and the suffering in hope of the transformation it might bring.[130]

In the contradictory climate of post-9/11 United States, where bor-ders are seen as under constant threat and the "outsider" something to be feared, Martinez reminds us that migration is "an awkward, messy, painful, sublime process," and yet for all that "It was, it is, an American process" from which everyone must learn:

> The migrants are a mirror in which we see the best and the worst of ourselves, our past and our future. They remind us over and again that there is nothing stable in our world: No state, no culture, no religion, no politics is immune from history and the way it shapes space and time.
>
> The migrants tell us that we are, all of us, always on the move.[131]

Or perhaps, to see it slightly differently, as Rosa Linda Fregoso has claimed, there is an even more profound possibility of a new "cultural citizenship" forming out of these complex dynamics: "These transnational immigrants are creating the conditions of possibility for the emergence of a new political consciousness, brewing in many of those hidden corridors throughout the new borderlands a consciousness that joins the ancient call for social justice everywhere."[132] As Urrea has said about the border, "I don't know what the solution is. I just want to show you. I just want you to know. . . . I just want to write haiku. But *the border keeps happening*" (emphasis added).[133] Whatever we think of this "happening," it may represent what Bowden, following a similar point made by both Néstor Garcia Canclini and Goméz-Pena, has called "the laboratory of our future," something fluid and beyond nations' control, constantly subverting the grid, defying surveillance, beautiful and horrific, and testifying to the immense will, spirit, and resilience of human beings in the face of immense suffering.[134] In Bowden's deliberately provocative, ambivalent image it is likened to a rhizomatic flower:

> A lush beautiful thing blooming color, hypnotizing the eye, flaunting style, oozing sex, and beckoning with lust and love. . . . But something has gone awry. . . . The flowers have become somehow monstrous. They have become blooms beyond taxonomy. They spread at will, crossing borders, boundaries, all known proprieties. . . . This inability to paste a simple label on the thing is driving officials almost mad. . . . Worse than the kudzu vine. Worse than the killer bee. . . . The scent seductive, thorns sharp, roots out of sight but running deeply and sinking into the earth and refusing to let go. No matter what.[135]

And for Bowden, as for Martinez and Anzaldúa, the official lines of the border are cut through by the "edge," by actual migration and practice, suggesting the "emergence of a place beneath the maps of nations and beneath the consciousness of rulers. . . . The very thing happening is what is being denied by the rhetoric of nations."[136] This comes close to Gómez-Pena's notion of a "new cartography," or what he later called "a moving cartography with a floating culture and fluctuating sense of self."[137] Actual life defies official rhetoric and the "virtual reality" of the border maintained by "nations": "We have become something else," Bowden writes, "something new because we are not dying, we are being born."[138]

But, as in all these border narratives, any new birth is painful and bloody, a fact highlighted throughout Bowden's work—"the edge is a jittery place full of heat, color, gore, change, collision, and lust. . . . We press on, being born, bleeding, listening to all the jukeboxes as the choppers whomp over our heads and flash the spotlights in the night."[139] As Bowden puts in *Juarez*, almost despite the pain, "The future has a way of coming from the edges, of being created not in the central plaza but on the blurry fringes of our peripheral vision" through "events in excess of our frames of reference."[140] Indeed, his metaphor for this change is a powerful, violent one, returning again to Anzaldúa's and Martinez's use of the earthquake for effect: "I felt the jagged rock in my mouth, faced up to the blood on my tongue, sensed the sounds struggling up from my throat . . . our tongues keep licking and licking that jagged lava . . . a secret universe is so alive the maps deny it exists." This "molten" cross-border breach of official, mapped, and gridded culture is Bowden's territory—unstable, edgy, "rising from the molten lava, the earth shaking"; "something new is emerging, something still seeking that word which will be its name. An orphan child of two nations, two ebbing nations, a jittery child. . . . An edge." Rather like the dance metaphor used earlier, nations are bound together and interdependent in this process, "Sometimes it seems like a marriage, sometimes more like a collision but still it keeps happening," and out of this violent "happening" the "edge" creates an unpredictable, rhizomatic space: "We are becoming. We are going toward something. But we are not there yet. We are an unfinished thing."[141] Bowden's words remind us of Deleuze's definition of a rhizome that "may be broken, shattered at a given spot, but it will start up again on one of its old lines, or on new lines," like border crossers, obsessed with "becoming" and the belief that "Becoming is always 'between' or 'among'—a spatial edge of flows and transfers, motion and collision, a border where differences overlap and are conjoined by an 'and'": "AND is neither one thing nor the other, it's always in-between, between two things; it's the borderline, there's always a border, a line of flight or flow. . . . And yet it's along this line of flight that things come to pass, becomings evolve, revolutions take shape. . . . . An AND, AND, AND which each time marks a new threshold, a new direction of the zigzagging line, a new course for the border."[142] Becoming within this space is "a bastard people, inferior, dominated, always in becoming, always incomplete," where "bastard" is not familial but "the process or drift of the races," the "invention of a people, that is, a possibility of life," an imagined people who are currently "missing" from the dominant cultural order and its regimented forms of expression and control.[143] For Gómez-Pena and others writing in the post-9/11 climate of a "war on terror," of a new "cartography of fear" (not hope), where the United States has, once again, become the global "sheriff," the "Robocop against the Global Evil," the possibilities envisioned in the borderlands seem more important than ever. The "borderization" of the world, where notions of hybridity, syncretism, negotiation, and intercultural dialogue circulate as people jostle for space and power in contact zones, is central to Gómez-Pena's work and, as we have seen, implicit in Anzaldúa's later writings, presenting some blueprint for what Martinez has termed "post-border cultures": "one huge borderland [where] traditions clash and meld."[144] Anzaldúa's discussion of "mestizaje," which offered an early vision of fused identities, is central to the "evolving [culture] . . . that transcends the demarcations of border patrols and free trade zones . . . a post-border culture . . . much *more than* a regional phenomenon. *More than* a geographical region . . . a cultural space created by forces that are not unique to this region, but part of a much larger, indeed global, evolution" (emphasis added). For Martinez, "mestizaje" is mobile, always "more than" one thing, an "ongoing process" where, to borrow from Deleuze, "becomings [might] evolve, revolutions take shape" in a multiple cultural space of mixing, not just of blood, but ideas, thoughts, feelings, fears, and aspirations—"a border, a line of flight or flow"—"a journey that has no end . . . the cultural version of perpetual motion not in theory but in practice." He would, therefore, agree with Gómez-Pena, who sees this rhizomatic process as having now gone "way beyond mestizaje," since the reality is no longer simply about fusion but about numerous interlocking and "overlapping subcultures" that indicate complex and shared spaces whose meanings are impossible to fix and which point toward a vital readjustment of our sense of nation, culture, place, and identity, acknowledging mobilities and routes as well as stabilities and roots in how America defines itself. "So then," writes Martinez, "to be American (north and south) is to move. To run away, to run towards, forever leaving, forever arriving, forever trying to return," but the "elemental irony" in all this is that "the 'Americans' whose own origins are a classic migrant story, are now the ones telling the Other Americans, the Mexicans [and other groups], to stop moving. . . . They will not stop moving." As all the borders of the world shift and the American West redefines itself within this mobile global terrain, perhaps there is truth in Martinez's claim that "All our backs are wet."[145]

3. WELCOME TO WESTWORLD
Sergio Leone's Once Upon a Time in the West

The American cinema constantly shoots and reshoots a single
fundamental film, which is the birth of a nation-civilisation.
Gilles Deleuze

The previous year, Baba had surprised Hassan with a
leather cowboy hat just like the one Clint Eastwood wore in
The Good, the Bad, and the Ugly—which had unseated
The Magnificent Seven as our favourite Western. That whole winter,
Hassan and I took turns wearing the hat, and belted out the film's famous
music as we climbed mounds of snow and shot each other dead.
Khaled K. Hosseini

Learning from Almería

An expanded critical regionalism like that explored in the previous chapters demonstrates that no region can be static or inward-looking, for it
needs to recognize forces beyond the nation, considering how the regional travels and dialogues with other cultures, circulating as it is consumed and re-produced in other forms. As the West is performed and
practiced outside its geographical and ideological boundaries (or grids),
as in Khaled Hosseini's Afghanistan-set novel The Kite Runner (quoted
above), it undergoes changes akin to the "wandering lines" described by
Michel De Certeau—"'indirect' or 'errant' trajectories obeying their own
logic . . . [creating] unforeseeable sentences, partly unreadable paths"—
and although they share a common "root" in the American West ("the
vocabularies of established languages"), "the trajectories trace out ruses
of other interests and desires that are neither determined nor captured
by the systems in which they develop." These trajectories (or routes)
beyond the grid demonstrate the rhizomatic potential of "westness"
exemplified, in this chapter, through the tactics adopted by Italian filmmaker Sergio Leone as he "poached" the language of the Western in the
1960s, creating an alternative "outside" within the existing framework of
the genre, with textual and ideological ruses that "circulate, come and
go, overflow and drift over an imposed terrain, a manoeuvre 'within the
enemy's field of vision.'"[1] From this he developed a "recycled," hybrid

genre known as *Western all'italiana*, or more colloquially as "spaghetti Westerns," "more cynical, ironic [than any Hollywood Western], like the *commedia all'italiana*."[2]

Indeed, the physical traces of these creations still exist, north of the city of Almería on the southern coast of Spain, inland near Tabernas, as the remains of the film sets used by Leone and other directors to produce hundreds of Italian (and Spanish) Westerns.[3] They have become quasi–theme parks like "Mini Hollywood," run-down, struggling sites like "Western Leone," or more impressive, still-used film sets like "Texas Hollywood" with its adobe church, clapboard main street, and saloon. Here you can find the impressive log home of the McBain family from *Once Upon a Time in the West* (now a saloon), the (rebuilt) stone arch where Harmonica's brother is killed by Frank, the bank of El Paso in *For a Few Dollars More*, and other locations that, even if not the originals, simulate the scenes from a hundred themselves-simulated Western films. This is the American West Leone created: a European version that looked authentic but, at the same time, had a particular quality of light, filmed in a unique manner to emphasize its stark, isolated beauty. The uncanny, disorienting experience of these places, even today, mirrors the effects of spaghetti Westerns—both familiar and unfamiliar, strangely unsettling, "more Western than Westerns themselves." Of course, the fact that these sites remain preserved and visited by thousands every year adds further to the circulation of the West as a global concept, as iconography and experience, as myth and simulation. Tourism further recycles Leone's vision, staging "live" shows on the streets of every site, imitating in (usually) stilted fashion the particular mannerist qualities of "spaghetti" acting styles: laconic, slow, packed with looks and glances, and explosively violent. In this, the "already-said" of Leone's pastiche and homage, learned from a studious comprehension of American Western codes, is played out again—simulated like a faulty copy—on a twice-daily basis in the dusty, hot hills of Almería by local people dreaming of elsewhere. But the copied copy is a perfect reminder of the West's existence as a complex, traveling concept, a rhizomatic formation crisscrossing continents, being constantly reconfigured and used in all manner of ways. Any sense of an original, authentic West has been displaced and disrupted by the effect of the hyperreal, like the streets of "Western

4. Neil Campbell, Texas-Hollywood (2005) (original in color).

Leone," where the real and the imaginary collapse into each other, creating a thirdspace from which interesting, critical questions emerge about the production and consumption of meaning, about the role of myth and icon, and about the persistence and fascination with all aspects of westness (see figures 4 and 5). For me, therefore, these sites inadvertently continue Leone's own filmic interrogations. The same sites Leone once used to signify the West still circulate within commercial culture as settings for low-budget television productions like *Lucky Luke*, postmodern films like Alex Cox's punk Western *Straight to Hell* (1986) or Alex De la Iglesia's wonderful *800 Bullets* (2002), music videos like Sting's "Cowboy Song," and most famously by reinventing the spaghetti Western as a Pepsi advertisement using David Beckham and assorted Spanish footballers. Appropriately, one of Leone's collaborators, Dario Argento, makes the point that most "spaghetti" filmmakers knew "Westerns only because of movies" and therefore were always engaged in imaginative reconstructions in their work, a critical screening of existing images reinterpreted and vital to the effectiveness of the films working with and against genre memory.[4]

One experiences Almería's sites today as a "post-tourist," a tourist not in search of some authentic or unique event but one who revels in the en-

5. *Neil Campbell, Leone's Almería (2005) (original in color).*

tirety of what tourism has become, a bundle of complex relations among place, representation, knowledge, and mystery. One does not go to Tabernas for a "real" western or Leone moment but instead for a layered series of artificial, constructed experiences that can oscillate between kitsch and iconography, between recognition and revulsion. The "playful" post-tourist in situ (like the viewer of a Leone film) "traverses a landscape," noting its "geometric complexities . . . jazzlike discordances . . . [and] variety of aesthetic contexts" with the "humorous eye for 'kitsch' as well," enjoying "the connective tissue *between* 'attractions' as much as the vaunted attractions themselves" (emphasis added), but in addition calls upon a vast range of other media-generated "landscapes" of sensation, knowledge, and imagination that, in the words of Arjun Appadurai, "transform the field of mass mediation because they offer new resources and new disciplines for the construction of imagined selves and imagined worlds."[5]

The post-tourist perspective alerts us to the potential for contestation and transformation, blending the actual and the virtual into "a constitutive feature of modern subjectivity," aware of multiple positions simultaneously, as "a tourist . . . not a time traveller when he goes somewhere historic; not an instant noble savage when he stays on a tropical beach; not an invisible observer when he visits a native compound" and, we might add, not a Western hero on a Leone film set. The post-tourist perspective, therefore, enables one to embrace *and* critique the experience as part of the dialogical process of being "in-between" both.[6] Alex Cox commented that the effect of the spaghetti Western was to provide "a *view* of a genre, as distanced and critical of its source as the best of comedies," further suggesting this capacity to move "between" forms with "a cynical and conscious undercurrent."[7] Maxine Feifer recognized that achieving "authenticity" was an archaic desire related to an impossible belief in the "real" and the "original" experience, now clearly altered (and enhanced) by the omnipresence of the global media in all its forms. Her examples help us realize there can be no authentic, true experience, whether as a tourist or more generally in life, since even the supposed authentic, as Nathaniel Lewis asserts, is a "cultural construction" sustained by "ideologically infused discourses and delusions," and "what we take to be authentic is a 'simulacrum,' a copy without an original."[8]

This post-tourist method, derived from the deep mapping of such simulated places, is a helpful approach to how we might interpret Leone's work as a whole, and in particular *Once Upon a Time in the West* and its key conceptualization of "cinema cinema," that is, films about films.[9] Interestingly, Wim Wenders commented that watching the film made him feel like a "Western tourist," generating a "strange feeling [that] turned me into a concerned viewer," making him aware not of the "surface" but "rather what lies beneath: the inner side of Westerns . . .

[where] something else glimmers." Almost inadvertently, Wenders articulates my point about the effect of Leone's film as it moves us between the "surface" and "what lies beneath," between the mythic grid and the more complex, rhizomatic "wandering lines" within.[10]

The endless recycling of western iconography as a global production of meaning was recognized by Leone; indeed, I believe it was central to his approach in the Dollars trilogy—*A Fistful of Dollars* (1964), *For a Few Dollars More* (1965), and *The Good, the Bad and the Ugly* (1966)—and to *Once Upon a Time in the West* (1968), the film he defined as "the summa of everything for me."[11] He once said, "America is really *the property of the world*. . . . America was something dreamed by philosophers, vagabonds, and the wretched of the earth way before it was discovered by Spanish ships. . . . The Americans have only rented it temporarily." Indeed, he continued, "the problems of America are the problems of the whole world: the contradictions, the fantasies, the poetry. The minute you touch down on America, you touch on universal themes."[12] This "property" is nowhere clearer than in the West and in the Western as a global phenomenon being reinterpreted in Leone's films that dared to assault one of the mainstays of westernness, its authenticity: "Like jazz and baseball, the Western was home-grown, as American as apple pie, the form that celebrated our pioneer and immigrant roots."[13] The "roots" of the West, which tie it to national identity formation, and the Western's expected coded formulae, which ritualize and dramatize these apparently essential American qualities (masculinity, capitalism, individualism, destiny, etc.), are undone by Leone, who uses them as the "ground" for his films, only to reroute them and thereby represent and explore ideological tensions inherent within the genre and, by implication, within notions of the complex discourse of westness itself. Just as the preserved sites of Almería act as material reminders of postmodernism's interest in simulation, intertextuality, and performance, they also create a sense of dislocation and distance, both effects associated with its philosophical positions. It is no surprise that Jean Baudrillard called Leone "the first post-modernist director," while Leone collaborator Bernardo Bertolucci referred to *Once Upon a Time in the West* as "the first and only postmodernist Western!"[14] The fixed and stable parameters of the Western, as a form of "grand narrative" defined in the canonical Hollywood Westerns of those like John Ford, are unraveled and interrogated by Leone's postmodern "cohesive creation of an imaginary multi-layered world, at once wholly familiar and wholly alien, horrific, comic and absurd," countering the homogenized universals of earlier films.[15] In John Storey's words, grand narratives function by "marshalling heterogeneity into ordered realms; silencing and excluding other discourses, other voices in the name of universal principles and general goals," while postmodernism's response is "a plurality of voices from the margins, with their insistence on difference, on cultural diversity, and the claims of heterogeneity over homogeneity."[16] Leone's films are never just about pastiche or nostalgia, never simply citing other films in an uncritical manner, but rather deploying these elements as tools of drama and interrogation, creating rich and playful texts that also delve into and analyze established ideologies, iconographies, and histories of the West.

Reaccenting the Western

In pursuing this postmodern process, Leone's work employs a persistent and critical "reaccentuation" of the Western genre, a term I borrow from Bakhtin: "Every age re-accentuates in some way the works of its most immediate past. The historical life of classic works is in fact the uninterrupted process of their social and ideological re-accentuation.... New images . . . are very often re-accentuating old images, by translating them from one accentual register to another (from the comic plane to the tragic or the other way around)."[17] Of course, the multiple locations, the dubbing of Leone's films, their use of different nationalities, and their deliberate examination of the "grammar" and "language" conventions of the Western genre make them constantly engaged in these processes of reaccentuation. This is further accelerated as the films travel between cultures, literally and metaphorically "translated" and circulated among different audiences. Bakhtin's process informs the "accented" cinema defined and developed in the postcolonial film criticism of Hamid Naficy. For Naficy, "accented" films are primarily Third Cinema texts informed by "prevailing cinematic modes" but simultaneously constituted by the "structures of feeling" of their directors "as displaced subjects and by the traditions of exilic and diasporic cultural productions." Out of this doubleness, a deterritorialized "accented style" emerges expressing mixed feelings reflecting tensions manifested in the director's position in relation to dominant cinematic and political systems. Naficy calls this position "interstitial" and argues that "accented" films "are created astride and in the interstices of social formations and cinematic practices" and by so doing exercise a "critical" eye over all sides, "expressing, allegorising, commenting upon, and critiquing the home and host societies and cultures and the deterritorialized conditions of the filmmakers." Indeed, one of the interstitial categories he discusses is that of "border consciousness" with its "hybridized," "cross-cultural and intercultural" subjectivities and its concern for "multifocality, multilinguality," drawing on Mexican American examples such as Gloria Anzaldúa and the films of Gregory Nava.[18]

While these definitions cannot be applied uniformly to Leone's work, the sense of the "accented" voice informing Naficy's theory does have some relationship to an Italian director working simultaneously within and outside a dominantly American tradition, genre, and set of audience expectations. Leone is "exiled" outside Hollywood, bringing an alternative set of values, practices, and political positions to bear on this most American of genres. His "border consciousness" deliberately employs specific border locations to examine colonial relations of power as well as to suggest his broader perspective of "exilic liminality," viewing issues and identities from "both sides," thereby creating a border vision.[19] As discussed in chapter 2, the borderlands signify the West as part of a wider region dramatically unfinished or contested, where the vision of progress often associated with the incipient town and founding community is replaced by dusty deserts, whitewashed villages, and spaces of transition (railroads, deserts, dusty back roads). In De Certeau's terms, these are the "places of transit, where 'borderline,' 'borrowed' or 'rejected' phenomena can be perceived" and opposed to "supposed or posited totalities," bringing to them a "corrective" and "bringing forth differences relative to continuities."[20] In this way, Leone, as an "interstitial" figure working between and across traditions, links Bakhtin's and Naficy's ideas, demonstrating how the accented and the reaccentuated overlap, as Taghi Modarressi has written: "The accented voice is loaded with hidden messages from our cultural heritage . . . [and this language] can build a bridge between what is familiar and what is strange. They

120

may then find it possible to generate new and revealing paradoxes . . . our juxtapositions and transformations—the graceful and the awkward, the beautiful and the ugly, sitting side by side in a perpetual metamorphosis of one into the other."[21] In many ways, therefore, Leone's capacity to work both inside and outside the accepted frameworks of the Western reveals a similar desire for "juxtapositions and transformations" that places the viewer *between* "accents," temporarily "exiled" from the comfort of generic conventions and their concomitant values, into a new uncanny cinematic thirdspace "bridging" the familiar and the strange.[22] This suggests both the political vision of Third Cinema and a clear indication of the postcolonial theory Naficy calls "third optique," a critical thirdspace that deconstructs and challenges binaries, presenting instead a cinema that is "multiperspectival and tolerant of ambiguity, ambivalence, and chaos."[23] This can be a zone of discomfort, where expectations are stretched and broken and ideologies destabilized and questioned, such as when *Once Upon a Time in the West* opens with a lengthy, almost speechless sequence that echoes familiar Westerns like *High Noon* (with the gang awaiting the arrival of their leader) but simultaneously reverses and distorts expectations formally and thematically with a stylized sequence heavily influenced by the surrealist artist Giorgio De Chirico.[24] In what Leone referred to as his method of "provocation," this gang awaits an enemy in a scene that Leone stretches out with a sound track of squeaking metal, dripping water, and buzzing flies, played out in a landscape of extremes: a vast timber boardwalk creating a stage on which these performers will act out their death throes at a harsh, barren desert station called Cattle Corner, with no livestock in sight.[25] In these uncanny, surreal spaces of contradiction—that is, as both familiar (as iconically "western") and unfamiliar (stretched and distorted) at the same time—Leone sets the film's critical tone: at once *of* the Western but always going beyond it, drawing the audience "outside" its boundaries into a slow, analytical interrogation of its formal qualities, its detail, its fictional component parts, its mythologies. As Christopher Frayling has put it, Leone "lovingly re-created [the Hollywood Western] before being turned inside out," and we witness this critical "folding" in this elongated scene.[26]

To this end, we recognize from a hundred Westerns Jack Elam (one of the waiting three) and certainly note the black gunfighter, played by Woody Strode, an iconic John Ford actor (most famously in *Sergeant Rutledge* and as Pompey in *The Man Who Shot Liberty Valance*). In the subtle reversals of this scene, they will die, stripped out of the narrative before it has truly begun, beginning the film's complex process of genre destabilization and erasure. In a similar manner, Leone's choice of Henry Fonda as his central villain, Frank, deliberately reverses the established audience perception of a typical Fonda type—clean-cut, decent, and honest. The "frame" of the Western, its iconographic and ideological grid, as a coded system of expectations and values is pulled askew here, as throughout the film, with Leone probing its structure from "outside" and proving that the genre cannot be complacent or contained. As Deleuze writes of painting, any framed "picture is also traversed by a deframing power that opens it onto a plane of composition or an infinite field of forces . . . all of which give the picture the power to leave the canvas." Indeed, Deleuze and Guattari connect this with literature's power, as defined by Bakhtin, to be "contrapuntal, polyphonic, and plurivocal compounds" traversed by multiple "voices" into hybrid textual fields that defy "framing" as they move outward.[27] Thus in reaccenting the genre Leone pays homage to its history while simultaneously renewing it with critical energy that connects it to a wider "plane of composition," that is, to forces and implications beyond its apparent frame.

A Postcolonial Western?

Paul Smith argues that the spaghetti Western represents the "only major and sustained revision of that central Hollywood movie genre, the western, that has been undertaken outside Hollywood and largely without its capital," and that it therefore stands as a "response" or "riposte" to "colonizing models on the part of what can effectively be called a subaltern culture (that is a culture whose structures and formations on many important levels are provoked by and forged in the shadow of a more dominant culture)." As a "subaltern commodity" it critiques the dominant culture and returns "to affect and alter production" in America, thus actively and dialogically engaging with the Hollywood tradition in complex webs of exchange, or what I earlier referred to as "cultural import-export."[28] This "return" demonstrates once again how iconography travels and mutates, is "used" and challenged within the complex circuits of cultural exchange across the "circum-West." Leone's Westerns were never anti-American, but their ambivalence and their multi-accented approach to an often overly regulated genre breathed new life into the form, opening it up to new possibilities and problems. Frayling refers to this transatlantic exchange as the "cultural roots controversy" because it was felt that American films were the "roots" of the Western, with sole access to what Krista Comer calls the "insider, regional discourse," and that everything else was merely a corrupt, bastardized version of the original.[29] The migratory and diasporic tendencies of the West's various discourses (of its "westness") undercut any notion of a "pure," authentic form interfered with by traveling genres such as that of Leone. Rather, corrupting the original, "authentic" Western and its claims of historical/national truths, as some American critics believed, the "spaghettis" offered something new, what Smith calls "deliberate transformations," through which the Western's range was extended and altered as it "traveled" into and out of Europe: "Again this is a procedure that is reminiscent of the way in which subaltern or colonial agents will not only lionize the American product or artifact but also at the same time turn it to different signifying ends and social functions within their own cultural systems."[30]

Employing ideas from postcolonial theory, Smith's arguments enable a view of spaghettis that rejects simple imitation as their objective and sees instead a series of complex relations between the films (on several levels) and the dominant Hollywood genre. Leone's *Once Upon a Time in the West* acts, to borrow words from Kobena Mercer, as a "dislocation of [American] national identity (and its narratives of manifest destiny) in a new era of globalization."[31] In their most extreme form, spaghetti Westerns are, according to Giuliana Muscio, a "counterattack on American cinema's own ground . . . [a] revenge on Hollywood" for having Americanized the Italian film industry for many years.[32] Under these terms, Leone's works can be read as distinctly postcolonial, portraying contests between those dominant forces—like Morton and Frank in *Once Upon a Time in the West* seeking to impose their single, seamless vision upon the world—and those other forces with contrary aims and purposes. The film's postcolonialist perspectives chime well with the growing alliances of social movements around issues of colonization both between and within nations (it was released in 1968). Leone's perspective from outside enables an interrogation of forms of internal colonization, as "first generation" colonizers (like the Irish McBains) are themselves colonized by the eastern capitalist Morton as he expands ever westward with his version of mechanized Manifest Destiny.

Morton, the crippled, capitalist railroad owner, is a curious paradox whose dream of mobility is to cross America from the Atlantic to the Pacific and to unify the nation by rail (for profit), and yet as a man he is diseased and dying of "tuberculosis of the bones," obsessed by time, immobile, and virtually rigidified by the brace he wears. Ironically, Morton, the "man with no legs" (whose very name suggests death), substitutes action and movement with money and technology; contained and fixed within his luxurious carriage, he imposes an elaborate, ostentatious eastern "home" upon the West. He is variously associated with a turtle (by Frank) and a snail (by Cheyenne), "easy to find" because "you leave a slime behind you like a snail, two beautiful silver rails." His dream of the Pacific Ocean is signified by the painting on his wall of surf and waves crashing on the shore—an image of fluidity, openness, and life that runs contrary to his actual condition of rigidity, fixity, and impending death. The full irony is captured when we see Morton moving within his carriage by means of an elaborate grid of metal above his head, a grid that both echoes his desire to own, order, and control the land outside and, as I have argued earlier in this book, reminds us of the framework of codes, representations, and discursive formations that have constructed the West's iconic presence in our minds, a coding that Leone interrogates relentlessly in this film. Morton's imperial grid, manifested as railroad, is his attempt to manage and control time, to harness the deathly void of the desert landscape across which he travels, and which mirrors his own slow demise, with a mapping process like that described by William L. Fox: "The land becomes landscape becomes map. At that point we're so distant from the land itself that it becomes merely a surface to be manipulated—to be inscribed, erased, written over, which is exactly what happened in America once we had even just begun to fully overlay the cartographic grid upon the West." The tool of empire, the railroad, was a "set of steel-ruled lines that recede into the vanishing point of the frontier, and that measured its progress by ties laid out every few feet."[33] This is Morton's absolute vision of order, as neat as the framed picture on his wall, the grid above his head, and the basic, brutal exercise of power he employs to achieve his ends within the film. Through him is made manifest what Patricia Nelson Limerick defines as "conquest," "the drawing of lines on a map, the definition and allocation of owner- ship . . . and the evolution of land from matter to property."[34]

However, Leone once said, "As Romans, we have a strong sense of the fragility of empires. . . . I admire very much that great optimist John Ford. . . . [A]s Italians, *we see things differently*. That is what I have tried to show in my films. . . . I see the history of the West as really the reign of violence by violence" (emphasis added).[35] It is Frank and Morton who represent this imperial desire as Manifest Destiny, "the reign of violence by violence," rolling out the grid as the ultimate sign of capitalism. Le- one's portrayal of Morton is brutal, representing, as he does, the inevi- table future of the West and the end of its more romantic, mythic phase. Morton's association with motion and time link his capitalist motivation with death; as he tells Frank, "I have no time for surprises," since his dis- ease drives him into "hasty" actions to secure the land he desires. It is his will that destroys the McBain family in the film's second act of slaugh- ter, in which the harmonious preparation for the arrival of Jill, the "new mother," at Sweetwater is cut short by Frank's killings, culminating in the murder of the young son Timmy. The great Fordian Western family narrative is interrupted as an entire genealogical line of inheritance is obliterated in favor of individualist gain. Frank's hired gun is bound up here with Morton's money and so the murder of the child is an extension of Morton's capitalist reach, a point underscored when Frank comments later about being behind Morton's desk; "it's almost like holding a gun, only much more powerful." Frank's goal is to make the transition from gun to desk and become a businessman, one even more ruthless than Morton himself. Morton and Frank enact, as colonial forces, what De Certeau terms a "writing that conquers," "a colonization of the body by the discourse of power" by which "the New World"—now in particular the American West—will be used "as if it were a blank, 'savage' page on which Western desire will be written. It will transform the space of the other into a field of expansion for a system of production."[36] With no signs of an indigenous Indian population except as remains, another phase of settlement, the colonizing Irish McBain family, is "erased" and the "page" cleared by the film's early action to be reinscribed with Morton's "story."

This colonial contact is most apparent as the film intercuts a number of key scenes: first, Frank's "rape" of Jill, prefaced with his having found the unfinished sign for the station McBain was planning for Sweetwater; second, Frank's row with Morton at the Navajo cliffs, where he knocks him down and claims he can "squash him like a wormy apple"; third, Cheyenne and Harmonica's mapping out of Sweetwater on the ground; and fourth, the auction of McBain's land. This sequence is framed by the simultaneous discovery by Jill, Cheyenne, Harmonica, and Frank of McBain's plan for Sweetwater, a railroad station and town built around the water he owns on his land. The symbolically important "empty (wooden) sign" ordered by McBain can now be given a referent in the film, one that explains Frank's and Morton's murderous desire. However, intercut with this scene is the so-called Navajo cliffs scene and Cheyenne and Harmonica's staking out of Sweetwater. The curious scene at the cliffs (cut from the original film but reappearing in the full version) allows Frank to assert himself over Morton by knocking him from his crutches into the dust he so despises. What is interesting is the location, clearly in the United States, and probably at Mesa Verde, Colorado—the site of a lost ancient race, the Anasazi (Ancestral Puebloans), whose decline and probable migration provides an ironic backdrop for Morton and Frank's quarrel. Their plotting marks another shift in the West toward a new era of business that, in turn, will destroy another "ancient race," its mythic heroes. And it is Cheyenne who opens the next scene, digging in the dirt, not for evidence of the Anasazi, but for the railroad tracks built in the desert bringing the new era ever closer. In the scene that follows, Harmonica marks out a basic grid for the new station, realizing McBain's "dream of a lifetime," one that he is desperate to complete for Jill, while stopping Frank and Morton acquiring the land. As this scene closes, Leone cuts to the "rape" of Jill by Frank.

Rape, power, greed, competition, land, loss, and violence all intersect and cohere in these scenes, telling a particularly impressive tale of the motivations and the struggles inherent in Leone's West, where what is at stake is the dream of a future tied inevitably to the revelations and erasures of the past. As Harmonica says of Sweetwater, "You don't sell the dream of a lifetime," and yet paralleling this he also says later, "I don't invest in land," as if to remind us that this is a world in which he will have no place and must only be developed by others after he has gone. Jill, the former prostitute, will, however, do anything "to save her skin" (including "performing" for Frank as a "willing" lover), for this is now her inherited dream, one she is unwilling to sacrifice. Her version of capitalism is clearly in contrast to Morton's, for although it is inherited from McBain, she seems less concerned with the question hanging in the air at the massacre—"Are we going to be rich, Pa?"—than with a communal giving, symbolized in her role as Earth Mother and water carrier.

The struggle of "minor languages" from within the majoritarian or dominant form (of "subaltern" perspectives, to use Smith's term), here embodied in Jill, Harmonica, and Cheyenne, parallels once again postcolonialism's desire to express the "zones of silence," as De Certeau puts it. Leone's urge as a filmmaker is like that of De Certeau's New Historian, a "prowler" working at the "margins" who "deviates" from the "powerful centralizing strategies" by reintroducing alternative perspectives from "outside," like Foucault or Bakhtin, from "sorcery, madness, festival, popular literature, the forgotten world of the peasant . . . all these zones of silence."[37] In *Once Upon a Time in the West*, Morton's vision, his "writing" of history, is linear and controlled, literally akin to the "two beautiful shiny rails" that mark his territorialization of the landscape, "written" from sea to shining sea, consuming everything in his way, and unwilling to entertain any alternative stories from the "forgotten world"—stories like Cheyenne's, Harmonica's, or the McBains' (the first two with direct and indirect Indian connections)—being swept aside by his singular vision of progress. His authority, both his power and his "authoring" of a particular imperial "gridded" vision, is governed by money, violence, and a ruthless assault on time. He comments again and again about how little time he has to complete his goal, and for this reason he overrides natural time and history in the same way his railroad carves its way through the landscape. His is a single, determined, totalizing, epic goal that will tolerate no "obstacles" and no alternative versions or "languages," mirrored perfectly in Morton's fixed body literally braced to look in only one direction, by the framed picture of the Pacific representing controlled nature, tamed within an *authored* frame, and also by the grid that Morton's mobility is contained by in his carriage running on fixed tracks.

In contrast to this fixity, Leone's film introduces heterogeneity and movement, the "traveling," impure elements that function to unsettle the single point of view. As De Certeau puts it, "the movement of documentation, that is, of smaller units, sows disorder within this order, escapes from established divisions, and brings about a slow erosion of organizing concepts . . . it '*produces* as it destroys.' Through the moving and complex mass that it throws into historiographical delimitation and which stirs things up there, information appears to involve a *wearing out* of the classificatory divisions . . . indeed, discourse no longer 'stands up.'"[38] De Certeau's analysis can be applied to Morton's historical "writing," his framed vision of accelerated progress in the West suddenly confronted by "smaller units" (the film actually refers to them as "small obstacles") challenging his vision through the "*slow* erosion" of his authority and power, to "stir things up" and "wear out" the "discourse" he represents until the crippled man, literally and metaphorically, "no longer stands up."

Just as Leone's slow film deliberately prolongs and stretches time, reminding us of the inescapability of history and the relations of past to present to future, these scenes all seem to contribute to a subtle analysis of motivation and desire. Morton and Frank try to short-circuit time through money and through violence while repressing the reality of their own mortality, figured as Morton's disease and Frank's crimes. But as the idea of "slow erosion" suggests, the repressed past will return, just as Harmonica's uncanny presence brings the past back into Frank's life and confronts him with the memory of his murdered brother and the consequences of his actions. The "smaller units" of history, as De Certeau called them, combine to deny Morton and Frank's belief that they can control or ignore time, presenting instead a contested vision that allows the dead to speak again—"Once Upon a Time." Thus the flashback of Frank's killing of Harmonica's brother literally "returns" slowly into the text at three key points, bringing the dead back as memory of and retribution for his murder and for the slaughter of the McBain family. These "small units" of time and history return to "make a place for the dead . . . [and] redistribute the space of possibility" within the new community emerging at the end of the film, "to use the narrativity that buries the dead as a way of establishing a place for the living," as De Certeau puts it.[39] This is suggested by the unusual shot at the McBain funeral from the grave upward to Jill in mourning, as if to remind us of the watching dead whose ghostly presence from the past is never lost to the film. Similarly, the red gingham tablecloths, which initially symbolized life and community at the McBain family feast, become the shrouds of the dead after their murder, returning finally as images of life again as Jill prepares to assume her role as communal mother. And it is the ghostly Harmonica, who always moves slowly, sliding in and out of the frame, and, as Janet Walker argues, is himself symbolically "resurrected" three times in the film, who kills Frank, avenging his own brother and the McBain murders, canceling out the businessman that Frank aspires to be.[40] These are the "spectral alternatives," to reuse Koolhaas's phrase from the introduction, reminders from the past that cannot be erased, as imperialism assumes, but which form the layers and meanings of the present and the future. Harmonica, as a form of the living dead returning from the past, has no further role in the film, and like all those of the "ancient race," and the film's specters of the past, he must now leave so that a "new" layer of history can be created by a "people to come," those not rooted in that past, but now freed from it and able to "become."

Leone's Dialogical Western

For some, Leone's analysis of capitalism and his interrogation of Hollywood codes constituted an "anti-Western"; for others, like Lee Clark Mitchell, it was all about "parody," "spoofing," and "wry mockery" of the classic Hollywood text via an "impudent route." Although Mitchell goes on to acknowledge Leone's "use" of the generic structure as a source of freedom from which he could launch into "a surreal sense of dismay at the genre," he concentrates too much on the Dollars trilogy at the expense of Leone's masterpiece, *Once Upon a Time in the West*.[41] These comments deny Leone's immersion in the genre's conventions and history and downplay his intention to engage with, interpret, "use," and develop the Western, to make it "travel" and insinuate itself along new lines of creative flight.[42] Perhaps Philip French's comment comes closest to understanding the potentially complex interculturalism of Leone's work: "It took from Hollywood, and it also gave back."[43] Leone's dialogical relationship with the Western is crucial to an understanding of ways by which he would both work with it and against it, a critical rhythm sustained by his status as an "outsider" whose timely "excess of seeing" would intervene in the Western in a number of fascinating ways. As Frayling puts it, "Leone's films are of interest partly *because* they attempt to criticise and redefine the 'rules' of the Hollywood Western genre—an attempt which could only have come from *outside* the Hollywood system."[44] These "rules"—the generic codes embedded in the Western, as in art, literature, and history, as we have seen—are synonymous with and rooted within an American national narrative, its cultural imaginary of westward expansion, Manifest Destiny, frontier conquests, settlement, and the bringing of light into a dark land. Yet as Frayling suggests, Leone cannot be "read" in quite this way, for his films move in and out of the established genre so that, as Smith suggests, their "displacement of the generic verisimilitude is put to the service of a displacement of the cultural imaginary that inhabits the generic conventions. Leone's westerns set up a larger gap between themselves and previous products than is easily tolerable in a single increment."[45] They are "excessive," moving beyond or outside expectations, norms, and predetermined frameworks, working as if to prove correct Derrida's comments on genre: "It is precisely a principle of contamination, a law of impurity, a parasitical economy . . . a sort of *participation without belonging*—a taking part in without being part of, without having membership in a set" (emphasis added).[46] This is exactly Leone's relationship to America as played out in his films' use and recycling of generic formulae. In a separate piece, appropriately titled "Living On—Border Lines," Derrida asks "What are we doing when, to practice a 'genre,' we quote a genre, represent it, stage it, expose its *generic law*, analyze it practically? Are we still practicing the genre? Does the work still belong to the genre it re-cites?" Partly in answer to these questions, he sees a generic process that "interrupts the very belonging [to a genre] of which it is a necessary condition."[47] Interestingly, Derrida views genre (appropriately for my argument about the

West) generally as rhizomatic or "folded," as "invagination," "an internal pocket" that "splits while remaining the same and traverses yet also bounds the corpus."[48]

In examining Leone's relations with the Western, these Derridean terms are helpful to understand how the genre is manipulated from this folded, inside/outside perspective as a means of interrogating the underlying assumptions and values that often go unquestioned within it. Frayling writes in a similar manner of the "appropriating and 'transcribing'" active in Leone's oeuvre as it works with and through ("re-cites") the generic codes of established Westerns, making multiple intertextual references in the process.[49] Thus Leone's "participation without belonging" enables a critical perspective upon the West as embedded cultural iconography, deliberately manipulating the generic memory of his audience and employing his own knowledge and image reservoir to raise ideological questions about how it has been represented and circulated. For example, in *Once Upon a Time in the West*, generic set pieces such as an immigrant family picnic (à la John Ford), replete with "Danny Boy," red-headed children, and red gingham tablecloths is rapidly undone through brutal violence from outside the scene (imitating Leone's own attack on the genre). Literally, from outside the "closed system" of the scene, with all its generic weight derived from audience knowledge and close intertextual references to films like *Shane* and *The Searchers*, comes a doubly shattering entry into the "frame" from "out-of-field"—of cinematic and generic rupture.[50] Recalling the earlier points about framing and deframing drawn from Deleuze, what Leone achieves in this rupturing scene is emblematic of the whole film's effects; in it, the blue-eyed child-killer, Frank, played by Henry Fonda, shatters our notions of the villain, overturns the Fordian family with violence, and reopens the possibilities of the Western as "critical" all in one moment. In a telling phrase, Leone referred to his deliberate choice of Fonda for the role because he felt "uprooted in his unaccustomed role."[51] Thus, Leone's "participation" in the Western invokes the history and expectations of the genre, while his lack of "belonging" allows him to interrupt it from outside the frame, and thereby reframe and "uproot" westness as both generic coding and ideological framework. Again and again in *Once Upon a Time in the West*, Leone challenges and expands this framing: by cinematography—with extraordinary close-ups, panorama landscapes, elaborate crane shots, and characters "sliding" into shot; by editing—whereby one scene appears to spill into or refer to a previous, unconnected one (such as Harmonica's apparent watching of Jill's rape); by his use of an Ennio Morricone sound track that interrelates with action, comments on characters and events, or impacts on the ambience and mood of the scene.

Roland Barthes, writing in the same year, 1968, that *Once Upon a Time in the West* was released, redefined the notion of text as "a multi-dimensional space in which a variety of writings, none of them original, blend and clash . . . a tissue of quotations drawn from the innumerable centers of culture." He continues by claiming that "a text is made of multiple writings, drawn from many cultures and entering into *mutual relations of dialogue, parody, contestation,* but there is one place where this multiplicity is focused and that place is the reader, not, as was hitherto said, the author. The reader is the space on which all the quotations that make up a writing are inscribed without any of them being lost; a text's unity lies not in its origin but in its destination" (emphasis added).[52] Barthes's phrase "mutual relations of dialogue, parody, contestation" echoes the effects of Leone's film, which draws the viewer into a demanding "production" of meaning based on the experience of a text "woven entirely of citations, references, echoes, cultural languages . . . antecedent or contemporary, which cut across it through and through." Intertextuality is set against "monologism," which "appears to be the Law," insisting upon a "network" of crossed-over relations, threads of meaning, and traces of possibility that engage the viewer in "play, activity, production, practice," "a practical collaboration" from which comes "*jouissance*"—"a pleasure without separation" of viewer/reader from text.[53] Barthes refers to the consequences of such "readings" in ways that seem also to describe Leone's film; he describes how "the *frayed* character" of texts can affect the reader/viewer as "an explosion: calls for contact and communication, positing of contracts, exchanges, outbursts of references, gleams of knowledge, dimmer, more penetrating impulses from 'the other scene.'"[54] Victor Burgin explains intertextuality in helpful terms, beginning with his view of text "seen not as an 'object' but rather as a 'space' between the object and the reader/viewer—a space made up of endlessly proliferating meanings which have no stable point of origin, nor of closure. In the concept of 'text' the boundaries that enclosed the 'work' are dissolved; the text opens continuously onto other texts, the space of *intertextuality*."[55] Leone's use of such intertextualities is vital to his work and resonates with Deleuze's comments on painting, a form the filmmaker understood and often referred to in his work: "The painter does not paint on an empty canvas, and neither does the writer write on a blank page [or the filmmaker on a blank screen]; but the page or canvas [or screen] is already so covered with preexisiting, preestablished clichés that it is first necessary to erase, to clean, to flatten, even to shred, so as to let in a breath of air from the chaos that brings us the vision."[56] In utilizing such "preexisiting, preestablished" images, Leone begins a process of critical destabilization of the genre through manipulation of its characteristic elements, dominated, above all, by masculine excess and its attendant violence.

Leone's much-discussed violence, always a component of the Western, becomes in his hands a method of erasure, of mutual destruction played out between his central male characters (and assorted extras), leaving the way clear for something else, something *not* to do with death, to borrow a famous line from the film, but rather life. Leone dramatizes in extremis a version of Richard Slotkin's "regeneration through violence" thesis, "the structuring myth of the American experience."[57] Thus the film moves through death, violence, treachery, revenge, and capitalist greed (as many Westerns do), clearing them all aside in the forms of its male characters and their actions, toward a utopian moment signified by the presence of the feminine—Jill McBain—and the possibility, however transitory, of the rebirth of the West, "a new dimension—the capacity for growth and change," as Alex Cox put it.[58] Indeed, Leone himself spoke of the film as a "cinematic fresco," as "my version of the story of the birth of a nation" acted by "the most worn-out of stereotypes: the pushy whore, the romantic bandit, the avenger, the killer who is about to become a businessman, the industrialist who uses the methods of a bandit."[59] These "worn-out" figures exit the stage to leave the whore to be transformed and transforming, to symbolize this "birth" of a new nation and the end of another world—"the beginning of a world without balls," as Leone put it.[60] The "ancient race" (as the film calls them) of mythic men linked in chains of brutality is "worn-out" to a point of erasure by their interconnected violence and make way, by the end of the film, for an emergent new West, leaving a strange masculine vacancy at its conclusion, a notion rare in Hollywood Westerns. Of course, what disappears is the excessively individual, mythic masculine figures, who are all, in different ways, "not the right man" (as Cheyenne says) to remain in Sweetwater and, in a version of familiar Western genre endings, "ride off into the sunset." The masculinity that remains is collective, multicultural, and laboring, the men who are building the station and the railroad, surrounding Jill as she offers them water, no longer mere drips, like those in the opening sequence of the film dropping onto Woody Strode's hat, but fresh, "sweet" water from her well. The fluidity and fecundity of water associated with Jill contrasts markedly with Morton's rigidity and his failed dream of the Pacific while reminding us of his desperately ironic crawl to a muddy puddle as he dies.

This self-consciousness constitutes Leone's "critical cinema" with its capacity "to shock the spectator into a questioning of what he or she is seeing, and a recognition of ideas which he or she can think about after the film is over."[61] Working by a Brechtian "laying bare the device," he reminds the audience by elaborate methods of the constructedness of what they are watching, or via "extreme stylisation" the "taken-for-granted" assumptions of the realist text are shaken by deliberate exaggerations of expression or chronology. In addition and alongside these methods, Leone's critical cinema contrasts the familiar mythologies of the Western with alternative, restructured notions, the effect of which, as Sarah Hill has put it, "undermines the traditional white/black hat binarisms of the genre to create a new form of western that is far more ambiguous."[62] One way this ambiguity works within *Once Upon a Time in the West* is through the use of visual quotations from other Westerns within the text, creating what Leone called "a kaleidoscopic view of all American Westerns put together."[63] The intended effect was akin to my earlier parallel with walking along the familiar streets of Leone's Almería film sets preserved as theme parks, only to turn a corner to see the false fronts, or the junk stacked behind them, or the nearby Coke machine for tourists to use. Shifting the audience from a homely and familiar scene to its antithesis, and to a breaking down of expectation, has the jarring effect of critical dislocation, of the cinematic uncanny: "to create the impression that the audience was watching a film they'd seen some-where before—only to jolt them with the realization that they'd never seen the story told in quite this way before. Again there was the mix of recognition and surprise, visual clichés and trompe l'oeil."[64] As I discussed earlier in relation to the framing process, Leone's critical cinema is full of such jarring moments that switch the viewer between violence and humor, pastiche and homage, irony and archetype with as much skill as the film's shifting sound track or scene editing. Barthes examines this in The Pleasure of the Text (1973), where he explores reading as a process of entangled joys and challenges, textual games and exchanges played out through the experience of the reader as "the cohabitation of languages working side by side . . . a sanctioned Babel." Leone's intertextuality is like Barthes's "circular memory" whereby texts interconnect and return upon each other in various, thrilling, and critical ways: "I savor the sway of formulas, the reversal of origins, the ease which brings the anterior text out of the subsequent one."[65] Leone's West is a carnivalesque, sur-real space of theatricality, performance, and parody where the spectacle is everything and the screen becomes a rich, experiential field of plea-sure for all the senses and for the mind, testing and puzzling at one and the same time.[66] Leone's parody is like that defined by Judith Butler, one that requires an intimacy with the form "that troubles the voice, the bearing, the performativity of the subject such that the audience or the reader does not quite know where it is you stand, whether you have gone over to the other side, whether you remain on your side, whether you can rehearse that other position without falling prey to it in the midst of the performance."[67] Once Upon a Time in the West is a Western reconfigured by Leone, partly as a projection of the American cinematic imagination and partly as a commentary upon it. This is, after all, not just cinema about cinema, as Frayling claims, but a Western about westness.

It is a profound example of the rhizomatic as I have defined and used the term in this book, for it is an epic examination of westness—of its myths, ideologies, traditions, generic codes, assumptions, and plea-sures—but one that exemplifies a vision derived from diasporic, trav-eling processes. In fact, the film itself had a collaborative, dialogic beginning with Leone, Bernardo Bertolucci, and Dario Argento "dream-ing together" and understanding that "cinema was changing, and that there was a need for people who wouldn't tell you the same stories in the same old ways," and achieving this by referring to "visual images and sensations rather than a lot of dialogue."[68] Thus, out of the combined minds of three artists evolved a "treatment," the focus of which was iconography—"visual images and sensations"—drawn from their collective "dream" of the West, already translated from the American Westerns they had enjoyed as cinemagoers. As Leone put it, "I was more in love with the idea of the American West than anyone you could imagine."[69] The simulated West of Hollywood productions would inform this new departure, with stock character types, recognizable events, and scenes, yet they would interrupt these generic codes as Derrida outlined above—"we quote a genre, represent it, stage it, expose its *generic law*, analyze it practically." The "Once Upon a Time . . ." of American mythology and of all the "staged" stories it told about its construction as a nation and canonized in Hollywood and other expressive forms would be dialogized by the ". . . there was the West" (the literal translation from the Italian title—"*C'era una volta, il West*"), by Leone's interest in historical accuracy and in its emergent era of economic boom. Thus the film develops as a collision of real and imagined discourses of westness, of the mythic West as the archetypes Leone associated with America and "Americanism" as a child—possibility, openness, straight roads, and honesty. Yet shadowing this desire is that other sense of loss and longing, for a West already being transformed—like that in Ford's *The Man Who Shot Liberty Valance*, a film Leone said he liked most of Ford's because "we are getting nearer to shared values," where politics, the railroad, and organized capitalism have intervened in the "wilderness" and the "ancient race of men."[70] As we watch the scene in *Liberty Valance* where Ranse Stoddard (James Stewart) runs for governor, Ford's and Leone's "shared values" are revealed through a West already simulated as a stage show with rodeo riders, lasso tricks, and slick politicians whose western "image" sells them to a public yearning for narratives of the mythic past like the one Stoddard has built a career upon. In representing the theme park–like "spectacle" of the West, Ford, at his most unsentimental, was recognizing the simultaneous attraction and regret inherent in the region (and its projection) within a global consciousness. Leone's shared values with *Liberty Valance* emerge clearly in one of its central lines: "This is the West, sir. When the legend becomes fact, print the legend." Here Ford acknowledged the fabled nature of the West as "always already" a mythic construction, an immense tale too big and complex to be contained by mere "fact" and, therefore, always overspilling any historical containment of "truth." What Leone strived to show, heightened by his own position as outsider/insider, was the double or dialogical nature of the West as precisely this bundle of inextricably linked "facts" and "legends," disappointments and spectacles.

As discussed earlier, Wim Wenders reacted powerfully to *Once Upon a Time in the West* as "the limit . . . a killer" of the genre, because for him it turned the Western into an abstraction with its slow, unraveling style and its attention to detail, creating the sensation of being "like a tourist, a 'Western tourist.'"[71] Of course, Leone knew only too well that the Western's images could not "signify themselves," for they had been exhausted through overuse and were taken for granted by their audience to the point that the genre had grown stale and repetitive in Hollywood terms. As I have shown, his answer was to revel in the clichés and the mythic architecture of an exhausted, familiar genre, simultaneously defamiliarizing them through the acts of abstraction and spectacle Wenders recognized as like the tourist experience. As we watch the film, we "index" and "drag," "cut" and "paste" from our collective cinematic unconscious of Westerns in the same way that post-tourists engage with their "destinations," creating a multiple and complex set of responses and opinions, both creative and critical, iconic and ironic. Thus Wenders's observation that Leone was no longer engaged with the "surface" of the Western but rather with "what lies behind: the inner side of Westerns" where "something else glimmers through" is a perceptive comment that he reads only negatively as "the death of a genre and a dream" but which provides, I believe, an important clue to the effects of Leone's critical cinema. Wenders's "strange feeling" reemerged later in his own "Western" films, scripted with Sam Shepard, *Paris, Texas* and *Don't Come Knocking*, precisely because he and we are constantly repositioned in these films to see through the unquestioned mythic structures, iconic themes, behaviors, and events, becoming like "post-tourists," able to experience westness critically and pleasurably without having to sanctify the values embedded in its "surface."

A Baroque, Transnational Western?

"Westness" as iconographic territory is commodified and represented everywhere in global culture, and Leone understood this, making *Once Upon a Time in the West* a complex, intertextual, folded text of over thirty quotations from films such as *Shane*, *The Searchers*, *The Man Who Shot Liberty Valance*, *High Noon*, and, very significantly, to Nicholas Ray's *Johnny Guitar*, a film that Bertolucci pointedly termed "the first of the baroque Westerns."[72] Recall from chapter 1 how J. B. Jackson was fascinated by the baroque, a form defined by art history as complex, ornate, theatrical, festive, "full of splendour and movement," with scrolls and curves that "writhe and whirl" as if they would "burst the frame." Such extravagant excess was, like Leone's cinema, challenging tradition in its efforts to "break the frame," and in the words of E. H. Gombrich, it aimed "to confuse and overwhelm us, so that we no longer know what is real and what illusion."[73] Deleuze has written much on the "philosophy" and aesthetics of the baroque in *The Fold*, throwing new light onto Bertolucci's comment, writing, "The Baroque refers not to an essence but rather to an operative function, to a trait. It endlessly produces folds . . . [it] twists and turns . . . fold upon fold, one upon the other" and is, therefore, connected with multiplicity, infinity, and endless reworkings. The baroque "moves between matter and soul, the façade and the closed room, the outside and the inside . . . a virtuality that never stops dividing itself. . . . Conciliation of the two will never be direct, but necessarily harmonic, inspiring a new harmony." The folds of the baroque connect the "high" and the "low" and "spill onto the outside"; it is "abstract art par excellence."[74] As with Leone's "folded" film text, each twisted surface is pleated so that it reveals something beyond itself, directing the eye and mind in different directions into and out of the film itself, "giving back" to America but also reminding us of the West's global status and influence. There are no easy, neat, "unfolded" surfaces left in Leone's film, for like the baroque, Leone is concerned to "lead the eye to confuse different orders of space and surface," creating a text that is "mannerist, baroque, spectacular, exhibitionist, performative, carnivalesque, camp, cartoonish, 'pop formalist'—a cinema of 'effects' rather than meanings, of playful excess rather than classical expressivity."[75]

Indeed, Leone himself has referred to how in his films "the sheer abundance of baroque images privileges surprise over comprehension" so that only "on a second viewing" would the audience "grasp more fully the discourse which underlies the images."[76] Leone's desire is clear from this: to challenge and redirect the audience through "surprise," to establish a dialogical process of "looking at again" (re-visioning) our first impressions to develop a "double" or folded moment of apprehension (not comprehension). Leone's underlying discourse of westness is played out in the film's elaborate geometry: "like a riddle taking the form of a rebus—with all the fine little component parts playing their part in the whole . . . all . . . revolving around the centre. Like a labyrinth. . . . It's a concept that appeals to me very much."[77] To see the film as a baroque puzzle, a rebus with its enigmatically hidden or disguised elements, is to understand how the film works both to utilize the "inside" of the Western genre and its established myths, while continually turning it to an "outside" to expose and expand the genre and to dialogize and globalize its possible meanings. It was in this spirit that Leone claimed that he wanted to liberate his audiences through a form of critical dialogue: "We are not *magisters*. The films we make ought to make people think. We are professional 'exciters.' But we are not directors of conscience. The audience should be allowed to draw their own conclusions."[78]

Just as Leone wanted to spark an active audience, Bertolucci has commented upon the critical exchange that the film demanded with the Hollywood Western itself: "I think he gave back to the proper Western makers the confidence that the Western can be a great movie. He gave back something that got lost . . . the innocence. He gave back a new identity to the Western, something that took off from Monument Valley, went to Almeria in Spain . . . and Cinecitta, and goes back after . . . a little travel to grow up."[79] The "travel" Bertolucci describes relates to the film's location in John Ford country (United States), Spain, and Italy, made with actors from the United States, Spain, and Italy, and drawing upon and developing rich traditions of many cinematic cultures, from which emerged "a new identity"—a hybrid text through which the West is translated and "given back" in generous aesthetic and political acts to America (and to the world), to its audience, and to movie history. Smith, in his discussion of the way the Western is "shifted, altered, and renewed" in its "spaghetti" form, echoes Bertolucci by adding that "genres as it were *migrate*," bringing Leone into line with Edward Said's and James Clifford's postcolonial sensibility discussed in the introduction, recognizing "traveling" as a useful concept for understanding the complex interactions of a postmodern, transnational world, "nourished and often sustained by this circulation of ideas, [as] . . . acknowledged or unconscious influence, creative borrowing, or wholesale appropriation, the movement of ideas and theories from one place to another is both a fact of life and a usefully enabling condition of intellectual activity." This reconceptualization of "travel" is one way through which we might rethink the West as a "circulation of ideas," mobile, and routed via different cultures and discrepant histories that revitalize and examine existing forms and ideologies. In Leone's hands, westness *becomes*, it travels as filmic and cultural reference, as complex aura, and as ideological pattern, blurring geographic boundaries between Europe and the United States, "creating a more fluid sense of cultural transmission and of the past."[80] His traffic between countries and forms, according to Marcia Landy, "exceeds literal geography, becoming another instance of the instability of categories" and, therefore, of his desire to split apart tired conventions and rediscover in the bones of old forms something new and creative.[81]

To this end, Leone's cinematic routes, his rhizomatic wanderings within and beyond the Western, belong to no single place; they are "unaccountable," to borrow David Thomson's word, because "where are they from? Who could have made them? Of what nation or age are they? . . . Neither American nor Italian, the clichés of the Western growl behind fluttering faces out of Giotto or Raphael."[82] *Once Upon a Time in the West* is literally a transnational creation filmed in Almería (Spain), Rome (Italy), and Monument Valley (United States), using actors from many different nationalities, producing a movie dubbed into many different languages and distributed all over the world. As a filmmaker, Leone has drawn influences from Italian neorealism, Hollywood genre cinema, and Akira Kurosawa's films in Japan, and, in turn, has influenced other international filmmakers.[83] This crisscrossing process has a variety of economic, aesthetic, and political effects. Economically, the film appealed globally to as wide a market as possible through its flexible production and universal themes, and it benefited the local areas where it was filmed. Aesthetically, the film refuses to follow the rhythms of Hollywood cinema, deliberately reversing and critiquing them in different ways, for example, by exploiting the size of the frame to its full extent, allowing the cameras to linger poetically over subjects, confronting the audience with breathtaking close-ups and swirling crane shots, and by choreographing dazzling rituals. Indeed, Leone seemed to comprehend that a multi-track medium like film could and should exploit all its elements—aural, visual, and literary—in the construction of a cinematic experience working on many levels. Politically, the effect of using different nationalities in the cast, for example, is crucial to the film, giving it an immediate multicultural impact, yet Leone goes further by deliberately miscasting actors whose ethnicity conflicts with their role. Most notably, Italians Gabrielle Ferzetti and Claudia Cardinale play Anglo-Saxons (Morton, the diseased capitalist, and Jill McBain, a New Orleans prostitute turned wife), while Italian Marco Zuanelli plays a Chinaman called Wobbles, Charles Bronson (Polish American) plays a half-breed Native American named Harmonica, and Jason Robards (white American) plays a Mexican bandit with an Native American name, Cheyenne! This determined playfulness with audience expectations and genre conventions is typical of Leone's approach throughout the film and acts to question our assumptions about the Western (and by implication about the West) by deliberately going against the grain, jumbling ethnicities to demonstrate the actual (but often hidden) multiculturalism of the West, while also asking us to question its traditional ethnic and gender stereotypes as portrayed by Hollywood.[84] How significant is it, for example, that Woody Strode, an African American, is one of the first characters we see in the film? Or that Jill McBain is placed at the very center of the film as a complex woman, resilient, undomesticated, independent, and sexualized? In these different ways, Leone translates the Western transnationally, mobilizing the genre from within its own defining characteristics and stereotypes so that its fixed codes are carefully turned around upon themselves, interrogated, and ultimately reimagined, particularly through the figure of Jill McBain, as we will discuss further later.

This transnational approach relates back to Leone's sense of America as "the property of the world" and its specific rendition in a deessentialized Western that consciously moves the audience between ethnicities and between deeply rooted expectations. As Adrian Martin comments, "Leone is ultimately not a practitioner of pure cinema . . . but rather a richly impure, hybrid cinema," since in his "hands, the classic genres become not only Pop Art friezes of iconographic signs and indices, but also a ritual procession of dramatic or 'scenographic' highpoints: 'clinches,' charged looks and gestures, moments of recognition."[85] Leone's work is choreographed ritual, constantly awakening the audience to the lost spectacle of the cinema as sensation and theatricality somehow lost in the modern world grown cynical and tired and to a film industry bound into formulaic and generic boundaries. However, Leone is not indulging in nostalgia for his "fairy tale" of the West; instead, he juxtaposes the mythic, enchanted West alongside a counterposition, an anti-mythography of disenchantment, death, corruption, and violence. The dialogue between and across such positions might be traced back to Leone's own statements about his reactions to "America," which epitomize this dual, "accented" perspective:

> In my childhood, America was like a religion. . . . I dreamed of the wide open spaces of America. The great expanses of the desert. The extraordinary "melting-pot," the first nation made up of people from all over the world. The long, straight roads—very dusty or very muddy—which begin nowhere, and end nowhere—for their function is to cross the whole continent. Then real-life Americans abruptly entered my life—in jeeps—and upset all my dreams. They had come to liberate me! I found them energetic but also deceptive. They were no longer the Americans of the West. They were soldiers . . . materialist, possessive, keen on pleasures and earthly goods.[86]

The western "dream" with its diasporic, spatial attractions is intercut here with a more "earthly" reality of power, greed, and ownership that resonates through Leone's films in diverse ways. The tensions of mobility and fixture, of imagination and materiality echo through these words, as through his films, and surface again in Leone's own words later in life: "I can't see America any other way than with European eyes, obviously; it fascinates me and terrifies me at the same time."[87]

This generic "traveling" is mirrored in the film's actual concern with migration and mobility, whether in the capitalist land-grabbing of Morton and Frank, the classical move of Jill McBain westward for a new life, or the nomadic wanderings of Cheyenne and Harmonica. Leone plays out a tense drama between mobility and settlement, understanding intuitively that this was the great American story wherein people sought some balance between the "routes" of diasporic migration and the "roots" of established, settled life. McBain's "dream of a lifetime" is, of course, about building a place of stability, putting down roots, and rearing a family (and making money), and it conflicts with a different dream, Morton's, also about money, but without the balance of community and family. The film's framing narrative is of the railroad sweeping from the Atlantic to the Pacific bringing with it a multicultural, migratory people. Although Leone recognized the inevitable era heralded by the brutal business of Frank and Morton, the film's final scenes offer some resistance to their power in the figure of Jill McBain, whose migration is related to settlement and most significantly, perhaps, to a "people to come" indicated by her generous provision of water to the multicultural railroad workers in the final act of the movie. Like a Greek goddess, an Earth Mother, Jill opens up Brett McBain's closed dream of family wealth to a new community yet to be formed—an imagined, utopian vision beyond the film, and perhaps beyond realization, but nonetheless a community emerging out of the nomadic actions (and sacrifices) of Harmonica and Cheyenne and the new domesticity of Jill, the whore-migrant turned communal icon, and in resistance to Morton and Frank. Through her as a point of conjuncture, Leone not only alters the genre balance of most Hollywood Westerns but also presents an imagined community, a fable of nationhood reimagined around a woman—multicultural, mobile, of the people. The violent machismo of the "ancient race" and their myths—the staples of most Westerns—have been erased from the film in preparation for this utopian moment, a moment that is, as Leone had wanted it to be, "about a birth and a death," something different and new emerging from the violence that precedes it.[88]

Although the new era is like a shadow hovering in the background of this moment, implied in Harmonica's comments that "other Mortons will be along," it is as if Leone provides a moment strangely out of time (a motif that has driven the film from its opening scene), a glimpse of what might be possible, a meeting of routes and roots, of settlement and mobility. I take this space at the film's finale to be a version of what Peter Hitchcock terms "transgressive imagiNation [sic]," which "exceeds, challenges, demystifies, or transcodes the components of national identity," negotiating an alternative transnational form as it "picks away at the imaginative grounds for their subsistence as an alibi for more egalitarian modes of socialization."[89] Through Leone's "insurgent imagination" a potential and different West emerges, providing "metaphors of transformation" whose function is to "allow us to imagine what it would be like when prevailing cultural values are challenged and transformed, the old social hierarchies are overthrown . . . and new meanings and values . . . begin to appear."[90] The final exchange between Jill, Harmonica, and Cheyenne condenses the implications and ambiguities of this meeting into sparse language:

> Harmonica: "It's gonna be a beautiful town, Sweetwater."
> Jill: "I hope you'll come back someday."
> Harmonica: "Someday."
> Cheyenne: "Yeah . . . I gotta go too."

The nomads move on (or die), and only Jill remains with the red gingham tablecloths, earlier associated with the death of her husband and family, now signifying the new life she is beginning as she steps out into the light and air of her emergent community, her "imagiNation." In the last of Leone's expansive shots, associated with Jill throughout the film, we see her in peasant's dress, surrounded by, and gradually merging with, multicultural workers, giving them water from her well in preparation for the community to come.

Deleuze's *Cinema 2* is helpful in exploring the significance of this finale as Deleuze comments on how film's role is "not that of addressing a people, which is presupposed already there, but of contributing to the invention of a people." In other words, film (like all the other arts) can imagine alternative ways of being, imagine a "people" whose existence is often denied or hidden by the official culture whose vested interest it is to assert their version of a people "already there," a people who correspond to some dominant, acceptable model. Classical Hollywood asserted a unanimous "people" in certain dominant genres, such as Ford's Westerns in Deleuze's example (along with King Vidor and Frank Capra), gathering at the river and building communities, yet it was "the neo-Western" that first demonstrated its "break-up" because "the American people . . . could no longer believe themselves to be either the melting-pot of peoples or the seed of a people to come." Instead, Deleuze argues, "modern political cinema" (and I would include Leone in this), developing in a postwar climate of change and increased social and political movements, was built on fragmentation and a questioning of "unanimity," understanding there was no *one* "people" but "always several peoples, an infinity of peoples" who cannot, and should not, be united into a "tyrannical unity." Deleuze believes that this awareness was often "hidden by the mechanisms of power and the systems of majority" in the West, yet it was "absolutely clear in the third world," where exploitation, minorities, and identity crisis were commonplace. It was, therefore, from the colonial and postcolonial world that some alternative sense of "people" emerges, having "to go through" and "work on" all the materials of the colonizer that has "swamped" that culture. The role of the "author/director" is "destroying myths from the inside," to show "the raw drive and social violence underneath the myth," producing "Not the myth of a past people [Leone's ancient race], but the storytelling of the people to come . . . to create itself as a foreign language in a dominant language."[91] Thus Leone's "foreign language," as an "outsider" filmmaker, exists within and interrupts the Hollywood Western's "dominant" one, becoming "minor" in the sense Deleuze defines it, and his storytelling ("Once upon a time . . . ") intervenes in the master (national) narrative of the West as settlement and colonization. As Leone "repeats" familiar Western tropes and themes he transforms them, for as Claire Colebrook writes, "A minor literature repeats a voice, not in order to maintain the tradition, but to transform the tradition," appealing to the forces of difference that produced the original work.[92] After watching Leone's films it is impossible to look at classic, "traditional" Westerns in quite the same way again, for an exchange has taken place between forms and affected the viewer with the energy of difference and critique. Within the film itself, Jill McBain, of course, represents this "foreign" or "minor" language—as woman—who remains at its finale as a figuration, with those anonymous others who surround her, a collective assemblage of the "people to come," attached to the "territory" marked out, but breaking out to form new territories too. The railroad's status suggests this in the final scene; being *of* Morton but also *of* these people who have made it and *of* Jill McBain, who appears, however briefly, to have assumed control.

The end of *Once Upon a Time in the West* therefore exists as "a plurality of intertwined lines," different stories with no unanimity, no absolute resolution.[93] The utopian moment, as I termed it earlier, is signified by the water carrier Jill McBain, whose life, stained by death, steps out of its shadow to offer nourishment and promise to the multicultural masses of "a people to come." Indeed, Jill's position in the film is often represented as strangely conflictive, with contrasting framings of her as, on the one hand, contained—such as in the kitchen or bedroom, most memorably seen from above through lace or when on a bed behind bars with Frank—or, on the other, shown through extravagant and expansive shot sequences, such as Leone's crane shot at Flagstone that follows Jill's arrival, or the journey to the McBains through Monument Valley. This tension indicates Jill's inside/outside status in the film and dramatizes her role as a precursor of the world to come, a world in which she will move *between* the domestic and the public, no longer defined only by social labels like "whore" or "mother," but able to assume an active place in the new community. History has been reconfigured in Leone's film to demonstrate, as De Certeau puts it, "A construction and erosion of units," a living contest between different forces (like Morton and Jill—who, of course, of all the central characters, never meet in the film), reminding us that "all historical writing combines these two operations."[94] Thus Morton's "history," his linear narrative of progress symbolized by the railroad's movement westward, and alongside him, the mythic histories of wandering gunfighters, are both problematized and eroded by the film's conclusions and by the possibilities of the emerging alternative— and as yet untold—histories present in the anonymous laboring figures who surround Jill at the end. As Deleuze puts it (echoing Appadurai), film has a vital part to play in the "acknowledgement of a people who are missing" from established history and representation; indeed, he adds, films are "contributing to the invention of a people," and, although never conclusive and probably, at best, only temporary here, this is the potentially radical vision rising at the end of *Once Upon a Time in the West.*[95]

Coda: Leone's West

My Name Is Nobody (1973), directed by Tonino Valerii and "supervised" by Leone, was the latter's final involvement with the genre. Set in 1899, the film deliberately engages with themes of ending and change, demonstrated by the choice (once again) of Henry Fonda as the aging, spectacle-wearing gunfighter Jack Beauregard, looking to leave the West for Europe.[96] The ironic "return" east epitomizes the film's interest in interrogating many of the established motifs and thematic patterns of both the American classic Western and its shadow form the spaghetti Western. Playing opposite Fonda was the Italian actor Terence Hill (Mario Girotti), famous for his role as comic-hero Trinity and now figured as "Nobody," with a deliberate reference back to Clint Eastwood's "Man with No Name" from the Dollars trilogy as well as forward to later neo-Westerns, *Dead Man* and *Smoke Signals*.[97] Like Leone's favorite Ford Western, *The Man Who Shot Liberty Valance*, *My Name Is Nobody* is concerned with "history" and "legend" as constructions.

As Frayling points out, *My Name Is Nobody* is full of references to other Westerns, as all Leone's work was, but one difference here is that Leone can now quote his own films, drawing himself into his elaborate referential game of intertextuality. Thus the opening sequence (directed by Leone) echoes many earlier films with slow, deliberate waiting and exaggerated sounds, as does its finale (with Fonda alone waiting for the train and having to kill the "wild bunch"—reversing the killers waiting for the train and for Harmonica in *Once Upon a Time in the West*). More than this, the film is obsessed with acts of seeing, with spectacle, with reflections (literally in windows and mirrors), but also as it reflects upon both the renewed genre and the traditions of the Western. Nobody and Beauregard's final shoot-out (itself an elaborate simulation engineered by Nobody to release Beauregard from the West) has to be witnessed on the street of New Orleans, so the scene is captured by a photographer whose camera frames the event, upside down, for the audience too. As the spectacle is stage-managed (or "directed"), like the whole legend-creation of Beauregard in the film, by Nobody, he ensures they are both "in-shot," becoming, as it were, a director within the film itself, arranging his players and controlling the mise-en-scène. There are fewer more self-reflexive films aware of the way the West and the Western have always been about spectacle, about simulation, about performance, turning itself almost as it formed into a mythic theme park of repeated icons. Watching the film intensifies the experience discussed above as akin to "post-tourism," reveling in its multilayered ironies, enjoying it just as we might a trip to Almería's film sets and mock shoot-outs. After all, with uncanny circularity this is precisely what is happening at the end of *My Name Is Nobody*, a mock shoot-out played out for an audience's pleasure as visual spectacle. It's no surprise either that a long mid-film sequence takes place at a carnival, "The Street of Pleasure," central to which is a Hall of Mirrors where Nobody and Beauregard battle with Sullivan's henchmen. Bakhtinian carnival turns the world upside down in order to expose its values and hypocrises, to alert us to the hierarchies and assumptions that structure the dominant social order. In many ways Leone's input into this film is concerned (as most of his films are) with at least some of these points. Indeed, Nobody himself is a comic trickster, a carnivalesque figure, engagingly irritating as he "disarms" the viewer and forces us to question his role and purpose and, wider still, that of the Western and its mythologies.[98] He is a "low" and vulgar figure throughout—always dirty, gulping food, urinating, and stealing. As the Italian actor playing the American playing the director playing the gunfighter, Nobody signifies the relationship of the spaghetti Western to its American counterpart. He is audacious, complex, irreverent, dialogical (he's a big talker), coarse, and exuberant, and Beauregard tries to resist his influence and remain aloof and "pure," but like the Hollywood Western (which he represents in many ways), he cannot avoid the "input" from Nobody. The "American" works with the "Italian," the old with the new, and Beauregard's legend is secured through the invention and stage skills of Nobody, and out of the unlikely mix something different is created. As Frayling puts it, "The Hollywood Western has come up against what looks like its negation, but has learned from the experience. So, the living legend can now retire to Europe with a good conscience."[99]

Leone's hybrid, dialogically critical cinema is being referred to here, and the continuing significance of the West as an iconic presence cannot be overlooked. In his lengthy monologue at the end of the film as he heads to Europe, Beauregard reflects (once again) upon the West and how it "used to be a lot of wide-open spaces, with lots of elbow room," populated by "romantic fools . . . [who] still believed that a good pistol and a quick showdown could solve everything," but all that has changed, like the "ancient race" vanishing in *Once Upon a Time in the West*, making possible a new West. As Beauregard says, "fellows like me . . . the same fellows you want to write up in history books," now hand it on, "it's your kind of time not mine," and "That's why people like me have to go: and that is why you fixed the gunfight with me—to get me out of the West clean. . . . What can you expect of a national monument!" This, Leone's last Western, like *Once Upon a Time in the West* before it, seems to be about ending, about the end of the genre, as so many critics have argued, but in fact both reaccentuate and stimulate the genre, showing what it is possible to achieve as forms "travel" creatively and imaginatively. When *Heaven's Gate* was greeted in 1980 as the death of the Hollywood Western for its economic infelicitousness, there was also a sense that it was actually too much like a Leone film to really succeed in the U.S. marketplace. Like Leone, Michael Cimino wanted to deal with big themes like greed, capitalism, brutality, and change, setting his film in the town of Sweetwater and daring to luxuriate in long set pieces (like the roller-skating scene) that defied the codes of the Hollywood tradition. Again, although seen as a "death of the genre" Western, like Leone, *Heaven's Gate* would, in time, be reexamined favorably, and its audacious form would stimulate a new generation of Westerns.[100]

Leone once said that "I wanted to show the cruelty of that nation, I was bored stiff with all those grinning white teeth. Hygiene and optimism are the woodworms which destroy American wood. It is a great shame if 'America' is always to be left to the Americans."[101] Ultimately, his position of "participation without belonging" in relation to the West permitted such a unique "outside" vision to emerge, a critical dialogue asking questions about the West as history and representation. As Roxanne Dunbar-Ortiz has put it in an article connecting U.S. intervention in Iraq with a long history of colonization, or "empire as a way of life," it is vital that Americans untangle the "roots" of empire from "accepted, conventional modes of thought . . . false patriotism and racism . . . and sophisticated theorems of both liberal and conservative economics, sociology . . . and history." To achieve this, "citizens of an imperialist country who wish to understand imperialism must first emancipate themselves from the seemingly endless web of threads that bind them emotionally and intellectually to the imperialist condition."[102] Perhaps one way to dismantle such a deep-rooted condition is to get outside that "web of threads" and intervene in the accepted modes of thought through challenging, dissonant images and awkward, complex dialogues like those manifested in Sergio Leone's films, and in particular in *Once Upon a Time in the West*.

4. "THE 'WESTERN' IN QUOTES"
Generic Variations

Its roots continue to spread under the Hollywood humus
and one is amazed to see green and robust suckers spring up in the
midst of the seductive but sterile hybrids that some would replace them by.
André Bazin

In the long run, feature films will be
the truly important documentaries of our time.
Wim Wenders

As I discussed in the previous chapter, Sergio Leone's films were seen by some as the death knell of the Western and by others as its regenerative force, breathing new life into a tired, mythic formula and seeing the genre as the site for cultural critique and counterhegemonic practice. The established generic grid of the Western proved elastic and porous enough for new filmmakers looking to utilize its broad expectations and codes for different purposes, building on the promising works of directors such as Nicholas Ray, Sam Peckinpah, and Robert Altman. Often these innovations came from outside the Hollywood mainstream, working, as André Bazin wrote, "under the Hollywood humus," from directors whose work was more eclectic and certainly not primarily associated with the Western. In working from within this established and major Hollywood genre, these films represent a version of what Deleuze and Guattari would call "minor languages" capable of a kind of "creative stammering" by which the codes are interfered with, causing "procedure[s] of variation"—"variables of expression and variables of content." Thus the established and taken-for-granted "major language" and codes of the Western genre are made to "stammer" in these renewed forms, drawing attention to its mythic constructs and to new thematics within the texts—"Conquer the major language in order to delineate in it as yet unknown minor languages." I would argue, however, that this is a continuation of Leone's filmic experimentation and his development of "critical cinema" in movies where the effect is "To be a foreigner, but in one's own tongue. . . . To be bilingual, multilingual, but in one and the same language." For filmmaking this involves the strategic manipulation of existing genre "language" and convention, "[u]prooting them from their state as constants," in order to challenge the viewer and expand the generic form and theme "towards the limit of its elements."[1] Such a process of variation or "mistranslation" from the established codes is what Deleuze calls a "line of flight... which affects each system by stopping it from becoming homogeneous" and creating some new perspective "different from that of the constants . . . an outsystem."[2] The dangers of genre are that it can become a closed circle of meanings, endlessly recycling ideological notions without reflection or questioning, and appealing to an ever-narrowing audience with set expectations. As we have seen throughout this book, the West has been a particular focal site for the inscriptions of national identity, and one of its primary mythic vehicles has been the Western generic "system." Thus generic traditions of community building, individual sacrifice, acceptable violence, hypermasculinity, and racial and gender division have too often become unquestioned elements within this system. What I propose here are filmic examples of rhizomatic generic lines of flight that shift the Western beyond its traditional boundaries, encompassing different perspectives, new themes, and more complex dialogical structures.

Although Leone had created his own "outsystem" by usurping the authority of the American Western in the 1960s, and innovators such as Altman, Peckinpah, and Eastwood had continued to explore the genre, it was in 1980 that Michael Cimino's *Heaven's Gate* attempted to unsettle this generic "circle" from within with a powerful, and much maligned, "new" Western that displaced traditional perspectives with a nonlinear, symbolic film rethinking issues of class, gender, race in ways that disturbed America's deeply held, mythic consciousness. Its rejection of traditional narrative in favor of "big impressionist blocks" that work rhythmically, requiring the audience to "participate imaginatively in its construction, to use our own judgment in making connections back and forth," gives the sense of the film as "an immense fresco" that may never be complete, since the wall may have "patches . . . left uncovered" and the space "could be infinitely extended." Overall, Cimino's sprawling architectural film, with its detailed building blocks, makes us work hard as viewers, denying us the ease of linearity and the clues and hooks of suspense, demanding instead our total immersion in his visual drama, which will "make no sense to us if our engagement is not continuously active and analytical."[3] Cimino's is a cinema of affect, best revealed when it is at its most cinematic, that is, not imitating everyday vision or simply following preexisting narrative forms, but maximizing its capacity as cinema to represent the world differently. Thus the generic system has to be continually disrupted to find new ways to present vision, to affect the audience, and to challenge ideas. Thus cinema is not about recording how we *do* see life but about challenging us to see it differently, making us see images, scenes, moments in ways we cannot in life—mixing image with sound, close-up, zoom, crane shot and intimate, personal event, slow motion, or some other "distortion" of vision. The organizing viewpoint shifts with the camera and can portray multiple positions of movement and time that interfere, as in Cimino's film, with "normal" linear events and causal actions, presenting instead a complex montage with its own rhythm. It is hard to impose any single vision (or grid) onto this, and indeed this would be an attempt to "master" the text in a way that parallels the desire of the elite in the film to possess the land and control people's lives. Cimino's ideal for film, as for his alternative community of Sweetwater, is "a flow of differing difference" like the scene at the roller rink (called Heaven's Gate) where all the different communities, generations, genders, and languages come together in a utopian moment. The reason Deleuze was so taken by cinema was that, like painting or literature, it had the capacity not simply to convey ideas but to create innovative possibilities for the eye and for perception, to create new affects and resist fixed points of view.[4] Of course, this can be unsettling and exciting, as we see in Cimino's extravagant episodes in *Heaven's Gate* that demand much from the viewer, particularly one schooled in the norms of Hollywood narrative cinema. The purpose is, as Deleuze would say, to "collapse and yet maintain the . . . empty frame" of the Western through a cinema of new thoughts *and* affects that "make us become with them . . . draw us into the compound" through a multiple and troubling "language of sensations."[5]

Just as the ideological West itself had become naturalized through its myths and representations, so one of its central signifiers, the Western, had become bound to linear codes and systems of theme and image that were sacrosanct and yet almost invisible in their authority.[6] In breaking the latter, one simultaneously challenged the former, one of the reasons Cimino's film, I believe, was criticized so virulently at the time of a newly resurgent conservatism in the White House under its mythic cowboy, President Ronald Reagan. In this sense, as Robin Wood comments, the film employs the Western to represent the "Death of a Nation" as opposed to Griffith's *Birth of a Nation*, offering none of the comforts of a national narrative born from dubious unity, but instead presents a chaotic and violent disruption born from greed, racism, and class war. What is on trial, therefore, was not simply a film but a whole series of deeply felt beliefs and stories about the significance of the West within the American national imaginary.[7] In addition to its impressionistic narrative blocks, symbolic scenes, and testing "flow" of images, Cimino's alternative Western outsystem begins in the Harvard yard, uses non-American actors (John Hurt, Isobelle Huppert) and Russian dialogue, and constantly shocks and surprises its audience by stepping outside Hollywood codes and "languages" to present a moving "elegy for a possible alternative America destroyed before it could properly exist by forces generated within, yet beyond the control of, democratic capitalism."[8] Like Leone's vision of Jill McBain and a gathering, multicultural community at the end of *Once Upon a Time in the West*, Cimino offers in *Heaven's Gate* a glimpse of a similarly radical and different West defined by the "multitude . . . as a social possibility" instead of the usual individual at odds with the community of most Westerns.[9] Ironically, the film was not just about the "Death of a Nation" but was subsequently held responsible for the "death of the Western" itself due to its failure at the box office and its bankrupting of United Artists. However, what it proposed was a magnificent and audacious assault on the "system" of the Western, its codes and values, expectations and themes, projecting instead a bold, transgressive approach that would, in time, inspire a new generation of equally impressive new Westerns, but with, as Jim Jarmusch put it, "the 'Western' in quotes."[10]

It is these "Westerns in quotes," with their various outsystems, that are the subject of this chapter, examining how what Jarmusch once called "peripheral Westerns" work in relation to the established and mythic genre while offering something critical and innovative.[11] As the post–*Heaven's Gate* Western struggled to reinvent itself, some of the most interesting work came from those willing to follow its many paths and "off-shoots" in different directions in films such as *Walker* (1987), *Unforgiven* (1992), *The Ballad of Little Jo* (1993), *Posse* (1993), *Desperado* (1995), and *Lone Star* (1996).[12] Alex Cox, a British director whose work has been much influenced by Leone, created in *Walker* a postmodern exploration of the inevitability of Manifest Destiny, paralleling the excursion of William Walker into Nicaragua in the nineteenth century with Ronald Reagan's foreign policy in the 1980s. With the punk sensibility also developed, as we will see, in Jarmusch's work, Cox appropriates the characteristics of the Western in order to explore its ideological undertow of violence, imperialism, and racism, deliberately using anachronistic references within the film to Coca-Cola, helicopters, Marlboro cigarettes, and *Newsweek* to make his points. Similarly, Cox's film is clearly an influence in Mario Van Peebles's "New Jack Western," *Posse*, which weaves contemporary events and themes, such as the L.A. riots and institutional racism, into a black Western format.[13] Van Peebles's use of Woody Strode as his narrator alerts us to his awareness of both Leone (*Once Upon a Time in the West*) and John Ford (*Sergeant Rutledge*, *The Man Who Shot Liberty Valance*) while developing his own counternarrative to mainstream and mythic histories.

In this section, however, I have chosen films across a decade (1995–2005) that create further rhizomatic outsystems in varying degrees, demonstrating the range of tensions created by shifts in tone and subject matter from the most extreme and radical transformation of independent cinema, as in American Jarmusch's *Dead Man*, to the subtle play of the sadly neglected *The Claim* by Englishman Michael Winterbottom, and finally to the mainstream but challenging adaptation of Annie Proulx's story "Brokeback Mountain" for the screen by Taiwanese-born Ang Lee. My intention in using such a mix of films is to show how cinema continues to interpret and interrogate the vast array of western iconography through its self-conscious use of the Western as a "traveling" genre.

Outsystem 1: *Dead Man* (1995, Director, Jim Jarmusch)

Jarmusch's *Dead Man* creates its outsystem from the Western genre by building on two key characteristics: first, that it has always been "a way of processing history for Americans and stamping ideology onto the film"; and second, that the "openness of the form and its inseparable connection to 'America' in the broadest sense" meant that its traditions could become "departure points for something that maybe subverts them or uses them in a way that's not necessarily formulaic." Hence, Jarmusch says, he will "take the things I am attracted to and weave them into something of my own."[14] Aware of the tradition linking the Western to the American national narrative, and equally aware of the constantly restated death of the genre after *Heaven's Gate*, Jarmusch weaves these positions into his film so that it becomes a reflexive commentary on the genre and on American values and myths, both resurrecting the Western and reframing its ideological values and possibilities. Coming from the independent film tradition, Jarmusch has consistently remapped and folded existing genres in this way—for example, the road movie in *Stranger Than Paradise*, the prison breakout film in *Down by Law*, and the gangster genre in *Ghost Dog: The Way of the Samurai*—as if self-consciously interrogating popular Hollywood forms in order to extract new life from them.[15] Thus, for Jarmusch the "inside" generic forms and associated memories can be productively revised, folded "outside" so that different, critical, and imaginative new texts emerge. In this respect, his arrival as a filmmaker in the mid-1970s shares much with the punk movement and in particular with the concept of "bricolage" as defined by critic Dick Hebdige, whereby "basic elements can be used in a variety of improvised combinations to generate new meanings within them." As John Fiske redefined it, "bricolage" is the actions "by which the subordinated make their own culture out of the resources of the 'other,'" a process I would extend to Jarmusch's filmmaking, which appropriately began with his using old film stock given to him by Wim Wenders for *Stranger Than Paradise*.[16] As a "bricoleur" Jarmusch plays with existing, familiar genres and tropes, stretching and twisting them so they draw attention to themselves, while creating innovative spaces in the text for audiences to reflect upon what they see and to connect their unconfirmed expectations to wider frameworks of meaning. This adds something to Greg Rickman's famous comment on *Dead Man* that it represented the "the Western under erasure," borrowing from Derrida's idea that language is incomplete, defective, and so always "under erasure"—"effaced while still remaining legible . . . destroyed while still making visible the very idea of the sign." In this process, Jarmusch "erases" (or subverts, if you prefer) the Western's traits while keeping "legible" his generic and cultural sources, so both remain in plain sight throughout, like the word itself crossed through. This helps in understanding Deleuze's idea of a cinema that both collapses and maintains generic conventions as well as Jarmusch's recent comments on *Dead Man*'s having "a lot of layers" present while simultaneously being erased.[17]

Jarmusch's "punk aesthetic" draws from this "outside" in ways that deliberately disrupt the ideological circuits of established genres, like the Western, injecting surprising, often quirky elements that jar and interrupt the ease and flow of familiar, national forms and archetypes.[18] In the dramatic but appropriate language of Deleuze, discussing Foucault, "Thinking does not depend on a beautiful interiority that would reunite the visible and the articulable elements, but is carried under the intrusion of an outside that eats into the interval and forces or dismembers the internal."[19] The dangerous "unity" of elements that "presupposes a beginning and an end, an origin and a destination that can coincide and incorporate "everything," requires forces from outside to intrude (as in Jarmusch's genre disruption) to create "a mixed-up state of agitation, modification, and mutation."[20]

Jarmusch refers to himself as a "mongrel" like all Americans, and he emphasizes this perspective in his work in order to see the "inside" and the "outside" and create this "mixed-up state" in his films: "America is made up of foreigners. . . . All of America is a cultural mixture, and although America is very much in denial of this, that's really what America is."[21] As a result, he claims to be drawn to European characters because "they're the essence of America," and sees his position as in-between, able to perceive America from both points of view: "I'm in the middle of the Atlantic floating around somewhere when it comes to the themes in my films." As a director Jarmusch has been much influenced by European filmmakers such as Godard and Wenders, and through their work he got to know American "outsider directors," as he calls them, like Nicholas Ray, Sam Fuller, Edgar Ulmer, and Robert Frank. In addition, *Dead Man* has a German/Japanese co-production and used German cinematographer Robby Muller, famed for his work with Wenders. As Jarmusch put it, "it's kind of a strange circular pattern, coming back to directors in your own country through directors in Europe," and yet this "weird circular thing" is a movement vital to his films.[22] In his "peripheral Western" *Dead Man*, coming at the genre from this outside position, this "circum-atlanticism" further emerges in a number of important ways through its central characters: William Blake (Johnny Depp), who is confused with the English romantic poet by Nobody (Gary Farmer), a Native American who has traveled to England, been schooled there, and learned the poetry of said Blake. The West in Jarmusch's hands becomes a fluid and transnational space, already affected by global shifts and movements, imitating the "circular pattern" that Jarmusch spoke of in the ways it traced complex cultural interactions across national boundaries.

These fascinations with the "outside" make *Dead Man* a traveling Western in many ways, beginning with the archetypal journey into the West by an incongruous naive character (the tenderfoot) seeking his fortune on the frontier, utilizing the director's own sense of feeling like an "alien" growing up in Akron, Ohio, "pretty much outside of things," and then discovering the world through travel: "I think travelling really opened up my imagination. . . . I love being in places where I don't have roots or don't know what is predictable."[23] This is precisely the effect he adopts for his central character *and* his audience in *Dead Man*, deliberately uprooting him from family and home and plunging him into an alien and disorienting environment, while simultaneously uprooting the audience from any comforting generic familiarity. Blake's innocence can be paralleled with the West itself in that Jarmusch wanted him to appear "like a blank piece of paper that everyone wants to write all over," just as Frederick Jackson Turner referred to the region as a "blank page" awaiting the inscription of "civilization." But, as the film reminds us throughout, you cannot trust writing, for too often it deceives and confuses. After all, the tenderfoot has traveled across the West on the strength of a letter soon rendered useless by Dickinson, the factory owner.

With deliberate echoes of the train in Leone's *Once Upon a Time in the West*, the lengthy pre-credit sequence follows Blake's train journey across America from Cleveland to Machine in the Pacific Northwest, tracing his gradual abandonment of the trappings of civilization the closer he gets to the end of the line. This sequence also introduces the powerful motif of "white man's metal" that provides a chain through the film—train, factory, guns, bullets—something that will eventually kill all its characters, including Blake (the "magnet for white man's metal," he calls himself) and Nobody. Jarmusch's protagonist is, however, initially an innocent, reading the *Bee Journal*, wearing an incongruous checked suit (a "clown suit," it is called later), and looking increasingly awkward as his fellow travelers become more gruff and brutal, carrying only guns, killing buffalo, and glaring at him. Out of the train window Blake watches a shifting wilderness landscape, from mountains, to forests, to deserts, with abandoned Indian camps and broken-down wagons, signs of "failed pioneer dreams" and "the history of possession and dispossession in the region."[24] At the climactic point of his journey the engineer delivers a surreal monologue comparing the view outside with that inside, suggesting a confusion between the inner consciousness and external events that sets the tone for much of the film to follow—a dreamlike, hallucinatory excursion further "West," where westness is much more than geography. Indeed, the engineer, as we realize later, also predicts the final scene of the film and the death of Blake—"Doesn't it remind you of when you're in the boat?" The immediate impact of this whole sequence, played out against the harsh, jarring guitar sounds of Neil Young's sound track, is one of dislocation for the audience (as well as for Blake), of being transported beyond our genre expectations and comfort zones and thrust into a confused and troubling whirl, a form of critical deterritorialization. What are we watching? Is it comic, tragic, surreal? Can I continue to watch? The engineer may, of course, supply the answers when he gives Blake three vital clues: that he's come "all the way out here to Hell" for a job that probably won't exist since "I wouldn't trust no words written down on no piece of paper," and that all he will really find out west is "your own grave." Hell, no trust in language, and death are what awaits William Blake on the frontier—no Promised Land, no mythic words to be believed in, only the dark inevitability of the grave. The idea of the West's association with rebirth, new beginnings, and rootedness is interfered with by Jarmusch, who commented in an early interview that "most Westerns really, thematically, are about death," as if he was already shaping Blake's journey in his imagination—the journey of a dead man into a dying land told through a dead genre.[25] As Geoff

Andrew argues, the film becomes "an elegiac poem for lost innocence and a meditation on different attitudes to death," but in addition it is clearly an astute commentary upon the pervasiveness of the West in the popular imagination and in the use of particular forms of westness in the formulation of national identity and political ideology.[26]

The end of the line, the terminus of western expansionist history, is Machine, which, as its name suggests, is a vision of industrialized hell, Blake's (the poet's) "dark, satanic mills," smoky, muddy, piled with skulls and coffins, all witnessed by the pale-faced Blake along with whores, pissing horses, gun-toting outlaws, and a forlorn mother and child begging in the street. These scenes seem to prefigure something of the "realist" mise-en-scène borrowed by David Milch for his HBO series *Deadwood*, an almost medieval, noirish scrabble for power and survival. The passive Blake has entered the "machine" of inevitability and, as the engineer has already indicated, his fate is sealed and he is as dead as the skulls and stuffed animals that populate mill owner Dickinson's office. Jarmusch defines a brutal West without redemption that culminates with the wounding of Blake at the hands of Dickinson's son Charlie, whose former girlfriend Blake has just slept with. When Blake finds a gun under her pillow, he asks, "Why do you have this?" To which she answers, as if prefiguring all the horrors of the film and the subject of Jarmusch's commentary, "'Cause this is America." In this gothic dark land a form of social Darwinism mixed with a relentless, violent inevitability immediately counters any naive vision of the West as opportunity. It is Al Swearengen's world in *Deadwood*.

Jarmusch's dying accountant now becomes an outlaw cut adrift from the world of Machine to wander further west, quickly hooking up with a Native American called Nobody, who in many ways, like Blake, runs counter to established stereotypes. This "outsider" figure, so often silenced and "dead" in Westerns ("the only good Indian is a dead Indian"), is given a central role in the narrative, immediately labeling Blake "stupid fucking white man," but is soon won over by confusing him with the romantic poet of the same name, someone he has long admired and quotes throughout the film. In Jarmusch's curiously upside-down world, Indians travel to Europe, speak English, read poetry, and refuse any subordinate role, and within this, for all its quirkiness, what emerges is a version of the West as a poetically imagined hybrid contact zone where conventional iconography, atmosphere, and action are reshaped. Everyone in the film is in motion—Blake and Nobody, the bounty hunters, traders, Indians—by train, canoe, horse, and on foot, and under these conditions encounters take place, often violent, but also over trade and exchange (the running joke about wanting but never having tobacco emphasizes this element). The fact that Nobody denies us the easy stereotype of the "grounded" Indian—close to the land, communal, and spiritual—is an important part of Jarmusch's determined efforts to subvert the supposed norms of the genre and all its ideological grids. In one speech, Nobody tells of his forced imprisonment in Toronto, Philadelphia, and England where he was paraded and exhibited in a cage, while simultaneously he "learned" from his captors, "mimicked them," and studied in a manner that predicts Homi Bhabha's theory of postcolonial mimicry. In this "the *ambivalence of mimicry* (almost the same, but not quite) does not merely 'rupture' the discourse, but becomes transformed into an uncertainty which fixes the colonial subject as a 'partial' presence," that is, incomplete and virtual. Thus mimicry is a "*double* vision that in disclosing the ambivalence of colonial discourse also disrupts its authority . . . [by] producing a partial vision of the colonizer's presence; a gaze of otherness, that . . . liberates marginal elements and shatters the unity of man's being through which he extends his sovereignty."[27] This resonates in our first sense of Nobody gazing on Blake and addressing him in English as "stupid fucking white man," ensuring that "the observer becomes the observed" as he quotes him the poetry of William Blake, which Blake ironically thinks of as "Indian mullarkey." In this sense, as Susan Kollin argues, Nobody is a "hybrid . . . world-wise, cosmopolitan Indian" who opposes the stereotypes of the savage Other, the vanishing American, and the stoic, noble wise man, and runs against the "dreary humanism" of white liberal representation (such as in *Dances with Wolves*), offering instead something closer to Gerald Vizenor's concept of the postindian as "native presence," "resistance," and "survivance" rather than colonial "absence" dictated through simulation and stereotype. In fact, Jarmusch claims that his intention was simply to present Nobody as "a complicated human being" with all the possibilities this suggests.[28]

Of course, at the same time, to return to my earlier points, Nobody's partial presence reminds us of the wider aims of the film as a generic mutation—"almost the same, but not quite"—working away at the frame of the Western as a source of new possibilities and connections beyond itself as "colonial" form, a "double vision," both inside and outside, to jolt the audience beyond the values defined by the traditions of the West into the realm of the "post-Western." Having followed Blake's and Nobody's surreal journey, we arrive at one scene that typifies Jarmusch's punk subversion of the mythic West's "sovereignty" with the scene at the trading post manned by the racist Christian (Alfred Molina). It is the moment before the circle of the narrative returns upon itself with the canoe on the river repeating the opening train sequence, and the arrival at the Makah Indian village repeating Blake's initial walk along the streets of Machine. At the apex of the narrative the scene is telling in its drawing together of traditions and their subversions. Here the trading post is infused with Christian hypocrisy and western racism, the hallmarks of Manifest Destiny, through the words of the owner who blesses Blake, tells him the ammunition is both guaranteed and "blessed by the Bishop of Detroit," and then curses Nobody, asking Christ to "purge" the earth's "darkest places from heathens and philistines." But unlike the tradition of the silent Indian, Nobody talks back to colonial power and sovereignty once again with a quotation from the poet Blake, denouncing his "vision of Christ" as "my vision's greatest enemy." Against a sign reading "Work out your own salvation," the preacher-capitalist denies tobacco to Nobody while willingly selling it to Blake, and tries to trick the latter into signing an autograph on a wanted poster while pulling a gun on him for the reward. Blake's response is crucial, for he turns the pen into a weapon, as if to enact Nobody's earlier plea for him to write poetry with blood, and drives it forcefully through the hand of the preacher, to reiterate Nobody's "vision" as opposed to that of the deceitful and callous trader. This scene's twists and turns, its playful, surreal elements, and its attack on many of the underlying ideologies of westward expansion demonstrate Jarmusch's purpose in the film.

However, despite this seemingly climactic moment in which Nobody and Blake work together to overcome the hypocritical preacher-trader, Blake is immediately shot again, thus denying us any sentimental "new" mythos of red/white unity (à la *Dances with Wolves*), and must begin the last phase of his journey. Indeed, Jarmusch refuses to offer any further concessions to the traditional Western, rapidly killing off all his characters and providing no revelation through Blake's passing.[29] Many languages and stories throughout the film, like the scars and markings on his body, have inscribed Blake's "blank canvas," but none of them represent conclusive self-knowledge or revelation in the form often found at the conclusion to Westerns. Blake is, in reality, as confused and dreamy at the end of his journey as he was at its beginning. At the very edge of the West, on the Pacific Ocean shore, Nobody tells him to "go back to where you came from" (back east, back to Europe, back to the spirit world), alone in darkness to complete both the cycle of the film and his cycle of life.[30]

Outsystem 2: *The Claim* (2000, Director, Michael Winterbottom)

Like Jarmusch's, Winterbottom's oeuvre is deliberately varied, "a body of work that constantly tests and challenges the boundaries of cinematic form and is highly conscious of its relationship to dominant models of filmmaking," and it is for this reason that both turned their attention to the Western as one of most influential and ideological of genres.[31] If the confused presence of poet William Blake acts to interfere with the smooth, mythic patterns one might expect from an American Western, forcing us to rethink and supplement our notions of westness in *Dead Man*, then what of one that utilizes a Thomas Hardy novel, *The Mayor of Casterbridge*, and translates it to gold rush California? Winterbottom's *The Claim* does just this, employing "outside thought" to further examine the cultural significances of the West as syncretic and transnational. For a British director whose diverse body of work has ranged across many genres, usually set in the United Kingdom, this marks an important exception, allowing him the opportunity to explore powerful themes in an intense and mythic landscape.[32] This is a distinctly transatlantic Western demonstrating "the inescapable hybridity and intermixture of ideas" and emphasizing "the instability and mutability of identities" from a position "between" cultures, drawing from Europe to comment on America and vice versa.[33] This is a further example of materials reviewed throughout this book that are not "content with the merely national" approach to the study of the West and seek a more mobile response to cultural and identity formations, situating events within international frames of reference so they "don't always 'bounce back' to us in the form of the nation state," as Krista Comer has put it.[34] Of course, in Hardy's novel, too, there is a transnational dimension, with characters having traveled from Canada and America to Britain, from Scotland to England, demonstrated most emphatically through the figure of Farfrae (who becomes Dalglish in the film), bringing mechanized agriculture to Casterbridge and contemplating leaving England for, as he puts it in the novel, "the other side of the warrld, to try my fortune in the great wheat growing districts of the West!"[35]

Such transatlanticism is translated into *The Claim*'s cast, too, which, like Leone's strategy in *Once Upon a Time in the West*, mixes established émigré U.S. stars with European actors to convey a wonderful sense of America in its westward, immigrant formation: Natassja Kinski (playing Polish) and Milla Jovovich (playing Portuguese) combine with the Scot Peter Mullan (playing the Irishman Dillon) and American Wes Bentley (playing the Scot Dalglish). Reminiscent too of *Heaven's Gate*, this fluid ethnic mix creates the sense of a community in transition, molding an identity out of the multiple experiences of the western diaspora.[36] Equally in its use of Hardy's novel as a source, it connects moods and themes across continents, such as encroaching modernity, global economic markets, migratory patterns, and ethnic diversity, allowing the one to illuminate the other in unexpected ways. The West is not, in this sense, exceptional, but rather symptomatic of larger global shifts and forces that move people around the world in search of different and better lives. For example, the incipient town of Kingdom Come, established by the ruthless Dillon, remote and encircled by the snowy mountains of the Sierra Nevadas, is strangely reminiscent of Hardy's Casterbridge with its self-made mayor Henchard at the heart of a similarly sparse and contained place: "It is huddled all together; and it is shut in by a square wall of trees, like a plot of garden ground by box-edging . . . untouched by the faintest sprinkle of modernism. It was compact as a box of dominoes."[37] Just as Hardy's work examined England on the threshold of the industrial age with its gridlike ruralism about to be changed forever, so Winterbottom's film excavates California, the West, and America at the moment of its modern development with the coming of the gold mines and the railroad. As Patricia Nelson Limerick has argued, mining has "long-range effects on the West": scattering immigrant populations, giving rise to conflicts, creating early forms of rapid urbanism, producing compressed social mixes of gender and race, and, she says, above all it "set a mood that has never disappeared from the West—get in, get rich, get out."[38] In the film, "modernism," as so often in the Western (as we have seen with *Dead Man* and *Once Upon a Time in the West*), also takes the form of the railroad being surveyed by Dalglish and which may, or may not, develop the settlement for the future as the "advance guard of empire."[39] The emphasis on mining and the railroad suggests the film's interest in the idea of the "the claim," here suggesting the claim upon the land itself as commodity to be exploited, and the instability of such communities, dependent on the longevity of the mineral deposits and the infrastructure of the railroad as a source of development. Winterbottom's film explores this instability as a defining aspect of the West as a place in which fortunes were made and lost, communities founded and abandoned, and lives secured or cut adrift. Another meaning of the "claim" implied in the film's title is that of Dillon trying to claim a legitimate life for himself, to establish "roots," despite his past, in the shifting landscape of this mining community. As occurs so often in examining the West, one is struck by it, in Limerick's words, as "a place of extraordinary convergence, one of the great meeting zones of the planet . . . [where] people from all over the planet met, jockeyed for position with each other, and tried to figure each other out."[40] The intense activities, mobilities, and frictions of the West as transnational, contested territory and contested narrative come through in *The Claim* as Winterbottom engages the audience in a dramatic rendition of the struggles between roots (settling down) and routes (passing through) played out in the snowy wastes of California, in a West that is already "global" in so many ways.

Indeed, Hardy's image of Casterbridge as a box of dominoes further informs the atmosphere of Winterbottom's Kingdom Come, both as a place of chance, gambling, and fierce competition and as an austere black and white space carved out of a hostile world. This is a blindingly snow-sheathed California contradicting its mythic associations as the land of sunshine and reversing the generic markers of Westerns as necessarily desert-bound, like Ford's or Leone's, creating instead a poised, fragile environment through which the action unfolds. There is a claustrophobic tension throughout the film echoing Hardy's familiar, imprisoning Wessex "engirdling," "screened," and "grizzled," with the snow sealing in the repressed emotions of love and violence simmering within Dillon's past and embodied in the town he has created.[41]

Like the novel, the film begins with the selling of a wife and child, but in this western version it is for a gold claim in 1849 California, a time when, as Winterbottom says, "California was essentially not part of America and everyone was an immigrant."[42] A poor Irish immigrant, Daniel Dillon, trades the only things he has—a wife, Elena, and daughter, Hope—for gold and for Kingdom Come, the settlement he establishes over the ensuing eighteen years, and in so doing, in the spirit of Thomas Hardy, seals his fate with an almost biblical certainty: "Thy Kingdom Come, Thy will be done. On earth as it is in Heaven." Thus the film begins with a brutal, gendered act of commerce upon which is built a community and a dream. Winterbottom's West echoes William Carlos Williams's statement, "History! History! We fools, what do we know or care? History begins for us with murder and enslavement, not with discovery . . . the spirit, the ghost of the land moves in the blood, moves the blood."[43] The promise of the future of the West and the American nation, like Dillon's life, is therefore based on a repressed dark and guilty past that will eventually return across the ghostly white snows to haunt him in later life. When the repressed returns as his wife and daughter, Dillon has to confront his past actions and in so doing expose the underlying greed and overtly masculine power that he represents. His wife, however, is dying from tuberculosis, the disease symbolizing the change about to disrupt his world, the "ghost" moving in the blood. The desire for land, wealth, and authority is here intensified through the almost godlike presence of Dillon, a dictator, who appears as judge and jury for the town, seen in the film whipping a man in the street or arbitrarily executing sleeping survey workers.

Winterbottom was attracted to these historical events because of the "blankness of the starting point," allowing him to place Dillon into a situation "where you could do anything . . . [with] no sense of there being any external law" and see what "moral decisions" he made.[44] Another meaning of "claim" in the film's title clearly also refers, therefore, to all those inscriptions people would impose on the apparently blank space of the West, whether it be Dillon's version, the impending grids of the coming railway anxious to join the nation at Promontory Point, or a new era heralded by Lucia's emergent town at the film's conclusion. In all this, Winterbottom examines the West as composed of competing human desires for control and order, for types of possession (over women, land, money), and for power, as if the protagonists are literally "writing" themselves onto the country's blank page, like Leone's railway boss Morton in *Once Upon a Time in the West*, as discussed in chapter 3 as "writing that conquers," inscribing their desire on to "a blank 'savage' page," transforming "the space of the other into a field of expansion for a system of production."[45] Indeed, *The Claim*'s advertising tag line was appropriately "Everything has a price." The film prefigures *Deadwood*'s obsessive interrogation of western "entrepreneurialism" (mining, whoring, gambling, assassination), corruption, and violence as the founding inscriptions of the region and its own second series' slogan, "Fortune comes with a price," echoed perfectly Winterbottom's dark, monochrome world.

The Claim's various "colonizations" are dramatized in connected scenes showing Dillon with his piles of gold bars, having sex with his girlfriend Lucia, breaking up with her in an effort to assume some new moral ground with his "reclaimed" family (who have returned to Kingdom Come some years later), and finally in a sequence showing Dalglish mapping the territory for the railroad and literally crossing Dillon's town off the map when they realize it is too dangerous to bring the railroad there. The combination of edits here is significant, setting up a chain of meaning vital to the events of the rest of the film—wealth, greed, sex, gender, power, land, control, hope, and failure. And in the midst of these scenes is the ever-present sense of violence that hovers over the whole film: Dillon hits Lucia, a man is blown up by "nitro" in the survey team, and in an amazingly prescient slow-motion shot Winterbottom shows a horse ablaze running in panic through the snow.[46] Attitudes to land are paralleled with gender politics here as Dillon seeks to control Lucia through offering her the saloon and gold for her continued cooperation, which she rejects with her counterclaim "I'm no whore." This scene operates to show how, among other themes in the text, the film examines "relations of difference and dominance" at work in the West and how constructions of gender were challenged by women like Lucia working outside society's "strictures of regulationism."[47] Later, Lucia and Hope, with some reference back to Jill McBain in *Once Upon a Time in the West*, emerge as strong feminine figures in the film, signifying different versions of the future, one an independent businesswoman, the other a potential wife and homemaker.

Dillon's urge in the film, however, is to redeem himself from the past and to establish a stability and respectability by building a town and rebuilding his family. His desire to establish roots is epitomized by literally moving a house down the mountainside to a new position in the town to impress his dying wife.[48] In one of the film's grand set-piece sequences the home is literally dragged by hand through the snow in an audacious gesture redolent of other grandees like Citizen Kane, Fitzcarraldo, or Jack McCann in Roeg's *Eureka*, with Dillon standing on its balcony orchestrating this conquest of nature and space.[49] He is, of course, ironically also trying to conquer time and history by winning back his wife and daughter, and these audacious gestures proclaim his insistent desire for authority and power, like the beautiful statues, drapes, and ironwork inside the house, artifacts derived not from the past he seeks to repress but from the civilization and culture he longs to be associated with. These are the markers of classical civilization, empire, and imagined respectability that he hopes will displace his own brutal past. However, it all merely contributes to the fragility of his environment, barely holding back nature with a few fragments of acquired classicism, and emphasizing Dillon's repressed past and ever complicated present. It is the railroad, "the mechanical handmaid" of the cartographic grid structure, that commands the power of that present and future, and without it Dillon's "kingdom" will not survive, a situation confirmed by sequences showing the approaching trains, like immense William Henry Jackson photographs, and the survey maps that have gridded out the land for future use.[50] As William Fox has written, as we noted earlier, "To map the land was, thus, in no small measure to claim it" and to transform "blank space," via the "rectilinear Jeffersonian grid" and its lines, paths, and routes, into a kind of "national nervous system."[51] In all these key sequences the action is pared down as in Ingmar Bergman's films, gestures slowed down by the snow, with the physicality of every movement emphasized and aestheticized, drawing our attention to every step and nuance. As Walter Benjamin says, film can expose "a different nature" than the naked eye wherein "an unconsciously penetrated space is substituted for a space consciously explored by man" with the camera revealing what he terms "unconscious optics" in the same way that psychology reveals unconscious impulses.[52] What we are seeing here, as if in slow motion, is history unraveling in ways that the "king" of Kingdom Come, Dillon, can no longer control. Thus the rugged individualism of the frontiersman myth that he represents is being overtaken by the corporate West of the railroad and Dalglish's cartographic science that we witness mapping a different landscape from that envisioned as Kingdom Come, a "grid [that] exercises authority over space by applying a ruler to it in all sense of the word." The Jeffersonian dream of the grid extending European democratic principles into the "void" of the West confronts an older dream of individual will and struggle against nature, and as the film suggests, both are suspect and exploitative.[53]

Winterbottom refutes the romance of nation building and the myths of western heroes for a cinematic style reminiscent of European art cinema (Bergman, for example); Robert Altman's wintry, fatalistic, and ultimately bleak western McCabe and Mrs. Miller (1971); and, of course, Cimino's Heaven's Gate. As Dillon's "kingdom" collapses with the shattering entry of the past, his wife's death, and his rejection by the railroad survey, the only consequence is violence and apocalyptic destruction—the literal erasure of his "inscription" upon life and land. In the film's climax, the stark monochromatic world, like ink on a page, is brought into a series of terrible/beautiful oppositions that suggest a version of the West that is radically anti-mythic, intercutting Elena's death with a wedding in the town, Dillon's burning of his dream with a new life beginning, and the railroad's inevitable progress with the old king's demise. Death and life, old and new, destruction and regeneration, snow and fire collide in these dramatic scenes marking the end of Dillon as he wanders alone and broken to die and freeze into the landscape itself. In a cruel repetition of his arrival in Kingdom Come before it was anything but a shack in the snow, he now returns to that past, to the endless nothing-ness of the blank, white ground where he is finally and fatally "rooted" in the earth. In Hardy's original novel, Henchard, "a blundering Titan of a self-made man," almost commits suicide, describing his situation in words that define Dillon's own predicament at the end of the film: "The whole land ahead . . . was as darkness itself; there was nothing to come, nothing to wait for . . . it was unendurable." The "writing" of civiliza-tion that Dillon had inscribed into the western landscape through his vision of a "kingdom" he now erases with fire, thawing out the frozen, repressed scene with violence, returning it all to nature as a new and dif-ferent town emerges near where the railroad passes in the valley below, a town no longer controlled by the masculine violence of Dillon but by the feminine Lucia (whose name suggests light), who names it Lisboa (after her Portuguese father and heritage). Winterbottom's film, like Hardy's novel, unfolds as a "drama of pain" using a borrowed narrative frame to examine western ambition and the tragic consequences of its deceit and relentlessness within a universal context.[54] Whether through Dillon's megalomania or Dalglish's railroad grid, the film presents an already exploited West like that defined by William Fox where humans have become so distanced from land that it appears as "merely a sur-face to be manipulated—to be inscribed, erased, written over, which is exactly what happened in America once we had even just begun to fully overlay the cartographic grid upon the West."[55]

In the film's final speech, however, Dalglish (the new, modern man) offers a eulogy for Dillon and for the era he represented: "They're like kings . . . pioneers . . . people like Dillon. They came out here when there was nothing, built these towns and ruled like kings."[56] Yet the film does not end there, for if it did, the vision of the pioneer West might remain a stable and romantic one locating the likes of Dillon as an unproblematic frontier hero, like the pioneers of the Turner thesis or the classic West-ern film, whose single-mindedness and violence was fully justified as the necessary tools of survival and nation building. Instead it offers us three final images: first, of Lucia's skeletal new town below; second, as the camera lifts away from it, we witness a mad human scramble among the debris as the townsfolk discover all Dillon's melted gold now lit-erally returning to the ground; and third, Dalglish and Hope walking through the thawed, burned-out town (Paradise Lost?), like some post-apocalyptic Adam and Eve, to begin some "rerouted" new life elsewhere beyond this kingdom. This final tension between Dillon's calamitous obsession with roots and an emergent alternative of some routes beyond his destructive vision offers no simple resolution but rather a dialogue between the greed and violence of the past and the possible new beginnings of "the next generation ... Americans."[57] In telling this story about the death of a town and a man who rises and falls in an instant, the film reminds us that the West was not always about expansion, success, and growth but also about "shrinkage, abandonment, and waste," and so in the ruins of Kingdom Come's "colonization" we might see the traces of the environmental damage, militarization, and corporate neglect of contemporary western lands: "The West, these places tell us, is not a region where Americans escaped history, not a region of inconsequential, quaint, and distant frontier adventure, and not a region permitted by Providence to escape failure. It is instead the region where we can most profitably study the interplay of ambition and outcome, the collision between simple expectation and complex reality, and the fallout from optimistic efforts to master both nature and human nature."[58] As we contemplate the ruins and ghosts of Kingdom Come as one part of the burned-out cycle of western expansionism, it seems to return us to the very start of the narrative, like a text to read again, asserting once more the schizophrenic vision of the West as dream and materiality, "ambition and outcome," "simple expectation and complex reality," its layers exposed and its multiple inscriptions present and starkly written on the land itself, perhaps reminding us that, despite the mythologies, "Failure is, indeed, a prime opportunity to *learn*."[59]

Outsystem 3: *Brokeback Mountain*
(1999, Writer, Annie Proulx; 2006, Director, Ang Lee)

Unlike my previous two examples, Ang Lee's *Brokeback Mountain* became, during 2006, one of the most discussed and award-nominated films of recent years on both sides of the Atlantic. Heralded by some as the first "gay Western," this aspect of the film often obscured many of its other, interlinked qualities that once again demonstrated the flexibility and durability of the genre. Lee has called it a "post-Western" because

"it's a Western, but it's not really a Western" and because he "wanted
to shoot straight, mainstream, [and go] somehow off-beat" at the same
time.[60] This perhaps explains his oft-made comment in interviews that
he made the film from the "middle," a position that enables many sides
to be examined and from which things diverge rhizomatically. In the
words of Deleuze, "A rhizome has no beginning or end; it is always in
the middle, between things, interbeing, intermezzo . . . a logic of the AND,
[to] overthrow ontology, do away with foundations, nullify endings and
beginnings. The middle is by no means an average . . . it is where things
pick up speed . . . a transversal movement that sweeps one and the other
away."[61] Lee's middle ground is no "average" but a space through which
the film positions its audience so they might be tested by a "challenge to
what we've been taught": about judging two homosexual characters and
about the powerful mythic framework within which they (and the audience—as westerners and/or as filmgoers and readers) have grown up.[62]

The film is an interesting convergence piece, bringing together three
diverse creative elements—director Ang Lee, writer Annie Proulx, and
scriptwriters Larry McMurtry and Diana Ossana—in what Proulx has
termed a unique "collaboration." From the "middle" of this creative mix
emerges a powerful and challenging development of the Western as a
movie genre, extending the written story outward into a transformed
visual text, indicating a formal rhizomatic process extending outward
from its original text. Proulx has written of how the script worked by
"richly augmenting" her story, "adding new flesh to its long bones"
and allowing it to emerge "not mangled but enlarged," and McMurtry
saw it as "augmenting and amplifying, adding texture and substance
where necessary."[63] McMurtry, who both scripted and co-produced the
film, brought a whole career of interpreting the New West to the project;
grounding the work in a knowledge and understanding already seen in
novels converted to film or television, such as Horseman, Pass By, The Last
Picture Show, and Lonesome Dove. Proulx had only a limited input to the
script through conversations with McMurtry and Ossana, clearly trusting
McMurtry, in particular, to bring to bear on her work his own sense of a
changing West of displacement, mobility, and economic shifts. Indeed,
she has written of McMurtry's "incomparable knowledge of the west's
mores and language" and spoken of the final script as "an exceptionally

fine screenplay."[64] McMurtry's various statements over the years about his own work suggest why he would have been well suited to the task of scripting *Brokeback Mountain*. For example, he has written that "the place where all my stories start is the heart faced suddenly with the loss of its country, its customary and legendary range," and of his sense of a West "whose principal myth was the myth of the Cowboy, the ground of whose divinity was the Range."[65] Later he would write in his aptly titled *Walter Benjamin at the Dairy Queen* of his curiosity "about the difference between new and old, and also the difference between dense and empty, open and closed, new country and old cities, no society and old society."[66] Like Benjamin, McMurtry has always been an astute observer of the power of myth and story and of how various media affect how we think and feel about ourselves and society, including "the transformation of the west into images of itself, Western movies and country and western songs" and even of the capacity for "overflowing the bounds of genre in many curious ways."[67] One way this is suggested in the screenplay is through McMurtry's references to other popular cultural texts to establish how the two central characters act and present themselves, as if part of their existence is always governed by the performance of a "western" archetype in a gesture, a pose, or an attitude. This is their conditioning as "men of the West," performing a masculinity already defined and reinforced by the images of westness in the media and culture. Thus in the script McMurtry refers to James Dean in *Giant*, Sam Peckinpah's *Ride the High Country*, Roger Miller's song "King of the Road," and Steve Earle's "Devil's Right Hand" to give a sense of the iconographic grid within which these men move. This combination of local knowledge, myth criticism, and awareness of the rhizomatic, uncontrollable nature of westness makes McMurtry a perfect contributor to the creation of the film. In his essay on the screenwriting of the film, for example, he comments on how he wanted to capture both the "seductive," "lyrical pastoralism" of the western landscape and the reality of the lives lived within and against this mythic frame: "The West of the great mountains, of the high plains and the rippling rivers, is very beautiful, so beautiful it tempts many not to see, or want to see, the harshness of the lives of the people who live in the bleak little towns and have to brush the grit of the plains off their teeth at night." On this point, too, Ossana and McMurtry comment on the importance of Richard Avedon's photographs in his book *In the American West*, claiming that its "stark, unromantic" images showing people whose lives are "forged and fashioned by hard places and rough times, served to inform our collective vision and overall tone for the movie."[68] In all these ways the film, augmenting the story, builds a sense of the postwar West as performed and represented, creating an elaborate frame of myth and countermyth within which people like Jack and Ennis actually live conflicted lives, unsure of their place within an apparently defined, traditional cultural map.[69]

Lee's oeuvre is often referred to as restless and "eclectic," ranging across genres and styles, rather like the work of Jarmusch and Winterbottom discussed earlier, unwilling to settle into any Hollywood-invoked niche despite working for large studios. This might, in part, derive from his Taiwanese roots and his desire to avoid becoming defined as an "ethnic" director. Instead, Lee deliberately mixes genres, eras, and styles of film—from *The Wedding Banquet*'s interracial gay comedy, to *Sense and Sensibility*'s study of English social class and manners, to the Civil War "western" *Ride with the Devil*, to 1970s suburban satire of *The Ice Storm*, to martial arts epic *Crouching Tiger, Hidden Dragon*, or the comic book angst of *The Hulk*. Thematically, however, there are links across such diverse texts: studies of social containment and social mores against which struggle alternative forces, a variety of troubled outsiders, the powers of nature, love, and loyalty. Indeed, Lee has commented that the constant themes in all his work are "conformism," "repression," and "the struggle . . . [of] behaving as a social animal."[70] As a non-U.S.-born director, Lee has been drawn to these themes and tensions as an "outsider," like Proulx herself, sharing what she has called the "invaluable" "outsider's eye" that can permit alternative perspectives to emerge.[71] What we have already seen at work to varying degrees in Leone, Jarmusch, and Winterbottom as filmmakers is this Deleuzian concept of "creative stammering," of being "a foreigner in one's own tongue."[72] Lee's work questions the centralizing, normalizing culture and vibrates with rhizomatic energy following its own paths outward; as producer James Schamus says, "We're always learning, always trying to acquire new skills, choose new genres, take ourselves in new directions."[73] Proulx refers to Lee as "not afraid to walk into dangerous territory" and Ossana refers to him as a "risk taker," all qualities that further suggest his creative outsider status.[74]

Proulx, like Lee, is also something of an outsider to the West. Born in 1935 in New England, she lived as a child in Connecticut, North Carolina, upstate New York, Vermont, Maine, and Rhode Island, and finally settled in Wyoming in 1993. From a French Canadian family, she has defined herself as "a roving citizen of the northern tier of the continent" whose life has often been characterized by travel rather than stability.[75] These factors contribute to her relationship with the West, which she always sees, to some extent, as an outsider. The original story, "Brokeback Mountain," was published in the New Yorker in 1997 and became part of the collection Close Range: Wyoming Stories (1999) developing particular themes from earlier non-Western works: "the failure of the limited economic base for a region," "the individual caught in a whirlpool of change and chance," "a trapped feeling," and "images of an ideal and seemingly attainable world the characters cherish in their long views despite the rigid and difficult circumstances of their place and time."[76] Her reputation until then had been as a writer whose work "traveled," from Newfoundland in The Shipping News to Vermont and New England in Heart Songs and Postcards, but with her own settling in Wyoming she began to write more specifically western stories, following Close Range with the novel That Old Ace in the Hole (2002) and the stories Bad Dirt (2004). They explore versions of the West that deliberately challenge conventional stereotypes and modern images of the New West, best introduced by the epigraph to Close Range from an anonymous rancher: "Reality's never been of much use out here." In this spirit she goes on to claim that "The elements of unreality, the fantastic and improbable, color all of these stories as they color real life. In Wyoming not the least fantastic situation is the determination to make a living ranching in this tough and unforgiving place."[77] Her work uses these "fantastic" elements to portray quirky, broken lives and oddball characters, mixing sardonic humor and deep understanding of the region and its landscapes to examine its continued dreams, hardship, disappointment, and corporatization, and in so doing to challenge readers' expectations and assumptions about what now constitutes the West. As she has said, "I watch for the historical skew between what people have hoped for" (those "images of an ideal and seemingly attainable world") "and who they thought they were and what befell them." She combines in surprising layers a transnational West of Australian-owned "Down Under Wyoming" tourist ranches and Global Pork Rind corporations, with archetypal timeless small-town lives barely surviving the "critical economic flux" but where "The present is always pasted on the layers of the past."[78] Her fiction, her "writing in layers," as she terms it, has been heavily influenced (by her own admission) by the French Annales school of history of Braudel, Bloch, and Febvre, who pioneered the minute examination of the lives of ordinary people and their everyday traces "against the *longue durée* of events," studying relations among the various, complex layerings of time, geography, and identity.[79] Many of these concerns are compressed in the story "Brokeback Mountain," whose prismatic focus is a homosexual love story around which swirls her familiar "whirlpool of change and chance."

The story captures this transitional West through the lives of two men, Ennis Del Mar and Jack Twist, "both high school dropout boys with no prospects," a "Pair of deuces going nowhere," whose lives are brought together in desperation for work and escape from a culture that seems to have no place for them. Raised in "the land of the Great Pure Noble Cowboy," as Proulx calls it, they are victims of the "cowboy myth" forming the "images of an ideal and seemingly attainable world" to which they are still attached. "Both wanted to be a part of the Great Western Myth," writes Proulx, "but it didn't work out that way."[80] The truth is, however, that these would-be cowboys are watching sheep, with Ennis an orphan whose family ranch has failed and Jack a wannabe rodeo star ("crazy to be somewhere"), living in the shadow of his father, "a pretty well-known bullrider [who] kept his secrets to himself," and both are caught with only the fading memory of "the idea of the close(d) range, the open, unfenced place that no longer exists."[81] For them, meeting in 1963, this Wyoming West is in limbo, a cold, repressed space determined by strict codes and duties, strangely detached from national and world events (the Vietnam draft is only mentioned briefly in the story) and yet clearly affected by them in terms of economic change and general insecurity. In Lee's film version, the town of Signal is bleak, bleached, windy, and desolate, with the opening scenes marked by near silence as Jack and Ennis shuffle awkwardly outside Joe Aguirre's trailer and later wander its main street with buildings resembling a simulated film set of a nine-teenth-century frontier town.

As so often in the classic Western, only the western landscape offers solace, a means to earn a living, and a route out of this stifling environment, or what Ennis calls being "caught in my own loop."[82] The "loop," of course, includes his unsatisfied life as a would-be cowboy and the socially constructed masculine duty defined by marriage, work, and family that means Ennis and Jack's sexual relationship, ultimately, has to remain another repressed "secret" in the West, up on Brokeback Mountain. In the film, more than in the story, these powerful social constructions are manifested through patriarchal figures—Aguirre, Jack's and Ennis's fathers, and Lureen's father—whose values provide a powerful aspect of the social "loop." In one scene Lureen's father, who refers to Jack sarcastically throughout as "Rodeo," insists on carving the Thanksgiving turkey and then deliberately contradicts his son-in-law's wishes that his own son not watch the football game on television, saying, "You want your son to grow up to be a man, don't you daughter? (direct look at Jack). Boys should watch football."[83] In another scene (in both film and story), Ennis recalls how his father had taken him to see the battered corpse of a neighbor beaten with a tire iron for living with another man. These are lessons about a patriarchal social order rooted in bigoted values and violence that for so long have been central to the western mythology of the frontiersman, the Marlboro Man, in "the land of the Great Pure Noble Cowboy." This is the "conformism and repression" that Lee wishes to examine in his film version and that Proulx refers to in interviews as America's "real, deep and vast" sense of violence.[84]

The violence in this post-Western emerges out of the clash between these repressive social restrictions and the desire for expression, most noticeably internalized through Ennis, full of "self-loathing and in denial," who represents "the conservative side of America . . . the biggest homophobe in the whole movie."[85] His inarticulate, repressed desire erupts into the film to remind us of the consequences of such a controlling social grid: pounding the wall with his fist when he separates from Jack the first time, beating two bikers at a fireworks display, pulling a man from his truck in the street, and raging at his wife, Alma, when she "overstepped his line."[86] As so often in classic Westerns, as Jane Tompkins argues, violence displaces language and emotion, revealing that which is absent.[87] In both film and story this tension opens a sustained and complex critique of such an unrelentingly surveilled culture of duty and behavior, typified by Joe Aguirre's panoptic watching of Jack and Ennis up on the mountain.

Typical of the Western genre, Proulx also manifests these tensions through the story's descriptive spatialities: Aguirre's "choky little trailer office," the "small apartment . . . up over a laundry" where Ennis lives with his wife, Ennis's final trailer, Jack's father's ranch ("a meagre little place"), and Jack's boyhood room ("tiny and hot"). This point is amplified in a conversation when the two men recall "the submarine Thresher lost two months earlier with all hands and how it must have been in the last doomed minutes." Their closeted lives, compared here to a claustrophobic undersea world, are like all the contained, stifling social spaces within normalized culture, and none more so than the conservative West. Everything in their lives is governed by boundaries, unspoken rules, and duties, so that when Ennis questions Jack about his "knowledge" of Mexico (and a suspected gay life there) we are told he was "cutting fence now, trespassing in the shoot-em zone."[88] In contrast to these defined spaces of control and surveillance, Proulx provides the wide-open spaces of Wyoming, where different rules apply and where, in a version of the genre's tradition "men can be men" in contact with nature. Of course, the irony here is that these men want to express their homosexual desire outside the boundaries of the fenced-in social "loop," and it is only in the natural world that this is appears possible, away from the judgments and prejudice of the social code, up on Brokeback Mountain with its "freedom-granting yet hostile landscape."[89] The landscape can, of course, be neutral and reassuring: "The cold air sweetened, banded pebbles and crumbs of soil cast sudden pencil-long shadows and the rearing lodgepole pines below them massed in slabs of somber malachite"; a space beyond the social: "There were only the two of them on the mountain flying in the euphoric, bitter air, looking down on the hawk's back and the crawling lights of vehicles on the plain below, suspended above ordinary affairs." But it can also be a "two-faced landscape" where they erroneously "believed themselves invisible," away from the surveillance of that world below, existing as if "suspended" in time, untouched by the loop of tradition and convention "a while way the hell out in the back of nowhere."[90]

In his film, as Lee put it, "We are photography," and the visual replaces Proulx's "internal depiction" with maximum use made of the natural splendors of landscape to suggest Jack and Ennis's love. We see them in relation to sweeping valleys, hillsides, and mountains, jumping naked into rivers, sleeping under the stars, and going about their daily routines in relation to nature's time rather than society's. Interestingly, much is made of Aguirre's relationship to time and numbers; his speech is riddled with references to their patterns, and it is he who imposes his "rules" on Ennis and Jack: "He didn't ask if Ennis had a watch but took a cheap round ticker on a braided cord from a box on a high shelf, wound and set it, tossed it to him as if he weren't worth the reach."[91] Time is about control, order, and the authority of a social system of work and profit whose implementation elevates Aguirre's panoptic power while diminishing that of Ennis and Jack. Up above this commanding social grid, Jack and Ennis enter a separate but temporary time zone made of natural rhythms and routines—weather, food, work, and ultimately love. Tellingly, later in the film, as the lovers struggle to maintain contact, a refrain is "there's never enough time," and when Aguirre sees their love-making he responds initially by "fixing Jack with his bold stare," as if drawing him down from his "flight" once again into the claustrophobic social frame. However, when they return from the mountain, Aguirre's fixed and controlled world and its embedded values have been ruptured: the sheep are all mixed up ("Some a these never went up there with you"), and "The count was not what he'd hoped for."[92] As both film and story demonstrate, society will not tolerate these "flights" into nature and constantly hauls them back to its reality until "Ennis felt he was in a slow-motion, but headlong, irreversible fall" into the West's normative "stoic life" of family, work, and prescribed masculinity. All the time, as in Proulx's story, the film contrasts the natural world with the dark interiors and cramped spaces below in the social world: cowboy bars, alleyways, supermarkets, apartments, trailers, dirt farms, and closets. In these spaces Ennis and Jack look awkward, stilted, and ill at ease as their "mountain" time is compressed into the crushing weight of domestic routines: Ennis's shabby apartment with a suspicious wife and screaming children which he prowls like a caged animal staring out the window, or Jack's bourgeois Texas home ruled by the "stud duck" father-in-law and a business-driven wife whose marriage could, we are told, be conducted by phone.

Through Jack and Ennis's tragic love story the mythic West represented in so many films and novels is scrutinized and the region's coded boundaries breached so that, as Proulx writes, "in a disquieting way everything seemed mixed" and, therefore, suddenly, problematic and no longer held within the static spell of mythologies and fixed rules.[93] Proulx has said that she hoped the story would "start conversations and discussions . . . to awaken in people an empathy for diversity, for each other and the wider world," and in many ways the reader and viewer has to rethink the parameters of the Western, adjust its "frame," to comprehend the inclusion of their desire with its "brilliant charge" of passion, "the years of things unsaid and now unsayable," and the terrible emptiness of their final separation, alongside their overt masculinities "infatuated with the rodeo life" and "a muscular and supple body made for the horse and for fighting."[94] Rather than the repressed or parodic sexuality permitted in some Westerns, as charted by Blake Allmendinger's book *Ten Most Wanted*, *Brokeback Mountain* wants its audience to confront its existence and to understand the intensity, exhilaration, and pain of this fundamental clash between the socially accepted and the hidden in the lives of Jack and Ennis and their families.[95]

The story's moving climax is worth examining by contrasting how the story and the film deal with its significance. In the story, Ennis visits the room of his secret lover, Jack, after his death to find their bloodied work shirts hanging inside one another in the "shallow cavity" of a closet in a "slight hiding place": "the pair like two skins, one inside the other, two in one." As he holds the shirts in his hands he attempts to resurrect Jack sensually with his "mouth and nose," only to find there was "no real scent, only the memory of it, the imagined power of Brokeback Mountain."[96] In the film, the scene is shot initially from within the closet looking out to Ennis seated by the window, as if Jack's ghostly presence remains drawing his lover toward the secret shirts. Ennis ducks into the closet (where he has lived metaphorically so much of his adult life), falling to his knees as if at some sacred altar to their love, and finally admits his feelings for Jack against all the austere weight of his repression and self-denial. All Ennis has left of his desire are his sensual memories contained now in the symbolic fabric of the two shirts, each one a separate but linked narrative, that together with the postcard he buys of the mountain and pins up in his trailer, generate his dreams of Jack as he once was, to "rewarm that old, cold time on the mountain when they owned the world and nothing seemed wrong." However, this memory and imagined power is fragile in the face of the story's ever-present social framework, manifested through Jack's stern, judgmental "stud duck" father, who refuses to let the ashes be scattered on Brokeback Mountain and instead insists they go into the "family plot."

In the story, as Ennis leaves the farm he describes the "family plot" (both a material place and a symbolic "narrative" of tradition and patriarchy) that will be Jack's last resting place as "fenced with sagging sheep wire, a tiny, fenced square on the welling prairie, a few graves bright with plastic flowers . . . on the grieving plain."[97] The cemetery, Proulx's final spatial grid, is restrictive, like so many others in the book and film, containing and defining Jack through his family's narrative, in an unnatural place of plastic flowers and fencing holding back the natural world, the only space within which he and Ennis could express their love. Lee excludes this scene from the film, whereas Proulx places great emphasis upon its significance. In the film more attention is placed on Ennis's return to his trailer and the secret "shrine" he has created from the postcard of Brokeback Mountain and the two shirts (now reversed) hanging in his closet. As the movie closes, Lee constructs an elaborate shot of multiple frames: the closet door framing the shrine, the postcard framing the mountain, the trailer window framing the world outside, and the screen itself framing all of these images for the audience. As we gaze on this tableau, its multiple layers (like Proulx's writing) suggest something of the "conversations and discussions" that the film provokes and the choices it leaves us with; however, like the grim "family plot" in the original story, the "real" world outside the trailer window is a long way from the "imagined" paradise of Brokeback Mountain; it is flat and dreary ("the great bleakness of the vast northern plains," as the script describes it), a still "repressed America, where gay men are forced to bury their personalities and violent conformism is the rule of the day."[98] It is within this dark, repressive social order that Ennis is convinced finally that Jack's death had been a violent and deliberate act—"So now he knew it had been the tire iron"—just another expression of a violently patriarchal culture.[99] Despite Ennis's redemptive tears and the audience's undoubted empathy, both Proulx and Lee suggest through their different emphases in these endings that the West is an unforgiving place still locked into its mythic iconography and dark history of excessive masculinity. Proulx has admitted her own pessimism, using a quotation from Paul Fussell, on seeing his first dead body, to summarize her sensibility: "and suddenly I knew that I was not and never would be in a world that was reasonable or just."[100]

Ironically, then, the "loop" Jack and Ennis longed to escape seems impossible to break, and it is rather confirmed by the "family plot," the still-closeted shrine, and the unforgiving landscape that frames them all. As Proulx puts it, "Nothing ended, nothing begun, nothing resolved." In this state of limbo, Ennis has only his dreams to hold on to, with their mixture of "grief . . . joy and release," and the shadow of violent repression, where even an innocent spoon "could be used as a tire iron." He is condemned to the western "stoic life," living in the space between his desire and the conditioning pressure of an unchanged world: "There was some open space between what he knew and what he tried to believe, but nothing could be done about it, and if you can't fix it you've got to stand it."[101]

5. DIALOGICAL LANDSCAPES
"Outsider" Photography of the West

There are a lot of things that Americans live with that they
never really see, because they are such a part of their culture. . . .
As an "outsider," however, I can drive around the desert southwest
and get excited about miles and miles of telephone poles—
telephone poles that the average American might take for granted.
Ridley Scott

Surmounting the Epic West

Joel Meyerowitz has written of how he believes photographs work: "You
picture something in a frame and it's got lots of accounting going on in
it—stones and buildings and trees and air—but that's not what fills up a
frame. You fill up a frame with feelings, energy, discovery, and risk, and
leave room enough for someone else to get in there. . . . A photo must
have room in it for entrance by outsiders, so that the photographer himself or herself hasn't built a structure that keeps you out, but instead has
left some crack that allows you the freedom to enter."[1] His emphasis on
the "entrance by outsiders" interrupting the "frame" and the "built . . .
structure" of the image is a useful summary of the kinds of photography
I wish to examine in this chapter. In some respects the works I will discuss are those with "cracks" that allow the fixed ideological frame to be
interrogated and critiqued. The "photo-grid" of the West, going back to
the nineteenth century, forms "a matrix of other visual and literary ways
of narrating stories" (such as Albert Bierstadt or Owen Wister), contributing "potent bits of pictorial shorthand" shaping a powerful regional
imaginary.[2] In a similar manner into the twentieth century, the work of
Ansel Adams presented a monologic, monumental vision of a preserved
wilderness devoid of humanity (except the photographer) and culture,
echoing Rosalind Krauss's definition of modernist "grids," discussed in
the introduction, "crowding out the dimensions of the real and replacing
them with the lateral spread of a single surface" of an idealized, "pure"
West.[3] Indeed, Martin Stupich has written that Adams's photographs
are like a "long monologue of brilliant diction and linguistic arabesque
. . . [like] photography made to celebrate photography. The pictures

were whole, conclusive, final—each glorious print was a complete and clear answer, but to a question I would never ask."[4]

This heritage has cast a monologic shadow over western photography, creating what Bakhtin would term an "epic" vision, "already ready defined and real . . . already finished, a congealed and half-moribund genre," looking backward to "[t]he epic absolute past" as "the single source and beginning of everything good for all later times as well." As in Adams's West the past is sacred, complete, and untouchable, "as closed as a circle" and with "no place . . . for any openendedness, indecision, indeterminacy . . . no loopholes in it through which we glimpse the future; it suffices unto itself."[5] The photographers I discuss in this chapter "reframe" the West to break open this "closed circle," reinvoke the "Other," and challenge epic distance with the details of the everyday, thereby questioning, as Giles puts it, "alignment with such 'monolithic' national narratives."[6] The "new" photography of the West, post-Adams, explores these "loopholes" to present an "anti-epic," anti-mythic vision created in dialogue with this tradition and its mediations, mutations, and simulations. In Adams's frozen idealization of place as a myth, as Edenic Promised Land, the West as culturally constructed, social landscape, a zone of contact and encounter where interaction and dialogue takes place at all levels, is, therefore, repressed. The eternal and sacred effect of the epic "grids" of his photographs with their "centripetal" pull to authenticity, origins, and tradition, can, however, be dialogized by the presence of alternative, "centrifugal" forces—bizarre, contradictory, and problematic "intrusions from outside"—always asserting the photographer's position in the construction process.[7]

The "closed circle" of representation, like Meyerowitz's limits of the photographic frame, can be breached and its "inside" turned outward to reconnect with a field of forces and images beyond itself, just as new photography dialogizes "the great *drama* of meaning [Adams's] photographs *enact*" (emphasis added).[8] Remember, "outsideness," as we discussed in the introduction, provides a different lens, confronting the cultural "givens" and myths that have taken on a dominant status, engaging in "a kind of dialogue, which surmounts the closedness and one-sidedness of these particular meanings, these cultures" with a new form of "creative understanding." My examples of American and European photographers are like "traveling aliens" developing this "creative understanding" which, according to Bakhtin, "raise[s] new questions for a foreign culture, ones that it did not raise itself," and through contact with these issues, "seek[s] answers to our own questions in it" while "the foreign culture responds to us by revealing . . . new aspects and new semantic depths." Thus both cultures might engage in a reciprocal relationship, a critical dialogue based on exchange and circulation. As the introduction showed, Bakhtin's "excess of seeing" is based on the recognition that I can see what you cannot see and vice versa, seeding his notion of dialogism, in which multiple "excesses" of sight and "voice," from outside and inside, are folded together, often conflictively, across and between established boundaries.[9] Hence the West should not be represented as a single, unified concept or uncomplicated national narrative but rather envisioned from multiple positions, inside and outside, questioning "essential" or originary knowledge and supplementing and extending critical understanding. Indeed, Mark Klett, one of the most significant post-Adams landscape photographers, reflects on Adams's photographic monologue in a similar manner, writing that "anyone who has visited the site of one of Adams' photographs knows that the romance of his landscape is often best experienced in the photographs themselves. The reality is quite different."[10]

Barthes argued that a photograph was "unary" when it "transforms 'reality' without doubling it, without making it vacillate . . . [with] no duality, no indirection, no disturbance." Its *punctum* was the "detail" whose "presence changes my reading" by interrupting, puncturing the system of representation, skewing the "frame" until the image is no longer "docile" but becomes active in the mind of the viewer, shifting the "unary" toward the "dialogical" through the "power of expansion." The *punctum* engages our senses, "constantly doubles our partial vision," shattering the apparent motionlessness of the photograph, unfreezing and mobilizing it by suggesting all that exists in relation to and beyond the singular, first (partial) sight. In Adams's work this might be the *punctum* of omission that reminds us of all he leaves out, or the crisp clarity of his tonal system that reveals an overly pristine West, but its function, as Barthes argues, "takes the spectator *outside its frame,* and it is there that it animates me" as a "subtle *beyond,*" a space in which the "dynamics" of the image, which by its very material, physical nature is static, are created from the interaction and dialogue of the spectator and the photograph (emphasis added).[11] This echoes an earlier essay in which Barthes explains that beyond the levels of "information/communication" and "symbolic/signification" there exists a "third meaning—evident, erratic, obstinate" which "cannot be conflated" and "exceeds" the "referential motif" of the image itself and "compels an interrogative reading." This "third meaning," like Bakhtin's "excess of seeing," is "obtuse," "the one 'too many,' the supplement that my intellection cannot succeed in absorbing; at once persistent and fleeting, smooth and elusive."[12] Ann Jefferson claims that meaning "bursts out of the frame," overflows its stasis, becoming more than its "obvious meaning," setting "the reader in motion, cast[ing] him loose."[13] Such photographic "thirding," to reuse Soja's term, can be seen "as an *accent*, the very form of an emergence, of a fold (a crease even)" acting as "a counter-narrative" to open up representations and announce the text as "multiple writings, drawn from many cultures and entering into *mutual relations of dialogue*" where the reader is "the space on which all the quotations that make up a writing are inscribed without any of them being lost," and thus "a text's unity lies not in its origin but in its destination."[14] Increasingly, western photography has grown weary of the Adams legacy and sought more complex, multiple, and dialogical renditions of place, an alternative perspective akin to Deleuze's description of a critical process concerned "to trace the lines of which it is made up, to determine the nature of these lines, to see how they become entangled, connect, bifurcate, avoid or fail to avoid the foci."[15]

"The Subtle Beyond": Robert Frank's West

Robert Frank, a Swiss Jewish photographer, arrived in the United States in 1947 torn between established postwar visions of America as a land of freedom and liberty, embodied noticeably in the West, and more suspicious and critical responses to social division and political consensus. Initially influenced by the Farm Security Administration photographers of the 1930s such as Dorothea Lange, Russell Lee, Arthur Rothstein, and Walker Evans, whose work in the West captured alternative images of human struggle, industrial agriculture, and natural disasters, Frank, by the 1950s worked with another "outsider" of French Canadian heritage and Beat sensibility, Jack Kerouac. Kerouac wrote the introduction to Frank's *The Americans*, made the film *Pull My Daisy* with him in 1959, and took a road trip with him in 1958 to Florida. Kerouac defined Frank's photographs as "*intermediary* mysteries," gestures of movement and fluidity *between* states, creating edgy dialogues through combination and juxtaposition, framing and reframing subjects, and in the relationships within and outside the image itself, an "art-form," claimed Kerouac, "not unlike my own."[16] Kerouac understood Frank's photography unlike any of the contemporary critics who were quick to dismiss the images, in the cold war spirit of the age, as anti-American with their "warped objectivity" and "one-sidedness." In contradistinction to these views, Kerouac saw the "double-sidedness" or dialogism in Frank's work, writing, "We . . . got out of the car to catch a crazy picture of a torn-down roadside eatery that still announced 'Dinner is ready, this is It, welcome' and you could see through the building to the fields the other side and around it bulldozers wrecking and working."[17] The sense of loss here is strong alongside possibility ("the fields the other side"), humor, and contradiction ("wrecking and working"), as if the outsider's eye has the benefit of seeing and knowing different sides—the iconic and the ironic, if you like. This recalls what Bakhtin admired in Dostoyevsky's dialogic "visualizing power" with its ability to "see everything in coexistence and interaction," seeing "many and varied things where others saw one and the same thing. Where others saw a single thought, he was able to find and feel out two thoughts . . . where others saw a single quality, he discovered in it the presence of a second and contradictory quality." In Dostoyevsky's world, as in Frank's, there was "profound ambiguity" represented as "complex and multi-structured . . . spread out in one plane . . . consonant but not merging or as hopelessly contradictory, as an eternal harmony of unmerged voices or as their unceasing and irreconcilable quarrel."[18]

In Kerouac's *On the Road*, Sal Paradise, searching for the promise his name implies, wakes up, literally and metaphorically, to the New World as an outsider heading West: "I was far away from home, haunted and tired with travel, in a cheap hotel room I'd never seen. . . . I was just somebody else, some stranger, and my whole life was a haunted life, the life of a ghost. I was halfway across America, at the dividing line between the East of my youth and the West of my future."[19] Frank, "far away from home" and "haunted" by his journey into America, was like Paradise's "stranger," a "ghost" drifting with his camera into the secret spaces of the everyday. Later Kerouac wrote of Frank, like a ghost, moving with the "strange secrecy of a shadow," capturing "scenes that have never been seen before on film" and, like Paradise, seeing "the dividing line[s]" of America.[20] Paradise's companion, Dean Moriaty, "a young Gene Autry . . . a side-burned hero of the snowy West," "a western kinsman of the sun," leads him "into the West," revealed as multiple and complex like the "sad poem" of Frank's photographs.[21] And as Kerouac put it, "Anybody doesn't like these pitchers don't like potry [sic], see? Anybody don't like potry go home see Television shots of big hatted cowboys being tolerated by kind horses."[22] Beyond the bland images of 1950s TV cowboy myths existed the profound and impure vision of Frank's West, a vision both tragic and joyous, ready to capture, like poetry, the necessary contradictions and anomalies of real life.

In key statements Frank articulated his ambivalent outsider vision, a position that allowed him an angle upon the mythic, national narrative embodied in so much western iconography, seeing how "the United States . . . signifies the kind of civilization born here and spreading elsewhere" and yet simultaneously that "Criticism can come out of love. It is important to see what is invisible to others. Perhaps the look of hope or the look of sadness."[23] Indeed, in one of his most recent interviews, Frank claimed, "I'm an outsider still. How does that song by Johnny Cash go? 'I'm a pilgrim and a stranger.' I like that. That's how it is with me, and it's too late to change now."[24] Although Frank is by no means a photographer only of the West, his dialogical cultural landscape images represent this outsider's eye—both pilgrim and stranger—interrogating the "thirdspace" of the West, the complex space *between* the real and imagined, mediated and material, captured in the 1950s' first flush of the media age. More than 40 percent of the photos in *The Americans* are, in fact, images of the West in which love and criticism, pleasure and pain, doubts and admiration, mingle in his ironic/iconic photographs examining being besieged by westness, creating "The truth . . . somewhere between the documentary and the fictional, and that is what I try to show. What is real one moment has become imaginary the next. You believe something you see now, and the next second you don't anymore."[25]

Like J. B. Jackson, whose work parallels Frank's (and Kerouac's) in many ways, Frank understood the West as a heavily invested space, brimming full of clichés and myths and so not a blank "canvas" for the artist to work with. His multiple Wests acknowledge all the preestablished givens and iconic western images while confronting and critiquing them in any new work: the neon-lit cowboy bars of Gallup, New Mexico; Native Americans on the road in Idaho; a Mexican staring at a Las Vegas jukebox; the faded glories of Bunker Hill, Los Angeles; the ravaged landscape of Butte, Montana; the isolated farms of Nebraska; the casinos of Elko, Nevada; corpses by the side of the road in Winslow, Arizona; roadside memorial crosses in Idaho; St. Francis blessing the gas stations and car lots of Los Angeles at sunrise; or an open highway in New Mexico. In this burgeoning postwar period, the most prevalent West was either the mythic cowboy country of 1950s television or the emerging New West of the Sunbelt economies and militarized Southwest. Frank's acute and uncomfortable juxtapositions "travel" *between* these binary positions of pleasure and death, poverty and wealth, motion and stasis, class and race, decline and change, creating instead unfinished, surreal, and tension-filled frames, demonstrating the capacity of the outside, traveling eye (the pilgrim/stranger) to see America's "fractured frames of reference, its infinite regression of half-lives, its proliferation of contaminated sites, its bounty of waste," simultaneously challenging and understanding the viewer's complex expectations and assumptions.[26] As Frank put it, recalling Kerouac, looking at his photographs should be "like read[ing] the line of a poem twice."[27] In this rereading or doubling process, Frank defines something of the outside eye's capacity to make us look again and look differently, to see the strange within the familiar, to perform the uncanny as we shift dialogically between the known and unknown, the mundane and the magnificent.

Once again this recalls Dean and Sal in *On the Road* discovering "the strange Grey Myth of the West" at Cheyenne's "Wild West Week" with its theme-park atmosphere mixing desire and deep disdain: "I was amazed, and at the same time I felt it was ridiculous: in my first shot at the West

I was seeing to what absurd devices it had fallen to keep its proud tradition"; or traveling through Central City with its "chichi tourists" and "Hollywood stars" attempting "to revive the place"; or to the "carnival of lights and wildness . . . lost in the brown halo of the huge desert encampment LA really is." Indeed, in Kerouac's words from the novel, Frank was attempting to unsettle the "smooth, well-ordered, stabilized-within-the-photo lives" by mobilizing within the frame alternative impressions—"the raggedy madness and riot of our actual lives, our actual night, the hell of it, the senseless nightmare road."[28]

To analyze and explain this I am going to use "Hoover Dam, Nevada, 1955" in some detail, even though it never made it into *The Americans*.[29] Sandra Phillips calls it "a stunning comprehension of the dilemma of landscape in the postwar West," but even this fails to do justice to its extraordinary impact and influence.[30] The location is Hoover Dam, Nevada, an iconic technological site providing water for the urban New West of Las Vegas, a tourist destination and a symbol of human control of nature, and yet Frank's oblique photographic style denies us the place itself, offering instead a representation in the form of a postcard in a rack. The rack belongs to the souvenir shop selling all manner of images and mementos, producing meanings for this place and other "western" spaces (like Kerouac's Cheyenne or Central City). The image Frank chose from the six negatives he shot there focuses on the rack of three postcards—of the dam, the Grand Canyon, and an atomic bomb blast—providing a surreal portrait of westness as sublime nature, sublime technology, and catastrophe, and, tellingly, all the possibilities *between* such stark portraits. Formally, the photograph confronts the eye with a layered collage of images—photographs, words, shapes, windows—all serving to disrupt a simple view, enacting Frank's frustration with what he later called the "square photo."[31] Frank captures in this multilayered "text" a narrative about the New West contained within and straining against another commentary about representation and the power of the image to circulate meaning. Within the frame of the photograph, multiple frames create a form of "moving" (or "traveling") photography that suggests the West as a space of interlocking and contrary narratives where tourism jostles with ecology and every natural wonder has become already a "Kodak moment." At Hoover Dam, people will photograph this site for themselves, buy others' images, listen to the tour guides, and read the books, drawing together all these elements into a discourse of the Hoover Dam, and, by association, of the West. The layered frame demonstrates Frank's determined effort to explore and explode the boundaries of photographic practice, to propose, as Barthes did above, the notion of reframed, excessive photography that "takes the spectator outside its frame . . . [where] I animate this photograph and . . . it animates me," creating a "subtle *beyond*."[32] Like Deleuze and Guattari's discussion of framing and deframing considered in relation to Leone's cinema, Frank's work gives "the picture the power to leave the canvas," creating "a disaggregation of the tonal plane" spilling out "beyond" its nominal frame, provoking the viewer and challenging established precepts.[33] His urge is to "break up the sovereign optical organization" (frame, order of composition, ideology, expectations) through the creation of a photographic "diagram" (to borrow another term from Deleuze) whose "lines and zones" inject chaos into the "givens" of art (or the "given" West), "like the emergence of another world" through a "catastrophe" that acts to "give the eye another power" creating the possibility of some new "rhythm" and order" in the work, beyond its bordered frame.[34] Thus Frank's Hoover Dam photograph redefines the West by turning tourist imagery against itself, portraying it as always-already mediated and multiple, irreducible to a simple, single frame or sensation and always part of a wider field of forces. As we "travel" through Frank's travel image, we are *moved beyond* the traditional awe and wonder of sublime nature in the Ansel Adams tradition to the technology that produces both a dam and a bomb—life and death, survival and annihilation. How do we process such information and the possible readings it establishes? This is the power of Frank's work.

In this sense Frank's rhizomatic method relates to my developing argument about a West defined as interacting lines rather than by any coherent or unitary space, as an unfinished "diagram" or moving cartography continually pushing against imposed boundaries and fixed, mythic narratives. As Deleuze and Guattari put it, "What's interesting, even in a person, are the lines that make them up, or they make up, or take, or create," and Frank's photographs always suggest these lines, the very multiple "storylines" that gave his last exhibition its name.[35] Frank once said he would "do all kinds of things so I wouldn't be stuck with that one image," since any single image (or meaning) reduces the complex, contradictory, multilayered experience of identity, life, and nature.[36] To this end, Frank's urge, as in "Hoover Dam," is so often a "deframing" and multiplication of the single, static photograph to produce sensations beyond it, creating Deleuzian "counterpoints" that transform the apparently immobile into the mobile, "creating a syntax that makes them pass into sensation that makes the standard language stammer, tremble, cry, or even sing . . . *the foreign language within language* that summons forth a people to come" (emphasis added).[37] Frank's friend Allen Ginsberg explained Frank's decision to move away from photography as sparked by getting "tired of looking through the camera, through like a frame. He wanted something larger. He wanted to be in the world."[38] Indeed, when Frank turned to filmmaking after *The Americans*, he wrote: "I will make a film . . . about photographs leading (me) to moving images. Fragments of saved up memories . . . *moving inside that frame*. Pushing towards another—scene— . . . *To reveal and to hide the truth*. A photograph is fiction and as it is moving it becomes reality" (emphasis added).[39] Like Leone and Jackson in their own fields, Frank provided "the foreign language within" to unsettle and trouble the established and "taken-for-granted" "language" of western representation. Julia Kristeva, under the influence of Bakhtin, wrote that the foreigner is the "space that wrecks our abode," an unhomely, uncanny presence "within us," but one vital to a recognition of difference and humanity.[40]

Hence, in another western photograph, "Los Angeles," the camera looks down, like a foreigner, onto a city street as a series of grids—pavement, building, rooftops—punctuated only by the neon arrow slicing through the center of the image and the striding figure below.[41] Both arrow and figure are moving out of frame in a surreal enactment of this familiar tension between grids and lines (of flight), death and life, dark and light, inertia and motion prominent in Frank's work and prefiguring the work of Los Angeles artist Ed Ruscha. Ruscha has often commented on those painters, photographers, and filmmakers, such as Kurt Schwitters, David Hockney, J. G. Ballard ("He cuts open the belly of what's going on and everything falls out on the floor"), Antonioni, Roeg, as well as Frank, who influenced him because of their "foreign" critical point of view upon America: "They knew more about the culture than we did. . . . Probably because they view it as strangers, and they see the kind of life that they don't have."[42] Ruscha's painting and photography have often deliberately re-represented icons of Americana—Wonder Bread, Standard Oil, the Hollywood sign, Sunset Strip, and parking lots—conveying what he terms (like Frank) his "love/hate" relationship with Los Angeles.[43] Dave Hickey argues that Ruscha's aim is to attack "standardization" through his "Standard Oil" paintings and to reclaim the overbranded image, to "restore the wonder to Wonder bread." The gas station "dispensed standards" and the restaurant served "norms," and so Ruscha burns them down, asserting the typical and the ordinary.[44] Frank clearly had a similar radical, critical intent in his work, a desire, if not to "burn it down," then at least to break the frame and connect everyday events with wider social issues such as racism and poverty, of "opening the host to his visitor." As Robert Silberman has written, Frank's western photographs were "radically different" from those of Ansel Adams, presenting "car photos, not horse photos, grab shots made with a 35mm camera, not the large format work favoured by the f.64 school. . . . [H]e saw the ironies created by cowboy culture as it moved through America" and in all this became the "first major revisionist of the iconography and formal approaches used to depict the American West."[45]

In "Rodeo—New York City" Frank shows how even in photographs it is possible to move inside the frame.[46] Like a still from an imagined Wim Wenders version of *Midnight Cowboy*, he fills the frame with contradictory information inviting a narrative: a cowboy, a New York street, the word "Dodge," a waste bin, traffic, an onlooker staring back at the camera. Here the West's public, mythic face—the Marlboro Man—is displaced, deterritorialized into an urban world where cowboys should not be, inviting questions about masculinity (the boots, the tight jeans, the belt, the cigarette) while challenging our narrow expectations about identity's relationship to place. It asks, can westness exist outside the West? The effect of the photograph is to point us, like the neon arrow, beyond the "frame" of expectations, to begin to rethink and re-vision the West from outside, and in so doing to reinvigorate the documentary tradition and engage directly with the emerging mediated culture, "to produce something that will stand up to all those stories but not be like them."[47] This sentiment is borne out in the following comment:

> I'd like to make a photo-film and work out *a dialogue between the movement of the camera and the freezing of the still image, between the present and the past, inside and outside, front and back.* . . . *Two houses. Two countries. Two points of view.* One is outside cultural life, the other right in it. One is the other's refuge. Both *are at the same time necessary and useless* . . . my photographs will become pauses in [my life's] flux, breaths of fresh air, windows on another time, on other places.
>
> I'd like to make that film. (emphasis added)[48]

As we have seen, Frank's perceptive use of dialogic perspectives created a "foreign language" that served to disrupt and question the ease of an already existing and established mythic language (in cultural discourse and photography), providing a dynamic starting point for later artists concerned with the function and purpose of the West in the imaginative construction of "America."

Frank's American Legacy

Architect Robert Venturi wrote in 1966 a statement that overlaps with Frank's vision in its challenge to representational essentialism and "purity":

> I like elements which are hybrid rather than "pure," compromising rather than "clean," distorted rather than "straightforward," ambiguous rather than "articulated," perverse as well as impersonal, boring as well as "interesting," conventional rather than "designed," accommodating rather than excluding, redundant rather than simple, vestigial as well as innovating, inconsistent and equivocal rather than direct and clear. *I am for messy vitality over obvious unity.* I include the non sequitur and proclaim duality. . . . *I prefer "both-and" to "either-or," black and white, and sometimes gray, to black or white.* A valid architecture evokes many levels of meaning and combinations of focus: its space and its elements become readable and workable in several ways at once. (emphasis added)[49]

Later he wrote *Learning from Las Vegas*, using the desert West's extraordinary visual culture to bring many of these concepts to life, finding in the heart of the New West, near where Frank had visited and photographed in the mid-1950s, the "messy vitality" and simultaneity that challenged comfortable norms and ideals. The "social landscape" of Las Vegas, "innovating, inconsistent and equivocal," full of hybrid, formal fusions, required its "readers" to look beyond established lines of thought and be open to other possibilities blooming in the excesses of the desert. Inspired by the work of J. B. Jackson, whose own photographs shared something of the spirit of Frank's work (see chapter 1), Venturi et al. registered a cultural shift away from dominant patterns of thinking and toward this challenging postmodern "messy vitality." Photography began to register this shift via its post-Frankian representations of the West in 1974 with Robert Adams's book *The New West*, in 1975 with the *New Topographics* exhibition, and in 1978 when Lewis Baltz published *Nevada*.

The 1975 exhibition *New Topographics*, for example, represented the West as building sites, roadsides, housing projects, motels, and industrial parks, commenting directly on Ansel Adams's belief in the emotional and spiritual "equivalence" one should record in landscape. Learning from earlier photographers like Walker Evans and Eugene Atget, the exhibitors represented "social landscape" as a complex, interactive space where difference existed "side by side" in the strangest ways, but they wanted to achieve it with emotional neutrality and an objective recording of the world around them. William Jenkins, its curator, used a quotation from Jorge Luis Borges to open the catalog, in which he pleaded for "plain stories" told in a "straightforward way" moving to the style of "anybody." This flat, stylistic anonymity, influenced by Ruscha's photographs, captured images of "man-made structures within larger contexts such as landscapes" and aimed to let the results speak for themselves.[50] Beyond the ideal, mythic western pastoralist landscape, these new photographic topographies of culturally produced space provided, alongside Jackson's new cultural geography and Venturi's pop-architecture, a focus for reconsideration in which modern industrial parks, trailer parks, suburban subdivisions, sidewalks, and driveways were provocatively juxtaposed with conventional western space, challenging both eye and mind within single frames or serial projects. There is no room for romance or nostalgia here, evidenced by Joe Deal's call to eliminate "the vagaries of sky and horizon" by creating "*undifferentiated space*" with the emphasis upon the "*ground-directedness* of these photographs." Similarly, Robert Adams describes a scene: "By Interstate 70: a dog skeleton, a vacuum cleaner, TV dinners, a doll, a pie, rolls of carpet. . . . Later, next to the South Platte River: algae, broken concrete, jet contrails, the smell of crude oil. . . . What I hope to document, though not at the expense of surface detail, is *the Form that underlies this apparent chaos*" (emphasis added).[51] Adams's notion of "Form" indicates the limits of much of this work, which controls the amount of "surface detail" it represents in order to maintain some semblance of overriding, undeniable form. Below the "apparent chaos" of the West, they seem to say, there still exists some wondrous narrative or "essence" that just might be restated and reclaimed through photography. As Adams wrote in *The New West*, "all land, no matter what has happened to it, has over it a grace, an absolutely persistent beauty. The subject of these pictures is . . . not tract homes or freeways but the source of all Form, light."[52]

Although the *New Topographics* exhibition continued a process of surmounting epic distance, in many respects, as Adams's comments above show, it held fast to conventional, underlying principles of fundamental "grace," "beauty," and "form" that could be attained *through* landscape. Adams's epigraph to *The New West* tells of how "things themselves / in thoughtless honor / Have kept composure, / like captives who would not / Talk under torture." Adams applies this sense of resilience and forbearance to the landscape itself, and photography's task is to show its ultimate "composure" and "honor." The lesson of *New Topographics* was to expand the notion of landscape still further and break the dominance of the "epic" view by representing the "already-written-on" West, so that instead of environment as "setting" it is better seen as "a speaking vestige of the movement of history" defined by the "inseparable unity and interpenetrability" of the human and the natural where "the locality [place] ceased to be part of abstract nature, a part of an indefinite, interrupted, and only symbolically rounded out (supplemented) world" and became instead "an irreplaceable part of the geographically and historically determined world, of that completely real and essentially visible world of human history."[53] Lewis Baltz, whose first photographic collection had recorded the industrial parks springing up amid the "edge cities" of the prosperous New West, referred tellingly to the "forensic objectivity" of his images, full of fragments, roadsides, dump sites, and overlooked spaces. Indeed, one critic referred to Baltz's work as "the remains of lost movies."[54] Baltz, clearly influenced by Frank, utilizes the western grid, showing his work as a series of wall grids, "echoing capitalism's mapping of the world in lines, graphs and charts," and then simultaneously challenging and teasing the eye and mind with contrary, discordant elements within each image.[55] For example, in "South Wall, Mazda Motors, Element No. 40" in his *The New Industrial Parks Near Irvine, California* (1975), shown in the *New Topographics* exhibition, the bizarre archaeology of western space is exposed on the gridlike, mirroring windows that resemble both individual film cells *and* the bars on some postmodern cage reflecting the landscape behind. The distant low hills and trees reminiscent of some earlier sense of the West are juxtaposed with the roads, cars, streetlights, telephone lines, and buildings that signify a "New" and very different, emergent West. The chunks of rock placed as Zen ornaments outside the Japanese factory are ironic fragments from those hills, the remains of an Ansel Adams landscape, now restaged as the artifice of global corporate consumerism.

Post-Frank western photography read cultural space as layered archaeology, constructed of formations of time and space, both human and nonhuman, in which "development, emergence, and history" are "interwoven with . . . signs of historical time—essential traces of human hands and minds that change nature."[56] Echoing De Certeau, they began to represent the West "composed by these series of displacements and effects among the *fragmented strata* . . . these *moving layers*" (emphasis added), arguing against the distanced epic view proposing an alternative vision built from the "everyday," whereby lived experiential "stories," "the world's debris . . . leftovers . . . fragments," "[t]hings extra and other (details and excesses coming from elsewhere) insert themselves into the accepted framework, the imposed order . . . [and where] The surface of this order is everywhere punched and torn open by ellipses, drifts, and leaks of meaning: it is a sieve-order." Thus, "within the structured place of the text . . . [are] produce[d] anti-texts . . . [and] possibilities of moving into other landscapes," which, I would contend, is the very function of dialogical photography as initiated by Frank and developed in these later photographic works.[57]

Photography can be sensitive to these notions of "presence/absence," "moving layers," "strata," and "leaks of meaning" without becoming a purely abstract form, by asserting and then challenging the relations between the image and the viewer with all their underlying assumptions and expectations. The "anti-text" existing within the text's frame, as we have seen with Frank's work, is a concept readily recognizable within the realm of photography that can, of course, actively employ diverse juxtapositions, contradictions, and anomalies to spur on and provoke the viewer/reader beyond his or her initial responses. As Victor Burgin rightly argues, "the photograph is a *place of work*, a structured and structuring space within which the reader deploys, and is deployed by, what codes he or she is familiar with in order to *make sense*."[58] This photography restates the West as "palimpsest," constituted by layered, archaeological sites with "no place that is not haunted by many different spirits hidden there in silence." The places of the West "are fragmentary and inward-turning histories, pasts that others are not allowed to read, accumulated times that can be unfolded but like stories held in reserve, remaining in enigmatic state, symbolizations encysted in the pain or pleasure of the body." These are the surreal and "stratified places" of Frank's photography that resist and question the notion of a return to origin and "source" that still hovers over the *New Topographics'* work.[59]

Another of the *New Topographics* photographers whose work projects this sense of critical "ground-directedness" was Stephen Shore (born in 1947), who refers back to Robert Frank and forward to Europeans like Michael Ormerod and Nick Waplington, whom I will discuss later. Shore's color images of the West resonate with social landscapes: small towns, old cinemas, gas stations, homes, streets, corners, intersections, and crossings (of wires, shadows and light, sky and earth, nature and culture)—indeed, the many everyday spaces where the static and the mobile interact and relate.[60] They are often still, poised images with the Hopperesque quality of a whole, complex narrative about to unfold or of one that has just happened and moved on. These are what Shore terms "uncommon places"; of course, these are, in fact, "common," everyday places that have an immense significance of *being* and a complexity revealed in their patterns, tones, and relations captured by his acts of traveling. This is Shore's world of the *uncommon* common learned from the same tradition as Ormerod—Atget, Evans, Frank, and pop art (Shore worked in Warhol's New York Factory from 1965).

Shore (like Baltz) has been much admired in Europe as well as the United States, with Germans Hilla and Bernd Becher, who were also part of the *New Topographics* exhibition, helping to promote him. Hilla Becher commented that Shore's photographs often return to points of crossing, and "The intersection is what America is . . . life intensifies precisely at the intersections. . . . Shore's photographs have something of the quality of a first encounter." Heinz Liesbrock adds: "I think he was able to see this country *with the eyes of a foreigner*, and was therefore able to show things in his pictures whose special characteristics are not recognizable to many Americans, but which have almost a mythical quality for us Europeans, things we've often investigated in film and literature" (emphasis added).[61] The European interest in Shore is based on the extraordinary sense of outsideness in his work, as if he is seeing the landscape through the lens of imagination and mediatized representations, staring with the lens at the very components of westness—the breakfast plate, the trailer, the tourist landscape, the motel, the roadside diner or billboard, the cowboy, the grid of streets, parking lots, or drive-in. Much influenced by Frank, Shore has spoken of feeling like an outsider and identifying with others whose journeys brought them into contact with the West, such as Jack Kerouac and Vladimir Nabokov, whose novel *Lolita* (1955) was a particularly important text for him and always seemed "so photographic."[62] In *Lolita* the same kind of iconic westness that appears in Shore's photographs is described through the eyes of another outsider, Humbert Humbert, and channeled via the author, a Russian émigré in America from 1940:

> all those Sunset Motels, U-Beam Cottages, Hillcrest Courts . . . a picnic table, with sun flecks, flattened paper cups . . . and discarded ice-cream sticks littering the brown ground. . . . I would stare at the honest brightness of the gasoline paraphernalia against the splendid green of oaks, or at the distant hill scrambling out—scarred but still untamed—from the wilderness of agriculture that was trying to swallow it . . . with a remote car changing its shape mirage-like in the surface glare, and seeming to hang for a moment, old-fashionedly square in the hot haze . . . dun grading into blue, and blue into dream, and the desert would meet us with a steady gale.[63]

Shore's "outside eye" penetrates the "mythic" America without nostalgia but with a certain disbelief and anthropological interest summed up in a story he tells about his first photographic road trip: "In 1972 I set out with a friend from Amarillo, Texas. I didn't drive, so my first view of America was framed by the passenger's window. It was a shock." Slightly removed behind the window, Shore saw the West as a series of framed images, in all their variety, everyday, iconic, hyperreal, and the consequences can be seen in the style of his subsequent work with its intense use of color and shape to represent the fullness and ordinariness of the landscape.[64]

Henri Lefebvre has written: "it is precisely because it [space] has been occupied and used, and has already been the focus of past processes whose traces are not always evident on the landscape," that it might appear "neutral," and yet "space has been shaped and molded from historical and natural elements. . . . Space is political and ideological. It is a product literally filled with ideologies."[65] Of all the *New Topographics* exhibitors, Baltz and Shore—almost despite themselves at times—demonstrate this ideological process in their images, presenting a West scored by shifting layers and fragments with none of the reassuring narrative unity of Ansel Adams or what even Robert Adams called "grace" and "absolute beauty." Lefebvre noted the need to reappraise the "everyday" so that "in each thing we see more than itself—something else *which is there* in everyday objects . . . something enfolded within which hitherto we have been unable to see." In seeing this "enfolded" thing, emphasized by its new context, our "awareness of this contradiction becomes more acute."[66] However, it is worth recalling Michael Holquist's comment that "An event cannot be wholly known, cannot be seen, from inside its own unfolding as an event."[67] Photography that came after the *New Topographics* exhibition had to go further in this ideological dialogue to provoke the viewer into "unfolding" the "enfolded" layers through a reengagement with the known and the familiar, since "it is in the most familiar things that the unknown—not the mysterious—is at its richest, and that this rich content of life is still beyond our empty, darkling consciousness, inhabited as it is by impostors, and gorged with the forms of Pure Reason, with myths and their illusory poetry."[68] This renewed impulse might, therefore, come once again from "outside" its own unfolding, as it had with Frank, through the lens of another European photographer, Michael Ormerod.

Frank's European Legacy:
Michael Ormerod—"Opened from the Inside Out"

Englishman Michael Ormerod's work as an "astonished foreigner" enacts a fascinating circum-Atlantic dialogue, probing western landscape, popular culture, vernacular space, community rituals, and people in the full knowledge of the double traditions of Europeans Atget, Cartier-Bresson, Bill Brandt, Tony Ray-Jones, and that of "social landscape" immigrant "travelers" and native commentators, John Gutmann, the Farm Security Administration photographers, Frank, Evans, the New Topographics exhibitors, William Eggleston, Joel Sternfeld, and Shore.[69] Paul Gilroy writes of how special critical power "derives from a doubleness . . . [an] unsteady location simultaneously inside and outside the conventions, assumptions, and aesthetic rules" that might equally apply to Ormerod's relationship to the West as it had once to Frank's.[70] Ormerod's photographic "routes" through the West are both geographical and intertextual, drawing into his work a complex but often playful layering of imagery acting as an arena for dialogue wherein the viewer engages with the work's many inflections and lines of flight. Like Frank's, Ormerod's images of the West make the established visual language of myth and nation "stammer," providing the "bilingual even in a single language" or "speaking in one's own language like a foreigner" so that what is known and "taken for granted" is reexamined and, perhaps, renewed.[71]

Ormerod's "practice of outside" is derived from a particular double view of America explained by his friend Geoff Weston: "Michael, like most of us [in Europe], definitely had a love-hate relationship with America. On the one hand he found it pretty seductive and on the other he found it almost gross in its indulgences, and I think some of that is fairly evident in the work."[72] Ormerod wanted to photograph this "dream-world" of the West, as Frank and others had, but now cognizant of the global specter of Americanization emerging as British critic Richard Hoggart pointed out in 1957 at the time Ormerod was growing up, with youth "living to a large extent in a myth-world compounded of a few simple elements which they take to be those of American life." Central to Hoggart's "shiny barbarism" was the imagery of westness via the comic book, the TV Western, and Hollywood movies all producing for Ormerod's generation, born in 1947, a "dream-world" functioning both as a cultural imperialist fear *and* as an alternative to the stuffy establishment values of conservatism, rationing, and repression in Britain.[73] With a public school education, Ormerod, destined for an upper-middle-class life in the world of commerce (his degree was in economics), found contradictory feelings pulling him to the "outside," to other perspectives, to left-wing politics, to photography, and to travels in America.

This dilemma was rehearsed in the 1950s by British critic Peter Reyner Banham, who was drawn to American design and popular culture but was simultaneously critical of its values and left with a mind "curiously divided" between "unavoidable admiration" for American "creative power" and production and the "equally unavoidable disgust at the system that was producing it."[74] In a powerful phrase, aligning his response to Frank and others discussed in this book, Banham referred to American pop culture as "the day of the outsider," offering energy and expression to those in Britain who had been defined and delimited as "working class" and providing a corrective to postwar Britain's "sloppy provincialism," an antidote to the "Moore-ish yokelry of British sculpture or the affected Piperish gloom of British painting," with "the average Playtex or Maidenform ad in American *Vogue* . . . an instant deflater of the reputations of most artists then in Arts Council vogue."[75] For Banham, as for Ormerod, the most extraordinary examples of this dangerous, alternative energy were to be found in the West, with its immense landscapes, its exotic and mythic "otherness," and, simultaneously, its constant reproduction of iconography as hypersimulation.[76]

In *Scenes in America Deserta*, Banham writes of how his views "alternated between elation and bewilderment," with "confusions as well as . . . enthusiasms" over a sense of westness coming from John Ford film classics that ensured he "knew what Monument Valley looked like," while science fiction supplied his feel for the desert.[77] It is precisely this uneasy and suspicious relationship to the West, "the combination of being an outsider and being an insider," that gave Banham his "prophet-without-honour-in-own-country-complex." As Whiteley puts it, "Perhaps the outsider-insider was one of the most impressive achievements of a 'both/and' approach."[78] Banham's western cultural landscape of the "insecure tourist," like Ormerod's, is concerned with the traces we leave in the process of intersection and contact, an attitude summarized in this short section from *Scenes from America Deserta*: "Where I differ is that the works of man always interest me as much as the landscapes in which they are wrought. The tire tracks in the sand, the old arastra by the gold mine's mouth, the grove where the station used to be, the shiny power pylons marching over the horizon, the old windmill in the canyon and the new telephone repeater on the peak, the Indian pictograph and the war graffiti, the trailer home parked in the middle of nothing, the fragment of Coalport china found in the sand at the bottom of the wash."[79] Echoing the visual world of Frank and the *New Topographics* exhibitors, Banham would later write on Richard Misrach's photography, commending its representation of "the real desert . . . stained and trampled, franchised and fenced, burned, flooded, grazed, mined, exploited, and laid waste" with "great visual beauty." Banham sees in Misrach the vital dialogic vision again, the tension between beauty and waste and the need to find a method to convey it in a single image or sequence. After all, he says, "we try to block out these manifestations of our presence, and lift up our eyes unto the hills beyond—hoping that they, at least, will still look something like the work of Ansel Adams. They don't, of course." Banham's "outsider" perspective called for a "both/and" vision that deconstructed the view that "discriminate[s] clearly between D and not-D, that which is deserted and without people, and that which is peopled and therefore cannot be desert."[80] Thus in a very photographic moment, sounding like a description of Ormerod's work, he describes the "deep satisfactions of the sunset" and alongside it "on the other side of the road or parking lot . . . a Didion landscape of moral anorexia, collapsed Chevrolets, and mountains of beer cans."[81] Banham's layered palimpsest projects a vision of westness as actual and/or imagined contact, as though the two are totally bound up together, reminiscent, as ever, of the multiple frames and juxtapositions within Frank's "Hoover Dam" photograph.

Banham's awareness of the West's simultaneity is mirrored (and extended) by another European, Jean Baudrillard, who wrote in *America*

(1986) that "the whole country is cinematic," a "mediascape" as much as a landscape, where everything already exists as representation. According to Baudrillard, echoing Banham, to understand Monument Valley one must recognize its "geology," its Indian history, and the films of John Ford, since "All three are mingled in the vision we have of it."[82] This multiple mapping of place, echoing De Certeau's palimpsest, is embedded in Ormerod's work too, with layers creating a complex, evocative visualization of history represented in his intertextual western images both familiar and iconic, while jarring us into a second or third look, a *re-vision* emerging between and within the image's apparent surface. To look through and across the stratified, detailed layers of an Ormerod photograph is to understand something of what De Certeau means when he writes that "epochs all survive in the same place, intact and mutually interacting," for it is as if their simultaneity and imbrication are represented within the frame as active, layered history.

> The kind of difference that defines every place is not on the order of a juxta-position but rather takes the form of imbricated strata . . . beneath the fabricating and universal writing of technology, opaque and stubborn places remain. The revolutions of history, economic mutations, demographic mixtures lie in layers within it, and remain there, hidden in customs, rites, and spatial practices. The legible discourses that formerly articulated them have disappeared, or left only fragments in language. This place, on its surface, seems to be a collage. . . . A piling up of heterogeneous places. Each one, like a deteriorating page of a book, refers to a different mode of territorial unity, of socioeconomic distribution, of political conflicts and of identifying symbolism.[83]

Ormerod's fascination with the West's "opaque and stubborn places," with the "hidden" "fragments," and with "heterogeneous places" relates to an awareness of untold histories, forgotten stories, and how "legible discourses" (or myths) construct a partial version of reality to exclude these diverse elements. Consider his image "Frontier—Rarin' to Go" (figure 6), in which we are invited to "read" its stratified space like an archaeological process, puzzling over the mix of elements within its frame "like a deteriorating page of a book" of western history.

6. *Michael Ormerod,* Frontier—Rarin' to Go *(date unknown) (original in color).*
Used by permission of Millennium Images, London.

Echoing Robert Adams's "Pikes Peak" gas station image in *The New West* with its partial sign "FRONTIE" dominating the image, Ormerod's ironic commentary goes further, increasing the detail and the juxtaposed resonance within the frame, suggesting how the sign's meaning (its *signifiers* and *signifieds*) has changed with time and space and now seems to sprout surreally from a bush. The dynamic history of this space as a roadside attraction (its "revolutions of history, economic mutations, demographic mixtures") is explicit here, embedded in its remnants: a closed-up brick building, a shed, some abandoned machinery, the debris of memory, and the sign itself, whose slogan reminds us of the spirit of the frontier and the desire for progressive westward motion. Yet the layers of the image suggest something beyond these readings in which the sign has a strange new meaning and one not necessarily ironic at all. Surrounded by the natural growth of trees, a blue sky and crop fields beyond, and shot in sharp daylight colors, irony is tempered by the indomitable human spirit that still moves on, is still "rarin' to go," up the road to the new silos one can see in the distant corner of Ormerod's image. The "collagist" intertext suggests the discontinuities of history, its comings and goings, booms and busts, leaving its bizarre traces of older dialogues on the land itself, gradually becoming themselves decayed and reclaimed by the trees and grasses growing all around. The human and nonhuman worlds are engaged through time and space, their individual elements perpetually bound together in a series of relationships that are often uneasy and destructive as well as joyous and productive.

With its overtones of familiarity and nostalgia, the photograph shares something with Baudrillard's West visited "in my imagination long before I actually came here," becoming what Geoff Dyer has called "a reprise and distillation . . . of dominant tropes of American photographs."[84] Yet this dreamscape is counterposed by a critical consciousness that scrutinizes the imagined place and interrupts the dreaming with an awakening sense of other, more complex forces of history and culture coexisting in the frame. If Ormerod's work is "cinematic," then what we have are akin to film "stills" fragmented out of the flow of the total movie and supplemented by visual interruptions that challenge comfortable notions of mythic completion and closure. In the "cinematic" country of the West, where "everything is transformed into images," the photographer must find ways to both document this tendency to simulation and engage with it creatively and critically within the photographic contact zone.[85] This dialogue is central to Ormerod's work, mobilizing the apparently "still" images in the mind of the viewer in ways that rupture the apparent familiarity and security of a scene in order, as Elizabeth Grosz put it, to "scatter thoughts and images into different linkages or new alignments," creating photographs that are "fundamentally moving, 'nomadological' or 'rhizomatic.'"[86]

Ormerod's photography shares something of Deleuze's comment on modern cinema in that his work "develops new relations with thought from three points of view: the obliteration of a whole or a totalization of images, in favour of an outside which is inserted between them; the erasure of the internal monologue as a whole of the film, in favour of free indirect discourse and vision; the erasure of the unity of man and the world, in favour of a break which now leaves us with only a belief in this world" (emphasis added). His work contains "an outside which is inserted between" established images and myths ("monologues") causing the viewer to look again, pause, reconsider and possibly "break" the "taken-for-granted" and the familiar that appears to be "whole" and unified. "It is the method of BETWEEN, 'between two images,' which does away with all cinema [read photography] of the One. It is the method of AND, 'this and then that.' . . . The whole undergoes a mutation, because it has ceased to be the One-Being. . . . The whole thus becomes . . . the force of 'dispersal of the Outside.'"[87]

This "outside" in Ormerod's West comes from its edges, geographically and socially, from small towns, half-built housing projects, roadsides, highway intersections, and parking lots. The supposed "neutrality" of the New Topographics exhibitors, with their cool, unemotional recording of the postwar West, is given a twist as Ormerod increases levels of tension and juxtaposition within the frames of his images, such as in his Albuquerque, New Mexico, planning board (figure 7). As we view this frame with its apparently familiar, gridded space, there is no single, "readable" text but rather a multiplicity of layers that intersect and overlap to represent the West as a series of constructions, a collage from which we, the viewer, must create meaning. A "found" architectural display board presents a variety of "languages" working dialogically to suggest an alternative "map" of fragmented "voices" combined to portray "landscape" (a key word visible in the photograph): words and images, photographs and drawings, plans and geological sketches, human and nonhuman presence. This clearly breaks with the normalized view of mapping, in which "the basic rule of legibility is that all symbols should be identifiable without any strain or ambiguity wherever they occur, [so that] in order to respond to a map symbol, the user perceiving the map image must be able to identify each symbol easily" (emphasis added).[88] The photographs within the photograph are images of the road, points of entry and departure, motion contained within the stasis of Ormerod's "final," but unfinished, image itself, all of which counter the tradition of maps-without-ambiguity. The overall effect of the photograph is incompleteness, a space full of edges (it is one of the words one can clearly read in the photograph), a rhizomatic spilling out in all directions without conclusion, suggesting, perhaps more accurately than a conventional map, the complex nature of the West as consumed and produced, real and imagined space. With strong echoes of the architec-

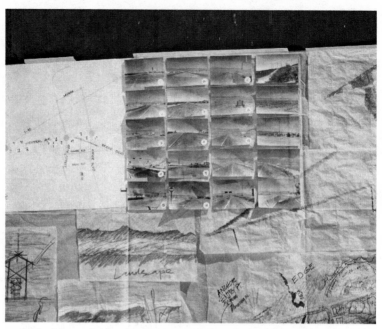

7. *Michael Ormerod, Albuquerque, New Mexico, planning board (date unknown) (original in color). Used by permission of Millennium Images, London.*

tural theory discussed in the introduction, Ormerod's image resembles Peter Eisenman's vision of architectural space as "dislocating," layered, always suggesting the "between" rather than any fixed or absolute and essential "text": "A dislocating text is always a second language." Like Deleuze and Guattari's insistence upon the "foreign language" within language, Eisenman sees the value of dislocation as a questioning of norms and assumptions, providing what he terms a "between text" with the capacity to violate "the maintenance of a system as a whole."[89] The photograph's "architectonics" shows westness as non-totalizable and fluid, dislocating the mythic "first language" with a critical "second," providing a multilayered, real and imagined cartography that can often be best appreciated from the outside looking in.

A further aspect of Ormerod's interrogation of westness is its mythic formations of progress, freedom, destiny, and individualism embodied in iconic, desired objects, like the car, the diner, and the road, which with time become old, unfashionable, and obsolescent. The photographic gaze falls upon the afterlife of the object as it rusts by the roadside, falls apart in the junkyard, or is simply bypassed or reified, and in so doing implicates the wider systems that produced and consumed it before they move relentlessly onto the next "new thing." Ormerod's photography intervenes, capturing this process in visions of a liminal West, on the edge, between past and present, at a "fold" where we can see the dynamic dialogue being played out: remnants of Main Street, broken commodities, and billboards become tragic reminders of rapidly disappearing worlds, hopes, and dreams that were once, in the past, themselves the cutting edge of fashion and modernity, but which now demonstrate capitalism's need for constant turnover and perpetual "progress." I see in Ormerod's western images what Walter Benjamin recognized in Atget's Paris photographs: "an index of dream-traces for the contemporary archaeologist excavating the residual ruins of modernity."[90] The "dream-traces" of the West remind us that the cycles of capitalism and its mythic versions of history also contain positive, human traits (original dreams, utopianism, pleasure) that, if wrenched out from their current use, might be reconfigured and transformed into something more meaningful. Photography can create this critical "pause" between life and death, a "stammer," a hesitation within the expected, offering, at best, fleeting moments of hope, realignment, and even redemption. With objects stripped of their "aura" as monuments to capitalism and the myths of "westness," they are repositioned, re-visioned as part of a wider social landscape in which power too might shift and decay.

Benjamin explained this notion of "aura" in relation to landscape's mythical uses (as in Ansel Adams earlier), since when looking upon a mountain range from "distance," "you experience the aura of those mountains" as "uniqueness and permanence." A different angle of vision or a closer look, as is so often the method of social landscape photography, might "destroy its aura" and change our relationship to its apparent mystery. As Benjamin wrote, photography and film can "burst this prison-world asunder by the dynamite of the tenth of a second, so that now, in the midst of its far-flung ruins and debris, we calmly and adventurously go traveling. With close-up, space expands; with slow motion, movement is extended. The enlargement of a snapshot does not simply render more precise what in any case was visible, though unclear: it reveals entirely new structural formations of the subject." The eye is freed to "travel" the image's elements, no longer controlled by the absolute reality of the "aura," released from a single vision to a plurality of reinterpretations so that meaning becomes a question of consumption and production, active and political, rather than a passive event. The viewer "reads" or "meets" (Benjamin's word) the text, engages dialogically with its multiplicity, and is part of the active meaning-making process that scatters the text beyond itself, beyond the frame. As Benjamin writes, this "enables the original *to meet the beholder halfway*" so that the "reproduced object" is "reactivated," given a new life, in the dialogic process the image has set in motion (emphasis added).[91] It is the detail within the photographic frame (like Barthes's *punctum*) that creates such tension, an effect described in Susan Stewart's discussion of narrative: "In the detail of movement we see the possibility of using detail to digress, to inscribe a circle around an object in order not to divulge it, and at the same time the possibility of using detail to tantalize. The digression stands in tension with narrative closure. It is *narrative opened from the inside out*" (emphasis added).

Ormerod's photographic "narrative" is digressive and open, challenging the viewer's perceptions from "inside" the familiar territory of western iconography, and yet, through an application of what Stewart calls "narrative looping" (a kind of Deleuzian "folding"), we are "detoured" to examine the detail, its context, its narrative threads within the frame, and ultimately to interrogate its ideological standing. Thus, as she goes on to say, using language well suited to our discussion of photography, "Instead of offering the reader transcendence, the digression blocks the reader's view, toying with the hierarchy of narrative events . . . recaptures the tedium of the journey, the incessant and self-multiplying detail of landscape, a detail which nearly erases the landmark by distracting the reader's attention" and thereby creating a "dialogue between inside and outside."[92]

Ormerod's Edward Hopper–like image, "Steppin' in High Fashions" (figure 8), demonstrates how detail functions in this way, presenting what were once "high fashions"—the dresses in the shop window—as poignant reminders of the endless cycles of production and consumption that underpin capitalism.[93] The clothes are strangely detached in the frame, hanging as if magically in a "closed" shop, on a deserted street, in an empty town, below a dingy hotel—objects now the obsolescent

8. *Michael Ormerod, Steppin' in High Fashions (date unknown) (original in color).*
Used by permission of Millennium Images, London.

remains of a previous time when they were, perhaps, fleetingly, indeed "high fashions." On the door is a notice "Welcome National Guard," linking this scene to the military-industrial complex that contributed greatly to the development of the postwar West and its system of values. Everything is separated, blocks (or grids) within the image (again, the former word is in the picture); fragments, apart, atomized—like the fire hydrant on the corner, the car, and the telegraph pole. These fragments interrupt the smoothness of a mythic small-town image, and the seamless "whole" is disrupted by Ormerod's montage of "blocks" that never quite fit back together again. The mythic western small town is both here and not here, caught in the image's frame in a jarring, uncanny sense that draws the viewer into its comfort zone of familiarity and detail while disturbing us with its strange, digressive elements. Within this field of complexity, Ormerod conveys a still beauty and "traces" of hope in the photograph, with its attention to detail, form, and color that, like the mannequins in the window, seems to reach out to the viewer, *almost* making a connection. The architecture is faded but grand, like the "fashions" (to the right of the image the letters "G *and*" ironically suggest this trace of remembrance), and the carefully painted fire hydrant suggests care and dedication. This is a lost world, hanging on to its former glories and its dreams of individual entrepreneurialism as reminders of human resilience, while the reality is of the shopping mall, the Golden Arches, and the suburbs somewhere just out of shot, and the relentless pace of change and "new" fashion in the New West. "We" are placed as viewers in this image, with a space between "us" and the shops inviting speculation about how we relate to its meanings—Do we feel nostalgic, or are we implicated in the system that creates such scenes?

Like Benjamin's essay, Ormerod's images strive to unsettle the mythic unities of the West, to explode "the homogeneity of the epoch . . . interspersing it with ruins—that is, with the present," to remind us of the discontinuous processes that have lead to the myths themselves.[94] Like J. B. Jackson, who wrote of "The Necessity for Ruins" within the landscape, Ormerod was attracted to the discarded, the surreal, and the incongruous as reminders of the decay and rejection of mythic, "monologic" fixing and to the recovery of an almost childlike appreciation of human potential and creativity. In Jackson's words, echoing Benjamin, "ruins provide the incentive for restoration. . . . There has to be an interim of death or rejection before there can be renewal and reform. The old order has to die before there can be a born-again landscape . . . redeeming what has been neglected."[95] Photography can trace the evidence of such "death or rejection," as in the fading western iconographies that haunt Ormerod's work, not simply to put them aside or to nostalgically appropriate them but to "redeem" them for new uses in a renewed landscape beyond the image itself. Whether at the frame's borders or in the actual geographies being explored, it is at the edges that things become unfixed, shabby, and fluid, with potential for change and irregularity, even for "heteroglot exuberance . . . where all is mixed, hybrid, ritually degraded and defiled" and yet "always *becoming* . . . mobile" because they are prone to the shifts of time, decay and renewal.[96] As Lefebvre writes, "Differences endure or arise on the margins of the homogenized realm. . . . What is different is, to begin with, what is *excluded*: the edges of the city, shanty towns, the spaces of forbidden games."[97] Ormerod's *re-stated* West is a space as capable of ending as of beginning, a "first sight" contained in every photograph and yet with a critical, satirical aspect cutting through any sentimentality or nostalgia. In revealing layers to set against the overly simplified, straight, evidential image, Ormerod asks the viewer to plunge below the surface, through the screens of myth and "effect," in order to see "the life beneath the ashes or behind the mirrors," a life brimming full of unresolved histories and contradictory, contested dialogues.[98]

New Western Globalism? Nick Waplington and Andrew Cross

For each generation of photographers the West has become more represented, a mediascape that tests and challenges creativity. As Dutch-born U.S.-based photographer Rudy Vanderlans wrote: "And when I look into the viewfinder all I see are Ruscha and Baltz and Baldessari and Hockney and Frank and Friedlander and Misrach and Deal and Evans and Owens and Lange and Wessel and Weston and Adams (Robert and Ansel). . . . And sometimes Curtis and Jackson and O'Sullivan."[99] As in Ormerod's photography, the West is always "westness," framed and reframed by others' photographs, films, advertising, and television, and thus to make images of these cultural landscapes is to acknowledge and work with this reality.

British photographer Nick Waplington made his reputation with Living Room (1991) photographing working-class culture in Nottingham, living with a family for four years and recording their lives with what John Berger called "baroque enthusiasm." Berger explained: "Baroque wanted to turn the earth-bound into the celestial, and to make human figures appear as at home in the sky as on the ground," suggesting Waplington's methodology later developed as another lengthy place-based project in the American West, Truth or Consequences (2001), where, as an outsider, he self-consciously documents and examines both a "real" western town and an "American photographic history" in which the documentary has been one of its most significant forms.[100] In this sense the photographs interrogate the apparent "truth" of documentary, or the "consequences" of comprehending that there may be no single, authoritative truth about this place or this region, revealing it as "a landscape of ready quotations," myths, and clichés, of an "already-represented" space within which "real" people still live. By labeling the collection

"A Personal History of American Photography from the Last Century," Waplington is fully aware of the mediated landscapes of the West and of the conventions and myths that have structured its meanings both for Americans and for the world. Without ignoring these "representations," he actively employs them, as does Ormerod, as a source of playful, creative understanding, with each image entering dialogues with the past, the present, and the future, recognizing that "his" "West," its "truth," is not unique or singular but part of a multiple, international discourse constructed from many voices and sources across time. Thus he comments: "My personal history of American photography would not be complete without a road trip. Las Vegas seemed the perfect destination. . . . I set out north on Interstate 25 to begin my journey across the desert." Acknowledging, as Ormerod had, the road trip as iconic, Waplington's travels are taken in a full post-tourist understanding of all the famous journeys taken before his (Frank's, Kerouac's, Hunter Thompson's) and of how the concept has become another part of the mythic frame of a globalized West.[101]

In 1998 his The Indecisive Memento emphasized the "journey as a work of art" and en route aimed "to tackle some of the stereotypes of documentary photography" that Waplington felt were often "completely pointless and antiquated." What he proposes instead is "being a tourist" less concerned with capturing the "decisive moment," for so long the supposed goal of all photography, and instead emphasizing the "non-moment . . . a Beuysian understanding of the world where the indecisive or chance encounters of life have become the decisive act." Here, updating Banham's position of the "insecure tourist" while invoking the surreal "indecision" of the everyday, the "Duchamp effect within photography," he uses traveling as a deliberate dislocation of self and values, a "way to force himself to consider new things and novel approaches as an artist" so that "travel has . . . afforded him a way out of the signature style."[102] Recalling the words of James Clifford, travel's "practices of crossing and interaction . . . troubled the localism of many common assumptions about culture. . . . Dwelling was understood to be the local ground of collective life, travel a supplement; roots always precede routes."[103] The entanglements of travel, both literal and epistemological, have specific outcomes for Waplington, presenting knowledge of the world as "con-

tingent and partial": "Everything is open and everything is possible . . .
to allow a natural movement and fluidity back into the work and break
down these aesthetic restrictions . . . to make pictures that ask questions
as opposed to pictures that draw conclusions."[104]

Instead of the "localism" of Living Room, Waplington's later work
"travels" and encounters, engaging with the transnational flows of commodities, people, and places that are the experience of the postmodern,
global economy. Waplington writes: "I find it interesting that the iconography of western graphics has seeped right through the world in
much the same way as the Roman alphabet did before it . . . a consumer
alphabet. . . . Everyone knows what the McDonalds sign stands [for] . . .
and it is that development that has become a sign of the homogeniza-
tion of world culture."[105] The Indecisive Memento (which was going to be
called Circles of Civilization) travels globally, at speed, tracing this branded
identity marked by the corporate capitalism of the ubiquitous Coca-Cola
or hamburger, captured in grabbed paparazzi images, often blurred and
deranged, of lifestyle and advertising, buildings, doors and windows.
Like a jet-age Frank in its anxious motion, the book is a "journey into
the absurdist spectacle of cultural frisson" moving us from close-ups
of burgers in São Paulo to Buenos Aires, Easter Island, Australian suburbs, and back to burgers, echoing Robert Adams, Lee Friedlander, and
Stephen Shore along the way. This is "a pop planet caught in Big Mac
conformity," deliberately provocative and jarring, as Waplington seems
to constantly unsettle himself as "author" as much as his audience. In
this process he shows "an artist's identification with what is alien and
his alienation from what he has already identified."[106]

It is this fascination with the alien, and his simultaneous recognition
of (and repulsion against) the familiar, that made Waplington's next
major project well suited to the American West, for here is a space intimately known and unknown through lived experience, the media generally, and photography especially. The choice of the town of Truth or Consequences as the focus for this collection serves a number of purposes:
first, it seemingly epitomizes the small-town "locale" brimming full of
the very values often associated with nationalism and exported through
Americanization and globalization; and second, and to a degree at odds
with this first impression, the town is a media construction renamed

from Hot Springs in 1950 in order to host the hit TV show's tenth-anniversary festival. This bizarre mixture of local values and global media savvy suit Waplington's continued ambiguous examination of cultural assumptions and values, permitting him to, in Clifford's words, "trouble localism." *Truth or Consequences* uses the perspective of the outsider, which, as Julia Kristeva wrote, "seeks that invisible and promised territory, that country that does not exist but that he bears in his dreams, and that must indeed be called a beyond," to engage with both actuality and dream, with local practices and global impulses, with represented and real lives, all intersecting in this particular western town.[107] Echoing Clifford, there is a sense that "location . . . is an itinerary rather than a bounded site—a series of encounters and translations" through which Waplington reiterates that life and the representation of life cannot be separated; any "reality" detached from this is impossible, and in the West, of all places, the lines blur everywhere.[108] The sequence of images creates an itinerary that moves us, as viewers, from the local outward and back again via circuits of iconography and reference. Like the German filmmaker, writer, and photographer Wim Wenders, Waplington recognized that in America, "However new it all was, it already seemed familiar," because it was a "Land made of images / Land for images," an observation that, as with all the Europeans examined in this chapter, created a healthy and productive ambivalence:

> How else but with ambivalence
> should one look at this country with its dream of itself?
> What other stance is imaginable
> Apart from "being of two minds"?
> I love this country . . .
> I'm also afraid of it.
> I'm happier here than anywhere else, but more distressed.
> It opens my eyes
> And I want to keep them closed.[109]

Like Wenders and many Europeans, "the first thing" Waplington "got to know about America were pictures." Recalling Vanderlans, however, the West is no longer merely refracted through the classics of "American photography" but is just as likely to be a hybrid of Marlboro adverts and

Edward Weston, John Ford and Walker Evans, a Route 66 road sign and a Timothy O'Sullivan image. This parallels Waplington's transnational focus, a continuation of his career fascination with globalization and corporatism, and his awareness, like Banham's, of Americanization as both cultural imperialism and pleasure, a space in which, as Wenders wrote, "vision was set free," but always simultaneously to "excess." Wenders, like Waplington, talks about the influence of Frank on his work, first, because he was a man with "a love-hate relationship with America, which is the European view, so to speak: a mixture of fascination and alarm. His pictures express that divided attitude very clearly"; and second, because he "seems to be able to take pictures out of the corners of his eyes."[110] This persistent doubling of vision ideologically and formally—present, as we have seen, in Ormerod and Frank—is extended by Waplington's globalized, "traveling" West, juxtaposing street parades and family "snapshot" portraits with more studied homages to precise, iconic, historical photographic moments. The local and global blur here, as do the inside and the outside, and as Doreen Massey has written, attempts to separate these elements artificially are pointless. What is required is a sense of place that is "extroverted" and not dependent on "some long internalized history," one that includes a consciousness of its links with the wider world, connecting local and global in a version of place as a "process" without boundaries.[111]

Wenders's photographs of the West capture a sense of ending, of "seeing something and recording it as if it were the last possible chance to do so," yet Wenders is also aware that "photography can be a horribly violent act" in its overuse of certain iconography. His example of the over-photographed, as so often, is Monument Valley, which he says "ought to be left alone for a hundred years so that someone can actually see the landscape again."[112] The desire, though commendable, is unrealistic and blind to the existence of westness as a constantly re-stated, re-represented textual formulation—whether it is the filmmaker's Monument Valley, the tourist's, the advertiser's, or the tribal elder's. Waplington's West, however, seems always aware of this westness as an absolute aspect of its global, commodified, mediatized condition, of "a world always already crowded with images."[113] Everywhere one looks there is an echo of another image. As Wenders put it, "John Ford's landscapes have been renamed 'Marlboro Country,' and the American Dream is an advertising campaign," where the "living breath of 'true images'" has been replaced by only "the bad breath of lies."[114] The difference is that Waplington refuses any nostalgic yearning for "true images," preferring instead to work through the archaeological palimpsest of images that continue to construct the West as "living breath"—as real and imagined space within which people live. What John Slyce has called the "burdened frame" through which we must view the West is the very topic at hand and is the challenge for Waplington and others working amid this "landscape of quotations."[115] Stewart defines "quotation" in ways relevant to Waplington's use of them: "Once quoted, the utterance [or image] enters the arena of social conflict: it is manipulatable, examinable within its now-fixed borders; it now plays within the ambivalent shades of varying contexts." She compares the quotation with the carnival in that "we see a process of restoration and . . . disillusionment, for the boundary of the text is both fixed and made suspect, and, because of the ongoingness of time and space, this placing is never complete."[116] Thus in Waplington's *Truth or Consequences*, the parade, which forms a human thread through the collection, reminds us that people live within this "museum" of iconography, not only looking upon it as a kind of spectacle but also constantly reshaping it and reinventing it as part of their everyday lives in the West. As I discussed earlier, the challenge is to examine those who have "framed" the West through images, creating their iconic grid, and to intervene in the process so as to acknowledge their impact while asking new questions, so that the "text is both fixed and made suspect." The "burdened frame," as always, can spill over and outward rhizomatically, or as Stewart puts it, "the quotation mark points not only inward but outward as well." Slyce recognizes this in his comment that the images "point towards something else—something that exists beyond their narrow frame."[117]

This then becomes the purpose of *Truth or Consequences*: to investigate and preserve (as all photography does to some extent) a sense of place, but to do so with a keen and active consciousness of its existence as lived space, mediascape, spectacle, and iconic space. For Waplington the West is common property, optical real estate, not exceptionalist or unique, existing in the imagination of us all, as unsurprising as the

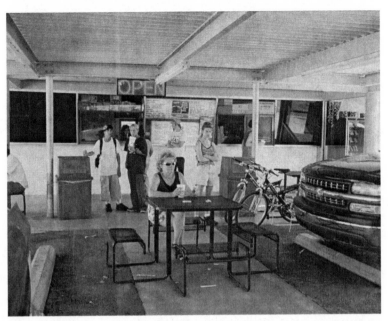

9. Nick Waplington, untitled, from Truth or Consequences (2001) (original in color).
Used by permission of the artist.

"Living Room" he photographed in his earlier works and as familiar
as the last movie, photography collection, or popular magazine we
glanced at. It is always also the actual lived space of people—those
we observe in the collection going about their ordinary lives—whose
own existence takes place within this place, those whose West is not an
object of framed study but the material subject of their lives. As we enter this collection we enter a landscape of traces in every sense: traces
of the marks left on the West by technology, human intervention and
imagination, commodification, exploitation, and those left by photographers "quoted" who have passed through to capture a "decisive moment" that somehow defined an aspect of the region, or of those made
by tourists and pleasure seekers, and indeed, all those who live and
work in this layered space. In one image from *Truth or Consequences* (figure 9)—part Sternfeld, part Misrach, part Duane Hanson, part Friedlander—Waplington captures a drive-in fast-food stand like an everyday tableau with a curious tension between the central female figure,
in shorts and sunglasses, and the four youths behind her, some with
arms folded, one looking at the camera, and the intrusive presences of

the Chevy truck and the two bikes, like mechanical customers waiting to be served. These tensions are ironically mirrored in the contradictory signs behind them: "No Loitering" and "OPEN."

In another photograph the West becomes open shelves of canned and dried goods—"Ranch style Beans," "Stagg Straight Chili Double Barrel Beef," "Casa Fiesta Refried Beans"—goods and brands that, at a closer look, are the familiar products of global multinational corporations found in most supermarkets.[118] In another, a low-level shot enlarges a bottle of Creamland Chocolate Milk to the size of a monument, as if to replace the expected monuments of the West associated with Ansel Adams so that western landscapes become ironic cultural spaces scattered with the remnants of consumer culture, tourism, and waste. As Benjamin wrote, "Living means leaving traces."[119] In Waplington's book the various traces collide and mix kaleidoscopically as our eyes traverse the images and the pages—from Eggleston to Frank to Misrach to Sternfeld to Baltz to Shore to Evans to our own tourist shots and our own unconfirmed echoes of other photographs (like those of Ormerod for me).[120] Through what Barthes called the "mutual relations of dialogue," we construct *Truth or Consequences* as complex westness in which no single meaning is insisted upon, since the text is plural, like Leone's films discussed in chapter 3, "woven entirely of citations, references, echoes, cultural languages . . . antecedent or contemporary, which cut across it through and through." Waplington's intertextuality, "in which every text is held, is itself being the text-between of another text," is set against "monologism [which] appears to be the Law." Thus the sequence *Truth or Consequences*, as it works on the viewer, reframes its "quotations" in a wider field of forces, linking *and* blurring lives with myths, the everyday with the apparently timeless, the iconic with the ironic, the local with the global, in a process like that defined by Barthes as an "organism which grows by vital expansion, by 'development' . . . [like a] network."[121] Ultimately, Waplington creates a hybrid visual "language" to tell an alternative history of family and place in the West (just as in *Living Room*), and does it here with every intention of paying homage to those whose eyes had first introduced him to America through photography and without whom he and we would have little visual information to work with.

10. Nick Waplington, untitled, from Truth or Consequences (2001) (original in color).
Used by permission of the artist.

Waplington's sense of westness is best summarized in the image of
the cowboy statue amid the signs "One Way," "Parking," and the red
hand stop (figure 10). This is the semiotic landscape within which the
collection works, the hyperreal West defined in Umberto Eco's *Travels in
Hyperreality* as "another, more secret America (or rather, just as public,
but snubbed by the European visitor and also by the American intellectual)" that "creates a network of references and influences that finally
spread also to the products of high culture and the entertainment industry."[122] In Waplington's version of the hyperreal, his "secret America,"
we enter a mirror world of familiarity, becoming actors in a half-recog-
nized drama, whereby Eco's "iconic reassurance" is made uncanny as
we slip from tourist vistas, to vacant lots and garbage, from pleasure
seekers and RV parks to abandoned shacks and suburban sprawl. Each
image offers some new "set," an angle offered upon the town, "diverse
meanings [that] run concurrently within the book and so eventually
become interwoven" like "different pieces of music that somehow join
together . . . different strands of work that have a common resonance
and yet deal with completely different issues."[123] The absolute "truth" of
Truth or Consequences is that there is none, for like the West itself, there is
always multiplicity and mixture, and despite its ever-constant claims of
"authenticity," only elaborate simulation.[124]

With this I return to Waplington's image of the cowboy statue in the jungle of signs and recall Kerouac's stunning response to *The Americans*, a book full of displaced cowboys: "Anybody doesn't like these pitchers don't like potry, see? Anybody don't like potry go home see Television shots of big hated cowboys being tolerated by kind horses."[125] The only "truth" in *Truth or Consequences* is the possibility that "potry" and the "Television shots" coexist and that photography permits the viewer to travel between them in full awareness that both construct and represent westness in a global, media age.

Another younger British photographer, Andrew Cross, has taken a different approach to the West in his work, creating a form of new epic that intersects and dialogues with those of previous generations. Here is a photographer born in 1961 whose work is in one sense quite distant in time from the breakthroughs of the *New Topographics* exhibitors and yet in many ways refers both to their work and to the Adams tradition they opposed so markedly. Cross's *Along Some American Highways* begins, significantly, on the road to Damascus, Pennsylvania, preparing us, even if only ironically, for the revelations ahead of a new vision of the overlooked ("by-passed") places at the roadside, and ends with "God Bless America" on another roadside verge. When viewing the collection one is struck by Cross's sense of "particularities," of representing roads as "place[s] in their own right," as well as by his sense of the scale and epic quality of western space. Perhaps unsurprisingly, given his subject matter, the book begins with a quotation from J. B. Jackson's essay "Roads Belong in the Landscape": "Roads no longer merely lead to places; they are places. And as always they serve two important roles: as promoters of growth and dispersion, and as magnets around which new kinds of development can cluster. In modern landscape, no other space has been so versatile."[126]

Cross's images are often of familiar "generic spaces" conveying aspects of westness—highways, intersections, signs, overpasses, and roadsides—but here shot in close proximity to the "traditional" natural landscapes within which they coexist—mountains, deserts, forests, and plains. Cross manages to convey hybrid western spaces, as in his stunning image "I-90 Exit 54, Washington" (figure 11), where the road and highway cut across an almost archetypal Ansel Adams's view of forest and snowcapped mountains balanced strangely by the scrub

11. *Andrew Cross, I-90 Exit 54, Washington (2003) (original in color).*
Used by permission of the artist.

and ragged edges in the foreground. Cross encourages us to "read" this western space as a palimpsest, with each angle of vision revealing another perspective, another layer of spatial narrative. His photographic road movie juxtaposes the shopping mall parking lots of California with Buffalo Bill's theme park in Nevada (see figure 12), with roadside culture and signage, stressing the implicit connections between roots and routes as the images direct us off highways via signs and intersections to the frayed edges of communities—often only hinted at by their fast-food outlets, strip malls, and storage sheds. In Cross's work, unlike Waplington's, humans rarely exist; the photographs concentrate rather on humans' constructions and viewpoints, not their actual lives. Whether his subject is American trains or highways, Cross cannot help but evoke romantic, emotive journeys of departure and arrival, yearning for Kerouac's open roads or Guthrie's boxcars, drawing himself and his viewers back through personal and cultural memories tinged with excitement and guilt. Cross works from within his own memories and imaginings of the West, drawing on his own journeys through England as a child projecting onto the iconic journeys implicated in any representation of the American western landscape.

12. *Andrew Cross, I-15 Exit 1, Nevada (2000) (original in color).*
Used by permission of the artist.

The romantic yearning and excitement so often associated in the European mind with the West is tempered, however, by an uneasiness that places the viewer "between" these responses, aware of the ideological baggage such romance carries in the twenty-first century, of the price of that supposed mythic freedom, and the reality of technology, economics, and class that actually determine and underpin these American cultural values. Cross's work consistently wrestles with such issues, pulling his viewers between these poles of mythic yearning and political recognition, asking in an understated, cool manner for us to look again, to literally and metaphorically re-vision our identities within landscape. Indeed, all his work is about "travelling between two places" (on railroads, roads, boats, planes, etc.), which is "somehow considered to be . . . negative," a view that for him "prevents us from looking at them properly." As Massey puts it in her essay in his book *An English Journey*, "Origin and destination are products also of the connections between."[127] Like Waplington and Ormerod, Cross wants to get away from the sense of place as "very fixed, traditional, and hierarchical" and to represent a more open and "different kind of space" that includes the banal, overlooked, and everyday, spaces like malls, highways, and airports, which are so often dismissed as functional and homogenized, existing simply "between two places." In what Marc Augé terms "non-places," Cross finds forms of westness that cannot be ignored and whose spaces grow ever more familiar to a globalized world of similar cultural landscapes.[128]

The significant dimension that Cross's work develops is an observation about globalization and the repetitions of architectural space as it travels from America into the world. Recall how Robert Frank, in his Guggenheim application, made before his road trips for *The Americans*, wrote that he wanted to observe "the kind of civilization born here and spreading elsewhere," as if he understood early on the significance of Americanization and its massive impact on the production of space. Cross's work charts the ways by which the brands, signs, and structures of the western highway, initially traveled as icons via art, photography, and film, are becoming increasingly recognizable within the lived landscapes of Europe and the rest of the world. The Marlboro Man has gone global along with McDonalds, the suburban "mallscape," Venturi's "decorated shed," and the endless containers of the logistics industry, to reemerge beyond the frame of the West in the landscapes of middle England, Germany, or India. So as we wander visually through Cross's collections, from page to page, we shift between difference and repetition, moments of intense unfamiliarity and jarring similarity to our own everyday experience, wherever we are in the world, provoking something of Augé's sense of a world where "people are always, and never, at home . . . [and] the frontier zones . . . no longer open on to totally foreign worlds."[129] So, although Cross is still an "outsider," his work demonstrates that globalization compresses the world and makes a once "unique" experience prone to repetition and familiarity, drawing the West ever closer to its ever-present circuits of representation and imagining. Just as Waplington's unavoidable awareness of global corporatism as the new iconography of westness is everywhere in his work, from canned goods and gas stations to fast food and clothing, Cross too provides a twenty-first-century reminder of a kind of "Best Westernization" of cultural landscape. A hotel chain once associated only with the western states is now global, its sign everywhere, spreading rhizomatically outward and back in the production and circulation of a complex circum-West of iconography and experience. As Appadurai puts it, "the United States is no longer the puppeteer of a world system of images but is only one node of a complex transnational construction of imaginary landscapes."[130]

In this respect, Cross's work examines both routes *and* roots, routes of commerce and exchange, of travel and transportation, of logistics and global marketing, while also considering how these processes affect identity, community, and our sense of belonging—roots. Of course, in Cross's work these are both local and global processes, just as the road can connect us to our most immediate and local worlds and also to the wider world beyond. This is a point made by Massey quoting Bruno Latour: "Is a railroad local or global? Neither"—because it can be both. Cultural landscapes reflect and constitute who we are, what we feel, and what we might imagine, and they are constantly being produced and consumed while, in turn, producing and consuming. Cross's work documents these changing landscapes without falling into the traps of romance and exotic travelers' tales, thus creating what he has termed a kind of photographic "anti-travel programme," emphasizing what others ignore, "the relationship between the objects of travel and the experience of travel," and examining "other kinds of landscapes which are otherwise considered irrelevant."[131] This entails, like a globalized J. B. Jackson, views across vast parking lots, along highways, down onto intersections, tracing the multiple routes of elaborate cloverleafs, or the still silence of a truck stop or fast-food outlet. Despite the inherent mobility of these landscapes, there is often a deliberate stillness to these photographs, ceasing the flow, rerouting the eye, creating moments in time where the visual experience *dwells*, encouraging the viewer to engage with the image or the film sequence. As always in Cross's work it is in moments like these that we shift from the banality of the everyday and the endless repetitions of the journey into another sphere where ironic and critical narratives are created, emotions and memories emerge, and our perceptions are shifted. Something we never noticed takes on a significance all its own, and juxtapositions disrupt the immediacy of the frame: the absolute beauty of an RV park in Nevada, the surreal absurdity of a sign reading "Wrong Way" on the highway, or the sheer immensity of the railroad carriages leaving Wagner Mills, Nebraska. Although in-

13. *Andrew Cross*, Rugby, North Dakota—The Geographical Centre of America *(no date). Used by permission of the artist.*

evitably always an outsider to the West he records, Cross reminds us, under globalization's glare, of what we have always known, that westness is translated everywhere in the real and imagined landscapes of everyday lives, as likely evident in Rugby, Warwickshire, as in Rugby, North Dakota.

6. STRATA AND ROUTES
Living on Reservation X

If a culture lives, it changes, it always changes. If a people live,
they imagine themselves always and in a new sense.
Gerald Vizenor

One story can never be all.
Sherman Alexie

To bridge is to attempt community.
Gloria Anzaldúa

Breaking the Ethnic Grid

Writing this chapter from outside the United States and as a white critic
has made me doubly conscious of my position in relation to the texts
I am going to discuss, very much aware (again) of my "outsider" status. At the risk of making errors, of which I am sure there are many, I
wanted to examine some notable critical positions and then to see how
they related to the most accessible of texts, contemporary Indian film.
Ironically, most of the books, films, and critical writings referred to in
this chapter have never been readily available in the United Kingdom,
so their impact will have been limited to a few academics or committed readers and fans. In some respects this has meant that the representation of the Native American has been even more circumscribed by
certain established images derived from literature, film, and television,
largely unchallenged, and taking on an increasingly fossilized character.
Perhaps, in this sense, Gerald Vizenor's arguments about how "indianness" is constructed, which I will discuss below, are strangely intensified in Europe, where the flow of texts and countertexts has been limited
and where the persistent stereotypes of the romantic, stoic, or vanishing
Indian have created a deadening archive of Native life. These romantic,
tragic, or New Age "indian" simulations have an international dimension reproduced and distilled in theme-park dioramas, museum exhib-
its, children's toys, computer games, "tribal mood music," advertising,
and in the Winnetou inventions of Karl May in Germany (recognized by
Vizenor) and its subsequent "ethnic drag" performed annually at Bad

Segeberg with its motto "Eine Stadt spielt Indianer" ("A town plays Indian").[1] Yet in performing versions of "indianness" as whites, in "playing" with identity, ethnicity, and "history," there might be useful critical perspectives to carry forward. As Katrin Sieg puts it, "Ethnic drag dramatizes social conflicts in the manner of a dream, through condensations, displacements, and distortions. Its relation to reality is indirect," yet such processes of identification, of "playing Indian," can have both a "hegemonic and subversive dimension." Rather like the perspective of post-tourism discussed in chapter 3, the "subversive" sense she claims comes via the spectator's awareness of the drag show's performance, its guises, offering a "critical vantage point from which the internal logic of nationality, race, and gender can be understood" and its "internal instability" recognized.[2] Thus the acting out of already established, clichéd roles that presume an authenticity and accuracy of detail as a way of honoring Native cultures can have an alternative, unsuspected, and critical effect by emphasizing the ethnic grid that contains and delimits identity rather than sustaining or empowering it. As Philip Deloria puts it, one will undoubtedly engage with the Indian as a reassuring marker of "something undeniably real" connected with notions of a "real Self," a "powerful indicator of the timeless and the unchanging," but also see that "Indianness" could be "an equally compelling sign of transformation, rebellion, and creation."[3] Such a shift between one perception and another has the capacity to fracture the grid, coming close to Vizenor's own radical intention to make Native people see how they have become constructed as "*indians*" (inventions, simulations, absence) by others and by themselves, within a wider U.S. and international context, so that they might be freed to "create new myths and stories about natives in diverse situations, who do not solely rest on *indian* simulations or romantic revisions."[4] As Vizenor argues, because all Indians are invented and "playing" roles, they too must recognize and interrogate the sources of that invention as a means of critique and an opportunity for new stories to be formed. The "ethnic drag" performances of "indianness" studied by Sieg at Bad Segeberg or their equivalents in other cultural texts can function as an important reminder to question notions of the "real" and the "authentic" and remain alert to the claims of any single or essentialized point of view. Thus any criticism, whether from outside or inside (of the United States or Native cultures), has to recognize the significance of these dual and related positions—hegemony/subversion, inside/outside, authentic/inauthentic—and chart a dialogic course through all sides so that many dimensions can be examined and utilized in the deconstruction of such a restrictive "ethnic grid."

Louis Owens's *Mixedblood Messages* contains an important discussion of how the "deadly cliché" of "frontier" might be "appropriated" and "transvaluated" for Native American studies so as to deemphasize its association with a terminal notion of the expansionist West defined by Frederick Jackson Turner in 1890, a moment that coincided with the massacre at Wounded Knee.[5] Instead of the straight line marking Manifest Destiny's furthest reach, Owens argues for "frontier" as closer to Mary Louise Pratt's concept of the "contact zone" as "social spaces where disparate cultures meet, clash, and grapple with each other, often in highly asymmetrical relations of domination and subordination." As Pratt has written, the "contact zone" version of the "colonial frontier" is intended to "invoke the spatial and temporal copresence of subjects . . . whose trajectories now intersect" in relations defined as "interactive, improvisational," and concerned with "copresence, interaction, interlocking understandings and practices."[6] Along these "seams" of contact, as Owens calls them, is a frontier space that is "multidirectional and hybridized," contested, "the zone of trickster, a shimmering, always changing zone of multifaceted contact within which every utterance is challenged and interrogated, all referents put into question." Whereas this space is "always unstable, multidirectional, hybridised, characterised by heteroglossia, and indeterminate," Owens's other term, "territory," stands in contrast to it, "clearly mapped, fully imagined as a place of containment, invented to control and subdue the dangerous potentialities of imagined Indians . . . the ultimate logic of territory is appropriation and occupation."[7] Owens adopts this frontier/territory coding to suggest the double containment of Indians on reservations and through their discursive emplacement within the dominant cultural order as simulated "Indians." Owens's "territory" expresses a material and discursive grid "bounded by discourse, articulated and controlled," through which Indians were neutralized, contained, and made static "within the trope of the noble and vanishing red man" before being "subsumed into the national metanarrative." The challenge is to resist this "ideology of containment" in all forms of representation and "to insist upon the freedom to reimagine themselves within a fluid, always shifting frontier space," "deconstructing rigid borders, slipping between the seams, embodying contradictions, and contradancing across every boundary."[8] Any effort to construct a static "Indian" in a moribund culture locked only in the essentialized past is akin to the play-acting at Bad Segeberg, its "ethnic drag," and must be met with oppositional energies asserting the fluid, multidirectional qualities of "frontier space" to break the grid of identity and break out of what Vizenor defines as the cultural process of "simulation" and "terminal creeds." The latter is the consequence of Indian "invention" and simulation from "static standards," with Indians "stuck in coins and words like artifacts. So we take up a belief and settle with it, stuck, static. Some upsetting is necessary."[9] As we saw earlier, Gloria Anzaldúa has referred to a similar need for "reframing the old story" through what she terms a "new tribalism" that, contrary to its initial implied meaning, calls for a growth in identity and community based on "propagating other worldviews, spiritual traditions and cultures" that enable us to reject "identity boxes" and "to rethink yourself in more global-spiritual terms . . . to retribalize your identity to a more inclusive one."[10]

Vizenor's version of this contained, "gridding" process comes through in his sense of a Native literature "pressed into cultural categories, transmuted by reductionism, animadversions and the hyperrealities of neo-colonial consumerism," with tribal cultures "invented as 'absolute fakes' and consumed in social science monologues. . . . [With] Social science theories [that] constrain tribal landscapes to institutional values, representationalism and the politics of academic determination." Thus complex, mobile, and multidirectional Indian cultures are reduced to the lowercase "indian," to "artifacts," simulations, "terminal creeds," an "absence," "invented from traditional static standards," and it is precisely because of this, as Vizenor argues above, "some upsetting is necessary." First identifying and then upsetting the grids of representation is at the forefront of Vizenor's writing as it hovers over the "ruins of tribal representations" striving to "surmount the scriptures of manifest manners with new stories . . . [to] counter the surveillance and literature of dominance with their own simulations of survivance."[11] The word "Indian" is a "colonial enactment," a "bankable simulation," a projection, a stasis of containment that denies, surveils, and ultimately creates only a powerful "absence," a "prison of false identities," or what I term an "ethnic grid" in American culture.[12] Vizenor's work in fiction and criticism demands a resistance to stasis and a willful, playful reassertion of Native mobilities of all kinds, for as he has said, "Cultures are not static, human behavior is not static. We are not what anthropologists say we are and we must not live up to a definition. . . . We are very complex human beings."[13] In part this emerges through the trickster stories that twist and turn, contradict and surprise in ways that "travel" between teller/listener or writer/reader, engaging us in a dialogic process, forbidding any passivity in our relations with the texts. He writes: "Trickster stories arise in silence, not scriptures, and are the *holotropes* of imagination; the manifold turns of scenes, the brush of natural reason, characters that liberate the mind and never reach closure in stories. Trickster stories are the postindian simulations of tribal survivance."[14] This "trickster hermeneutics" is present both in the content of Vizenor's stories and in the form of his new critical language, inflected with poststructuralist notions of *différance* and deferral of meaning, echoing the work of Derrida and Deleuze and Guattari, deliberately seeking to "move" the reader into uncharted linguistic fields, forcing us to rethink established terms of reference and reconsider the values carried by them. Vizenor is another Deleuzian "minoritarian," a "stammerer of language . . . a foreigner in one's own language. Constructing a line of flight . . . of variation which affects each system by stopping it from being homogeneous."[15] As noted previously, Deleuze's concept of "minor literature" refers to "that which a minority constructs within a major language," to the rejection of cultural "unanimity" and dominant voices, asserting the presence of the "missing" people, those below the radar of power and systems of the majority who can be "invented" through sustained imagination, literature, and art to "supplement" a "presupposed" and "inert" national consciousness.[16]

As we read Vizenor from essay to essay, from book to book, there is a process of folding, refolding, and unfolding taking place, a complex outflowing of ideas that occurs "between" claims and points, moving the reader across language in rhizomatic threads and interconnections. Thus "the *manifold* turns" above, the "*creases* outside the institutive surveillance and sway of government," and the "*tease* [that] must reverse modernist theses, models of the social sciences, and the narratives of native absence" are all strategies of writing and telling that Vizenor employs to challenge these "inert" grids of representation and propose a "transmotional" Native presence of "survivance" and "sovenance" (emphasis added).[17] This echoes the Deleuzian discussion of the fold as an image of multiplicity and complexity that resists containment and expands the grid: "The problem is not how to finish a fold, but how to continue it, to have it go through the ceiling, how to bring it to infinity."[18] Such is the purpose of Vizenor's tricksterism in its resistance to all singularity, its refusal to accept the "vanishing," absent "*indian*," preferring to chart the "folds" of Native community and identity as dynamic, shifting, and variable, "a virtuality that never stops dividing itself," "the variable curve that supersedes the circle" of simulation.[19] As John Rajchman puts it, "The strategy is . . . to introduce something into . . . or 'implicated in'—the gridded space, which it cannot contain, which leaks or spills out from it, linking it to the outside." For Vizenor this is the "trace" of Native presence, despite the effects of manifest manners, held in stories, always in motion through their production and reception, eternally adaptive and syncretic.

The endless simulations charted in Vizenor's writing emphasize the inevitable existence of gridlike structures of language and power, but as with Deleuze, his constant struggle is to find the "leaks" and "folds" of complexity that are hard to contain and that "at any point or moment break out of it and cause it to be reframed."[20] As Deleuze and Guattari wrote in their study of Kafka, "Expression must break forms, encourage ruptures and new sproutings. When a form is broken, one must reconstruct the content that will necessarily be part of a rupture in the order of things."[21] Vizenor has said that this too is the function of his comic/ trickster writings: "I think we should break out of all the routes, all the boxes, break down the sides. A comic spirit demands that we break from formula, break out of program . . . break out of all restrictions . . . even break out of their blood . . . break out of the mixture in their blood . . . break out of invented cultures and repression," and to achieve this his "folded" texts energize writing with the oral tradition's twisting, tricky tales.[22] As Elvira Pulitano summarizes, "Like tricksters, writers must constantly unsettle, contradict, and unglue the creeds of authoritative discourse," setting words and concepts in motion to defy fixity and to question territorial separatism and nationalism by asserting "the ability to move in the imagination, the ability that establishes a sense of presence for Native people."[23] Vizenor's imperative is to promote Native identities as "becoming," unfixable, and "not mere statutes, inheritance, or documentation," the *indian* as "archive."[24] The latter refers both to the dominant culture's processes of containment and control and to the tribal overemphasis on legalism, territorialism, and inward-looking blood quantum politics, which, for Vizenor, serve always to reduce the possibilities of "native presence" and confident survival. His work is endlessly, "teasingly" mobile and "deterritorialised"—linguistically and imaginatively—always anxious to glimpse "the mighty curve of the unnameable" and to demonstrate that "Natives have always been on the move, by necessity of sustenance, and over extensive trade routes; motion is a natural right, and the stories of visionary transmotion are a continuous, distinctive sense of sovereignty."[25]

Countering this Native "transmotion" is the "territorial" process of reductive simulation embedded both in representation and in the material enslavement of reservations, or what Vizenor also calls "exclaves."[26] Yet, despite these acts of "severance," the reservation exemplifies a contradiction for American Indians, with connotations as both "home" and "a negotiated space set aside . . . by oppressive colonial governments to isolate them, to extricate them from their cultural habits, and to save them from the vices of the outside world." Ironically, the isolation of such a "reserved" space on the margins of the dominant white culture helped maintain Native language and culture as "traces," despite the often prisonlike conditions of a landscape of control and surveillance. Reservations resemble Owens's sense of "territory," presenting another manifestation of the grids discussed throughout this book, maintaining boundaries that, as Gerald McMaster points out, functioned as forms of border control: "We could not leave the reserve without a pass, we were prisoners, and could barely survive. There were gates on the fence around the reserve."[27] In Sherman Alexie's script for Chris Eyre's film *Smoke Sig-*

nals (1998), which I will discuss in detail below, this serious sense of containment is transformed into a joke as Thomas Builds-the-Fire and Victor Joseph plan to leave the reservation for Phoenix: "You guys got passports? You're leaving the rez and going into a whole different country, cousin," to which Thomas answers "But it's the USA," to which the retort is, "Damn right, and that's as foreign as it gets. Hope you got your vaccinations." In that film, at a key moment when the two young Coeur d'Alene Indians have been arrested for suspected assault and drunken driving and are supposed to conform to all the ingrained stereotypes of the troublesome red man, Thomas claims "we was framed." Typical of the film's subversive and self-conscious use of humor, Thomas employs a clichéd film-script response to answer the police accusations while at the same time announcing the ways in which those very stereotypes act to "frame" and enclose Indians within the dominant culture.

Reservation X

As we have seen, however, such grids or frames can be adjusted and reframed to create new, creative spaces, whether literally on or off the reservation, adapting Native community and identity in accordance with a changing, postmodern, global culture. As McMaster puts it, echoing Owens's "frontier," Native "community is no longer fixed, unified, or stable . . . it exists in a state of flux," and identity "is seen as multiple and mobile against the stable and homogeneous concepts of the past," and under such conditions "We may say that we are from there, when really we are from here; tomorrow we will be from over there. Similarly, we can no longer define ourselves as this or that; we are now both and more." McMaster's term for this shifting condition of "both and more," with its echoes of Vizenor's plea for "transmotion" or "active presence," is "Reservation X," an idea adapted by McMaster from Shelley Niro's film script for *Honey Moccasin* (1998) and defined as "a reality of place for contemporary Indian people, a community that is *at once fictional and real*, but nonetheless a place with a story." The "X" too is a historical reminder of the mark placed on treaties by Indian chiefs whose hands were guided by others, it "signified articulation; it left a *trace* . . . it was contradictory; it indicated inarticulation. These Xs created the reserves" (emphasis added). The X signifies a "fictional and real," "both and more" space and carries within it the "trace" (a word Vizenor, via Derrida, favors too) of history and deception, but not embalmed as "tragic victimry," for it also marks a kind of erasure, a crossing through of those signifiers allowing other creative forms to emerge. Out of this matrix is created the energy of "the new reservation narrative" exploring Indian identity and community as no longer marginal but central, "a frontier of difference and a place to which one can always return" and thus, "by inverting the stereotype of the reserve as somehow outside the core of the state, a new, enabling trend occurs."

In a similar way, the notion of "the rez," according to McMaster, has come to signify more than just an actual place, used by younger urban Indians to represent "a cool Indian community. . . . [Its] hip-hop style abrogates our old understanding and infuses it with new, powerful, and ironic messages. . . . [Creating] a term of appropriation and articulation, of taking something and using it to advantage . . . it signifies the idea as much as the complexities, paradoxes, and contradictions of living on the rez."[28] The multidirectional and hybridized sense of the "frontier" defined by Owens thus takes the form of Reservation X here, a theoretical perspective coined about artists that can be ably extended to writers and filmmakers too, to all those, in fact, experiencing and expressing the tensions of contemporary Indian life, "in between two centres"—reserve and urban, red and white. Borrowing from the theories of Homi Bhabha and Edward Soja (discussed in the introduction and chapter 1) and developing ideas already expressed in his essay "Border Zones: The 'Injun-uity' of Aesthetic Tricks," McMaster refers to this powerful "in-between" existence as "third space" wherein these artists "see, borrow from, and articulate within two spaces" shifting across cultural lines and traditions, sometimes questioning and subverting, seeing boundaries as "permeable" and culture as a "changing tradition."[29] This "third space," rather like Owens's "frontier space," is "a perceptual space for various practices, including 'resistance' and the articulation of 'self-identity' . . . a zone of 'in-between-ness' . . . where shifting allegiances criss-cross permeable grids or boundaries, and where identities are to be understood as 'nomadic subjectivities.'"[30] Thus Reservation X is no grid of state power or frozen tradition but rather exists "out of reach of the usual codifications . . . [not identified] by numbers, by ID cards, nor by a place on a map, but by something less measurable and more meaningful . . . [both] dislocating and relocating of the artist's voice." As Charlotte Townsend-Gault writes, developing McMaster's ideas, this is a "virtual place" and a "source of energy" for those artists who "resist any single way of shaping and framing what they have to say" and who wrestle "with discourses of art and tribe, with traditions old, new, and invented, with finding ways to draw on old meanings while allowing for new meanings, with power struggles over memory and anger." As she goes on to say, what is played out within Reservation X is "extreme difference as the non-negotiable basis for identity and participation in a universalizing global culture to which all differences contribute."[31]

In the various essays in McMaster's edited volume *Reservation X*, any fixed notion of Indian community or identity is problematized, recognizing, as Mary Longman says, that "there is no fixed address for Reservation X," and opting instead for a more mobile, transformative notion that, while understanding the significance of traditional ways, also embraces global communication and social shifts. One of Longman's artworks is entitled "Strata and Routes" (figure 14), a sculptural installation showing two tree trunks with roots sprouting at each end. The piece was inspired by a little rock she had seen embedded and entangled in the roots of in an overturned tree, a "found" object that suggested to her much about contemporary Indian life, identity, and community. The two trees were placed together, layers (strata) of rocks repositioned at the center acting as sutures, and a large rock placed on top of the tree (covered with photographs of the artist's family) with roots growing all around it. In this schematic piece, Longman ties together nature, family, and community in a process that is both of the earth (*rooted* below) and of the sky (reaching upward and *routed*). As McMaster comments, "The homophones *routes* and *roots* are resonant. Perhaps Longman wants us to know that we follow many paths, yet we will always find home."[32] Applying terms and ideas drawn from postcolonial and diaspora theory, McMaster interprets Longman's work as understanding the "in-between" not as a "selling out" of the old ways or a ditching of tribal cultural identity but rather as an affirmation and evolution drawing on more than a single cultural "repertoire," as Stuart Hall terms it, by people who increasingly "belong to more than one world, speak more than one language (literally and metaphorically), inhabit more than one identity, have more than one home; who have learned to negotiate and translate *between* cultures" and as a result, "speak from the 'in-between' of different cultures, always unsettling the assumptions of one culture from the perspective of another, and thus finding ways of being *both the same as* and at the same time *different from* the others amongst whom they live." The concept of a pure, untouched, and authentic culture and tradition is modified here by the same influences and exchanges of Pratt's "contact zone" (including violent conquest, trade, resistance, assimilation, acculturation, and hybridization), and although the actual reservation experience might still form a key definition of "home," it is not the only one where identity and place are constantly redefined as "both and more." The version of tradition as an "a one-way transmission belt; an umbilical cord, which connects us to our culture of origin" is a linear concept of culture, when an alternative version, like that presented as Reservation X, for example, sees "culture as moving, not in a line but through different circuits."[33] What this recognizes, like the work of Stuart Hall and Paul Gilroy writing about black culture, or Anzaldúa on Chicana/border cultures, is that to talk of culture as reaching back to some absolute point of origin where everything was pure and "authentic," so that all subsequent transformations are merely irrelevant dilutions, is to limit and restrict how traditions evolve and "travel" along various complex routes. In Gilroy's terms, therefore, cultural survival is about "roots" *and* "routes," looking both "inside" *and* "outside," both "down" *and* "outward," following, in Longman's artistic example, the strata *and* the routes. Commenting specifically on this artwork, Longman has said that the stones were "diverse identities" and the strata were "the evolution of the past to present" and that in the double-ended tree trunk she imagined "one hybrid form" wherein "The roots of ancestry evolved into routes of life passages. The dangling, tiny end roots on the top trunk indicate a further growing, as if they were delicate nerve endings waiting to experience."[34] This is a rhizomatic vision through which "desire moves and produces," but when it is contained or stunted it becomes like a rooted tree ("arborified"), and "Arborescent systems are hierarchical systems with centers of significance and subjectification, central automata like organized memories," suggesting the "weariest kind of

14. Mary Longman, Strata and Routes (1998) (*photograph of installation*).
*Matrix G, rocks, cottonwood, fir, and photo emulsion, 153 x 184 x 153 cm.
Collection: Mackenzie Art Gallery. Used by permission of the artist.*

thought."[35] In Deleuze and Guattari's work the "tree" signifies "rigid segmentarity" a "principle of dichotomy" and binary logic, the "structure or network *gridding the possible*" (emphasis added), against which, as we have seen, they argue for the rhizome, yet contending that "they are inseparable, they overlap, they are entangled," and "every society, and every individual, are thus plied by both segmentarities simultaneously: one molar, the other *molecular*" (as in Longman's installation).[36]

Such a description echoes the words of Pulitano, who writes of how contemporary Indian authors "attempt to re-create/reimagine the dialogic quality of the oral exchange" in their works, producing "substantially multi-generic, dialogic, and richly hybridised works, texts that shuttle back and forth between worlds and worldviews and 'mediate' strategies that challenge Western ways of doing theory."[37] And yet she, like myself, recognizes that many Indians would argue against such ideas of hybridity and incorporation of non-Indian ideas (often termed mixed-blood or cross-blood theories), seeing them as a dilution of authenticity and a compromise that veers away from a Native American "tribal" criticism or literature "rooted in land and culture, sensitive to the needs of community, and creating resistance movements against colonization."[38] A critic such as "separatist" Craig Womack rejects cross-cultural exchange in favor of a "Red," tribalcentric critique, arguing that what he is interested in is a "Native literary nationalism" to reclaim "the 'mental means of production' . . . [so long] owned, almost exclusively, by non-Indians" and to work "from within the nation, *rather than looking toward the outside*" (emphasis added). He refutes the notion that there is only a Native world "filtered through contact with Europe" as "assimilationist ideology, a retreat into sameness and blending in," and prefers instead to assert Indians as "not victims but active agents in history, innovators of new ways . . . of thinking and being and speaking and authoring." As he goes further, however, his language echoes Longman's installation and commentary: "tribal literatures are not some branch waiting to be grafted onto the main trunk. Tribal literatures are the *tree*, the oldest literatures in the Americas, the most American of American literatures. We *are* the canon." His image rejects the possibilities or significance of "routes" in favor of the valorization of "roots" and of an "arboreal" vision of culture, a binary vision that positions "us" against "them," seeing a Native sovereignty that "roots literature in land and culture" as the vital "inside" and anything else as an irrelevant and intrusive "outside."[39] Pulitano suggests that this approach essentializes Native discourse, "does not let the discipline evolve," and ends up "parroting the master's language, but with the terms reversed and without 'signifying' any difference." She refers to Womack as a nativist, deliberately connecting his ideas with postcolonial theorists who define this term as meaning those who believe that "colonialism needs to be replaced by the recovery and promotion of pre-colonial, indigenous ways."[40]

Womack stresses that in his vision "Sovereignty . . . like the oral tradition, is an ongoing, dynamic process, rather than a fixed creed, and evolves according to the changing needs of the nation," and he writes of the "application of tradition in radical new ways."[41] However, Pulitano accuses his approach to the oral tradition of being too inward-looking, an "attempt to fix traditions . . . as markers of authenticity" rather than to recognize the "ongoing transformation of stories" as signs of their endless adaptability and vitality. Identity and community, in other words, are in danger of being represented, through these approaches to the oral tradition, as static and closed up in time and space, curiously imitating the stereotypes so often presented in dominant cultural texts of "indianness."[42] Her argument with Womack is that through his analysis of oral stories he "becomes the insider claiming to present the correct meaning of the story merely on the basis of an authentic Native perspective" and thereby essentializes Creek culture and "fixes that tradition as a cultural artifact." His refusal, she argues, to look "outside" ignores the complex relations and contacts that have contributed in multiple ways to the constructions of Indian identity, community, and evolving tradition. For Womack, the "outside approaches" have often reduced complex Native stories to mere ethnography, seeing it as a problem to be solved with social science's "unique set of rules that apply to static cultures located in the past rather than viable nations facing contemporary political realities."[43] However, as we have seen, Vizenor's contention is that anything that fixes Native culture as an artifact or museum piece is to be resisted, whether it be the dominant white culture or tribes themselves, for "Exclusion by natives is not resistance; the simulations of a native presence, as a separation of the past, are not acts of courage or resistance," and "The reservation politics of sanguine modiation and blood count names is a curse of exclusion and dominance."[44]

Womack writes: "Perhaps it is time to dig in, to entrench ourselves with what we have inherited from our home cultures," a sentiment that Pulitano takes to underline his essentialism.[45] Womack's position is that cultural strength and survival necessitate this "entrenchment" in tribal traditions, since Indian literature was defined for too long "from outside our community . . . applying their principles of literature to these Native works." What is needed, he claims, is "a local, grassroot-level dialogue between the text and the community in which it's set," because then "you get so much more out of it . . . reading with a sensitivity to local Native issues, relevant to our people."[46] Yet he is keen to emphasize that Native stories do not "always remain the same" and that when they are seen in this light they place Indians in "a 'pure versus tainted' framework" in which the old oral tradition is seen as a pure expression of "Indianness" and writing is seen as tainted. The consequence of this, he argues, is to lock Native studies into "a system that does not allow the discipline to evolve," making it easy for the myth of the "vanishing Indian" to persist, suggesting they existed only in the past, in another closed world. In fact, Womack's position is clear on this and a lot closer to writers like Vizenor, arguing that from tribal "local" experience, grounded in an oral tradition, this "pure versus tainted" framework can be challenged, since "by *redirecting our language* we can use our energies to concentrate on cultural survival rather than cultural disintegration" (emphasis added). And despite the Creek-centeredness of *Red on Red*, Womack concedes as it progresses that to have roots in the Creek nation does not preclude a relationship to the world outside it, and that such roots can, in fact, as he argues in his section on Joy Harjo, "vitalize" writing from the "foundation" outward to indigenous struggles on a global scale. "Harjo's Creek grounding strengthens her pan-tribal vision," as her writing "is following a story map, travelling through Creek narrative," but refusing to be boundaried by any "quick, romantic 'ancestral moment,'" since for her, memory "should result in telling and speaking, and, especially, resisting, a combination of imagination, words, and deeds."[47] As I will show later in this chapter, this process of "redirecting language" and connecting across and beyond tribes can be extended to the cinematic stories of Chris Eyre, which work against another established tradition wherein Hollywood had spoken for and defined the Indian, producing what Ward Churchill calls the "emulsification of native cultural content."[48] Indeed, Eyre comes closest to the realization of Vizenor's hope for "an original postindian script [that] might overtake the simulations in any movie."[49]

Womack's own "redirection" of language comes through in the "intertexts" that occur throughout *Red on Red* when a playful "oral" writing emerges that, contrary to Pulitano's argument, seems to point forward and to generate exactly the dynamic quality Womack emphasizes as a

Native literary characteristic. This is in the form of letters written between Jim Chibbo and his friend Hotgun that are interspersed throughout the "serious" literary text. A clue to their inclusion is offered in the
introduction, when Womack writes of Chibbo, "He's not satisfied with
explicating Creek texts if he has never tried his hand at creating anything
Creek himself" and then tells us that "Jim tries to tell a few funny stories
here and again to consider the most serious critical issues in the book
without becoming mean hisself [like a university professor]." The letters aim "to get to the heart of matters quicker by funning each other
than by writing literary criticism." These are, like the "grassroot-level
dialogue" he has spoken of, Creeks writing about Creeks rather than a
"bunch of mongrelized mixed-bloods who weren't sure if they were Indians as they muddled about in some kind of hybridised culture, serving
as the footpath between whites and Indians."[50] An early example shows
how in these creative critical sections Womack comes close to a trickster style familiar in Vizenor's work (despite the dig at the "mongrelized
mixed-bloods"). Characters discuss smoking, and one, Stijaati, holds
up "his red-and-white package of Marlboros," asking, "How's this pack
of cigarettes like Chebon's book?" The answer is, "It ain't," because
"Chebon's book about the Red, not the white." "Ain't that a little naïve? A Red book?" asks Big Man. "Only if you believe white always swal-
lows up Red. I think Red stays red, most ever time, even throwed in with
white. Especially around white. It stands out more." In the humor of
this exchange, with its playing with and punning on words and acutely
observed cultural politics, Womack performs what he argues Native
literature must be, political and collective, "part of sovereignty: Indian
people exercising the right to present images of themselves and to discuss those images."[51]

Thus, in stressing the essentialism and the particular vision of tribalism in Womack's work, Pulitano emphasizes her preference for writers like Vizenor, Greg Sarris, and Owens, and in so doing she misses
Womack's awareness of a "routed" culture too, aware of its relations
with others, constantly "re-storying" itself precisely in order to survive
and prosper in such an environment. "Digging-in," as he terms it, does
not mean cutting oneself off from the world, but rather, as Deleuze and
Guattari put it, developing a strategic "minor literature," "Writing like

a dog digging a hole, a rat digging its burrow . . . finding his own point of underdevelopment, his own *patois*," meeting the dominant culture from a position of strength, solid in the knowledge of specific traditions that are themselves relevant and forward-looking.[52] As Womack said in a 2005 interview, revealing a pronounced shift in his views, "All our Indian skills are still active, but it's not just that old cliché of the Indian with a blanket. Before it was Either/Or. Now, there's no conflict between the two cultures, Western and Indian, we move in both worlds."[53] My sense is that Womack expresses here a sentiment similar to Longman's notion of "strata and routes," that empowering mix of tribal grounding in specifics (the "molar"), in the stones and earth, alongside the rhizomatic ("molecular") extensions interconnecting and moving outward. Although he has a reputation as a "local" tribalist, Womack sounds increasingly like what McMaster was describing in his Indians who are "both and more," aware of the increasing need for connection "between two cultures," following both "strata and routes" on Reservation X. Deleuze and Guattari offer another approach to the direction I perceive here in their discussion of "minor literature," arguing that it always functions in relation to major language "in order to place it in a state of continuous variation (the opposite of regionalism)," that is, seeing the work of minor language as rhizomatic and deterritorializing rather than as merely "regional" and contained by narrow, specific "tribal" (their word: "ghettoizing") uses. As they put it, "Use the minor language to *send the major language racing*," to move and vary the "constant" and "standard" forms of the established and dominant system, creating an "outsystem" always directing us beyond any purely "local" or "regional" concerns toward some "potential, creative, and created, becoming . . . crystals of becoming . . . to trigger uncontrollable movements and deterritorializations." What I sense, even in Womack's work, is the recognition of these processes of evolutionary encounter as central to a dynamic and vibrant Native culture, engaging rhizomatically from roots to routes, to discover the "pass-words beneath order-words . . . to transform the compositions of order into components of passage."[54]

As McMaster writes, "Syncretic/hybrid possibilities have been dismissed as tradition-less," when in fact they often provide opportunities to reexamine and reinvent traditions of "community" with artists who "live, create and appropriate between two or more spaces" as a "tactical position," using this border zone as a creative arena making works that are "self-referential . . . deploy self-parodying devices that poke fun at the clichés, stereotypes and conventions of (Native) representations" through a combination of what De Certeau calls the "esthetics of 'tricks' and an ethics of *tenacity* (. . . refusing to accord the established order the status of the law)."[55] For McMaster, as for Vizenor, what emerges in this border zone or frontier is the trickster, "the spirit of disorder, the enemy of boundaries," and today's tricksters are artists "political and activistic," "not just carriers but innovators of culture, living 'betwixt and between' several cultures and communities."[56]

Chris Eyre: "An Insurgent Native American Counter-cinema"?

In his films, Chris Eyre often uses trickster figures and other narrative and thematic devices to enable him to pursue his interest in the "betwixt and between" of contemporary Indian cultures, the tensions and politics of reservation life in a national and global context. Vizenor wrote in 1994 that "Manifestly, movies have never been the representations of tribal cultures" but are instead "the muse of simulations, and the absence of humor and real tribal cultures."[57] In the visual memory bank of the world "The *indian* is an imprinted picture . . . a cultural concoction of bourgeois nostalgia and social science evidence. Cultural pageants, dioramas, and museum presentations pictured the fugitive *indian* in the archives of dominance." Whether through photography or later film, the consequences for the Native was the same, a stasis and containment with "capturable native motion" leading to an "aesthetic servitude, an eternal *indian* simulation" through the lens of the "manifest camera."[58] In Ward Churchill's infamous phrase, the movies provided a "cinematic colonization" through their "Fantasies of the Master Race," translating the earlier work of ethnography and anthropology through the camera lens in order to fix Native Americans in a "time/space compression" in which tribal differences, geographies, and language are ignored for the portrayal of generic "indianness." Cinema was a perfect vehicle for the continued, strategic erasure of Native identities behind a mask of simulation and impersonation, with white actors playing Indian, ancient cultures either ignored or romanticized, and human complexity reduced to

crass stereotypes of Indians as savage, stoic, mystical, or simply vanishing. Under the surveillance of Hollywood and embedded in the rigidified generic codes of classic or "new" Westerns, Indian stories at the
movies "become indistinguishable in the end, following as they do a
mutual trajectory to the same destination within the master narrative of an
overarching 'American Story'" (emphasis added).[59] The narrative paths
of Westerns, with their "mutual trajectory," form a critical element of the
"gridding" discussed throughout this chapter, which can be challenged
by the "redirection of language" and the assertion of a multidirectional-
ism that breaks apart this single perspective.

Perhaps this has begun to change with the cinema of Chris Eyre, an
Indian filmmaker whose first movie, *Smoke Signals*, addresses some of
these concerns, exercising humor as part of an armory against simulations. The multidirectional sense of the "frontier space" is at stake in an
overly static version of Indian culture, whether through the simulations
of a dominant white culture or through an over-essentialized depen-
dence on the "gymnastics of authenticity."[60] Film can contribute greatly
to a new multidirectionality, pointing outward from a grounded base
in tribal culture toward global concerns, aware both of the demands of
indigenous traditions and of the relevance and usefulness of popular
media. To be an Indian in the twenty-first century is to live "in part out
of what remains of his tribal lore, in part out of the mythology and science created by White men to explain him to themselves," in the full
glare of mediatized simulation and excessive representation, and amid
the proliferation of stories and accumulated tribal battles over blood
quantum and sovereignty.[61] *Smoke Signals* understands this position and
navigates paths through these issues with authority and humor, helping
to forge what Churchill has termed "an autonomous native cinema."[62]
Churchill ends his book *Fantasies of the Master Race* discussing the film;
Beverly R. Singer begins her study of Native American film and video,
Wiping the War Paint Off the Lens, interpreting *Smoke Signals* as a watershed,
because "for the first time" a generation was witnessing "American Indian actors playing American Indian characters, saying words written by
American Indian screenwriters, and following direction from an Ameri-
can Indian director"; while Jacquelyn Kilpatrick defines "The American
Indian Aesthetic," in part, by using the film.[63] What this film and other

movies directed by Eyre, such as *Skins, Skinwalkers, The Thief of Time*, and *Edge of America*, achieve is the translation of complex theoretical and cultural ideas and debates into an "accessible" medium while blending the comic and serious. His films engage their audiences (both Native and non-Native) with many of the concepts underpinning the work of Vizenor, Owens, Womack, and others discussed above, showing, ultimately, a commitment to Native community, family, and tradition, or what Jace Weaver calls "communitism." This means "proclaiming and living our commitment to Native community and values. . . . [i]n the stream of history to which they belong and thus be better understood and appreciated . . . [and] better able to embrace and assimilate the thoughts of Others and of the dominating culture without losing our roots." This "communitism," he continues, is "related to Vizenor's 'survivance' [and] Warrior's 'intellectual sovereignty,'" combining "community" and "activism" so that "literature"—and, I would add, film—has a "proactive commitment" to community both locally and globally, contributing to the promotion of communitist values and to the "healing of the grief and sense of exile felt by Native communities and the pained individuals within them."[64] To explain this position further, Weaver draws on postcolonial theory and the work of Homi Bhabha, who argues, using the ideas of Renée Green, for "community envisaged as a project—at once a vision and a construction—that takes you 'beyond' yourself in order to return, in a spirit of revision and reconstruction, to the political conditions of the present."[65] Bhabha's point, like Vizenor's, is that this sense of community is not a static one but is rather constantly formed and re-formed from an "in-between" position that "prevents identities at either end of it from settling into primordial polarities," recognizing the value and relations of the past, present, and future as complex, hybrid dialogues.[66]

In *Smoke Signals*, scripted by Sherman Alexie from his collection *The Lone Ranger and Tonto Fistfight in Heaven*, Eyre creates a film that is communitist in its portrayal of Coeur d'Alene reservation life, family bonds, and friendship and yet achieves this through framing the text within a familiar Hollywood genre, the road/buddy movie, and with a series of self-conscious references to the generic Western tradition. From this position "in-between" cultures, Eyre aimed at "touching something that doesn't exist in cinema and that is the representation of contemporary Native America."[67] In part, as Eyre has commented, his work reflects his own background as a white-adopted Cheyenne/Arapaho, educated off the reservation: "I'm an amalgamation of two worlds and I think looking at two sides of things that I can't separate has given me that sensibility called 'humanity.' It transcends culture and race, in the end what you're left with is Skins or Smoke Signals."[68] In the latter film the "two worlds" are manifested in different ways, both locally through Victor and Thomas (the former a "stoic" warrior type, the latter a sensitive trickster-storyteller) and more globally as the contrast between life on and off the reservation. Alexie has actually commented that the Victor/Thomas duo represents "a sort of schizophrenic multiple personality of myself."[69] Significantly, the film adopts the road/buddy genre as a means of exploring and testing out these tensions between different "worlds," literally moving its characters across time and space for six days of (re)creation (i.e., both fun and rebirth). As Alexie has said, he wanted to deliberately suggest mythic journeys in the European tradition both in "high culture" through the Bible, the Iliad, and the Odyssey, and in popular culture through established road-movie formats of Thelma and Louise and Midnight Cowboy. Yet in their use of flashbacks Eyre and Alexie add a dimension to this formula, suggesting "The way time works in Indian culture . . . more circular, so that the past, the present and the future are all the same thing."[70] This technique of seamless edits shifting the viewer from present to past to future, Alexie admits, was "borrowed" from John Sayles's Lone Star (1995), a film whose central theme is the exploration of a community in transition on the U.S.-Mexico border. The community in transition in Eyre's film thus emerges through the circular journey of its "twinned" characters "born of fire," moving them through their pasts toward their futures and forms of reconciliation. The dissolve edits emphasize visually the relations in Eyre's work between past and present, tradition and evolution, a technique that moves the viewer from point to point, creating another "bridge" across which divisions are interrogated and connections found.

In addition, the film retains and uses Native creation/emergence and journey motifs and other sacred images (circularity; the elements fire, earth, water, and air; trickster; etc.). Through these methods the film "travels" in many ways, creating a version of what Vizenor calls "transmotion," that is, the invocation of memories, stories, songs, and visions, a "virtual cartography" that works in dialogue with and opposition to the conventional cultural grids imposed from colonial "mappings." Leaving the reservation without "passports" identifies a shift into new territory within which Thomas's stories and visions provide a "virtual cartography" for Victor's gradual transformation and reconciliation with his dead father, Arnold Joseph, whose ashes they go to collect in Phoenix. Rather than accept the "passive representations" of Hollywood "indians," Eyre, like Vizenor, produces a film of "active creations" in humor, friendship, and ultimately healing that engages directly with many of the "fixed" simulations that have reduced tribal communitism to static stereotypes.[71] Hence the film self-consciously references other Westerns, most noticeably *Little Big Man*, with its line "It's a good day to die" refigured in three different ways in *Smoke Signals*: "Sometimes it's a good day to die and sometimes it's a good day to play basketball," "It's a good day to be indigenous," and "Sometimes it's a good day to die and sometimes it's a good day to have breakfast." At other points, Victor accuses Thomas of being obsessed with *Dances with Wolves*, implying it has given him his mystic view of tribal life, while Thomas refers to them as not "The Lone Ranger and Tonto," but "Tonto and Tonto." Intertextuality in the film is deliberately dialogical, demonstrating Eyre's and Alexie's awareness of Vizenor's concepts of "aesthetic victimry," simulation, and absence and their crucial understanding of the iconography within which all Native peoples function. In an example of intertexts at work in the film, Arnold (played by Gary Farmer) asks Victor who his favorite Indian is, to which he replies, "Nobody." Nobody was also the name of the Indian played by Farmer in Jarmusch's *Dead Man* (see chapter 4), a film that Eyre has called "a really amazing stream of consciousness film."[72] Such patterns of reference function to reinforce Eyre's aim to be a "bridge to other people who aren't like us," developing and extending familiar cinematic codes to new ends, reframing structures and knowledges to create his own version of Reservation X's complex, layered domain. Indeed, *Edge of America* (2003) literally brings together one minority (African American) with another (Indian) in a dramatic racial contact zone, as teacher Kenny Williams arrives to teach and coach basketball on the Navajo Three Nations Reservation. In this Eyre draws on various cinematic traditions—youth movie, underdog sports story, racial "clash of cultures," and healing tale—while folding them into his framing narrative of reservation life, family bonds, and communitist empowerment.[73] His willingness to incorporate different traditions within his populist films evidences his interest in bridging cultural divides while remaining true to the Indian community.

In *Smoke Signals* and *Skins*, for example, every time a television is seen it is showing a Western, and at one point Thomas comments tellingly, "The only thing more pathetic than Indians on TV is Indians watching Indians on TV." Eyre has spoken of how "Victor and Thomas are definitely conscious of themselves in the over culture. . . . It's always about how the over culture wants to portray Indians, and it's usually in a romantic vein—and I definitely don't want to go there. . . . There's Native America and then there's America's Native America . . . [with] Indian-head icons on fruit boxes and Cherokee this and Cherokee that." Beginning with *Smoke Signals*, Eyre is consciously moving his audiences away from this "over culture" view, presenting instead "Indian people like anybody—complicated people."[74] Thus in another scene we see a typical Western film landscape like that associated with John Ford, but instead of Indians on horseback we have Victor and Thomas on foot with regular clothing, arguing and telling stories. This disjunctive use of landscape happens elsewhere in Eyre's work, deliberately toying with audience expectations, such as the opening of *Edge of America*, where a classic roadscape through Indian country seen through a car windshield is disrupted by the realization that it is an African American in the car—an incongruous, outsider figure suddenly upsetting our imagined, comfortable "Indian" assumptive world. At the same time, we are hearing the African American Neville Brothers on the sound track singing "Sons and Daughters" with lyrics that themselves cross the cultural line, suggesting themes central to Eyre's work: "Can't stop running water. Can't kill the fire that burns inside. Can't deny our flesh and blood, don't forsake our sons and daughters." As the film will suggest, its central African American character is running away from his past as a "black man in America," arriving in Indian country as "lost-er than you know" (as a Native character puts it). He gradually comprehends a parallel struggle over identity and culture on the reservation, the recognition of which allows him to come to terms with his own anger and to become finally part of another community, draped in a specially made Navajo rug into whose weave is integrated a black male figure alongside Native people.

Although his work can often seem oversentimental and drawn toward these themes of recovered community, family, and healing, Eyre refuses to ignore the complicity of Indians in their own representation, showing through Victor in *Smoke Signals*, for example, how easy it is to play out expected stereotypes. Wherever they occur, as Alexie has said, "icons are an oversimplification" and need to be interrogated with humor and irony.[75] In one scene, Victor tries to teach Thomas how to be an iconic "real Indian," saying, "get stoic . . . you've got to look mean, like a warrior, as if you've just got back from killing a buffalo." When Thomas points out that their tribe fishes for salmon, Victor concedes that "Dances with Salmon" just doesn't have the same impact. Victor performs an Indian identity based on an extreme, scripted image of "Indianness" just as Thomas also plays the role of mystic storyteller. The difference is that Thomas is more self-aware, comic, a provocateur whose trickster role is to bring Victor to awareness and the possibility of some reconciliation, some healing. The trickster is a mobile, fluid figure, always undercutting the sentimental, able to "send the major language racing," well suited to represent the "in-between" position, moving "betwixt and between" definitions, marking a total unwillingness to be fixed in one place by "order-words," presenting a portrait of *postindian* artists as Vizenor would define them: "We come after the invention [of the *indian*], and we are the *postindians* . . . [who] create a native presence, and that sense of presence is both reversion and futurity." Looking backward and forward, "tricky and ironic," the trickster is the "intransitive motion of shadows."[76] Thomas's self-aware tricksterism is revealed when he expresses his condolences about Arnold's death: "Hey, Victor. I'm sorry about your dad." "How'd you hear about it?" "I heard it on the wind. I heard it from the birds. I felt it in the sunlight. And your mum was just in here crying." This plays with both white stereotypes and Indian simulations as mystics, showing the capacity of penetrative parody and ironic, critical commentary. In this, as Eyre has said, "Thomas is the trickster figure . . . likened to the jester" (a role developed through Rudy and

Mogi in *Skins*), the figure who enables Victor's journey (by supplying the money for the trip), propels the narrative through his stories, and shadows him along the way. In the film, during the "motion" of the bus trip on their way to Phoenix, when Victor has persuaded Thomas to be a "real Indian," free his hair, and be "stoic," they both return to find two cowboys in their seats. After failing to get them to move, Thomas comments ironically, "I guess the warrior look doesn't work every time," because "cowboys always win." Significantly, however, it is just after this that Victor and Thomas invent their chant "John Wayne's Teeth" ("are they real, are they plastic, are they steel"), utilizing humor as a mechanism of resistance rather than simply recycling the iconic warrior stance.

Thomas constantly sets Victor's identity in motion toward new meanings, unfixing him from his static/stoic existence enacting *différance* whereby the verbs "to differ" and "to defer" (postpone) are both suggested simultaneously.[77] Through the trickster (Vizenor's Native *différance*), Native identity is seen as mobile, always different and deferring itself into more stories, and unable, therefore, to become fixed and contained. The trickster "arises in agonistic imagination; a wild venture in communal discourse, an uncertain humor that denies aestheticism, translation, and imposed representations."[78] Thomas is the trickster figure of "transmotion," combining these vital elements in one being, as occurs so often in trickster narratives. In a long speech while walking across the Arizona landscape to Arnold's trailer, Thomas condenses Indian colonial history as a tale of movement away from Columbus, Custer, and Truman's atomic bomb testing on Native lands, and even from Neil Armstrong arriving on the Moon. As he says, "we just keep walking." Thus "Native transmotion races as a horse across the page, and the action is a sense of sovereignty"; it is the "source of survivance" that literally provokes Victor's change through stories taking the film backward in time to the events that have shaped their lives and forward through visions that offer forms of reconciliation (most noticeably the dream of Arnold Joseph at Spokane Falls). Motion through stories, visions, dreams, humor, actual journeys, and processes of change is vital to counter those static "over culture" images and to prevent tribal community appearing as enclosed, anachronistic, and one-dimensional in relation to the United States and beyond. As Vizenor writes, "the ideas and conditions of motion have a deferred meaning that reach, naturally, to other contexts of action, resistance, dissent, and political controversy" and are not "mere territoriality." Sovereignty as motion is "never granted by government" in treaties or courts, for "it is a natural human right that is not bound by borders" or controlled by passports; it is "visionary" and "does not embrace inheritance or tenure of territory."[79] As Victor's mother, Arlene, says in *Smoke Signals*, "You know how Indians feel about signing papers." This takes us back to Womack's work to some degree, to the sense that Indian culture is determined first and foremost in relation to territorial and tribal land as sovereignty claims (roots). What Vizenor suggests is that this requires supplementation, with sovereignty restructured to include "vision" and the less tangible characteristics of cultural strength (a sense of roots *and* routes—of "transmotion") so that what is challenged is both a Euro-American framework *and* the tribal categories of nationalism and blood quantum modiation, both of which, in different ways, seek to contain and fix Native identities and communities.

The trickster, Thomas Builds-the-Fire, as a key "storier of presence" who constantly "moves" the imagination, enacts "an ideal healing force, one that disrupts and confronts [Victor's stoic/cynic self] while creating the possibility for a discourse that is communal and comic."[80] He constantly provokes Victor, in the flashbacks of their childhood, forcing him to confront his past, often causing violence ("When Indians go away they don't come back. . . . *Last of the Mohicans, Last of the Winnebagos*") or asking questions about Victor's absent father ("What do you know about fire?" "Why did he leave? Did he hate you?"). Clearly, his role in the film is to stir Victor's anger while also reminding him of his of tribal affiliations and, most significantly, his father's positive qualities, using stories about Arnold protesting against the Vietnam War in Washington and getting two years in Walla Walla for "being an Indian in the twentieth century," taking him to Denny's in Spokane, or looking like Charles Bronson. Victor's worldview is founded on anger and cynicism ("People are awful, there'll rob you blind . . . you can't trust anybody") born out of his violent childhood in a home defined by alcoholism, abuse, and absence. His father's leaving home is a key motif for the film that forms the basis for the narrative journey and for the ultimate reconciliation. Thomas's questionings—his erosion of Victor's defenses with humor and stubborn persistence—culminate in his decisive statement just before the car wreck: "Maybe you don't know who you are. Just hanging around the reservation for ten years. . . . You make your mother cry." Shortly after this, Victor runs for help as another part of his healing "ceremony" and undergoes a series of flashbacks that draw him closer to a different perception of his father, who "went back into the burning house to look for you," ending with a vision of Arnold holding out his hand to lift him up from the road (and from the past into the present). As the two return to the rez, Victor now says, "Let me hold on to Dad," marking his personal transformation and reconciliation with his dead father and with the past. As Eyre has said, "It's a story about forgiving our fathers. And more so, it's a story about home," with Thomas always understanding what home means but Victor having to discover it. Indeed, as Victor picks over Arnold's few belongings in his trailer, he finds a family picture with the word "Home" inscribed on the back, a moment that results in Victor's cutting his "warrior" braids as a sign of his shift to a new identity (and mirroring his father's own hair-cutting after the initial fire). Thomas in the voice-over refers to this moment as a "ceremony" now over, further highlighting Victor's important shift "from denial to being angry . . . the first step towards healing."[81]

This suggests the personal journey of Victor and Thomas, "children born of flame and ash," toward understanding and healing, with the motif of fire a key marker of their stages of discovery, from the fire that kills Thomas's parents, started accidentally by Arnold, through the ritualistic purification by burning of Arnold's trailer, to the transportation of his ashes from Phoenix back to the reservation, then split half and half, with some scattered in the river at Spokane Falls so he might rise "like a salmon." Fire is also suggested in the film's title, an ironic reminder of stereotyping and also a message about communication, "about calls of distress, calls for help," for as Alexie has said, "that's really what this movie is about." In translating aspects of his novel into the film, Alexie admits he was at a different point in his own life, having given up alcohol and willing to move away from representing the traumas of "addictions or dysfunctions within the community," toward "looking for the causes of that behavior," creating "more of a whole journey [in which] you get there and you get back."[82] Owens famously accused Alexie of being a

"Chief Doom" Indian presenting "just one side of Indian existence . . . conform[ing] readily to Euramerican readers' expectations that American Indians are doomed by firewater," and although, as Alexie has admitted himself, this might have some truth in his early work "soaked in alcohol," his collaboration with Eyre shows a significant shift toward examining different perspectives with humor and healing.[83] Kilpatrick follows the Owens line in her comments about the film as "devoid of much hope for the future," missing its central point: to deliberately present Indian communities and individuals as complex and variable, not static and defined by good/evil dichotomies.[84] This is what Alexie meant by the "whole journey" in the film, one that moves the audience through a series of episodes of revelation as the past is drawn into the present, like the car driven by the Native girls Velma and Lucy in the film moving backward to go forward, a metaphor for the way the narrative functions. The loss and absence of the "vanishing" Indian father, in part a deeper metaphor about Indian historical defeat and cultural erasure, has to be retrieved and reworked rather than allowed to fester as an open wound in Victor's static life on the reservation. Within the film, the motif of lying marks this transition, moving Victor from his view of Arnold as a "liar" and of white culture as lying to his community, toward a modified position when a white woman vouches for him after the car wreck and a white policeman sides with him, and amplified in Thomas's final question: "Do you know why your dad really left?" This brings Victor's more conciliatory response, "He didn't mean to, Thomas." These words, like the cutting of his hair, connect Victor back through time to his father, who at the beginning of the film has saved Thomas from the fire but, when thanked for doing a good thing, says, "I didn't mean to." In a clever reversal Thomas now "saves" Victor and, in his final voice-over "vision" of the future, as the camera pans across the landscape, comments on this complex theme of reconciliation: "How do we forgive our fathers? Maybe in a dream. Do we forgive our fathers for leaving us too often or forever? . . . Do we forgive our fathers in our age or theirs? Or in their deaths, saying it to them or not saying it." In the midst of this voice-over we see Victor throwing Arnold's ashes into the raging river from the literal (and metaphoric) bridge in an act of hope and rebirth, recalling Thomas's earlier vision of rising like a salmon. With this visual trace in our minds, Thomas's final words have a pertinent and, as ever, provocative meaning: "If we forgive our fathers, what is left?" Perhaps what is left is healing, forgiving both Indian and white "fathers" so that some "bridge" can be formed out of the purifying ceremonies of fire and water, and perhaps what is left is the warrior literally poised on the bridge over the raging river, crying out in relief and anger, or perhaps it is the motion of the camera and the river driving us on to an equally uncertain and irresolvable future. These possibilities, the film's signals of smoke, are, I believe, what Eyre meant when he commented that he was particularly interested in "where the movie ends," since it was "really a beginning point for a lot of the Pandora's Box, as it were, of what is Indian Country and how . . . it relate[s] to America."[85] Like Vizenor, Eyre in many respects refuses "monologic realism and representation," opting instead for "alternative actions and responses," encouraging the viewer to engage further with the text and follow its many lines of flight.[86]

The final gesture of *Smoke Signals* is repeated at the conclusion of Eyre's second film, *Skins*, as Rudy stands atop Mount Rushmore with his arms raised having just poured red paint down the face of George Washington, the mythic "father" of the United States. As a commentary on the healing suggested in his first film, this again presents us with a "Pandora's Box" of possible interpretations, from resistance to reconciliation, marking an interesting political shift in Eyre's work.[87] In *Skins*, which is based on Adrian Louis's 1995 novel of the same name, Eyre again took on and transformed an example of what Owens calls "Chief Doom" literature, "paint[ing] the most despairing and destructive picture of Indian America we have yet seen."[88] Indeed, Elizabeth Cook-Lynn attacked Louis as "anti-Indian," guilty of "demonizing our own people . . . self-flagellation . . . self-loathing."[89] As he did with Alexie's prose, Eyre deliberately challenges himself to adapt Louis's dark text into a potentially "bridging" work portraying, without doubt, the complexities and struggles of reservation life, but tempered by reconciliation and hope. As a post-9/11 film ending with such a gesture of resistance, it has been criticized as an anti-American statement, but Eyre has been quick to correct this in a very particular way, stating that it is ultimately "a very patriotic movie because it makes a mockery of the patriotism that's found waving a flag on your front porch in middle America" and reminds Americans, "as we run around the world as the world's humanitarians," of the "hy-pocrisy" closer to home in Indian country.[90] For him, "patriotism . . . is about exercising your right to speak or to exercise the democracy that you have in an effort to make what we have better in this American fam-ily," to "dialogue about how to make our country better." In order to do this, he continues, Americans must know their own history, especially concerning Native Americans, rather than "sweep [it] under the rug."[91] This suggests also Eyre's commitment, not to "self-loathing," but to use his film narratives to interrogate U.S. ideological grids and Indians' em-placement within them.

Thus *Skins*, like *Smoke Signals*, charts reservation life and the journey of two men (here brothers, Rudy and Mogie Yellow Lodge) toward forms of redemption, but its context has a much more overt cultural politics and historical edge that the film unravels within its narrative. Eyre's purpose was clear: "It's not about romanticizing who we were. It's about look-ing at who we are, or some of what we are, and reclaiming the good with the bad, in order to *move forward*. I'm not leaving it to the American public or the white liberal to say who we are" (emphasis added).[92] This process of movement ("transmotion") takes many forms in the film, as in *Smoke Signals*, such as in representing the reservation as diverse and complex, combining traditional ways, poverty, and violence with univer-sal popular cultural forms and lots of humor. Mogie wears a Madonna "Like a Virgin" T-shirt throughout the film, boys listen to rap and rock on their beatbox, and Rudy is nicknamed Rudolph the red-nosed rein-deer by Mogie and said to look like Jay Leto and act like Clint Eastwood and Rambo. Although distinct and "sovereign," the reservation is con-nected to the wider United States and the world in a way that allows Eyre to make further political connections in terms of the film's final scene especially. This place and its people are not statically trapped in the past, except by the limitation imposed on them by social and eco-nomic deprivation and cultural stereotypes. In another sense, the film "bridges" through its production, for as Alexie has pointed out, it was a "multicultural" film—"he's [Eyre's] Cheyenne, who was adopted out and raised by white folks, making a movie based on a book written by a Paiute who lives on the Lakota-Sioux rez [with] a screenplay written by a white woman on a movie produced by white people and financed by European money."[93] His point is that "an insurgent Native American counter-cinema" has been for Eyre rather more of a cooperative action, a hybrid (or "mixedblood") creation from the very beginning, working between various lines of demarcation, which in different ways contribute to the challenging of fixed or closed perspectives.

Its setting on Pine Ridge Reservation immediately enables the film to draw upon the history of Wounded Knee as a reference point: "one of the icons of what Indian country is," says Eyre, a place with immense social problems as well as "spiritual strength . . . in those communities." This is all part of Eyre's sense of what he calls "dialogue" (another facet of his "bridging" or "in-between" position), that is, of presenting different facets of reservation life while refusing to "shy away from the issues."[94] Once again, utilizing his position "between two places" as a "bridge," he dramatizes through the struggle between brothers Mogie and Rudy (as with Victor and Thomas, or Kenny Williams and Annie Shorty in *Edge of America*) a version of what he has described elsewhere as a motif of "Two Spirits" exploring differences and tensions within the community and within value systems.[95] The film opens with a series of "dialogues" established, with actual footage from N BC *Nightly News* of the poverty and alcoholism on Pine Ridge and President Clinton talking of the "tools and support to get done what you want to do for yourself"; between the iconography of Mount Rushmore and the site of the massacre of Wounded Knee; and more generally between perceived images of "indianness" and the often brutal hardships of the contemporary reservation. These historical tensions prepare the audience for the central "dialogue" played out in the film between Mogie and Rudy, brothers divided by their differing responses to this experience of objectification and "victimry" (by TV documentary and politicians), tribal history, and political action.

The title *Skins* had a specific meaning for Eyre, suggesting something of the dialogic structure of this film, "defin[ing] what the word means to Indians" (brotherhood, community, belonging) while reminding them of "the forces that live around them."[96] Rudy is associated with those "forces" through the trickster spider, a Lakota spirit, who will "sneak up and mess with your life," something Mogie had told him after he was being bitten as a child. The reemergence of the spirit as spider and later as a stone that knocks Rudy out marks a significant development in his life, as he takes on the role of a vigilante to placate his growing frustration at conditions on the reservation. Rudy is a contradictory figure in true trickster fashion, a tribal policeman *and* a vigilante, an upholder of law *and* a transgressor, torn between laughter and anger, between a brutal, abusive past and survival in the present. In one scene after Mogie's buddy Verdell has been killed by a bear trap, a Native woman calls Rudy "Clint Eastwood," underlining still further his confusion of identities. Through him Eyre "offer[s] a social commentary in an effort to improve who we are as Americans," forcing the audience to confront their own assumptions about Native identity while witnessing Rudy's struggle with himself and his brother, and seeing the diverse aspects of reservation life in the process.[97] In the course of the film, as Rudy becomes more frustrated with the reservation's problems (its "terminal creeds" of violence, alcoholism, abuse, and poverty) and with the law offering little or no solution, he turns both to the direct action of vigilantism (beating up two murderers and burning down a liquor store) *and* to the spiritual ways of tribal religion, seeking guidance from a medicine man who tells him "Human beings don't control anything, spirits do," visiting a sweat lodge, and making tobacco-tie charms against the influence of the trickster spider. Through these actions Rudy articulates the modern Indian moving between worlds, forging a community in which the old ways and modernity might find some confluence, mutuality, and harmony. This is a constant theme in Eyre's work, emerging centrally in his adaptation of Tony Hillerman's novels *Skinwalkers* (2002) and *The Thief of Time* (2004), in which he develops the two tribal cops Jim Chee and Jim Leaphorn as representative aspects of this cultural balancing act. Chee is a trainee medicine man in *Skinwalkers*, referred to as "a cop . . . a medicine man . . . confused," seen participating in various rituals and ceremonies, wary of the dead, and constantly in conflict with his superior, Leaphorn, who is a skeptical, urban Indian of reason and logic, seen (rather tellingly) Googling the word "skinwalkers" to discover something that Chee knows intuitively. In fact, Vizenor used a quotation from Vine Deloria as an epigraph to his book *Earthdivers*, which fits well with this facet of Eyre's work by claiming that modern Indians are engaged in a "schizophrenic balancing act wherein one holds that the creation, migration, and ceremonial stories of the tribe are true and that the Western European view of the world is also true. . . . [T]he trick is somehow to relate what one feels to be with what one is taught to think."[98]

Something of this "balancing act" in Skins is dramatized through Mogie, who is also a trickster figure, despite his (literal) terminal status as an alcoholic. He is always associated with harsh laughter, telling stories, and being deliberately offensive and provocative, flaunting the drunken Indian stereotype that Rudy despises, talking of "pissing his pants," abusing and fighting with his brother, whom he accuses of being assimilationist, pouring beer and ash on the picnic pig roast, and boasting of his sexuality. Like his brother Rudy, though, he is full of contradiction: a youthful football star, Vietnam vet, and family man, now broken down by alcohol and poverty, and yet still questioning of power (the tribal cops, government, white history), politically astute, able to pass on oral history (in trickster form) and love to his son, Herbie. In one key scene, for example, Mogie is seen watching a TV Western and recalling his friendship with one of the Indian performers, which in turn leads him to a description of the testament of American Horse after the Wounded Knee massacre. The shift from "indian" simulation to testimony once again emphasizes the balancing act being played out in the film, as Eyre draws us closer to the "drunken Indian" stereotype while simultaneously presenting a rich, complex, "tricky" character. As Eyre has said about Mogie, he wanted the movie to be "about humanizing an untouchable," "an honouring of a man's life . . . [an] Indian character [that] embraces who he is, despite everything that's going on," expressing "pride and redemption," with humor, in an ambiguous and complex identity.[99] And yet in achieving this Eyre knew you had "to own the good, the bad, and the ugly of yourself . . . all parts of myself that I don't like, but [that] makes me whole as a person."[100] Rudy and Mogie perform this dialogic function in the film, enabling Eyre (as with Victor/Thomas and Chee/Leaphorn) to investigate varying traits of Native culture within contemporary America, employing trickster surprise and humor as a significant tool in this process. Its effects are best described by Mikhail Bakhtin: "Laughter demolishes fear and piety before an object, before a world, making of it an object of familiar contact and thus clearing the ground for an absolutely free investigation of it. . . . Basically this is un-

crowning . . . the destruction of epic distance . . . one can disrespect-
fully walk around whole objects."[101] Humor allows us to be closer to
the world, to investigate it intently and without masking; it strips away
the "simulation" and performs the "balancing act" between "terminal
creeds" and survival, carrying people forward, challenging us with "stories of survivance."

In the final scenes of the film, Rudy's trickster-vigilantism and Mogie's political-social outrage fuse in an act of spectacular protest art
based on the latter's earlier-stated desire to "Blow the nose off George
Washington at Rushmore." Cook-Lynn has described Rushmore as
the "epitome" of colonial "arrogance" and central to what Indians in
South Dakota call "the desecration tour," "the tourist temple of the pro-
fane."[102] Rudy desecrates the desecration by throwing red paint on the
president's face, thereby simultaneously "bloodying" the nose of the
U.S. "father" and turning him "red." This marks Rudy's reconciliation
with his now dead brother in a gesture of protest against the "hypocrisy"
of the national monument that famously includes no Native figures.[103]
In his protest Rudy defiantly raises his arms into the air and shouts (as
Victor does in *Smoke Signals*), remembering his past in a series of flashbacks, and culminating in a vision of the young Mogie reborn and on the
road heading away from the reservation. This moment is ambiguous,
an "end in motion," requiring the viewer to speculate on its meanings,
and whether it is a futile gesture, a sign of resistance, or a cultural and
personal assertion, it permits Eyre to maintain a vital openness to the
film.[104] Perhaps clues come in two ways: first through the sound track,
whose lyrics speak of "making a noise in the world" where "everyone
has a song"; and second through the camera as it pans across the landscape linking this one action with a wider world outside and to the monument's claims as a statement about democracy. Rudy literally makes his
mark on the "face" of America, stands up for the rights of all people to
be heard and to be included in history. For Eyre, as I said earlier, this is
"patriotic" in a real sense rather than in the frenzied, partial way often
assumed after 9/11, a way that includes a recognition of Native presence.

When the film was completed, Eyre took it on the road to Indian reservations in his "Rolling Rez Tour" to reach the widest Native audience
and engage in debates around the film's issues. However, elsewhere in

the climate of post-9/11 United States it was seen as anti-American in a time of global terror, as if linking Eyre's work with the furor over Ward Churchill's essay "Some People Push Back: On the Justice of Roosting Chickens" (2001), which made connections between the attacks in New York and Washington and the long struggles of Native peoples in the United States.[105] Eyre's defense is that ultimately his film is an affirmation of democracy and dialogue, of speaking out for fundamental rights in the production of better communities in which history is acknowledged and understood, not hidden, where beliefs and traditions are valued, and where all people can and must work together to move the world forward. This begins with his desire to make films "about the spirit of sustaining my own race of people," but through this to direct us outward to more global issues of trust and dialogue, a theme he has more recently incorporated in both Edge of America (2003) and his Smithsonian "signature" short film, A Thousand Roads (2005). The very title Edge of America and the way it was represented on the film titles (with a distinct vertical line between "Edge of" and "America") suggests Eyre's intention to once again explore division and bridging. Of course that line functions, as in Derrida's work, as a borderline that both divides and connects, an idea echoed in the work of Gloria Anzaldúa and exemplified by the anthologies This Bridge Called My Back ("I am a wind-swayed bridge, a crossroads inhabited by whirlwinds") and This Bridge We Call Home.[106] Her preface to the latter dwells on the metaphor at length: "Bridges are thresholds to other realities, archetypal primal symbols of shifting consciousness . . . passageways, conduits, and connectors that connote transitioning, crossing borders, and changing perspectives. Bridges span liminal (threshold) spaces between worlds, spaces I call nepantla . . . in-between space, an unstable, unpredictable, precarious, always-in-transition space lacking clear boundaries."[107] Although Eyre never theorized in quite this manner, his comments about creating a "bridge to other people who aren't like us" and his consistent concern for dialogue and journeys of healing and reconciliation draw him close to aspects of Anzaldúa's borderlands sensibility. The reservation exists at the "edge of America," a cutting edge akin to Owens's reappropriated, contested, and equally "unstable" "frontier wherein discourse is multidirectional and hybridized" in contrast with the assumption of "territory" "clearly mapped, fully imagined as a place of containment."[108] It is no coincidence that Williams, in *Edge of America*, is seen struggling to find his way with an official map in the early scenes of the film as he relocates himself on the reservation, while a Native woman tells him "you are lost-er than you know." What constitutes home is a persistent theme in Eyre's films, relating, I would suggest, to his interrogation of identity and cultural belonging. Community is about inclusion, not separatism, about reaching outward while still valuing tradition and the "old ways"; recalling Jace Weaver's words discussed earlier, it makes us "better able to embrace and assimilate the thoughts of Others and of the dominating culture without losing our roots."[109] As Anzaldúa writes, "we define who we are by what we include—what I call the *new tribalism.* . . . Staying 'home' and not venturing out from our own group comes from woundedness, and stagnates our growth. To bridge means loosening our borders, not closing off to others. Bridging is the work of opening the gate to the stranger, within and without" (emphasis added).[110] Thus in *Edge of America*, Williams, lost and referred to as a "black sheep," travels and "bridges" to find a new "home" (appropriately, initially a mobile one in the film, later anchored down by the tires supplied by Native boys) as part of the reservation. In a crucial scene, Cuch (Wes Studi) takes Williams to Shiprock ("the center of two worlds") to explain that "the creator scattered us to the four winds so we could prove we're human by finding our way home. Sometimes you have to go all the way round to find your way [home]."[111] In this scene, Cuch echoes the sentiments of Luci Tapahonso, who has written of her work as a vehicle for reversing the diaspora begun after European invasion, "residing away from my homeland, writing is the means for returning, rejuvenation, and for restoring our spirits to the state of 'hohzo,' or beauty, which is the basis of Navajo philosophy."[112]

This notion of healing is akin to Anzaldúa's "new tribalism," an expanded notion of home that includes and embraces difference through dialogue. But this cannot be a one-way relationship of only learning from Native culture, for that would deny the idea of "bridging." The other side of the dialogue shows Williams as "coach" empowering the downtrodden team, inculcating values of winning and pride, and encouraging them to "spin stories" and lose their "hip-hop attitude" in favor of working together. His simultaneous realization about himself applies universally to the shifting consciousness of the film: "I had the whole world worked out, I knew exactly who my enemy was." Williams's shift is measured in his relations with Annie Shorty, Cuch, and the basketball team he coaches, but most of all with the traditional "elder" Mother Tsosi, whose weaving contains within it a symbolic "flaw" that in many ways relates to the wider significance of Eyre's film. She tells Williams he likes things "his own way," echoing his admission of believing he had the world "worked out," categorized, and framed by his own prejudices, and goes on to tell him of the "imperfection" deliberately built into the Navajo rug, because otherwise "my spirit would be trapped in a perfect design. A flaw lets it out. Flaws keep our feet on Mother Earth." No individual and no system can or should be designed perfectly, for that would trap the spirit and contain the self; they need a "spirit outlet" and a means to get outside this "grid" that promises perfection and absolute order, to remind us of our imperfect humanity. Eyre's films maintain and utilize this "outside"/"outlet" as a device of reflection and questioning.

In *Edge of America* Eyre has opened out the themes of his earlier films to connect to wider issues of race, prejudice, and struggle, showing how life inside the reservation cannot go on without reference to forces beyond it. As Anzaldúa puts it (as an intentional response to 9/11), "Effective bridging comes from knowing when to close ranks to those outside our home, group, community, nation—and when to keep the gates open." Eyre's work is always about home, group, community, and nation and aware of this tension between closure and openness, but above all he shares with Anzaldúa a desire for better communities and nations, breaking through lines of separation to find "links," for "where others saw abysses, they saw bridges spanning those abysses."[113] This desire is clear too in Eyre's *A Thousand Roads* (2005), where four Native stories from Manhattan, Alaska, Peru, and New Mexico reveal shared and universal concerns: "Indian country is really all of us. Wherever we are in this world, we're travelling together on this journey down a thousand roads, all leading home."[114] Despite the difficulties of making films in a Hollywood-dominated climate, Eyre has continued to find ways—through television, cinema, and museum-sponsored work—to produce movies that explore serious and often complex themes in ways that refuse to be simply drawn back into stereotypes and which remain accessible to a wide audience. As he has said, "With my work I like the shades: very rarely are our thoughts really black or white except in the case of our own bias and the limitations of our own experience. We tend to be so limited in our perceptions of what AMERICA is. We don't know about our own history, about being real with those that aren't of us. We need some more social/shared understanding and laughter. There is no one truth to our diversity."[115] In these sentiments Eyre directs us to many of the important features of his films: their refusal to present Indian life as limited, static, or simply a "binary" of us/them; their interest in "diversity"; and their projective vision of shifting perceptions toward "social/shared understanding and laughter." Although strongly rooted in reservation life and tribal culture, Eyre's "communitism" is never inward-looking at the expense of a wider vision, and in this it shares something of Anzaldúa's notion of "new tribalism," "something beyond just nationalism while continuing to connect to our roots . . . nationalism with a twist. . . . It's saying, 'Yes I belong. I come from this particular tribe, but I'm open to interacting with these other people'" (see chapter 2). This is a vision born from being "in-between" many identities, as Eyre has argued consistently, signaled by Anzaldúa's term "nos/otras" suggesting how previously distinct categories have created a "frame of reference" in need of disruption, so "Now 'us' and 'them' are interchangeable. Now there's no such thing as an 'other.' The other is in you, the other is in me. . . . Both traditions are within me . . . we cross into each other's worlds all the time. . . . We all of us find ourselves in the position of being simultaneously insider/outsider. The Spanish word 'nosotras' means 'us.' In theorizing insider/outsider, I write the word with a slash between nos (us) and otras (others). . . . Hopefully sometime in the future we may become nosotras without the slash."[116] In *Edge of America* Eyre gives his clearest indication of this direction in his work, bringing together the racism of and toward both blacks and Indians within the film, showing how mutual understanding and knowledge can bring about change in the "frame of reference," a "bridging" process between cultures and stereotypes that begins to disrupt the "slash." In one exchange a Native woman explains to the black coach Williams, "You are angry because you are a black man in America. Well, we are Indian, get over it and get on or get the hell out." However and wherever it occurs, Eyre asserts this capacity for "seeing double," as Anzaldúa terms it, "first from the perspective of one culture, then from the perspective of another. Seeing from two or more perspectives simultaneously renders those cultures transparent," creating a space in which you are "no longer seeing the world the way you were enculturated to see it," and so gradually "as you struggle to form a new identity, a demythologisation of race occurs. You begin to see race as an experience of reality from a particular perspective and a specific time and place (history), not as a fixed feature of personality or identity."[117] Building on the recurrent "Two Spirits" in his films, Eyre's processes of "seeing double" returns us to Vizenor and Owens and their struggles against the "fixing" of identity within an ethnic grid, and their creation of "transmotion" that is maintained and developed in Eyre's works, honoring tribal cultures but without denying their dynamism and evolution. This sense is best captured in the final shots of many of his films that draw the audience away rhizomatically into the landscape itself, along rivers, into mountains, and across deserts, as if to remind us all of a "potent sense of interrelatedness" and that "The pulse of existence, the heart of the universe is fluid. Identity [and community], like a river, is always changing, always in transition, always in nepantla. . . . You begin to define yourself in terms of who you are becoming, not who you have been."[118]

7. POSTWESTERN GENERATIONS?
Douglas Coupland's "Plastic Radiant Way"

This is why the imaginary and the real must be, rather, like two juxtaposable or superimposable parts of a single trajectory, two faces that ceaselessly interchange with one another, a mobile mirror. Thus Australian Aborigines link nomadic itineraries with dream voyages, which together compose "an interstitching of routes," "an immense cut-out [découpé] of space and time that must be read like a map." At the limit, the imaginary is a virtual image that is interfused with the real object, and vice versa, thereby constituting a crystal of the unconscious.
Gilles Deleuze

The Double West

Mike Davis writes of how the belief of Native American prophet Wovoka in the Ghost Dance as an apocalyptic reminder of the instability of a white West is still alive and evident as one surveys the "artificial world" of L.A.'s "neon landscapes"—"Turnerian history . . . stripped down to its ultimate paranoia," he calls it. But as he reminds us, in the Ghost Dance tradition "this end point is also paradoxically the point of renewal and restoration."[1] This association of apocalypse and renewal, of ending and beginning, has a curious resonance for this chapter as I continue my efforts to show how westness is figured in a range of texts. For here I wish to consider how urban writers associated with "blank generation" or Generation X, whose work is often seen as nihilist, might be seen as contributing greatly to a rhizomatic rereading of what constitutes the West. The epigraph from Deleuze suggests my approach here, charting "the imaginary and the real" Wests as "juxtaposable or superimposable parts of a single trajectory, two faces that ceaselessly interchange with one another, a mobile mirror." Thus, juxtaposed with the apocalyptic is always something else shadowing it, a "ghost dance" of the "virtual," some potential within the destructive that for Douglas Coupland, the central focus of this chapter, is always associated with the multiple implications of westness.

The Led Zeppelin epigraph to Bret Easton Ellis's L.A. novel *Less Than Zero* (1985) reads, "There's a feeling I get when I look to the West," directing us to its acute observations of an excessive, self-obsessed, consumerist culture where life is defined less by relationships and memories than by billboards, designer labels, and MTV. The utopian hopes and dreams of the "Sunshine" region have been broken, wasted, or rewritten as "Noir." The novel's first words are "People are afraid to merge on freeways in Los Angeles," a comment that both sets the tone for what is to come and pays homage to Ellis's major influence, Joan Didion, and her *Play It as It Lays*.[2] In the first of a series of stunning motifs that conclude the novel, Ellis writes of "a street called Sierra Bonita in Hollywood" where "people saw ghosts; apparitions of the Wild West" haunting the wealthy suburbs, with Indians on horseback, carrying tomahawks, intruding, like the return of the repressed, into the self-obsessed lives of these "new frontiersmen."[3] In L.A.'s new frontier, history has been forgotten in the headlong rush into the future, where environmental destruction and genocide are simply the price paid for the good life experienced by the book's young characters. Yet the past will not "disappear here" (a recurring slogan in the novel), for it remains, haunting the mind of Clay, the central character, and the streets of Los Angeles like these ghostly Indians, or the "covered wagon" that caused a man to crash his car into a palm tree. The West, in all its real and imagined pervasiveness, cannot be evaded, becoming translated here into the Indian *and* covered wagon intervening into the glossy, gridlike order of suburban streets and lives like the return of the repressed. The turmoil of Ellis's West, torn between past, present, and future, is reflected in the landscape that intrudes into the fragile human environment, like a sinister reminder of that past, of "houses falling, slipping down the hills in the middle of the night," of "little girls" singing of destruction—"*Smack, smack, I fell in a crack . . . Now, I'm part of the debris*"—all mirrored in the novel's atmosphere of careless, human brutality, "of parents who were so hungry and unfulfilled that they ate their own children." The apocalyptic present and the repressed past erupt into the novel as a wake-up call to those, like Clay, living within the contradictory, simulated spaces of this New West where feelings have been replaced by advertisements. At one point his contained, troubled self is likened to "this glass paperweight with a small fish trapped in it, its eyes staring out helplessly, almost as if it was begging to be freed, and I start to wonder, if the fish is already dead, does it even matter?"[4]

270

As the novel closes, images accumulate to reinforce this sense of the West's uncanny capacity to unsettle and disrupt its own "homely" dreamscape. Juxtaposed with a trip out to "an old deserted carnival" and the sound of a coyote howling in the desert are an Elvis Costello poster with its "eyes . . . slightly off-center," echoing F. Scott Fitzgerald's eyes of T. J. Eckleburg in The Great Gatsby, looking down upon the room emblazoned, ironically, with the word "Trust," and a tourist poster of California "old and torn down the middle and tilted and hanging unevenly." This powerful montage spells out a vision of the contemporary West as a tension-filled space of lost dreams: part carnival, part degraded, lopsided illusion, part ghostly, natural past. At this moment, seemingly provoked into reflection by these images, Clay believes "it was time to go back," to the East, to his own personal past, and also into the forgotten past of the West, to understand how this world "so violent and malicious" was formed.[5] These contradictions in Less Than Zero can be seen in the novel's double use of Palm Springs: as Clay's childhood home visited because "he wanted to remember the way things were," but also the place where his father goes for a tan, a hair transplant, and an expensive face-lift, which "looks pretty healthy if you don't look at him for too long." Palm Springs functions as an important counter to L.A.'s depthlessness, a kind of "Twilight Zone" signifying a conjunction of past and present, on the edge of the desert with its resonant reminders of another intrusive, more primal West of coyotes, rattlesnakes, wind, and intense sun: "if you looked past the house and into the desert, all there was was blackness. No cars passed and I thought I saw a rattlesnake slither into the garage. The darkness, the wind, the rustling from the hedges . . . all had an eerie effect on me and I ran inside and turned all the lights on and got into bed and fell asleep, listening to the strange desert wind moan outside my window."[6] From "outside" Clay's contained and uniform world comes an alternative West that produces genuine emotion in him, provoking memory, fear, and a more poetic language in stark contrast to the fragmented, stifled forms used elsewhere in the narrative.

This "double" West, simultaneously utopian and apocalyptic, that Ellis began to explore through the language of a new youth culture is, I believe, crucial to an understanding of Douglas Coupland's work, beginning with Generation X (1991), a novel also set in Palm Springs. It is as if Coupland, picking up on the Ellis image of Clay's father, wants to examine the ambivalent landscapes of the New West precisely and deliberately *"for too long,"* journeying into them, reflecting upon them, and dramatizing his findings in fiction and essays. The youth cultural malaise of Ellis's "brat pack" boomers is now refocused around Coupland's Generation X busters, whose goal is to question and seek meaning in a western twilight zone overrun with consumer waste and rampant mall culture, but enticingly edged by the blank spaces of the desert. These are the *shin jin rui,* the "new human beings," a new generation "purposefully hiding itself" from the mainstream, "camouflaged" in the space of the West and able to reflect critically upon the rat race it despises.[7] To pick up on Ellis's image, it is as if the look of the Elvis Costello poster is the starting point for this Xer sensibility; "looking out the window, *beyond,* into the night, and his face looks almost *alarmed* at what he might be seeing, the word 'Trust' above the worried face" (emphasis added).[8] As I will suggest throughout this section, Coupland's exploration of the West involves an ambivalent attempt not only to register alarm at the products of Ellis's world but also to reflect upon that world and look beyond it in search of renewed trust and the redemption of hope. As Douglas Rushkoff put it in quite Deleuzian terms, "GenX refuses to mourn. . . . Instead, we celebrate the recycled imagery of our media and take pride in our keen appreciation of the folds within the creases of our wrinkled popular culture."[9]

GenX West

Coupland's work as a whole wants to examine the world at this point "less than zero" and try to fathom how it arrived there and where it might now lead. The West, as in Ellis's fiction, encapsulates America's dream of modernity, of progress, human perfectibility, technology, individualism, and conquest, the ultimate expression of the New World vision, humanity's "second chance." However, Coupland wants to record this failure *and* see beyond it, to generate some redemptive possibility. The ghostly, apocalyptic figure of Jared in *Girlfriend in a Coma* sums this up very well: "Most people, given a second chance, fuck it up completely. It's one of those laws of the universe that you can't shake. People, I have noticed, only seem to learn once they get a third chance—after losing and wasting vast sums of time, money, youth, and energy . . . but they still learn, which is the better thing in the end."[10] The notion of the West as Manifest Destiny, as something "given," like a gift, contributes to this failure, for Coupland implies it led to false security and waste when, in fact, "Destiny is what we work toward," always containing within itself something *virtual* ("ideal but not abstract, real but not actual").[11] As Rob Shields writes, "The virtual implies a willingness to believe in the reality of dreams, and marks the concern with history and the past as well as creative change," and out of this matrix Coupland's writings contribute to and extend western studies, echoing Deleuze's epigraph at the same time.[12]

Initially, Coupland explores the West and its component discourses (its westness) from a position of ambivalence, a Generation X "position" ironically aware of the simultaneous layers of history, mythic baggage, mediation, and transcendent promise, but in subsequent works this is reviewed from different and varied perspectives. What Rushkoff, sounding like Deleuze, called the "folds within the creases" become the minute details and everyday hiddenness that Coupland's work brings to the surface in its multiple explorations of the West's "recycled imagery"—from Disneyland, to Los Alamos, to Silicon Valley, and from Gap culture to beauty pageants. In *Life after God*, the specific western context is made most explicit:

> It was the life of children of the children of the pioneers—life after God—a life of earthly salvation on the edge of heaven. Perhaps this is the finest thing to which we may aspire, the life of peace, the blurring between real life and dream life—and yet I find myself speaking these words with a sense of doubt.
>
> I think there was a trade-off somewhere along the line. I think the price we paid for our golden life was an inability to fully believe in love; instead we gained an irony that scorched everything it touched. And I wonder if this irony is the price we paid for the loss of God.[13]

Coupland has further defined his sense of irony as "to have the ability to contain opposing ideas inside your head without going crazy," famously echoing Fitzgerald's *The Crack-Up* (see introduction) and suggesting the kind of "double vision" I have discussed throughout this book.[14] With the old certainties gone or under question, this "doubling" irony helps in the quest to comprehend the consequences of the promise, of "the price we paid for our golden life" in the West, contributing to a doubting style that interrogates the complex and layered nature of this experience without resorting to any single solution or fixed answer. This is, in the final analysis, a life *after* God, *after* Manifest Destiny, and *after* the neat lines of the frontier myth and its many "gridded" forms have been incorporated into a mediated, plural West where stories overlap and mutate constantly. It is, indeed, a *postwestern* sensibility (*after* the [traditional] West) formed in total awareness of the simulated and mythic narratives that have constructed the discursive West and yet retrieving something from within them of beauty and value to contribute to alternative creations and emergent new stories. Again and again, the question surfaces, what is the price we paid for this West?

Coupland's outsider status adds to my catalog of voices already discussed in this book whose work refracts any settled or unitary vision of the West through divergent, quizzical views. As a Canadian born on an air force base in Germany, Coupland further contributes to this doubting style, marking his work with what Robert Kroetsch once called "a shadowed writing," always uneasy and aware of the presence of others and the attractions of their world, while having long ago abandoned any "sentimentalizing [of] the mono-culture."[15] In his version of what Paul Giles called "looking both ways," Coupland has developed an ambivalent, critical, and questioning stance through which to examine the West and "the price we paid for our golden life" at the millennial junction of the twentieth and twenty-first centuries.[16] As the quotation above shows, Coupland is aware of the dominant and pervasive narratives of the West as a place of promise and renewal both inside and outside the United States, whether through images of the old frontier days, the 1960s hippie era, or even *Melrose Place*, and understands the need to analyze these "scripts," since "Ours was a life lived in paradise and thus it rendered any discussion of transcendental ideas pointless. Politics, we supposed, existed elsewhere in a televised non-paradise; death was something similar to recycling."[17] "Maybe," he writes in *Generation X*, "we were all promised heaven in our lifetimes, and what we ended up with can't help but suffer by comparison."[18] The reality is that the West has for so long functioned as an archetypal metanarrative, a big story now condensed to absurdly reduced "blips and chunks and snippets on bumpers," to clichés and mythic fragments endlessly circulated with increasingly less meaning by each generation. Coupland's West is part of "this weird global McNugget culture . . . [where] our ideas and objects and activities [are] being made of fake materials ground up and reshaped into precisely measurable units [and] entered into some rich guy's software spreadsheet program."[19] Thus Coupland's Xer critical sensibility, beginning with "an irony that scorched everything it touched" and then developing through other modes of commentary, including "transcendental ideas," "politics," and "death," supplies a powerful set of postwestern tools and approaches that enable us to examine the meanings of westness from vital, multiple, and contradictory perspectives.[20] Rushkoff's definition of Xer sensibility is a helpful guide to Coupland's initial impetus as a potential postwestern critic:

> GenX is a life philosophy designed to help us cope with the increasingly and disorientingly rapid deflation or our society, both financially and culturally . . . to reject the traditional values and linear reasoning of the dominant culture . . . [and] to derive meaning from the random juxtapositions of TV commercials, candy wrappers, childhood memories, and breakfast treats . . . to deconstruct and delight in the Toys R Us wasteland of cultural junk while warding off the meaningless distractions of two-party politics, falling interest rates, and phantom career opportunities.[21]

Living in this world, Coupland's characters are confronted by the contradictions of a postmodern West full of rampant technologies, extreme commodification, cosmetic surgery, nuclear landscapes, pollution, and simulation *as well as* the persistent, traditional stories of "freedom," "choice," and new starts associated with the region. Thus in *Generation X*, West Palm Springs is described like a Stephen Shore or Michael Ormerod photograph: "a modern ruin . . . an abandoned Texaco gasoline station surrounded by a chain link fence, and lines of dead *Washingtonia* palms that seem to have been agent-oranged. The mood is vaguely reminiscent of a Vietnam War movie set."[22] In *Miss Wyoming*, Cheyenne, famously visited in Kerouac's *On the Road* (see chapter 5), is described as an archetypal New West town: "past a thousand KFCs, past four hundred Gaps, two hundred Subways and through dozens of intersections over-loaded with a surfeit of quality-of-life refugees from the country's other large cities, with nary a cowboy hat or crapped-out Ranchero wagon to be seen in any direction."[23]

The residual potential energy of this hybrid, conflictual culture is too often sanitized, reduced, and contained (what Rushkoff called "defla-tion"), making it feel like a one-dimensional, framed "color cartoon," with bodies entrapped in offices like "veal fattening pens," "speckled in sores and zits . . . colons so tied in knots that we never thought we'd have a bowel movement again. Our systems had stopped working, jammed with the odor of copy machines, Wite-Out, the smell of bond paper." The photograph Andy has above his desk in *Generation X* typifies these images of fixed lives: "my *framed* photo of the whaling ship *crushed* and *stuck*, possibly *forever*, in the glassy Antarctic *ice*" (emphasis added).[24] In these images of containment, stagnation, and disease, Coupland's am-bivalent Xers convey the horror of fixity, of the West's potential and en-ergy immobilized by a gridlike existence of ruins and malls, conditioned and emptied out of all alternative, meaningful stories, afflicted by what he later terms "denarration."[25] In *Shampoo Planet*, one character imag-ines a world (rather like this one) where "History repeats itself" and hu-mans are obsessed by "organizing . . . [and] building fences around bits of land," while another describes "the extraterrestrial tangerine grid of Los Angeles" with its "amber palms and freeways . . . legislated memo-ries of Disneyland." Similarly, in *Polaroids from the Dead*, Los Angeles is where "grids overlap other grids overlap grids? Aqueducts, power lines, freeways, signage," and in *Miss Wyoming* it is "fast food America and its endless paved web."[26] This raft of images culminates in his scathing portrait of Brentwood, Los Angeles, a place with no memory, a "place where there is no 'here,'" an orderly, simulated world with its "covenant of invisibility . . . a consensual denial of civic randomness and chaos," "designed to emulate the country," and with a "chocolate box of archi-tectural styles." This is the "West Coast . . . a laboratory of denarration," where in "denarrated" spaces, like Brentwood, one dominant narra-tive has taken hold, yet below the surface (or amid the grids) of such structured, contained environments, Coupland finds a secret history of trauma, of Marilyn Monroe, O. J. Simpson, and the Menendez brothers revealing a startling counternarrative, a hidden story.[27] Richard Linklater, a westerner himself, who directed Slacker and is often bracketed with Coupland as the creator of Gen X, has commented in a similar way that, contrary to popular myth, his generation "had everything to say but was saying it in a completely new way. It was a multitude of voices coexisting and combining and all adding up to something that certainly 'meant' something but couldn't easily be classified."[28]

Like Linklater's "multitude of voices," what Coupland's characters desire and the author aims to present is the friction that fiction creates, to escape and reimagine their "streamlined narrow-mindedness" and to reenergize their lives through the remobilization of existence along various, uncertain paths in search of "feeling," memory, love, and beauty. Even the drugs don't work anymore (as they might have done in the sixties) and are just another form of containment and fakery, what one narrator calls appropriately "cosmetic surgery of the brain."[29] In a world of global standardization and uniformity where something as complex and contradictory as the West has become just another McNugget or theme-park experience and everybody wants to be a celebrity, there is a desperate need for reinvention and alterity, for challenge and provocation, for "dreaming of another world where complex issues refuse to masquerade as oversimplicities."[30] Coupland's work shares much with Arjun Appadurai's ideas about how "The imagination is today a staging ground for action, and not only for escape," "projective . . . a prelude to some sort of expression." Perhaps the West has always stimulated "imagination," "action," and "escape" to different degrees, so it is unsurprising that Coupland should so often invoke it in his novels as a space for renewal, for "the imagination as social practice," as Appadurai puts it. However, Coupland's utilization of westness in his work is "neither purely emancipatory nor entirely disciplined but is a space of contestation," constantly challenging his characters who live in-between the ruins of the mythic Old West and the New while still functioning.[31]

Coupland's work captures these curious contradictions of living in a New West that not only has a fixation on the Old West's myths and dreams created by other generations in what seems like "another universe" but also has the everyday experiences of a region polluted by atomic and chemical industries, riddled with crumbling malls, and McJobs. How does one live, his characters ask, in a world where real-life disaster movies "are all projecting so vividly inside our heads" and the whole region is suffering from "information supersaturation"?[32] The danger is of a "denarrated" region—or, more accurately, a region whose stories have become so all-pervasive to become almost irrelevant, *over*-narrating itself into oblivion. Just as Marilyn Monroe, according to Coupland, became "post-famous" through a similar process of "information overload," so the West has become postwestern, its stories taken for granted and worn thin in the telling, leaving only "a certain blankness in the eyes," demanding some radically new and different stories to form.[33] Coupland's work is interested in exploring this dual process of postwestern denarration and the possibilities of emergent and residual stories being revalued or promoted. One way characters cope with this in *Generation X* is by creating a parallel, "storied" West, "a sad [denarrated] Everyplace" called "Texlahoma . . . a mythic world . . . [in which] to set many of our stories," a composite of all the characteristics of the contained and contradictory society they aim to then enliven and redeem with new stories.[34] Ironically, in quite a traditional manner, Coupland's work exposes and critiques the postmodern West and then seeks to re-invent it, to redeem it through new stories, questions, and quests that carry his characters beyond stasis and fixity and toward renewal and hope. Like Walter Benjamin's work, Coupland's writing might be seen as engaged in the fictional dialectic of breaking apart *and* rescuing myth, exposing damaging western mythologies while simultaneously redeeming those elements within worth holding on to—the dream that is still present at the awakening.[35] As Claire says in *Generation X*, "it's not healthy to live life as a succession of isolated little cool moments. 'Either our lives become stories, or there's just no way to get through them.'" What matters is "to tell stories and to make our own lives worthwhile tales in the process."[36]

Coupland is, however, always wary (as are his characters) of seeking any absolute truth, any point of essence or origin that might claim to fully explain their lives or the West in which they live. Instead, his work is arranged in different configurations that draw attention to these myths while dialoguing with them. The stories created are not coherent or overarching but may be "assembled in startling juxtapositions which engender surprise and recognition"; thus in their discontinuous and fragmented forms these stories "give the lie to forms of representation and historical practices which emphasize only continuity and progress."[37] To borrow a conceptualization from Deleuze, Coupland's work can be seen as "cartographic" rather than "archaeological" in that it is not concerned with penetrating down through the layers to some final point of truth about the West or about identity (its essence or roots) but instead uncovers how both are like maps, "superimposed in such a way that each map finds itself modified in the following map," revealing "impasses and breakthroughs . . . thresholds and enclosures . . . trajectories and becomings." The political "unconscious" revealed through Coupland's work is not one of "commemoration," looking back to origins, but one of "mobilization" whose objects "take flight rather than remaining buried in the ground."[38] The stories and the critique "mobilize" thought, sending the reader's mind off in all directions, and yet always simultaneously aware of the mythic framework from which these lives are in flight. One way this can be seen in action in his work is through its transnational qualities, with characters who travel both within the West and beyond it, bringing back from "outside" ideas, objects, and stories that contribute to a continually adjusting sense of identity and place (their "inside"). Thus in *Shampoo Planet* Tyler visits Europe and notices on his return how his photographs show a "trend . . . of corporate logos having quietly inserted themselves into my memories. U.S. pizza franchises. . . . Cowboy cigarettes and courier vans . . . 'cola totems'—cylindrical poster pillories papered to resemble cans of cola." His comments on this are revealing: "Strange how I never even noticed these logos while I was actually there, but now I'm home there's no way to excise them from my hard-copy memories." In the same book, European tourists go West wearing "cowboy hats, ironed cigarette-legged jeans, and tan suede cowboy boots," "drifting through town 'discovering the Wild West' while maxing out *Papa's* Crédit Lyonnaise bankcard."[39] As people travel in the global age they carry with them and exchange stories and images of westness as pop-cultural capital, like forms of financial transaction, recycling myths and stories, and coming to moments of epiphany about Americanization and transnational affinities. What Coupland understands, above all, is the West's currency, its constant mutation, and its global reach as a "traveling" and fluent discourse.

In *Generation X* he constructs an intensive map of stories told by his young characters who have escaped the confinements of their parents' world to "become" something else in the desert of Palm Springs. As Deleuze writes, it is "becoming that turns the most negligible of trajectories, or even fixed immobility, into a voyage; and it is the trajectory that turns the imaginary into a becoming."[40] Writing or storytelling, like all art, can achieve this mixture of "trajectories and becomings," laying out paths to follow whose directions are multiple and unknown. In this sense, Coupland's work often appears fragmentary because it is moving "in the direction of the ill-formed or the incomplete," actualizing writing/stories as a process that relates to lived experience, and hence to the notion of "becoming," not as a final point, but always as "between" or "among." In this way writing is a "bastard" form, belonging to no single root, no originary "parents," but always divergent and rhizomatic, "the process or drift" that creates "paths" to follow through and beyond the work itself.[41] As a character in *Life after God* puts it, "It felt good to be moving . . . to look for the drift-stuff."[42] Coupland's characters are endlessly "voyaging," seeking out new places from which to "reformat" their lives, imitating the "dream" of the West for a new "awakened" age where total immersion in the old "traditional templates" is no longer sufficient and where the "drift-stuff," with all its inherent uncertainties, may be their most adequate alternative.[43] Throughout his work we encounter the West's "reductive materialism" while being encouraged to see beyond it and "substitute an expressive materialism" that "might create multiple new paths or synapses, not already given—new connections."[44]

In *Generation X* the West still offers the possibility of a "clean slate" from which to build these new connections/stories, continuing to act as a landscape through which people might transcend the crushing weight of a history written by others. Coupland still acknowledges the association of youth with the West, sending his new generation to the desert to "deprogram" themselves from their inherited lives. The expectations inherent in this history further add to the containment of his characters, who long for "less past" and "to erase all traces of history . . . [to] just empty my brain. . . . Clean your slate. Think life out. Lose your unwanted momentums." Thus, in rejecting other people's "history" and their "legislated nostalgia" (dreams, expectations, and myths) imposed from outside, they might "try and read the letter inside," creating alternative stories that "dream" different histories.[45] In *Miss Wyoming*, both lead characters, Susan Colgate and John Johnson, whose "cosmetic-sounding" surnames suggest the artificiality of their lives as Hollywood celebrities, seek alternative paths by disappearing and reinventing their identities away from the "land of gold."[46] John is described like the character in Coupland's story "In the Desert," "walking the country's burning freeways, its yawning malls, its gashes of wilderness, its lightning storms, its factories and its dead spaces" with his stated goal "to erase myself . . . stop being me . . . to disappear."[47] Susan survives a plane crash and wanders away to a temporary, alternative life, away from "the plastic strand of failed identities she'd been beading together across her life," hoping to be "reincarnated," to "meet Jesus" or at least to be "off the hook" as a "failure or a puppet or a has-been celebrity."[48] Both enact self-erasure, like *Generation X*'s talk of erasing history and having a "clean slate," as if to attempt a new start and to begin life again in a reworking of the greatest western dream of turning one's back on the Old World for a New World future. As a European tourist puts it in *Shampoo Planet*, "in the States you're allowed to redo history—erase your tapes and start over again; make a first impression twice."[49] However, as Coupland's work is keen to testify, such erasure is impossible, for to be human is to learn to live with the world's complications, its histories, and its disappointments, seeing them as the layerings of existence along with love and hope. One cannot permanently opt out and choose one life over the other; one must juggle all these lives and identities. As Jean-François Lyotard puts it, it is vital to practice "a resistance to simplism and simplifying slogans, to calls for clearness and straightforwardness, and to desires for a return to solid values," since such a return to simplicity is impossible in such a complex, layered world. Instead, people must learn to live with complexity.[50] Thus Susan and John *can* change, finding love and renewal in the novel, but they cannot "disappear" (like Ellis's L.A. youth) or evade their social commitments to others, or the vital, complex relations that define them as human beings (with family, friends, and history). John is, therefore, appropriately mocked for his desire to escape "on the road" in terms that suggest something of Coupland's own ironic commentary on the Beat generation and on how Xers were often perceived in his earlier work: "The road is *over*. . . . It never even *was*. You're thinking like a kid behind a Starbucks counter sneaking peeks at his Kerouac paperback and writing 'That's so true!' in the margins."[51] However, although total transformation might just be a Kerouacian fantasy, Coupland nonetheless exposes his characters to alternative lives, "as if seeing [their] country for the first time," breaking apart their fixed and segmented worlds and mobilizing them in different ways.[52]

Renewal and Restoration?

The arena for Coupland's characters' "dreaming" is an alternative West that, in *Generation X*, for example, stretches way beyond the United States, traced by the lines of flight from Oregon, to Manitoba, to California, to Nevada, and to Mexico—acting as an antidote to the cluttered and over-defined U.S. West associated with "history . . . turned into a press release, a marketing strategy . . . a cynical campaign tool," a place where houses get confused with shopping malls.[53] Ironically, Palm Springs with its plastic surgeons, German tourists, and "no weather like on TV" epitomizes this manufactured, mediated "history" of the West from which the novel's trajectory moves outward seeking alternative, rhizomatic stories that break off from this version in search of others. Of course, the romantic idea of a new start, as we have seen, is a very western dream and one that, although imagined by Coupland's characters, is unachievable in real terms. What they can achieve, however, is the critical realization of their conditions and a constant reiteration of alternative models of existence (or "stencils," as Coupland calls them) to put alongside the established order of things, to intrude, if you like, into the gridlike structures of the West.[54] Thus in *Shampoo Planet*, Tyler sees in Graumann's Hollywood "a simulated version of its own history—a new structure pretending to be an old structure" and describes Hollywood Boulevard as "a puree of franchise environments and out-and-out sleaze . . . encrusted with crushed hamburgers, IV needles, and lost maps—Disneyland with lesions."[55] And yet amid all this critical, apocalyptic imagery, as an earthquake strikes the city, he senses something else existing, something indestructible, L.A.'s "collective dream": "Cars roll down the city's roads, plants grow from the soil, wealth is generated in its rooms, hope is created and lost and recreated in the minds and souls of its inhabitants, and the city continues its dream and searches for those ideas that will make it strong." Sounding a little like Mike Davis, Coupland articulates the residual hope in a lost world that is like the last chapter of *City of Quartz* (1990), where Fontana, California, is described as "[r]ising from the geological and social detritus that has accumulated at the foot of the Cajon Pass . . . the regional antipode to the sumptuary belts of West L.A. or Orange County."[56] Examining the "deeply emblematic local history" of this place reveals in its layers of dreams, boosterism, decline, and reinvention a political and social archaeology that tells a complex narrative about capitalism in the American West. Davis examines the "human residues" from industrial landscapes that had once dominated Fontana, which in its boom time of the 1940s "was a colorful but dissonant *bricolage* of Sunkist growers, Slovene chicken ranchers, gamblers, mobsters, over-the-road truckers, industrialized Okies, *braceros*, the Army Air Corps . . . and transplanted steelworkers and their families," and by 1946 even the original nucleus for the Hell's Angels motorcycle gang. However, the decline of the Kaiser Steel empire left the area a desolate "landscape of randomly scattered, generally uncollectable (and ungentrifiable) debris: ranging from Didion's creepy boulders to the rusting smudge-pots in phantom orchards, the Burma-Shave-era motel names (like 'Ken-Tuck-U-In')," and massive redeveloped subdivisions. Most powerful of all these remnants of the past for Davis is the circus wrecking yard with the bits and pieces of California's amusement parks, which he sees as a "summary, unsentimental judgment on the value of its lost childhood" in which "the past generations are like so much debris to be swept away by the developers' bulldozers."[57]

The loss and anger felt in Davis's book is apparent, but his efforts to record these moments before they are swept away forever represent a further aspect of his project as a historian connecting his "lost childhood" nostalgia for the past and his Benjaminian desire to study its debris and the wreckage. For Benjamin and Davis, the writer is a historian/ragpicker whose work takes in the overlooked and the hidden, the historical materialist "concerned with the salvation of objects and people from the oblivion of forgetting, with collection and recollection" and resistance to the "fragmentation of experience . . . the growth of modern amnesia."[58] It is as if, as in Benjamin's work, and as I discussed in the photography chapter, at the moment of ruination when the surface crumbles and the world decays, Coupland sees another process of what Davis calls "renewal and restoration," where sustaining elements survive and can be reused for the future. Tyler in *Shampoo Planet* understands this double vision of the West most consciously when reflecting upon it from outside, from his visit to Europe when he realizes how much he misses "the Cowboy Bar atmosphere—its New World cow-rolling-on-a-spit sizzle . . . the country-and-western brutality that sometimes feels like freedom, sometimes feels like hell." This perverse doubling or dialectic of freedom and hell is what Benjamin saw in the cities of modernity and what Davis and Coupland see reiterated in the contemporary West.[59]

It is important that *Generation X* includes Mexico as part of its western cartography, presenting an actual space beyond the containment of the United States in which characters experience this doubling (or *folding*) as an emblematic hybridized border culture, "a newer, less-monied world, where a different food chain carves its host landscape in alien ways I can scarcely comprehend."[60] In this disorienting, amorphous contact zone, the controlling grid is fractured (always an impulse in Coupland's work as we have seen) and overdetermining stories are scattered by the hybrid energies of creative necessity—"a landscape punctuated by oxidized, spray-painted and shot-at 'half-cars'—demi-wagons cut lengthwise, widthwise, and heightwise, stripped of parts and culturally invisible . . . fences built of whalebones, chromed Toyota bumpers, and cactus spines woven into barbed wire."[61] Here, as in Kerouac's *On the Road*, is the "outside" of the U.S. West that cannot be detached from its "inside," uncannily folded together, and which Coupland's characters experience as necessary elements in their regenerated sense of "history." Histories, stories, and lives are here woven together, interdependent, uncertain, and dialogic in ways that cut across the settled, frozen, and "taken-for-granted" world that they have tried to escape. As Elizabeth Grosz writes about Deleuze's sense of the "outside" in philosophy: "Thought results from the provocation of an encounter. Thought is what confronts us from outside, unexpectedly. Thought confronts us necessarily from the outside, from outside the concepts we already have, from outside the subjectivities we already are, from outside the material reality we already know." Thought and reflection rupture the settled world as Andy, the chief narrator of *Generation X*, "encounters" the borderlands, challenging his sense of identity, reality, and all their "usual configurations," forcing him "outside the systems in which [he has] a home."[62] As ever, his response to what he calls this "new landscape" is to invent two stories. The first is "The Young Man Who Desperately Wanted to Be Hit by Lightning," about a man who reenacts the westering process, "goes West" rejecting his old life in a "boring job for an unthinking corporation" "to travel across the prairies in a beat-up old Pontiac in pursuit of storms, despondent that he might go through his entire life without being struck by lightning." Once again echoing the journeys of *On the Road* or *The Grapes of Wrath*, the story is unfinished, for this man is still looking, questing across Kansas or Nebraska, roaming "the badlands" of the West in search of illumination in the lightning flash. The second story is not about motion at all but about being grounded on the rocks of Baja, in "perfect silence" with a connection "like a guitar string" between his brain and the sky and being offered a silvery fish by a "happy-looking pelican." Both stories suggest a refusal to accept the status quo, the fixed and defined singular landscape of an already-scripted past and an already-finished people, proposing instead a multiple and folded culture and identity constructed from "routes" *and* "roots," of endless striving *and* contented stasis, both the lightning *and* the rock where the virtual and the actual coexist. Remember, these two stories are a response to what happens at the border, in Calexico, where cultures collide, and are a direct reaction to the book's questions about how to live in an increasingly reduced, stratified world.

However, alongside these textual stories and their inherent ambivalence, Coupland provides a third narrative stream in the "border" of the text itself: slogans, definitions, and images that act as a commentary on the novel's actions and ideas, coming, once again, from "outside."[63] Thus in this section's marginalia, where Mexico appears to offer a curious *heterotopia* for Andy, Dag, and Claire, another vision appears, defining their romantic escape as "Emallgration: Migration toward lower-tech, lower-information environments containing a lessened emphasis on consumerism," or as "Terminal Wanderlust: A condition common to people of transient middle-class upbringings. Unable to feel rooted in any one environment, they move continually in the hopes of finding an idealized sense of community in the next location."[64] Whether we interpret these comments as being directly about the main story or not, Coupland offers them as in the spirit of so much of his writing, as "little bombs that, when they don't explode in one's face . . . scatter thoughts and images into different linkages or new alignments without necessarily destroying them," aiming to "problematize, challenge, and move beyond existing intellectual and pragmatic frameworks." These textual interruptions "shake things up, produce realignments" generating a process without resolution, further adding to Coupland's multilayered, dialogic, "fundamentally moving . . . rhizomatic" manual of possibilities: of escape and new life, redemption and hope, love and beauty, and simultaneously a guarded and ironic reminder of the exoticization of the "Other" as a form of colonial nostalgia and the romantic yearning for new beginnings.[65] He provokes the "thought" of readers, allowing us no place of ease, no settlement, but only a perpetual problematization of the discursive, doubled West, for which, in John Rajchman's words, "there pre-exists no consensus, no 'we think,'" offering instead a multilayered "diagram" full of divergent lines "making a *carte* that is not a *calque*—a map that is not the 'tracing' of anything prior, but which serves instead to indicate 'zones of indistinction' from which becomings may arise."[66] The West, in these terms, is mobile and irreducible to a unified perception, an endless proliferation of connections, weaving in and out of different forms, feelings, and representations, mixing the new, the unthought, and the outside with their opposites, asserting the "foreign" within any presumed identity.[67]

In the novel's final, immensely symbolic chapter (*without* marginalia), Coupland echoes another classic American westward journey, that of the Joads in *The Grapes of Wrath* as they enter Techachapi, California, after their trek across the Mojave and see "the great valley below them . . . green and beautiful, the trees set in rows, and the farmhouses . . . the morning sun, golden on the valley" and "stood, silent and awestruck, embarrassed before the great valley. . . . It's California."[68] The promise of the West for the Joads is translated into its postwestern version in *Generation X*, with the land "transformed by agribusiness into a food factory; its abundance chemically stimulated by various technologies" that serve the corporation, not the individual, but there remains the flickering possibility of some new hope.[69] Andy's journey takes him through "Imperial County" from the desert to "this region's startling fecundity," to "Mecca" where he receives "a farmer's forgiveness" for stealing a "warm orange," has a "vision" of a "thermonuclear cloud" (which turns out to be the burning stubble of a field), has his head cut by a swooping white egret, and falls to his knees with blood on his fingers. In this massing of religious and apocalyptic imagery, Coupland prefigures his later work and suggests once again his theme of possible redemption: the search for lives better than those offered by corporate, consumerist America and a world of simple acts of beauty and power. The latter is typified by the scene that closes the novel—the hugs of retarded children like "an instant family . . . adoring, healing, uncritical," a "crush of love . . . unlike anything [he] had ever known."[70] As the ironic, hip Xer marginalia subside in this last chapter, Coupland's desire for the renewal of wonder takes his work back to the earliest dreams of the West as a space of possibility, radiance, and new beginnings. Curiously, and despite his reputation as a postmodern ironist and surveyor of consumer culture, Coupland's work, as we have seen, so often points to a *new* New World emerging out of the West, out of a human desire for moving beyond what is often presented as *all there is*, and toward a reclaiming of affect, "the search for depth and meaning . . . the sacredness of friendship, the spontaneous and selfless expression of love, and the value of narrative itself."[71]

In *Life after God*, Coupland once again explores characters who yearn for lives beyond fixity, seeking new "auras" by undertaking journeys through the West in a time "after God," when all the old "stories" seem inadequate or duplicitous. The book's form itself is a chain or "fold" of stories that connect and diverge, endlessly stimulating the reader with quirky flights of philosophical, existential questionings and everyday descriptions that provoke, challenge, and surprise. The tone is set in the final words of the first section: "stories of these beautiful little creatures who were all supposed to have been part of a fairy tale but who got lost along the way."[72] Once again the rediscovery of some meaningful "tale" within which to live is a guiding principle of the book, for as one character puts it, "there is a secret world just underneath the surface of our own world," and Coupland's fiction probes and details that surface in order for us to glimpse below or through it to other possibilities. The "surface" of this New West is akin to that defined by Fredric Jameson as postmodern culture: "new depthlessness," "commodity fetishism," "the imitation of dead styles," "the culture of the simulacrum," and "aesthetic colonization."[73] This is what has to be both described, as Coupland clearly does in all his fiction, and resisted, if only through a reengagement with affect, redemptive energy, and the assertion of what I will term here the "virtual." "I think," says one of the narrators in Life after God, "the people to feel saddest for are people who once knew what profoundness was, but who lost or became numb to the sensation of wonder—people who closed the doors that lead us into the secret world—or who had the doors closed for them."[74] Different methods are used throughout his work to reclaim sensations of wonder and reopen these doors, but fundamentally the goal is to jar us out of our "lostness" or entrapment in the "scheduled life" and expose alternative layers of possibility by "snapping" the "cord of normalcy."[75] "Our curse as humans," he writes, "is that we are trapped in time . . . forced to interpret life as a sequence of events," and so the book explores ways of intervening in this linearity: for example, through the capacity to "stop time," becoming "frozen in mid-motion," and so slowing down the accelerated culture enough to reclaim life; or through "dreams in which I am flying . . . [to] float and move" (like the pelican and egret at the end of Generation X) to find transcendence from the "bonds of Earth" and the "body."[76]

The most "western" section of Life after God is called "In the Desert" and reveals how difficult it is to transcend the complex materials of everyday life, once again announcing Coupland's dialogue between groundedness and flight (roots/routes; actual/virtual). The narrator drives from Las Vegas to Palm Springs through the "bigness of the landscape . . . counting the Rothkos of skid marks of long-dead car collisions on Interstate 15's white cement lanes," and here in the conventional space of pilgrimage and redemption "Nothingness was very much on my mind." Yet the world intrudes into that "nothingness" as he is bombarded by "radio stations from all over the West—those fragments of cultural memory and information that compose the invisible information structure I consider my real home—my virtual community" (emphasis added). This reminds him that identity in the West is not about one place or one thing, nor about some absolute grounding in historical truth, but as much a construction of unstable, mediated fragments, and, therefore, to presume one can exclude these and somehow live outside them is to deny the reality of existence in all its messy complexity.[77] As he writes in *Polaroids*, "What would it be like to have never had these commercialised images in my head? What if I had grown up in the past or in a nonmedia culture? Would I still be 'me'? Would my personality be different?" As he goes on to say, there is an "unspoken agreement . . . that we're not supposed to consider the commercialised memories in our head as real, that real life consists of time spent away from TVs, magazines and theaters." Thus as the narrator journeys across the desert in "In the Desert," he carries with him, along with the drugs he is smuggling (like so many Coupland characters), an identity in flux, continually responding to the information that surrounds him, information drawn from the landscape, climate, nature, as well as all the technologically mediated culture he consumes. To resist this process is pointless and deluding, for "Everybody travels everywhere. 'Place' [in its traditional, rooted sense] is a joke." In this *new* postwestern culture, old, static notions of place are redundant, since "home" is just as likely to be "a shared electronic dream of cartoon memories, half-hour sitcoms and national tragedies . . . [with] no fixed home in their mind."[78]

Katerberg's question "Do people in his stories transcend their own corrosive, ironic self-obsessions? Will they find somewhere to call home? Or do they remain tourists, ever on the move?" reflects a rather lopsided view of Coupland's work and assumes some ideal based on conventional concepts of stable, rooted home and identity.[79] In fact, although Coupland's work generates these questions constantly, I am not certain the answer falls so neatly into one or the other position. Home and identity are reimagined by Coupland, as so often in the texts I have discussed within this book, just as the West is in his fiction, as much more than rootedness, a concept that inevitably leads back to certain mythic notions of nationalism—"a history selectively strung together in a narrative form [with] . . . founding fathers . . . quasi-religious texts . . . rhetoric of belonging . . . historical and geographical landmarks . . . official enemies and heroes."[80] Instead, it becomes about seeing "dwelling as a mobile habitat, as a mode of inhabiting time and space not as though they were fixed and closed structures, but as providing the critical provocation of an opening whose questioning presence reverberates in the movement of the languages that constitute our sense of identity, place and belonging."[81] Coupland's voyagers in the desert, his exiles and nomads, deliberately echoing the Joads and Kerouac's heroes, are in search of a better life after God, living in what Edward Said calls "a secular and contingent world," and so have come to understand that "homes are always provisional. Borders and barriers, which enclose us within the safety of familiar territory, can also become prisons, and are often defended beyond reason or necessity. Exiles cross borders, break barriers of thought and experience. . . . Exile is never the state of being satisfied, placid, or secure. . . . Exile is life led outside habitual order. It is nomadic, decentered, contrapuntal; but no sooner does one get accustomed to it than its unsettling force erupts anew."[82] Remember the earlier description of "radio stations from all over the West—those fragments of cultural memory and information that compose the invisible information structure I consider my real home—my virtual community." In this Coupland perhaps comes closest to this exilic sense of "home" in a global age, a sense echoed in Lyotard's comment that "When a culture starts to coagulate as the spirit of a people, as a real country . . . this . . . ceases to be West."[83] It is no longer the West as settled, defined, and gridded but something altogether more diasporic and folded, constituted by a multiplicity of representations and stories, as distorted and fragile as the radio waves across the desert or what Lyotard calls the possibility of "ungriddable space."[84] Here Coupland's sense of postwestern identification echoes that of his contemporary Rubén Martinez, discussed earlier, who has written of identity like the border radio stations "that fade in and out, playing rock, techno, hip hop, oldies, and the Mexican border forms" and "occasionally the signals cross" mixing Pedro Infante with Johnny Cash and where "Vicky Carr's purr hovers like a ghostly harmony over Elvis Presley's croon . . . the soundtrack of a vast space and time."[85]

Coupland's work, as we have seen, consistently examines these tensions between this fluid, mediated culture, a more traditional rooted existence, and dreams of transcendence that point his characters beyond both. His West is about complex negotiations across border lines—for example, in Life after God, learning to live with the fact that despite what their parents' generation might have believed, moving to the West Coast did not mirror "the end of history."[86] Thus when his car breaks down in the desert, the narrator of "In the Desert" undertakes a walk during which he meets a strange drifter who offers him food and guidance in an almost biblical manner that gives him "something to believe in after there is nothing to believe in."[87] The wilderness can still act as a reminder of "a larger part of myself that I can always visit," a sense of "purity" against modernity and the accelerated culture, like in the final moments of Life after God where the narrator walks naked into the river rediscovering a sensation from his youth "pretending to be embryos, pretending to be fetuses . . . we floated in the warm waters," in a gesture that is part baptism, part return, part annihilation, finding in this final action a means to float and fly beyond the "gravity" of his existence. In Microserfs this transcendent desire recurs through computers helping us to "dream our way out of these problems" toward some "earthly paradise—the freedom to, quite literally, line-by-line, prevent humanity from going nonlinear."[88] Yet, as we have seen, in the final analysis it is the "nonlinear" that may indeed provide the alternative to the contained world in Coupland's work. Although there is a romantic pull in many of his stories to some perceived "home," some point of origin, some stable and rooted existence (a very "western" dream), few of his characters ever achieve it, and they never seem more satisfied than when they are searching, moving, and questioning the very culture that ultimately has an enormous investment in that sanctioned stability—its economic and social center. These are the paradoxes of Coupland's take on the West as the epitome of this cultural dilemma, the condensation of the New World dream: yet it is a New World brimming full of contradictions, in equal measures persistent powerful hopes and dreams and simulation, celebrity, and disappointment. In many ways, what Coupland's fiction does in relation to a comprehension of the complexities of what westness means is akin to the piece of black glass used by impressionist painters. He describes it thus at the end of Miss Wyoming: "Whenever they were unsure of the true color of something, they'd look at its reflection in a piece of black glass. They thought that the only way they could ever see the true nature of something was to reflect it onto something dark."[89] His fiction has consistently "reflected" on the "dark" disappointments and overblown expectations of the (New World) West's promise and subsequent simulated, commodified, and polluted landscapes, not simply to ironize or dismiss them but by traveling through them, living them, reflecting upon them, in order to see some "true color" still present and worth holding on to.

This comment comes as Susan Colgate and John Lodge Johnson begin a new life together at the end of *Miss Wyoming*, "heading away from where they had been before," as the latter recalls "a single moment during his time in the wilderness" which had otherwise been "romantic and naïve." Thus against the "dark" failure of his "Kerouac routine" he salvages one "true color" in the form of an aesthetic vision "facing west" as the rain, dust, and sun combine to create a premonitory vision pointing "backward" but also forward for his and Susan's new beginning: "the sun was radiating black sunbeams down onto the Earth, onto Interstate 40 and the silver river of endless pioneers that flowed from one part of the continent to the other."[90] Coupland's consistent interest in the "pioneer" dreams of the New World West and its convoluted promise and ever-present history is echoed here as John and Susan begin another pioneer voyage, another road trip, not toward any particular place, but rather finding in mobility an adequate representation of the West's contradictory spaces: "John felt that he and everybody in the New World was a part of a mixed curse and blessing from God, that they were a race of strangers, perpetually casting themselves into new fires, yearning to burn, yearning to rise from the charcoal, always newer and more wonderful, always thirsty, always starving, always believing that whatever came to them next would mercifully erase the creature they'd already become as they crawled along the plastic radiant way."[91]

Through the eyes of one Canadian "stranger," Coupland's work allows an engagement with the "mixed curse and blessing" of the West as "a race of strangers" who all, in different ways, struggle with their inheritance, as real, material place and as immense and complex virtual cultural construction within a global age. As one of the chapter headings for *Generation X* puts it, "Quit Recycling the Past." These are characters whose reality is globalized and where once-"stable" concepts like history and geography are continually questioned by experience: "what is geography to Harmony or Pony or Davidson, who speak to people all over the planet every day all at once on their computer nets and modems? Or what is history to Mei-Lin or Gaia, who receive seventy-five channels on the families' dish-TV systems?"[92] For Coupland, the experience of westness incorporates these realities, producing restless and questing characters of internal exile, diasporic and migratory, permanently unsettled with no absolute point of "home," family, history, rootedness, and authenticity. Yet the despair of modernity is offset by learning to live with these feelings, accommodating a sense of identity and community that is not entirely tied to these desires, more able to live "in-between" them and, therefore, better equipped to struggle along life's "plastic radiant way." John Ulrich argues that the term "Generation X" "marks precisely this paradoxical borderline status (inside and outside, within and against the mainstream), with 'X' capturing the dual sense of negation and freedom and 'generation' signifying a kind of hyperbolic assertion of subcultural, rather than demographic, solidarity." He adds: "X here marks an impossible spot, both inside and outside mainstream American culture, for which we have no preestablished terminology or identity—until now."[93]

Although it is not a western novel directly, Coupland's most inventive, ambitious novel to date, *Girlfriend in a Coma*, certainly reflects upon themes already established, building on many of his previous ideas and impulses as a writer to create a fiction in which the apocalypse actually happens and the world is destroyed, leaving only a small group behind as survivors. As if picking up on Mike Davis's Wovoka Ghost Dance, this literary conceit allows him to experiment with one of his favorite devices, the "outside" voice, here not simply "Polaroids from the Dead" but narrators—in the form of Jared, a ghost, and Karen, a coma "returnee." Rather like science fiction or a revamped version of the "impossible spot" discussed above, this permits an interrogation of this world from positions and knowledges *beyond* it. Transcendence now becomes not the goal of his characters but the actual "X" position from which his narrators speak about the world, moving "both inside and outside mainstream American culture." In a perverse twist, Coupland destroys the old New World in order to see how people might create a new one out of the rubble, and allows these unworldly voices to comment on it all. His survivors become the new pioneers: "I guess this is what the continent looked like to the pioneers back when they first came here. . . . A land untouched by time or history. They must have felt as though they were walking headlong into eternity, eager to chop it down and carve it and convert it from heaven into earth." As Jared, the ghostly narrator, says, "The New World was the last thing on Earth that could be given to humankind," and as the novel suggests, each subsequent generation has misused this gift and failed to fulfill its immense promise "to take mankind to the next level [through] newer, smarter, innovative ways of thinking and living and being." Hence, in the novel Coupland imagines a third chance to recover the New World without complacency, rejecting their old "static" lives of "videos . . . junk food . . . pills" within which one had "an acceptable level of affluence . . . entertainment . . . [and] a relative freedom from fear . . . [but] nothing else," and grasping the opportunity to begin again, to "clear the land for a new culture—bring your axes, scythes and guns." Once again, though, as at the end of Miss Wyoming, this potential renewal rejects a purely rooted culture, for as Jared says, "You're going to be forever homesick, walking through a cold railway station until the end, whispering strange ideas about existence into the ears of children. Your lives tinged with urgency, as though rescuing buried men and lassoing drowning horses. . . . There aren't enough words for 'transform.' You'll invent more." Out of this Coupland draws a potent call for change and different ways of thinking: "We'll be begging passers by to see the need to question and question and question and never stop questioning until the world stops spinning. We'll be adults who smash the tired, exhausted system. We'll crawl and dig our way into a radical new world." In these extraordinary visions—"this jumping-off point toward farther reaches"—Coupland hands the world back to people and says "You're indeed what comes next," learn by your mistakes and change it for the better, make a new New World built not on established answers and preformed patterns but on eternal questions and spiritual quests and along imaginative lines of flight.[94]

In these ways, Coupland's Xer cynicism and irony was merely the beginning of a process of questioning the waste of the western New World dream, sharing something of Deleuze's ambition "to lighten, to unground, to release the fresh air of possibilities, to combat stupidity and cliché . . . [becoming] a philosopher not of negation but of affirmation—not of mourning and absence, not of sad, tired ironies, but of humor and life."[95] Coupland was once asked if his writing was a "tool to make greater sense of the world," and his reply was simply "Yes. That's the only reason."[96] Similarly, as he wrote of the artist Shannon Belkin's work, in terms equally applicable to his own, it has "a sense of mission and the air of wanting to find a new destination"; it is "both an end and beginning; this is always the most interesting point in any artist's evolution."[97] Indeed, at the end of *Girlfriend in a Coma*, Richard's mind fills with the following words: "*Focus ahead . . . jettison everything. Leap forward. You have a mission.*"[98] In his first novel, *Generation X*, a visit to a Vietnam memorial, "A Garden of Solace," seems to suggest this desire for mission and destination, here imagined as a yearning to create "a remarkable document and an enchanted space," a space with a genuine "connection to a past of some importance" and yet one that is still capable of mystery and magic, of "coiled pathways" and "juxtaposed narratives" capable of articulating "disintegration, reconstruction, and reintegration" all at the same time.[99] Repeatedly in Coupland's fiction there is a willed mission toward some "new destination," usually uncertain, unfixed, and multilayered, and yet something that promises "both an end and beginning," like the finale of *Shampoo Planet* with its many surreal references to the flood and the ark, and the reassuring exclamation, "Wake up—*the world is alive.*"[100]

Conclusion: Virtual Architecture

Coupland's accumulation of western spaces, both documented and enchanted, rooted and routed, apocalyptic and redemptive, might be related to Foucault's concept of "heterotopia," that is, a potential space in which "fragments of a large number of possible orders glitter separately in the dimension, without law or geometry," and "create a multiplicity of tiny fragmented regions" where "things are 'laid,' 'placed,' 'arranged' in sites so very different from one another that is impossible to find a place of residence for them, to define a common locus beneath them all." With no "place of residence"—that is, no clear sense of "home" or rootedness—this vision is "disturbing," unsettling our sense of "language" and our usual reliance upon stable categories, singular patterns, and a "grid of identities."[101] It therefore functions as a "mythical and real contestation of the space in which we live," presenting a curious, layered new "architecture" constituted by "juxtaposing in a single real place different spaces and locations that are incompatible with each other."[102] Nathaniel Lewis speculates about this as a vision of the "literary West," calling it a "glaring *madness*" and "a frightening, ecstatic *beauty*": "Even though no 'common locus' exists, no True West, we can still luxuriate in the 'glitter' of the disorder and marvel at the dislocation of familiar arrangements."[103] Recalling my discussion of Koolhaas's and Tschumi's notion of delirium in the introduction, this is also the direction of Coupland's work, toward a renewable West of madness and beauty, in Lewis's words, "fluid, disruptive, elusive, and ultimately beyond the containment of representation or reading," beyond the containment that from *Generation X* onward has been a central concern in his writings and against which his work continuously struggles. The madness and beauty is there in Coupland's desire for "a strand of magic moments strung together, a succession of mysteries revealed," despite recognizing the West as a space of human failure and loss. His work strives to jolt us, like the survivors of *Girlfriend in a Coma*, out of our habituated grids and to see things differently: "In the frazzle of modern life, which is getting faster and faster, there's no denying it, the ability to reflect on it is getting lost."[104] Whether through extraordinary plot events, irony, humor, quirky everyday images, or transcendent, wondrous moments, his work is forever fabricating narrative spaces that force us to reflect, and potentially to redeem those dreams worth salvaging, like "children who fell down life's cartoon holes . . . dreamless children, alive but not living," and to bring them out "on the other side of the cartoon holes fully awake," perhaps even enchanted again, to discover they "were whole."[105]

Coupland's narratives follow such rhizomatic, imaginative paths, redeeming a vision of westness as enchanted, if full of holes; a set of energies that resist fixity in their literal and metaphoric textual mobilizations. Coupland's work echoes Derrida's comments on Tschumi's architectural *Folies* in Paris's Parc de la Villette: "The route through . . . is undoubtedly prescribed, from point to point. . . . But the structure of the grid . . . leaves opportunity for chance, formal invention, combinatory transformation, wandering"—for Lewis's madness (*folie*) and beauty—

for "other spacing" that challenges us constantly to reflect on a West that is "mobile, light and abyssal, foliated, foliiform. Foliated folly, foliage and *folle* [mad] not to seek reassurance in any solidity: not in ground or tree," but only in the rhizomatic sense of striving, multiplicity, and connection. In his fictional voyages through the West and their encounters with its many mediated landscapes and mythic foundations, Coupland creates a literary "architecture of heterogeneity, interruption, non-coincidence," or what Tschumi terms an architecture of "disjunction," and through this we encounter the West as it "constructs/deconstructs," seeing its various "pieces separate, compose and recompose." The "architectonics" of the West, its established hierarchical grids of meaning, identity, myth, narrative, and assumption, are here "put in question" by the madness and beauty of Coupland's eccentric texts as they reflect and reveal, "affirm and engage," and, ultimately, in Derrida's words about Tschumi, "maintain, renew and reinscribe," even "revive perhaps, an energy which was infinitely anaesthetized, walled-in, buried in a common grave or sepulchral nostalgia."[106]

Without dismissing or destroying the West's long and significant history and mythology (its grids), Coupland manages a journey through and between its points, following the twists, turns, and folds of its multiple lines without the need to settle on any single one, but instead appreciating their divergence and the possible directions to which they might alert us as we travel on. As Rajchman writes, "Multiplicity thus involves a peculiar type of com-plexity—a complexity in divergence—where it is not a matter of finding the unity of a manifold but, on the contrary, of seeing unity only as a holding together of a prior or virtual dispersion." So it is, I believe, in Coupland's rhizomatic vision, where what is sought is the "divergence" and "dispersion" embodied in the "virtual/actual" West rather than the supposed, imposed mythologized "unity," not as any single, reified originary point but always as an array of potentials, its "virtuality" ("the movement of a question that opens onto new uncharted direction," the "force of the past always still with us in the present"), unfolding in our lives, confronting us with questions to which we don't know the answers in advance.[107] Surely this is why the desert is always so important in Coupland's work, beginning in *Generation X* as the space to which his characters retreat as "the equivalent of blank space at

297

the end of the chapter."[108] For here away from the clutter and babble of life they might "write" alternative stories and find release in these imagined or virtual worlds, for "The desert is . . . not an endpoint, the ground zero of social implosion, but a beginning point—it's on the margins, in the desert, where the narrative begins. . . . [It] is . . . born of the desire to recover the social and the sentimental, to reinscribe it in a new space that, rather than ecstatic and visible, remains subtle and private."[109] Indeed, as Rajchman reminds us, "To virtualize . . . [the West] is thus not to double it but, on the contrary, to multiply it, complicate it, *release other forms and paths in it*" (emphasis added).[110] This idea of "release," of "mobilization" and "flight" into a "new space," takes us back via Deleuze to the image of potential at the end of *Girlfriend in a Coma*, "this jumping-off point toward farther reaches," and further back still to Ellis's "Trust" poster in *Less Than Zero*, and the look I claimed sets Coupland's voyage going: the eyes of alarm and reflection that fix us and direct us beyond the broken world, "outside" it so that we might comprehend better the "inside," finding in the relations of both a healthy and inspiring "complexity in divergence."

CONCLUSION
On "The Crystal Frontier"

There's a little bit of the West in all of us.
Wrangler jeans commercial

The world that is best is the most "multiple," the most virtual.
John Rajchman

The quotation mark points not only inward but outward as well.
Susan Stewart

Western *Folies*

Jean-François Lyotard's postmodern experimental text *Pacific Wall* begins with a description of the University of California, San Diego library as a "transparent jewel" with its "walls of glass" pointing in all directions, both "internal" and "external," radiating both total vision and knowledge "without problem or hindrance." However, his narrator goes on to think more about this elaborate crystal grid as a "maze" or labyrinth whose refractions and angles draw the eye away from the books, "behind the western face," from inside to outside and back again, until "it begins to jump from one to the other, and the suspicion arises you've been had. And that getting in or out is impossible for the precise reason there is no in or out." In fact, the narrator argues, this strange dialogic relationship "traces new passages in this web of words and things. You're adding something to the labyrinth." Inside this maze of mirror-like refractions and despite the "quality of its classifying system," the narrator reads (like us) a text that is itself "a collection of . . . approximations, far-fetched metaphors, unexpected linkages, gross errors and misconceptions, and delirious reasonings," believing he might be able to "restore its readability." In this multifaceted description Lyotard comes closest to understanding the kind of West I have suggested in this book: a complex discursive space that appears transparent, clearly represented and archived in a thousand canonical texts of history, literature, film, photography, art, geography, and every other form, and yet as one looks closer within this apparent clarity other forces emerge, spilling out and provoking "new passages" and connections to be made. This, to me, is the position of anyone attempting to comprehend the American West, to "restore its readability" and fix its meanings. The consequence of this process is, however, not to produce a coherent metatext that explains and defines its object of study but rather something closer to the rhizomatic endeavor I have traced across the preceding chapters, an intricate architecture always "adding something to the labyrinth" through what Mark C. Taylor terms a "riot of supplements."[1] Despite the spatial grids defined in the "absolute West," as Lyotard terms it—the library block, the stacks of books, the California cities like "a checkers game," with "highways [and] squares marked off," and those who "survey and allot . . . organizing, delimiting" space—there are counterforces simultaneously at work in a "relentless undoing of established patterns and combinations."[2] In fact, at America's western edge, Lyotard's "Pacific Wall," settlement and rootedness are always potentially unstable, the region an "island of forgetting," "temporary montages, precarious products of cultural bricolage soon to be swept away," and what remains is an "always-displaced serenity" or "unbearable" mobility. In contrast, according to Lyotard's narrator, when "a culture starts to coagulate" and become "rooted" it "ceases to be West," since in his precarious and mobile sense of westness its spaces must be "continuously replotted" and "undecidable," added to with "excess" and "surplus" because "a surplus rebuffs any attempt to construct coordinates."[3]

These spatial-architectural concepts take us back to where I began in the introduction, discussing how one might see Rem Koolhaas's critical quest for the "delirious" within the modernist grids of New York as a model for comprehending the West as a space in constant tension between mythic coherence and arrant mobility. In Lyotard's West the initial impression is of controlled structures and the "safety of sameness," whereas within the refractory folds and crystallized, prismatic forms of the library there exists something "more Piranesian than Mondrianesque" in which one can "assume the traces of an ungriddable space" within the apparently "homogeneous gridded space."[4] This represents the layered, "baroque" West always breaking out of the containing grids of definition, fixity, national certitude, and mythic closure, a labyrinthine West that refuses to be any single thing and which I wish to further address in this final section with a return to the abstract poetics of architecture and the apparently rather more prosaic experience of popular music. Through these distinct and yet strangely connected examples I wish to present a final set of possibilities to expand the "architecture" of western studies as a truly critical regionalism seeking constantly new directions and offshoots, connections and insinuations. In truth, what I am ultimately closer to proposing here is an "anarchitecture" or "transarchitecture" of western studies.

Swiss-born architect Bernard Tschumi, whose ideas I touched on in the introduction and chapter 7, has long desired, along with collaborators Peter Eisenman and Jacques Derrida, to free architecture from its associations with stability, permanence, and eternal values, ideas embedded in modes of thinking and speech such as the "foundations" of society or the "structure" of thought. Echoing Koolhaas's notion of "delirium," Tschumi's preferred vision is of an architecture affected by bodies in motion, by mobility, change, and transgression rather than by frozen, sedimented, contained, and "gridded" versions. As Tschumi put it once, he likes the "bad stories . . . murder stories," not the comfortable, safe stories; the dangerous, subversive narratives that take off in all directions to challenge the static, framed ones so often dominant in our perceptions of architecture (and culture).[5] His desire equates to my vision of the West, of westness as ungrounded, restless, and mobile—rhizomatic—constantly reframed and reinvented in a manner akin to the experience of cinematic montage, association, and suggestion, with "any point of a rhizome . . . connected to anything other."[6] Indeed, Tschumi's architectural/cultural theory (as in Deleuze) draws upon the cinema (or "film space") to express his sense of movement, juxtaposition, and layering, since "though cinematic sequence is structured, it is not fixed and, therefore, harbors an instability that can be both creative and destructive."[7] As Tschumi puts it, traditionally architecture "designs" and orders space through grids and frames, as does film, and yet the latter reminds us that frames can be manipulated, "mixed, superimposed, dissolved, cut up, giving endless possibilities to the narrative sequence" and so provide a new possibility for dynamic architectural forms and for human experience.[8] If, as Tschumi argues, architecture longs for permanence and transcendence, then the pyramid is its perfect form, and yet he takes from Georges Bataille's work the idea that insecurity is ever present and that its form is the labyrinth that undermines every pyramid. Like Lyotard's refractory library in *Pacific Wall*, Tschumi writes of the labyrinth, "One can never see it in totality, nor can one express it."[9] Refusing to see the world as settled form, Tschumi prefers the idea of "montage," a labyrinthine "discontinuity" of fragments "permitting a multiplicity of combinations. . . . Inscribing movement" through what he terms "cinegrams."[10] In other words, as I have said many times in this book, the frame or grid can become flexible, can, like most forms, travel and disperse. As Mark C. Taylor has written, "Tschumi's appropriation of the grid" in his designs, especially for the heterotopic Parc de la Villette in Paris, "is subversive . . . turning the grid against itself, he uses it to open rather than to close structure." "While the grid traditionally has been used to center and ground structures by providing a secure foundation, Tschumi employs the grid to create a decentered structure that is 'utterly discontinuous and often unpredictable.'"

As I discussed earlier, Tschumi introduces the *folie* ("folly" or madness) into the grid; a disorderly refusal of absolute design and control, "neither inside nor outside the grid . . . [folies] dislocate the structure within which they are inscribed."[11] In contrast with the stories and histories of the West, which strive to create an order, harmony, and synthesis of its multiplicitous and complex strands of meaning, Tschumi's *folies* act to counter totalizing, stable syntheses seen as the core of architecture. Derrida's appreciation of Tschumi helps to underscore this parallel, for Derrida sees that "this architectonics of invariable points" operates "beyond . . . architecture," establishing an "indisplaceable effectivity" in need of critique.[12] The *folies* operate, however, says Derrida, "to put in question, dislocate, destabilize or deconstruct the edifice of this configuration," that is, all that has "given architecture meaning," of all those meanings "naturalized . . . bequeathed to us . . . [that] we inhabit . . . forget[ting] its very historicity . . . [becoming] common sense itself."[13] Influenced by Derrida and Deleuze, Tschumi explores the limits of architecture, determined by a sense of "a dispersed and differentiated reality that marks an end to the utopia of unity," linking him subliminally, but crucially, with this study of the West, endorsed by his comment that his liminal architecture was about "BORDER CROSSING . . . where reality meets fantasy, reason meets madness, life meets death. (Border crossing is erotic)."[14]

In the cultural "architecture" of the West, its "designed" and ordered mythic texts and structures (its various monuments and cultural "pyramids") have given it its recognized and often unquestioned shape and history, yet into this it is vital to introduce, as I have done throughout this book, those texts that deviate from the established and canonical grid, interjecting various forms of "outsideness" and "folly" into how "westness" is defined. Derrida argues that Tschumi exposes architectural meaning "to the outside and spaces itself out in what is not itself," utilizing the *folies* to "maintain, renew and reinscribe architecture . . . [and] revive, perhaps, an energy which was infinitely anaesthetized, walled-in, buried in a common grave or sepulchral nostalgia."[15] Viewing this expanded version of westness is akin to the experience Tschumi desired of Parc de la Villette, wandering along its "cinematic promenade" snaking its way through the park: "Strolling along the cinematic promenade, one frames and reframes scenes in an alternative sequence: gap/closure/gap/closure/gap. . . . At each movement along the way the meaning of the fragments shifts and slides until it becomes completely undecidable."[16] "La Villette," Tschumi writes, echoing my sense of westness, "is a term in constant production, in continuous change; its meaning is never fixed but is always deferred, differed, rendered irresolute by the multiplicity of meanings it inscribes," and "the programmatic content is filled with calculated distortions and interruptions." As Tschumi's prefixes "cross," "dis," and "trans" suggest, the "programme" of presumed, fixed, contained "space" has to be constantly interrupted or "disfigured," as Taylor puts it, in order to reveal its possibility. However, echoing Gloria Anzaldúa's plea in *Borderlands/La Frontera*, Tschumi always sees a double motion of deconstruction and construction in his work, since "Deconstructions would be feeble if they were negative, if they did not construct."[17]

Taylor's unusual, rhizomatic, layered text *Hiding* draws precise parallels between architectural theory and the West in a section that juxtaposes, montages, and superimposes together a discussion of Tschumi's architectural theory and the experience of contemporary Las Vegas's "architainment," extending some of the ideas I have addressed and opened throughout this book. In the themed environments of the Strip, the West's postmodern capital, Taylor sees the equivalents of Tschumi's "cinegrams": fluid, multiple renditions of reality and the imaginary through the various screens, simulations, and performativities of Las Vegas's spectacular landscapes. As the West continues to redraw itself as the extraordinary post-tourist spectacle of Las Vegas, one cannot avoid the wondrously impure collisions and blurring of imagescapes, bringing together Robert Venturi, Tom Wolfe, Siegfried and Roy, canonical art treasures, *CSI: Crime Scene Investigation*, and Celine Dion into a surrealistic hybrid mix, a *folie*, experienced as one moves along the "cinematic promenade" of the Strip with its pyramid Luxor Hotel towering above and its labyrinthine experiences of the street below.[18] Tschumi wants architecture to be "cinegramic," like "images from a film that does not exist," as Taylor writes, and in Las Vegas it is as if those images have indeed found a sequence in its baroque foldings, as the "cinematic morphs into the virtual" and "Film layered upon film generates a space in which passive observers of cinema become active players in virtual games that know no end."[19] The various "frames" and grids of Las Vegas—its streets, buildings, screens—have given form to the notion of "immersive environments," creating on an urban scale cinema's dream of unboundedness, of a cinematic promenade consistently bursting out of its structures, suggesting "secret maps and impossible fictions, rambling collections of events all strung along a collection of spaces, frame after frame."[20] Las Vegas, as Taylor's work implies, is the embodiment of Tschumi's Parc de la Villette vision, within which, "though structures remain stable, everything is in motion. Simultaneously complete and incomplete, closed and open . . . a stage set for interactive media . . . [where] people who stroll along the cinematic promenade actively participate in the construction of imaginative spaces in which they dwell."[21] Similarly, Las Vegas's extreme West is the labyrinth resembling Tschumi's theories of an architecture where "infinite screens render the real imaginary and images real . . . an intricate assemblage of superimposed surfaces."

Taylor's point is that Las Vegas and Tschumi's theory mirror one another (like the words and images on the page of his book) and actually fuse and overlap (as they do before our eyes as we attempt to read his deliberately dialogically structured text), bringing to life the theory in the "transarchitecture" of Las Vegas. Along and off the Strip "a narrative montage of great complexity explodes" and we are "mobilized in a scenography of passage (transference, translation, transgression from one place to another, from a place of writing to another, graft, hybridization)."[22] Tschumi is comfortable in his assertion that architecture must challenge "eternal forms and secure foundations," "not to find answers but to learn to live with the impossibility of solutions," to comprehend that the interface between the virtual and the real has always been complex and uncertain, and that in our present age "To think virtually is to think differently."[23]

In Las Vegas's western *folies* one might argue that the grid has gone delirious in the ways Koolhaas suggested: presenting no "assembled totality" but rather epitomizing the grid as expanded form, crossing over and through as a kind of permeable, woven fabric (as Derrida asserts), "twining the threads of a chain" because "[a] weave always weaves in several directions, several meanings, and beyond meaning," "spacing a multiplicity of matrices or generative cells whose transformations will never let themselves be calmed, stabilized, installed, identified in a continuum . . . [and] point[ing] towards instants of rupture, discontinuity, disjunction."[24] Perhaps, to modify Dave Hickey's comments, "Las Vegas is a wonderful lens through which to view [the West] . . . [since] what is hidden elsewhere exists here in quotidian visibility," "the heart of the drift . . . the last refuge of unsanctioned risk and spectacle—the wellspring of our indigenous visual culture—the confluence of all the hustle and muscle . . . [where] Contingency is all."[25] In understanding this complex experience of Las Vegas's "electrotecture" we get closest to the heteroglossic, incomplete West examined in this book, a real and imagined, actual/virtual, rhizomatic space, "articular rather than anchored, compositional rather than unifying, immanent rather than transcendent, contingent rather than essential, and spectral rather than given."[26] It is the urban West as "event," a term Tschumi favors and defines as "a turning point—not an origin or an end," a "twenty-four-hour-a-day continuous invention," a "spacing" of and for "happening," where things can "take place," according to Derrida, as "sequence, open series, narrativity, the cinematic, dramaturgy, choreography."[27] In his rumination on Derrida's and Tschumi's architecture of events, Edward Casey argues that at its heart is the sense that "it continues to occur," always happening and refiguring "now" ("maintenant") but also "maintaining," as if to define it again as both "routes" and "roots," occurring and maintaining simultaneously. This transarchitectural event-happening, epitomized in the West's fastest-growing city, Las Vegas, resembles then the westness I have been charting in this book, for it refuses to be contained by its gridded forms and "folds out (ex-plicare) in forming the event, refusing to remain confined to any simple location by expanding outward in accordance with the event it embodies."[28]

In the labyrinthine complexities of the "West as Las Vegas" my sense of westness is confirmed, for it "exposes its containing grid as 'constraining' or 'framing' . . . [while] always exceeding it, surpassing it, or overflowing it . . . linking it to the outside. In this way the grid becomes only a dimension of the folding of the space in which it figures."[29] Here, the crystal prism of Lyotard's library is reconfigured as Las Vegas's delirious digital pleasure dome of laser shows and promenades, with the crystal dispersing into the million LCD screens flickering as "fantasies fold into fantasies to create worlds within worlds" in "a virtual potlatch of meaning."[30]

Calexico's Crystal Frontier

Space is definitely the place, and we try to let the music breathe and capture the feeling in the room.
Joey Burns

Let in a breath of air from the chaos that brings us the vision.
Gilles Deleuze and Félix Guattari

The art of this text is the air it causes to circulate between its screens.
Jacques Derrida

Interestingly, Derrida has written of the "sound-tracks" and "image-tracks" of architecture and explained his work with Peter Eisenman for Tschumi's Parc de la Villette project as "Choral Work," a multifaceted play of meanings at whose heart is the notion of the spatial as, in part, musical, or "choral"—"an architecture for many voices, at once different and harmonized in their very alterity"—and yet as "chora," irreducible, uncontainable, and always exceeding frameworks and definitions, a "bastard structure . . . at the same time looking like a paradigm and at the same time looking like a copy. . . . It is neither one nor the other . . . beyond philosophy . . . beyond the dialectics . . . chora is space, spacing."[31] Perhaps, then, it is through the musical and choral that one might comprehend a more tangible example of the West as "a virtual potlatch of meaning," exceeding the grid and constantly reaching out beyond the nation to engage with other forms and cultures in what Paul Gilroy terms "intercultural conversations." These dialogues derive from musical encounters, the creative "in-between" whereby different traditions and experiences intersect and fold with "their unsteady location simultaneously inside and outside the conventions, assumptions, and aesthetic rules" they are associated with.[32]

Music can, I believe, articulate and perform many rhizomatic tendencies through the "syncretic expressive cultures" I have been exploring in this book, revealing what George Lipsitz calls "sedimented networks and associations beneath the surface of the seemingly disconnected world of commodified musical production."[33] As music disperses across cultures and through the experience of the listener, it breaks and reconnects, forming different strands that confound any claim to authenticity or "purity," a concept at the heart of Tucson-based band Calexico's music. Indeed, John Convertino, one of its members, has commented, "What is the authenticity of America? That's what I love about music: there is no ownership. No one can [lay] claim—although many people do—to certain styles of music. It's all been borrowed from so many sources."[34] And this is similarly a characteristic of the specific spatial and cultural flux of the desert borderland of the Southwest where they work. As Joey Burns, the other central figure in Calexico, has said, "It's the West" that creates their hybrid music as the band responds to its diasporic culture, taking "traditional styles and twist[ing] them and mak[ing] them completely their own," while "not trying to keep this old West thing alive."[35] As *High Country News* put it in 2004, Calexico is "composing the new Western," contributing through their music to "a new literature of the Southwest," developing a complex, hybrid style that "forms a sort of grout that cements all the fractured tiles and asphalt and broken glass into a coherent mosaic," mixing multiple, global sounds precisely because "the frontier story no longer rings true" and there is a need to produce music so that a "region some see as hopelessly divided can be united."[36] The all-encompassing grid of a sedimented western mythology that has often appeared as a reassuring inwardness for the United States is, as so often in this book, displaced and exceeded aesthetically as the "inside" of an American western discourse is confronted by an "outside," and although still present, its framework is nonetheless deframed and reshaped through Calexico's music.

Named after the border town between the United States and Mexico famously visited in Coupland's Generation X, Calexico is a literal and metaphoric place of crossing, and the band's musical development is a testament to how the West can be viewed as a transnational, global contact zone, a complex petri dish of influences and nuances. They are similar to the earlier Los Angeles Chicano band Los Lobos, whose music "tried to straddle the line between the two cultures, creating a fusion that resonates with the chaos and costs of cultural collision," percolating with "persistent bifocality, juxtaposition of multiple realities, intertextuality, [and] inter-referentiality."[37] For Calexico, however, the possibilities of a "Cosmic American Music" (once called for by Gram Parsons) have expanded with a global culture constructed of "objects in motion" where objects can be "ideas and ideologies, people and goods, images and messages, technologies and techniques" exchanged in "a world of flows."[38] Their music and the structure of feeling that surrounds it, as I will discuss below, contributes to what we might term the "transnational imaginary," the "as-yet-unfigured horizon of contemporary cultural production by which national spaces/identities . . . are being undone and imagined communities of modernity are being reshaped."[39] Always stretching the musical grid through overlapping identities and with a sense of the local as always an "inflection of a transnational phenomenon," their work navigates significant paths out of the political bind of overwhelming nationalism or localism, folding ever outward into new collaborations and ever-changing forms.[40] The borderlands, as we have seen, are the starting point for an alternative vision of the West and America as "not a nationality but a trans-nationality, a weaving back and forth of innumerable threads of all sizes and colors, across conceptual boundaries whose colors bleed and shade into each other."[41] In the apt words of Iain Chambers, "Music permits us to travel . . . draws us into the passages of memory . . . [and] overflows the containment of our concepts . . . form[ing] a contrapuntal score that sounds out circumstances in the creation of a mobile individuation and community." Chambers's phrase for the effects he begins to describe here, of the way music transports the listener into and out of all manner of imaginaries, is the "nomadology of sound," revealing parallels to identity itself as "shifting, combinatory . . . an ever present, ever unfolding, bass line; a rhizomatic figure, a fugue drawn from the languages that transport and sustain us, a solo and improvisation on the energies that unfold and devolve in the world (rather than an isolated work that withdraws and redraws the world into the single and constant note of the self)."[42] In this complex metaphor Chambers suggests the power of music—"the bearer of alterity," as he calls it—to move and challenge our ways of thinking and feeling about identity, nation, and community, allowing us "to temporarily exit from *the narratives that frame us* in order to re-negotiate our 'home' in them" (emphasis added).[43]

Thus in Calexico's shifting, Deleuzian "nomadology of sound" we might begin with the political song "Sunken Waltz" that opens *Feast of Wire* (2003), with its Spanish guitar and polka beat and political lyrics speaking of its narrator lost in corporate Los Angeles, who "washed my face in the rivers of empire" and "made my bed on a cardboard crate down in the city of quartz," "prayed it would rain and rain / submerge the whole western states / call it a last fair deal / with an American seal / and corporate hand shake." With the self-conscious use of Donald Worster's New Western history eco-text *Rivers of Empire* alongside Mike Davis's scathingly Marxist *City of Quartz*, Calexico projects a critical regionalist vision of the contemporary West, driving music beyond its usual boundaries, connecting it with a wider cultural political domain as they compose not simply the new western but the postwestern. In "Quattro (World Drifts In)" the West is tied to a global culture where "the world drifts in and the world's a stranger" and people are living in a place "occupied and invaded," while in "Black Heart" the border crosser might "trip on the fence post line / sifting through the remains." While their lyrical journeys constantly return to themes of escape, running, struggling, and corporatization, where "hope's broken at the knees . . . and the world's made of dust and dust it will return" ("Close Behind"), the music carries us across many boundaries—from mariachi ("Across the Wire") to synthesizer ambience ("Black Heart," "Attack El Robot! Attack!"), to western sound track ("Close Behind"), to dub reggae ("Dub

Latina"), to pop rock ("Not Even Stevie Nicks"), to cool jazz ("Crumble")—creating the uncanny tension between aural freedom, hybridity, and social and economic constraint embedded in its themes. It is as if as we listen, we are drawn into the soundscape, which offers the possibility of productive diversity, hybridity, and creativity to set against the often bleak messages of the lyrics, which tell of despair and loss.

Burns has admitted as much of their album *Garden Ruin* (2006), whose very title suggests a "paradise lost" theme, acknowledging the lyrics are pessimistic, whereas "musically there's a lot of hope, a lot of positives. Contrast is really important for me."[44] This contrast between destruction and survival provides an engaging dialogic tension echoing Chambers's description of the affective power of music: "Sounds and voices that arrive from the edges of my life, the frontiers of my experience, manage to impose an interval in my understanding. Here music casts me elsewhere, opening a breach in the institutions and habits of the quotidian. Suspending the prescriptive, music permits a possible inscription in a gap in which one takes leave from the predictable in order to recite, and thereby, resite, a language, a history, elsewhere."[45] In the creases and folds of Calexico's desert operas "the prescriptive" is suspended and music opens out, "resites," into possible "new points of departure," offering "an exit from the constraining immediacy of the everyday world" through no single, neat passage but along "all sorts of byways . . . [that] digress and then digress from the digression."[46] As Chambers has written, such hybridized music creates "a musical and cultural conversation in which the margins are able to reassess the centre while simultaneously exceeding its logic," leading to "unexpected extensions and configurations; a multi-lateral . . . series of exchanges."[47] From their earliest album, *Spoke*, through to *Garden Ruin*, their music has consistently explored such diverse byways alongside a varied cultural-political fascination with all manner of intertextuality and dialogical border-crossing aimed at articulating "borders or . . . no borders or the juxtaposition of the two contradictions."[48] One finds it in their self-conscious references to a wider cultural "border" tradition in literature, art, and politics as well as in their increasingly apparent recognition of the West's relationship to global issues and other complex frontiers.

I take the title of this final section from the Calexico song and video

"The Crystal Frontier," which first appeared on *Even My Sure Things Fall Through* (2001) in two versions, "widescreen" and "acoustic." Deleuze and Guattari describe the crystal form as one that "expands in all directions" where "both exterior and interior are interior to the stratum," suggesting the complex multiplicity of the borderlands of Calexico's work while linking it to Lyotard's crystal library discussed above.[49] This also locates the band's fascination with mediatized iconography in the broadest sense: of the American West reiterated as music and film, myth and story, art and literature, all of which figure to varying degrees in their work. The title, however, is not theirs, but derives from Carlos Fuentes's "novel in nine stories," *The Crystal Frontier* (1995), charting multiple crossings (literal, metaphoric, and emotional) across the border, which Calexico "reaccentuates" by adding references to earlier journeys of Cabeza De Vaca and Fray Marcos de Niza in search of Seven Cities of Gold in the Southwest and by relating it to global events. For Fuentes, the border is a "crystal frontier"—alluring, refractory, complex, and increasingly transparent and permeable. It is traversed by all classes, for all reasons—"an illusory, crystal border, a porous frontier through which each year pass millions of people, ideas, products—in short, everything."[50] This is a space where businessmen and gangsters, doctors and maids, laborers and border guards intersect and are kept apart, like an "ironic community," as Fuentes calls it, "separated by the crystal frontier" and curiously connected by it too. In the title story, a Mexican cleaner, Lisandro Chavez, in Manhattan working on a glass skyscraper "like a pyramid . . . a Teotihuacan made of glass," sees a white woman, Audrey, in her office, and they are mutually attracted, "imagining each other" through the crystal cultural cage. Never actually meeting or touching, the two experience an intense, erotic moment as "their lips united through the glass" in a metaphor that epitomizes Fuentes's testing of these paradoxical cultural boundaries and links his vision with the similar explorations in Calexico's musical narratives and soundscapes.[51]

Sounding rather like Rubén Martínez, another of Fuentes's characters, a young Chicano writer, José Francisco, asks of the border, "What belongs here and also there? But where is here and where is there? Isn't the Mexican side his own here and there? Isn't the same on the gringo side? Doesn't every land have its invisible double, its alien shadow that walks at our side the same way each of us walks accompanied by a second 'I' we don't know?" Out of this dialogical tension emerges his identity as a Chicano writer, and in the final scene of his story, apprehended by the joint forces of the U.S.-Mexico border guards, his papers are emptied out from the international bridge and begin "to fly . . . like paper doves . . . flying from the bridge into the gringo sky, from the bridge to the Mexican sky. . . . To the river, to the moon, to the frontiers . . . until they found their destination, their readers, their listeners, their tongues, their eyes." In this gesture of dispersal and transgression, the words that shattered the symmetries of the border standoff, like José's "victory shout," "broke the crystal of the frontier" with a shattering reminder of possibility, of words reaching some "destination." As Fuentes writes, "let the words fly, poor Mexico, poor United States, so far from God, so near to each other."[52]

Calexico's music develops similar complex responses, both to the U.S.-Mexico border's "deep history" and to notions of transnational, global shifts and connections wherever they occur. Through their music, the group seeks routes to break the crystal frontier and let words fly.[53] As Burns put it in 2006, discussing the song "Roka" on *Garden Ruin*, "this idea of immigration doesn't so much pertain to our own back yard, but it's global," and Calexico's work has always expressed these cross-cultural, transnational elements, "draw[ing] from influences from all over the globe. . . . We try to broaden the musical horizon as often as we can."[54] Based in Tucson, a town where "there's always people in transition," they utilize such mobility in the music they create, mixing alternative country with mariachi, spaghetti Western sound track with electro, cool jazz with earthy folk, Portuguese fado with Fleetwood Mac, punk with lounge. One of the key inspirations for this vision came from the same source as that also described by Chambers, the 1993 Algerian Tony Gatlif's film *Latcho Drom* (*Safe Journey*). The film, which traces the movement of gypsy musical traditions across the globe, had a profound effect on Chambers, taking him to a "threshold of an elsewhere that opens my world to the disturbing presence of something that I recognise but which flees my desire for comprehension." The film's music and images create a disruptive "event that evades the closure of my understanding" for him, a sentiment echoed in comments by Burns on the same film, which he credits with provoking his understanding of the connections between apparently different musical styles and traditions, from "Link Wray, Ennio Morricone, [to] Amalia Rodriguez and Mariachi Vargas." It is this cultural connectedness *and* difference across the time and space of global borders that offers hope for Calexico, providing a strategy for defeating the "closure of [our] understanding," and, sounding like both Chris Eyre and Gloria Anzaldúa, to potentially "bridge a gap."[55]

Their disorientating musical soundscapes, often cinematic and sweeping, fold forms that challenge the listener's preconceptions about what the West might be, interrupting "this old West thing," acknowledging in some ways so many of the lines of flight I have examined throughout this book. As one reviewer put it about their album *The Black Light*, it is "part road trip, part redemption tale—like a Jim Jarmusch rewrite of West Side Story . . . there's elements in the half-vocal, half-instrumental mix of Palace and Smog, *The Third Man* and *The Wild Bunch*, Kurt Weill and Ennio Morricone."[56] As this suggests, their music has a strong pull to the cinematic, creating soundscapes that deliberately refer to Morricone's spaghetti Western sound tracks with their instant touchstones of folk themes, popular forms, and stylized, almost stereotypical arrangements signifying the imagined West, such as *Feast of Wire*'s "Close Behind." In videos for their music, such as "Ballad of Cable Hogue," named after Sam Peckinpah's 1970 film, they go even further, creating a pastiche of a spaghetti Western film, utilizing the setting of "Pioneertown" and drafting in French singer Marianne Dissard to play the femme fatale.

The conscious use of instrumentals also gives their music a distinct and unusual quality that Burns has specifically described as present in order to "transport the audience," providing "a spatial sense" and a "unique flow" that is "cinematic" because "it kind of helps provoke daydreams," enabling the music to "travel" and make important intercultural connections as well as consistently refer back to a mythic western past. Their work moves in the traffic between such worlds, always "painting a soundtrack . . . [to] invite the listener in and interpret"; however, in the spirit of Tschumi's architectural spacing, "We're into leaving open spaces" so that those "daydreams" and mythic resonances cannot remain unquestioned. Their use of hybrid forms, pastiche, and relentless shifting across musical, cultural, and linguistic boundaries prevents any comfortable retreat into prescribed notions of nation, identity, or place but instead insists on a more edgy approach—"Continuity is nice. Contrast is better," as Burns puts it.[57]

For Calexico these points of reference are to a complex aural, visual, and oral westness in the same way that their work consciously echoes the layered West constructed from the fictional landscapes of Cormac McCarthy's border fiction, the tough new journalism of Charles Bowden, or the "autoethnography" of Rubén Martinez and Luis Alberto Urrea. Urrea, for example, is referenced directly on *Feast of Wire* with a sleeve note "Thank You" (as are Bowden and Martinez) and specifically in the song "Across the Wire," which refers to "a whole lake of sleeping children" in its lyrics.[58] As Burns has said, narrative is vital to their work, providing a mechanism to avoid using "I," "me," or "you," as he puts it, preferring to "hear something else, something in a different language or a different expression," so that the stories come from "outside" "from the angle that a character from a Cormac McCarthy book might take. Or maybe the narrator observing people coming together in areas like this [Tucson]."[59] *The Black Light*, for example, as Burns puts it, "was a tip of the hat to . . . Cormac McCarthy" (who gets a "Thank You" on the cover), taking characters of "innocence and naivety out of their element," such as Billy Parham and John Grady Cole in McCarthy's border trilogy, transforming them "through these horrific but uplifting experiences."[60] Elsewhere they have recorded the traditional song "All the Pretty Horses" on 2001's *Aerocalexico*, from which McCarthy took the title of one of his border novels. Interestingly, Bowden writes in *Blood Orchid* that "I can only get started writing if I think it is music."[61] Music is, therefore, only part of the complex architecture of Calexico's work, since such intertextual connections are part of a dialogic strategy to draw the listener into a network of cultural forms that, in different and intersecting ways, represent the West from "inside/outside" and as complex and global.

Hence, Calexico's slogan, "Our soil, Our strength," might suggest at first glance a very inward-looking ideology, whereas in fact it stands as a grounding for their transnational, routed perception of how the West in all its mediatized forms belongs to a wider, global community, with its myths and tensions linked to more universal themes. In this way, their music is a further example of how, according to Liane Lefaivre and Alexander Tzonis, critical regionalism works: "as an engagement with the global, universalising world, rather than by an attitude of resistance," "a constant process of negotiation between the local and the global."[62] Even the band itself is a mix of regions and nationalities, "combining a whole spectrum of dynamics and backgrounds, culturally and musically," with Burns from Montreal via Los Angeles and Convertino from Long Island via Oklahoma, and other members from the United States and Germany, along with sometime collaborators from France and the United Kingdom.[63] As if mirroring an expansive notion of the West as always already multiple, Calexico's career has been marked by a willingness to work with others' material as well as to collaborate on various projects, both theirs and others'. Their songs have been remixed by others, like the Gotan Project and Jazzanova, while they in turn have recorded and performed songs by Nick Drake, Love, Alison Goldfrapp, Link Wray, Mark Eitzel, and most notably the Minutemen. The latter's song "Corona" from *Double Nickels on the Dime* (1984) shows Calexico's dynamic interpretive power, elevating the Latino rhythms from the original, raw San Pedro post-punk sound and adding a full mariachi orchestral treatment. The song's lyrics "The people will survive / In their environment" seem amplified by the border sounds, so that the implicit criticism of "the dirt, scarcity, and the emptiness" of those living to "our South" folds back into the whole Calexico oeuvre, showing how much D. Boon's original song was responding to his experience of border politics and the tensions between the rich North and the poor South. What Burns has called the "eclectic" punk West of angry Minutemen songs like "Untitled Song for Latin America" mixes with their jazzy instrumentals like "June 16th" and the Spanish guitar of "Cohesion" and, together, alongside "Corona," show the overall influence on Calexico's developing sound, but as with any reworking, as Burns has said, it was always about "reinvention," about "making it in their own style."[64] Music's capacity is here imagined as a processive exchange, "it is rewritten, becomes somebody else's place, somebody else's inscription."[65]

Calexico's work is often also produced collaboratively through close working with other groups and performers, such as Mariachi Luz de Luna, the Amor Belhom Duo, Giant Sand, or Iron and Wine, and constantly melds and experiments with different musical forms, as in their remix productions discussed above. As Burns says, "I like bringing all those aspects to this location, the greater Southwest, bringing them all together and then seeing what you can do."[66] When one of the band members, German Volker Zander, refers to the "whole utopian place Calexico represents," he means the creation of a community onstage and in the studio with a set of values and meanings resonating with notions of collaboration, hybridity, and intercultural conversation—a borderless world derived from crossing and recrossing those borders that exist yet can be overcome.[67] In fact, Convertino has made the point that it's a "full circle" to have Germans playing mariachi music, since so much Mexican music had its origins in European accordion and polka styles.[68] The politics of this musical "communion" rejects the closed world of "locals only," embracing syncretism, "taking elements from all over and bringing them together" with "respect and preservation at the same time that there's adaptation and accommodation . . . varieties, new styles of music that are being formed."[69]

This hybrid vision forged in the contact zones of musical production and consumption is reinforced by Calexico's use of the art of Victor Gastelum on their album covers. Described as "a huge inspiration," his work is about "blending hybrid forms" and creating images that "transcend the canvas and allow for overspray into everyday life," paralleling the "musical combinations" and melded forms of their music itself.[70] Gastelum grew up in a Mexican American family and was, like Burns, influenced by U.S. punk bands like Black Flag, the Minutemen, and Husker Du, and it is these "hybrid expressions" that emerge through his graffiti-stencil images combining street life, mythology, and religion in simple, stark, provocative pictures. As the artist says, he likes "to mix iconography to create my own icons" to convey "the whole picture of what is going on in this time and place."[71]

What begins in the West and on the Mexican border for Calexico resonates globally in the need for greater understanding and mutual respect, a perspective the group attributes to "traveling" outside the United States and experiencing the "different slant" provided by other cultures until any one-dimensional, narrow perspective is counteracted. As they put it, "Hollywood seems like it's on some imaginary planet . . . and TV news, it's so artificial; it's such a hoax." Their music is concerned with the tensions between a monologic, inward vision and a heteroglossic, outward one: "So when we talk about politics we're both learning a lot from each other's culture, and what's being projected on the screen. . . . America is . . . entangled with all this media wire, and all this manipulation through the media. We're [the United States] kind of isolated, too. Drifting out there a little bit from reality."[72] Through collaborations that extend their own musical spheres, Calexico deliberately explores this "entangled" culture and "broaden[s] the musical horizon," finding "more diverse paths" to pursue, paths that break the kinds of isolation referred to above, turning the West continually outward once again, so that the "world drifts in."[73]

Calexico's music challenges this closed world in ways that echo the ideas of Bakhtin, who wrote of the need for "heteroglossia to wash over a culture's awareness of itself and its language . . . relativize the primary language system underlying its ideology and literature and deprive it of its naïve absence of conflict." This process will "sap the roots of a mythological feeling for language," argues Bakhtin, and only after this has happened does a national culture become "conscious of itself as only one among other cultures and languages."[74] The consequent alternative vision born in coexistence and "openness in the cultural diversity" suggested here is akin to Anzaldúa's notion of "new tribalism" in which the "eclectic and individualistic" might find some place.[75] For Anzaldúa, the borderlands sparked her awareness of broader, globalized connections, of "interacting with other cultures and ideas," allowing her to "see beyond just nationalism" and to break out of the kind of isolation identified by Calexico. As she puts it, "we live in each other's pockets and not in isolated ethnic plots. We depend on exchange of goods, ideas, and information," and from this position of always being "in-between" emerges a different vision, a "new tribalism" bridging cultural exclusiveness and cultural inwardness.[76] Calexico, whose very name echoes this "in-between," border position, deliberately use their musical and cultural alliances to travel across established lines, to "illustrate," as Anzaldúa has said, that "we're in each other's world . . . affected by the other . . . we're all dependent on the other" and need to create a "language to speak about these new situations, the new realities," because "There's no such thing as pure categories anymore." As

Calexico suggests, "Even My Sure Things Fall Through," and their music, like Anzaldúa's writing, is more engaged in "disrupting categories" than in fretting over their loss or purity, since "categories" are rhetorical grids that "contain, imprison, limit, and keep us from growing" and so need to be overturned, becoming "impermanent, fluid, not fixed . . . not something that's forever and ever true."[77] Calexico's music, like Anzaldúa's work, is a testament to the "transformational multiplicities" defined by Deleuze and Guattari, capable of "overturning the very codes that structure or arborify it . . . right down to its ruptures and proliferations, . . . [making it] comparable to a weed, a rhizome."[78] As Burns has said recently, "Any band that gets pegged with any kind of characteristic that they're known for, you have to challenge that and you have to go beyond the description."[79]

Out of the disruption of categories (like the one-dimensional notion of the West) and the articulation of new identities and spaces comes a questioning of definitions of "insider/outsider," shifting the emphasis from division toward what Anzaldúa calls "a geography of hybrid selves."[80] One senses this in Calexico's almost endless variations of their own music, re-recording songs in different versions and styles, with different speeds, rhythms, vocal styles, personnel, some live, some studio-bound, as if deliberately experimenting and disrupting any sense of a sacred "original" or authentic song. Music is open and dialogical for Calexico, or as one of their songs put it, a "Gift X-change," part of a fluent stream of sound constantly shifting in ways reminiscent of Deleuze and Guattari's sense of music as potentially "causing particles to spin off the strata, scrambling forms by dint of speed or slowness, breaking down functions" and using familiarity ("a machinic assemblage" of recognized melody or form) "in order to take it to the bursting point," proceeding "kinematically and affectively, sweeping away a simple form by adding indications of speed to it."[81]

In the current climate of a "war on terror" and with the increased closure of borders, Calexico's music is informed by a still wider political need to break through such inwardness, since "There's always hope the more everybody gets in contact with each other and finds out information and shares stories, and kind of embrace[s] the whole world and all the various cultures and differences. You find that people whether they're

in Mexico . . . or Iraq . . . are independent human beings . . . that don't
have feelings of hatred."[82] On *Garden Ruin*, Calexico criticizes George W.
Bush, a president whose westness has become his badge of honor and
his use of western mythology and rhetoric a key platform of his post-9/11
strategy. Here, though, the band associated so clearly with western imagery and music uses such iconography to counter the impact of Bush's
government (its "cruel, heartless reign"), producing a more overtly political record with "monsters lurking all over it, even in the pretty bits,"
as Convertino has said.[83] Here the songs resonate with post-9/11 angst,
doubt, and mistrust, speaking of "nightmare news" and the "weeds of
discontent [that] choke a broken landscape," of dark days, the "darkest I've seen," where cities sprawl, storms howl, and Poe-like omens fill
the air. Yet the collaborative production, the airy, almost pop-like music,
contrasts with the pessimistic, apocalyptic lyrics, offering directions out
of the ruined garden, some possibility of renewal and hope. Far from
one-dimensional, the band maintains the dialogic struggle always present in their work, refusing to slide into comfortable continuities, but
rather preferring the contrasts and the entanglements of a complex
postmodern world.

In the sleeve notes to his album *West of the West* (2006), a collection of
California songs, Dave Alvin expresses something of the spirit of Calexico's version of "new tribalism." He makes the point that the "roots" music tradition from which he comes, with its strong "bloodlines" in folk,
rock, jazz, and blues, is now a changing tradition in the multicultural,
transnational culture of the West, continually evolving and hybridizing,
as music always does. The California West, he acknowledges, has always
been a "mix of cultures, beliefs, and attitudes" with the crazy diversity of
landscape and social institutions, as well as "the eternal hopes and disappointments of growing up in a mythical promised land." Yet, as he puts
it, echoing many of the lyrics on Calexico's *Garden Ruin*, "the landscapes
that shaped these songwriters have vanished or changed drastically. . . .
Small towns are now big cities sprawling beyond the horizon. . . . Musical styles change with the landscapes and population but the tradition
continues. Children of Cambodian immigrants compose hip-hop verses
on the streets of Long Beach while young Mexican immigrants sing
narco-corridos in the barrooms of Stockton. Right now . . . somebody

is writing the next generation of songs with California bloodlines."[84] In this there is no terminal sense of regret or loss, no nostalgia for some essential western moment when the "tradition" was pure and absolute, but instead, as with Calexico's permanent musical revolution, a sense of "the living memory of the changing same," which in Gilroy's words strikes a "balance between inside and outside . . . the different practices, cognitive, habitual, and performative, that are required to invent, maintain, and renew identity [community and nation], an irreducibly modern, ex-centric, unstable, and asymmetrical cultural ensemble that cannot be apprehended through the Manichean logic of binary coding."[85] Once again, I return to Gilroy's expressive imagery of roots and routes to link Alvin and Calexico with many of the works explored elsewhere in this book, for in their musical forms they both acknowledge a debt to roots music while simultaneously generating new routes away from any fixity or resolved, contained grid. In the spirit of Alvin's friend and collaborator John Doe, the positive side of roots music is its "simplicity" and relation to the past, but its negative side is its belief that "someone else's culture is more valid than your own."[86] In choosing to "frame" their version of twenty-first-century westness, Calexico and Alvin (along with many others) opt for rhizomatic "routes/roots" music, a renewed "Cosmic American Music" flowing outward *and* inward as a series of layered connections that value many cultures and many "pasts" and refuse to settle for just one.[87] In the words of Lipsitz, "identities could be changed . . . one was not bound by bloodlines, nationality, or occupation," and through all forms of performance one might be "challenging the legitimacy of static identities inherited from the past."[88]

Recalling Deleuze and Guattari's interest in the restless styles of the baroque and my uses of their ideas earlier in this book, it is perhaps worth adding that Chambers has also drawn parallels with the baroque and certain forms of rock music, claiming that "it is music that plays at the confines of a precarious world that is no longer either unique or unequivocal . . . music that plays at the border; a sound at the crossroads of musical genres and cultural identities, caught between worlds, confronting their consolations." How like the experience of listening to Calexico this is, whereby in their version of local/global westness we are drawn into "an aesthetics of excess that overflows the frame of prescribed reason and cultural restraint, and strains across the frontier, seeking an elsewhere, an encounter with alterity." In the traveling of hybrid sounds, "clarity and conclusion is thwarted" by the spiraling of musical mixing "out of ordained structures into the unmapped insistence of the corporeal and the contingent; there to encounter the promise of the possible."[89]

Throughout this book I have tried to suggest how the West travels, changes, and refuses to be contained by nation, geography, or mythology, and my final example has been that of music, because it permits a real and metaphoric "line of flight" outward through its production, performance, and consumption. Music can be rhizomatic in so many tricky and productive ways, as Chambers describes so powerfully above, refusing to stand still, inviting and pushing the listener beyond comfortable frames of reference, and confronting us with the unexpected. As Deleuze and Guattari put it, using an architectural model, music can create "the sonorous house and its territory" and yet simultaneously "deframe" or "deterritorialize" that musical space until "We pass from the House to the Cosmos."[90] The "refrain" can be a sign of musical reduction and sobriety, a "calming and stabilizing . . . center in the heart of chaos," a musical "circle" or "a wall of sound" keeping "chaos . . . outside," but as a complex and entangled form it can also create the opportunity for new flight and reinvention, opening "the circle a crack . . . [to] let . . . something in" from that very "outside" until "One launches forth, hazards an improvisation . . . ventures from home on the thread of a tune."[91] Ronald Bogue describes this deterritorializing, deframing potential of music as a natural process "fashioning rhythmic characters and melodic landscapes from sonic materials, their deterritorialization of refrains proceeding through diverse becomings."[92]

Perhaps the entangled and complex architecture of westness I have described in this book comes closest to these poetic renditions of music as an ambivalent form with no single trajectory, creating instead a series of lines and rhythms, always moving, crossing, and folding, like "a series of competing tales that compromise and undercut one another." The West, as it travels through discursive formations and national territories, cannot be contained within any single story or version, because "stories do not exist in some sort of fixed isolation, but are instead always bordered by some other story."[93] Indeed, in trying to articulate and suggest these complex mappings of westness as a new "architecture for area studies," I am drawn back (and forward) to metaphors employed by the diverse voices used in this conclusion: to Lyotard, Calexico, Fuentes, Tschumi, Taylor, and finally to Deleuze and Guattari's discussion of music, which, echoing all those above, utilizes the notion of the crystal. As Deleuze and Guattari put it, the crystal "forms by interiorizing and incorporating masses of amorphous material," echoing the sense of the West as an ingathering of peoples, cultures, ideas, and traditions, and yet, as they go on to add, "the seed of the crystal must move out to the system's exterior, where the amorphous medium can crystallize. . . . In short, both exterior and interior are interior to the stratum."[94] The inside and outside relate and exchange properties in this process, and the crystal is the "in-between" or middle through which energies pass and move, and its form "expands in all directions" as if constantly expressing the virtual within the actual.[95] In musical terms, the refrain is "a prism, a crystal," for "It acts upon that which surrounds it . . . extracting from it various vibrations, or decompositions, projections, or transformations. . . . [It] has a catalytic function" creating contrary impulses—"augmentations and diminutions, additions and withdrawals, amplifications and eliminations." Indeed, they argue, as I have of the West, the refrain can be seen "moving from the extremes to a center, or, on the contrary . . . from a center to the extremes, and also to travel these routes in both directions."[96] This double motion of the refrain is what Deleuze and Guattari value, loosening the "bad" refrain with its repetitive, conformist patterns ("Opening the assemblage onto a cosmic force"), deterritorializing it from its established "closed circle," and recognizing in the process that "the cosmic force," an inherent virtuality, "was already present in the material, the great refrain in the little refrains."[97]

The shifting motion of the crystal—forming and deforming, transparent and refractory, geometric and fluid, layered and solid—that Deleuze and Guattari link to the musical refrain works equally to express poetically my sense of the West-as-process in all its surprising intricacy. In the introduction I inquired into the possibility of a "system of westness," when in the final analysis, as Deleuze and Guattari put it, "We can never be sure . . . for we have no system, only lines and movements," and any true reflection must explore the "imaginary and the real . . . like two juxtaposable or superimposable parts of a single trajectory, two faces that ceaselessly interchange with one another, a mobile mirror."[98] For ultimately it is here, "At the limit" between real and imaginary, inside and outside, fixed and fluid, at the very "interstitching of routes," that Deleuze and Guattari, echoing Anzaldúa's nepantla, situate the possibility of "becoming" and change, "thereby constituting" what they term "a crystal of the unconscious."[99] In coming to terms with the complexity of such conceptualizations one comes closest to a truly expanded critical regionalism as a way of comprehending the West in the twenty-first century and beyond as part of "an emerging planetary culture," and to this end I would suggest, along with Deleuze and Guattari, that "It is no longer a matter of imposing a form upon a matter but of elaborating an increasingly rich and consistent material, the better to tap increasingly intense forces. What makes a material increasingly rich is the same as what holds heterogeneities together without their ceasing to be heterogeneous."[100]

NOTES

Introduction

1. Edward Said, *The World, the Text, and the Critic* (London: Vintage, 1991), 226, 241.

2. Dick Ellis, "Be a Crossroads: Globalising from Within," *49th Parallel: An Interdisciplinary Journal of North American Studies* 8 (2001), http://artsweb.bham.ac .uk/49thparallel.

3. Charles Bowden, *Blood Orchid: An Unnatural History of America* (New York: Random House, 1995), 113.

4. James Clifford, "Traveling Cultures," in *Cultural Studies*, ed. Lawrence Grossberg et al. (London: Routledge, 1992), 99, 100 (emphasis added). Clifford's idea of the "ethnographic frame" relates to my discussions of the grid and the frame elsewhere in this introduction.

5. Paul Gilroy, "Route Work: The Black Atlantic and the Politics of Exile," in *The Post-Colonial Question*, ed. Iain Chambers and Lidia Curti (London: Routledge, 1996), 17; Mary Louise Pratt, *Imperial Eyes* (London: Routledge, 1995), 6–7.

6. Clifford, "Traveling Cultures," 100; Pratt, *Imperial Eyes*, 7.

7. Paul Giles, "Transnationalism in Practice," *49th Parallel: An Interdisciplinary Journal of North American Studies* 8 (2001), http://artsweb.bham.ac.uk/49th parallel.

8. These are key terms in John Tomlinson's assessment of globalization in his *Globalization and Culture* (Cambridge: Polity Press, 2000), 1–15, 14.

9. Tomlinson, *Globalization and Culture*, 28; Clifford, "Traveling Cultures," 100–101.

10. Giles, "Transnationalism in Practice," 4.

11. James Clifford, *Routes: Travel and Translation in the Late Twentieth Century* (Cambridge: Harvard University Press, 1997), 3.

12. Tomlinson, *Globalization and Culture*, 30, argues that deterritorialization is a globalizing process that "weakens the ties of culture to place," acting as a way of uprooting such myths and traditions.

13. Bowden, *Blood Orchid*, n.p., 18, 260, 262.

14. Bowden, *Blood Orchid*, 29.

15. Clifford, "Traveling Cultures," 101.

16. For more on this see my "Producing America: Redefining Post-tourism in the Global Media Age," in *The Media and the Tourist Imagination: Converging Cultures*, ed. David Crouch, Rhona Jackson, and Felix Thompson (London: Routledge, 2005), 198–214.

17. Owen Wister, *The Virginian* (New York: Signet, 1979), 92–93. For more discussion of *The Virginian* see Neil Campbell, "Wister's Retreat from Hybridity," in *Reading The Virginian in the New West*, ed. Melody Graulich and Stephen Tatum (Lincoln: University of Nebraska Press, 2003).

18. Frederick Jackson Turner, "The Problem of the West," in *Frontier and Section: Selected Essays* (Englewood Cliffs NJ: Prentice-Hall, 1961), 75.

19. Frederick Jackson Turner, "The Significance of the Frontier in American History," in Turner, *Frontier and Section*, 46.

20. Richard Slotkin, *Regeneration through Violence: The Mythology of the American Frontier* (Middletown: Wesleyan University Press, 1973), 8.

21. Bowden, *Blood Orchid*, 8–9.

22. Gilles Deleuze and Félix Guattari, *A Thousand Plateaus* (London: Athlone Press, 1996), 16, 15.

23. John Rajchman, *The Deleuze Connections* (Cambridge: MIT Press, 2000), 98.

24. Roland Barthes, *Image/Music/Text* (1977; London: Fontana, 1979), 148.

25. Gerald Vizenor, *Fugitive Poses* (Lincoln: University of Nebraska Press, 1998); see also Michel Foucault, "Two Lectures," in *Power/Knowledge* (London: Harvester Wheatsheaf, 1980), for his discussion of alternative history, or what he terms "genealogy."

26. Kathleen Stewart, *A Space on the Side of the Road: Cultural Poetics in an "Other" America* (Princeton: Princeton University Press, 1996), 20.

27. Foucault, *Power/Knowledge*, 82.

28. Rajchman, *The Deleuze Connections*, 99–100.

29. See Rajchman, *The Deleuze Connections*; and Gilles Deleuze, *Francis Bacon: The Logic of Sensation* (London: Continuum, 2004).

30. Rajchman, *The Deleuze Connections*, 100; John Rajchman, *Constructions* (Cambridge: MIT Press, 1998), 15, 16.

31. Deleuze quoted in Rajchman, *The Deleuze Connections*, 21, 22.

32. Bowden uses the term "schedule" to define a dark vision of a world under control (*Blood Orchid*, 158). Later in his work he employs the term "rules" to represent this similar rigidified sense of social control, assumption, and regulation. See Charles Bowden and Michael P. Berman, *Inferno* (Albuquerque: University of New Mexico Press, 2006).

33. William L. Fox, *The Void, the Grid, and the Sign* (Reno: University of Nevada Press, 2000), 61–62.

34. Fox, *The Void*, 91, 129.

35. Fox, *The Void*, 95, 109, 115.

36. J. B. Harley, "Deconstructing the Map," in Trevor J. Barnes and James Duncan, *Writing Worlds* (London: Routledge, 1992), 243, 245; Rick Van Noy, *Surveying the Interior: Literary Cartography and the Sense of Place* (Reno: University of Nevada Press, 2003), 12.

37. William Least Heat-Moon, *PrairyErth* (London: Andre Deutsch, 1991), 11, 10, 15, 16.

38. Rosalind Krauss, "Grids," in *The Originality of the Avant-Garde and Other Modernist Myths* (1986; Cambridge: MIT Press, 1991), 19.

39. Gilles Deleuze and Félix Guattari, *What Is Philosophy?* (1994; London:

Verso, 2003), 187–88; see also Jacques Derrida, *The Truth of Painting* (Chicago: University of Chicago Press, 1987), on framing.

40. Deleuze and Guattari, *What Is Philosophy?* 187, 188, 190–91. The use of "uncanny" houses in western texts—particularly films—relates well to this metaphoric tension between the established and the open. I am thinking of Malick's iconic Hopper-like house in *Days of Heaven* or Philip Ridley's use of dwellings in *The Reflecting Skin*.

41. Fox, *The Void*, 117; Krauss, "Grids," 22.

42. D. H. Lawrence, "Chaos in Poetry," in *D. H. Lawrence: Selected Literary Criticism*, ed. Anthony Beal (London: Heinemann, 1955), 90.

43. Deleuze and Guattari, *What Is Philosophy?* 203.

44. Lawrence, "Chaos," 90.

45. Robin Blaser, "The Practice of Outside," in *The Collected Works of Jack Spicer*, ed. Robin Blaser (Santa Barbara: Black Sparrow Press, 1975), 276, 278.

46. Elizabeth Grosz, *Architecture from the Outside: Essays on Virtual and Real Space* (Cambridge: MIT Press, 2001), 65.

47. Michel Foucault, "Maurice Blanchot: The Thought from Outside," in *Foucault/Blanchot* (New York: Zone Books, 1990), 17–18, 21–22, 54, 55, 57.

48. Gilles Deleuze, *Essays Critical and Clinical* (London: Verso, 1998), 109–10. This idea is discussed in relation to "minor literature" throughout the book (see chapters 2 and 3 in particular).

49. Guy Vanderhaeghe, *The Englishman's Boy* (London: Anchor, 1997), 16, 27, 110, 107.

50. Vanderhaeghe, *The Englishman's Boy*, 109.

51. Vanderhaeghe, *The Englishman's Boy*, 282, 309, 28.

52. Mikhail Bakhtin, *Speech Genres* (Austin: University of Texas Press, 1986), 7.

53. Mikhail Bakhtin, *Art and Answerability* (Austin: University of Texas Press, 1995), 22, 15, 23, and Holquist's introduction, xxvi.

54. Derrida, *The Truth of Painting*, 56, 57.

55. Michael Holquist, *Bakhtin* (London: Routledge, 1991), 31.

56. Rem Koolhaas, *Delirious New York* (New York: Monacelli Press, 1994), 9–10, 11. The extension of architecture into the political, social, and cultural was central to the work of the Situationists, who were a major influence on Virilio, Koolhaas, and Tschumi. See N. Leach, "Virilio and Architecture," in *Paul Virilio: From Modernism to Hypermodernism and Beyond*, ed. J. Armitage (London: Sage, 2000), 73–74.

57. Gloria Anzaldúa, whose work I examine later, referred to her own writings as "my own feminist architecture" in *Borderlands/La Frontera* (San Francisco: Aunt Lute Books, 1987), 22.

58. As I suggested earlier, Foucault had an enormous influence on Deleuze's thinking and vice versa.

59. Michel Foucault, *The Archaeology of Knowledge* (London: Routledge, 1997), 31–33, 37, 39, 70.

60. Koolhaas, *Delirious New York*, 17, 20, 21.

61. Koolhaas, *Delirious New York*, 87, 89, 87, 97, 104.

62. Koolhaas, *Delirious New York*, 105; Gilles Deleuze and Félix Guattari, *Anti-Oedipus: Capitalism and Schizophrenia* (1972; first English translation, 1977; London: Athlone Press, 1996).

63. Claire Colebrook, *Gilles Deleuze* (London: Routledge, 2002), 5.

64. Deleuze and Guattari, *Anti-Oedipus*, 266–67; Gilles Deleuze, *Negotiations, 1972–1990* (New York: Columbia University Press, 1995), 23–24.

65. Paul Giles, "Transnationalism and Classic American Literature," PMLA 118 (2003): 63; Theodor Adorno, *Negative Dialectics* (1966; London: Routledge, 1973), 406, 172. Foucault, in his essay on Deleuze, "Theatrum Philosophicum," writes: "The circle must be abandoned as a faulty principle of return; we must abandon our tendency to organize everything into a sphere." In *Language, Counter-memory, Practice* (1977; Ithaca: Cornell University Press, 1993), 165–66.

66. F. Scott Fitzgerald, *The Crack-Up* (Harmondsworth: Penguin, 1976), 39. This is also the most quoted Fitzgerald story in Deleuze's work (see *A Thousand Plateaus*, 198).

67. I discuss "thirdspace" at length in chapter 1.

68. Koolhaas, *Delirious New York*, 173, 197, 241–42.

69. Theodor Adorno, *Minima Moralia* (1951; London: Verso, 2005), 74.

70. See Paul Giles's call for the "surrealization" of American studies in *Virtual Americas* (Durham: Duke University Press, 2003), 88.

71. Foucault, *Archaeology of Knowledge*, 42.

72. Koolhaas, *Delirious New York*, 245. Interestingly, New Western history reminds us to some extent that cities are western, and some of its well-known writers have written about urbanism in this "askew" way. See Patricia Nelson Limerick, "What Raymond Chandler Knew and Western Historians Forgot," in *Old West—New West*, ed. Barbara Meldrum (Moscow: University of Idaho Press, 1993).

73. Rajchman, *Constructions*, 20.

74. Derrida, *The Truth of Painting*, 22, 23, 54.

75. Rajchman, *Constructions*, 20–21. Here Rajchman is discussing the architectural theory of Peter Eisenman.

76. Derrida and Eisenman's collaboration was instigated by Tschumi, who won the competition to design the Parc de la Villette. Derrida wrote an essay on Tshumi's work, "Point de folie: Maintenant l'architecture," in *Rethinking Architecture*, ed. Neil Leach (London: Routledge, 1997); Bernard Tschumi, *Architecture and Disjunction* (Cambridge: MIT Press, 2001), 174–75; Jacques Derrida and Peter Eisenman, *Chora L Works* (New York: Monacelli Press, 1997), 135; Rajchman, *Constructions*, 21.

77. Tschumi, *Architecture and Disjunction*, 175, 195, 179, 194.

78. Derrida, "Point de folie," 326, 328.

79. Tschumi's work has many parallels to that of Paul Virilio, whose early architectural ideas in the 1960s also valued what he called the "theory of the oblique" as a means to break down the two accepted forms of architecture (the Euclidean space of the horizontal and the vertical) so as to achieve a third alternative—the "oblique." Virilio's interest in space and architecture led him to a detailed examination of the virtual as a further extension of physical, actual space. In other words, the virtual takes one outside the grid once more. Tschumi, *Architecture and Disjunction*, 196.

80. Tschumi, *Architecture and Disjunction*, 203; Derrida, "Point de folie," 328.

81. Derrida, "Point de folie," 331.

82. Tschumi, *Architecture and Disjunction*, 217–18.

83. Stuart Hall, "New Cultures for Old," in *A Place in the World?* ed. Doreen Massey and Pat Jess (Oxford: Oxford University Press, 1995), 181. A useful study of some of these ideas can be found in Susan Stanford Friedman, *Mappings: Feminism and the Cultural Geographies of Encounter* (Princeton: Princeton University Press, 1998), chapter 6.

84. Massey quote in Hall, "New Cultures for Old," 186.

85. Clifford, *Routes*, 23.

86. Paul Gilroy, *The Black Atlantic* (1993; London: Verso, 1996), 6, 7.

87. Jan Nederveen Pieterse, "Globalization as Hybridization," in *Global Modernities*, ed. Mike Featherstone, Scott Lash, and Roland Robertson (London: Sage, 1995), 64.

88. James Clifford wrote his "Notes on Travel and Theory" in 1989 and "Traveling Cultures" in 1992. Gilroy published *The Black Atlantic* in 1993. Gilroy, *The Black Atlantic*, 17.

89. Rosaldo quoted in Joseph Roach, *Cities of the Dead: Circum-Atlantic Performance* (New York: Columbia University Press, 1996), 29. Original in Renato Rosaldo, *Culture and Truth* (1989; Boston: Beacon Press, 1993), 20.

90. Gilroy, *The Black Atlantic*, 30, 19.

91. Paul Gilroy, "Diaspora and the Detours of Identity," in *Identity and Difference*, ed. K. Woodward (London: Sage, 1997), 328.

92. Gilroy, *The Black Atlantic*, 29, 31.

93. Gilroy, "Diaspora," 331.

94. Hall, "New Cultures for Old," 207.

95. Clifford, *Routes*, 24, 25, 2, 30, 251.

96. Bharati Mukherjee, *Jasmine* (1989; London: Virago, 2001), 81, 77.

97. Gilroy, *The Black Atlantic*, 96, 102, 198, 199.

98. Giles, *Virtual Americas*, 2, 3, 5, 6.

99. Giles, "Transnationalism and Classic American Literature," 63.

100. Giles, *Virtual Americas*, 6.

101. Giles, *Virtual Americas*, 7. Giles quotes Arjun Appadurai at this point to emphasize the advantages in an alternative "disjunctive" model that acknowledges

NOTES TO PAGES 31–34

(like Gilroy) global flows, mobilities, and the various complex routes that identities and nations follow. I discuss Appadurai later in this section and in chapter 1.

102. Gloria Anzaldúa, "Now Let Us Shift . . . the Path of Conocimiento . . . Inner Work, Public Acts," in *This Bridge We Call Home: Radical Visions for Transformation*, ed. Gloria Anzaldúa and Analouise Keating (London: Routledge, 2002), 549; Adams quoted in Giles, *Virtual Americas*, 7; Giles, *Virtual Americas*, 11, 14.

103. Giles, *Virtual Americas*, 18. The concept of "in-between," "middle," "interface," or "thirdspace" will resurface throughout this book in the work of many of the writers, critics, and artists under consideration. As Deleuze and Guattari put it, "A line of becoming has only a middle. The middle is not an average; it is fast motion. . . . A becoming is neither one nor two, nor the relation of the two; it is the in-between, the border or line of flight." *A Thousand Plateaus*, 293.

104. Shields quoted in Giles, *Virtual Americas*, 18.

105. Rob Shields, *The Virtual* (London: Routledge, 2003), 12, 14. Although not using this language, Nathaniel Lewis's *Unsettling the Literary West: Authenticity and Authorship* (Lincoln: University of Nebraska Press, 2003) undertakes a similar process.

106. Giles, "Transnationalism and Classic American Literature," 64. This process, as I argue at length in chapter 1, can be seen at the heart of J. B. Jackson's work, where "geographical integrity" is constantly critiqued by taking the "stranger's path" into overlooked and disregarded spaces.

107. Giles has referred to this as "a replenished, more complete version of American Studies, where the negative polarities of exclusion are annealed and the multiple languages of America brought, either sentimentally or dialogically, into accord" ("Transnationalism in Practice").

108. Giles, "Transnationalism and Classic American Literature," 64.

109. John Carlos Rowe, "Globalism and the New American Studies," in *Post-Nationalist American Studies*, ed. Rowe (Berkeley: University of California Press, 2000), 30–31.

110. Giles, "Transnationalism and Classic American Literature," 65, 72.

111. Giles, *Virtual Americas*, 263.

112. Gilles Deleuze and Claire Parnet, *Dialogues II* (London: Continuum, 2000), 11, 75. The phrase "poor, lonesome cowboy" appears to derive from the French cartoon cowboy character Lucky Luke, whose catchphrase it was.

113. Deleuze and Guattari, *A Thousand Plateaus*, 520 n. 18.

114. Deleuze and Parnet, *Dialogues II*, vii–viii.

115. Deleuze, *Francis Bacon*, 104–5.

116. Rajchman, *The Deleuze Connections*, 40.

117. Deleuze and Guattari, *A Thousand Plateaus*, 7.

118. Deleuze and Parnet, *Dialogues II*, 30, 36.

119. Deleuze and Parnet, *Dialogues II*, 37, 38, 39; Henri Lefebvre, *The Production of Space* (Oxford: Blackwell, 1991).

120. Deleuze and Parnet, *Dialogues II*, 39, 48.

121. Deleuze and Guattari, *Anti-Oedipus*, 132–33.

122. Deleuze and Guattari, *A Thousand Plateaus*, 186–87.

123. Deleuze and Parnet, *Dialogues II*, 24, 25.

124. Derrida, "Point de folie," 331.

125. Turner, *Frontier and Section*, 43; Deleuze and Guattari, *A Thousand Plateaus*, 20, 16, 6, 21, 25.

126. Gilles Deleuze, *The Fold: Leibniz and the Baroque* (Minneapolis: University of Minnesota Press, 1993), 20, 19, 6, 35, 120, 123, 16.

127. Clifford, *Routes*, 11.

128. Vizenor, *Fugitive Poses*, 22. As we will see, Vizenor describes Native American identity as "transmotional," created "in 'dialogical relations' with many others, with nature, and with those who must bear the *indian* simulations of dominance," and perhaps any consideration of the West must likewise find a similar "dialogic circle" that allows for the many intersecting and diverging elements to construct its own unfixed and unstable presence.

129. Doreen Massey, *Space, Place and Gender* (Cambridge: Polity, 1994), 155, 137, 152, 155, 154, 155–56; see also Doreen Massey, *For Space* (London: Sage, 2005), 9.

130. Arjun Appadurai, "Grassroots Globalization and the Research Imagination," *Public Culture* 12, no. 1 (2000): 7.

131. Turner, *Frontier and Section*, 61.

132. Appadurai, "Grassroots Globalization," 7, 8.

133. Rajchman, *Constructions*, 20.

134. Grosz, *Architecture from the Outside*, 66.

135. Anzaldúa, "Now Let Us Shift," 541, 544, 549, 548–49.

1. Toward an Expanded Critical Regionalism

1. Neil Campbell, *The Cultures of the American New West* (Edinburgh: Edinburgh University Press, 2000), 2.

2. Clyde Milner, "The View from Wisdom: Four Layers of History and Regional Identity," in *Under an Open Sky: Rethinking America's Western Past*, ed. William Cronon, George Miles, and Jay Gitlin (New York: Norton, 1992), 222.

3. Arjun Appadurai, "Grassroots Globalization and the Research Imagination," *Public Culture* 12, no. 1 (2000): 7.

4. Gunter H. Lenz, "Towards a Dialogics of International American Culture Studies: Transnationality, Border Discourses, and Public Culture(s)," *Amerikasstudien/American Studies* 44 (1999): 18.

5. Wilson quoted in Paul Giles, *Virtual Americas* (Durham: Duke University Press, 2003), 63.

6. Stephanie Foote, "The Cultural Work of American Regionalism" in *A Com-*

panion to the Regional Literatures of America, ed. Charles Crowe (Oxford: Blackwell, 2003), 26, 27, 30, 38, 26, 38.

7. Patricia Nelson Limerick, "Region and Reason," in *All Over the Map: Rethinking American Regions*, ed. Edward L. Ayers, Patricia Nelson Limerick, Stephen Nissenbaum, and Peter S. Onuf (Baltimore: Johns Hopkins University Press, 1996), 84, 96, 99, 95, 99.

8. See http://regionalworlds.uchicago.edu for more information on this project.

9. Appadurai, "Grassroots Globalization," 5.

10. Arjun Appadurai, "Disjuncture and Difference in the Global Cultural Economy," in *Global Culture: Nationalism, Globalization, and Modernity*, ed. Mike Featherstone (London: Sage, 1990), 296.

11. Appadurai, "Grassroots Globalization," 7.

12. Sita Ranchod-Nilsson, "Regional Worlds: Transforming Pedagogy in Area Studies and International Studies" (2000), 8, http//www.regionalworlds.uchicago.edu/transformingpedagogy.pdf.

13. Kenneth Frampton, "Towards a Critical Regionalism: Six Points for an Architecture of Resistance," in *Postmodern Culture*, ed. Hal Foster (1983; London: Verso, 1990), 1983, 16.

14. Frampton, "Towards a Critical Regionalism," 20, 21, 22, 23, 25.

15. Kenneth Frampton, *Modern Architecture* (London: Thames and Hudson, 2002), 315; see Chris Wilson, *The Myth of Santa Fe: Creating a Modern Regional Tradition* (Albuquerque: University of New Mexico Press, 1997), on forms of modern regionalism in New Mexico.

16. Liane Lefaivre and Alexander Tzonis, *Critical Regionalism: Architecture and Identity in a Globalized World* (Munich: Prestel, 2003), 10.

17. Catherine Slessor, *Concrete Regionalism* (London: Thames and Hudson, 2000), 16.

18. Frampton, "Towards a Critical Regionalism," 17.

19. Fredric Jameson, *The Seeds of Time* (New York: Columbia University Press, 1994), 204, 205, 201.

20. Frampton, *Modern Architecture*, 314, 315.

21. Frampton, "Towards a Critical Regionalism," 17, 21, 22.

22. See Wilson, *The Myth of Santa Fe*, 305; Frampton, "Towards a Critical Regionalism," 26.

23. Frampton, "Towards a Critical Regionalism," 21, 26.

24. Lefaivre and Tzonis, *Critical Regionalism*, 7, 21.

25. In *The Myth of Santa Fe*, 274–91, Wilson discusses the debates within Santa Fe over modern regionalism and in particular cites the influence of John Gaw Meem from the 1920s, whose architecture stressed the importance of site, local materials, and climate. Mumford visited Santa Fe in 1962, and J. B. Jackson had a home there and reported the debates in his journal *Landscape* (see 257–58).

26. Liane Lefaivre and Alexander Tzonis, "Lewis Mumford's Regionalism," *Design Book Review* 19 (Winter 1991): 3, 1, 2, http//www.bk.tudelft.nl/dks/publications.

27. Lefaivre and Tzonis, *Critical Regionalism*, 34.

28. Lewis Mumford, *Roots of Contemporary American Architecture* (1952; New York: Dover, 1972), xi.

29. Lefaivre and Tzonis, *Critical Regionalism*, 34.

30. Quoted in Lefaivre and Tzonis, *Critical Regionalism*, 35.

31. Lefaivre and Tzonis, *Critical Regionalism*, 35–36, 38.

32. Quoted in Lefaivre and Tzonis, *Critical Regionalism*, 38–39.

33. Lefaivre and Tzonis, *Critical Regionalism*, 39.

34. Cheryl Temple Herr, *Critical Regionalism and Cultural Studies: From Ireland to the American Midwest* (Gainesville: University of Florida, 1996), 18.

35. Slessor, *Concrete Regionalism*, 19, 20.

36. Lucy Lippard, *The Lure of the Local* (New York: The New Press, 1997), 37.

37. Frampton, *Modern Architecture*, 327; Herr, *Critical Regionalism and Cultural Studies*, 8, 18, 9.

38. Edward Soja, *Postmodern Geographies* (London: Verso, 1989), 189.

39. Edward Soja, *Thirdspace* (Oxford: Blackwell, 1996), 16. Other writers, such as Mike Davis in *City of Quartz* (London: Verso, 1990) and Peter Reyner Banham in *Los Angeles: Four Ecologies* (Harmondsworth: Penguin, 1971), can perhaps be seen as "new regionalists," particularly as I go on to define it here (see chapter 4).

40. Krista Comer, *Landscapes of the New West* (Chapel Hill: North Carolina University Press, 1999); Krista Comer, "Taking Feminism and Regionalism toward the Third Wave," in Crowe, *Regional Literatures of America*, 112–13.

41. Quoted in Lefaivre and Tzonis, *Critical Regionalism*, 35 (emphasis added).

42. Alison Calder, "Getting the Real Story: Implications of the Demand for Authenticity in Writings from the Canadian West," in *True West*, ed. William Handley and Nathaniel Lewis (Lincoln: University of Nebraska Press, 2004), 59. Calder in turn echoes Paul Gilroy's notion of "cultural insiderism" discussed in the introduction—rhetorical strategies that emphasize ethnic difference and ethnic homogeneity, nationality, national belonging, nationalism—an intense localism whereby the national is condensed and heightened as the presence of the regional and the local (of Texas as the "nth" degree of Americanness, for example).

43. Comer, "Third Wave," 114 (emphasis added).

44. Lippard, *The Lure of the Local*, 6.

45. Jane Desmond and Virginia R. Dominguez, "Resituating American Studies in a Critical Internationalism," *American Quarterly* 48, no. 3 (1996): 475–76, 476–77.

46. John Carlos Rowe, introduction to *Post-Nationalist American Studies*, ed. Rowe (Berkeley: University of California Press, 2000), 8.

47. Lefaivre and Tzonis, *Critical Regionalism*, 34.

48. Mary Louise Pratt, *Imperial Eyes* (London: Routledge, 1992), 4, 6–7.

49. John Carlos Rowe, "Post-Nationalism, Globalism, and the New American Studies," in Rowe, *Post-Nationalist American Studies*, 30.

50. Comer, "Third Wave," 113; Dick Ellis, "Be a Crossroads: Globalising from Within," in *49th Parallel: An Interdisciplinary Journal of North American Studies* 8 (2001), http://artsweb.bham.ac.uk/49thparallel/backissues/issue8/coll_ellis,htm. David M. Jordan, in *New World Regionalism* (Toronto: University of Toronto Press, 1994), claims that regionalism is marginal and therefore "necessarily proceeds from a de-centred world-view," since it functions "in opposition" to "a world beyond regional borders" (8). This is only sometimes true and cannot be taken as a universal truth of regionalism. After all, can't it engage with the world?

51. Rowe, "Post-Nationalism, Globalism, and the New American Studies," 31.

52. Michael C. Steiner and David M. Wrobel, "Many Wests: Discovering a Dynamic Western Regionalism," in *Many Wests: Place, Culture, and Regional Identity*, ed. Wrobel and Steiner (Lawrence: University of Kansas Press, 1997), 17.

53. Lenz, "Towards a Dialogics," 17. Under these terms, one can legitimately promote the reconceptualization of critical regionalism in the way that Audrey Goodman suggests we might, to "function as what Immanuel Wallerstein calls 'an antisystematic movement,' an experimental and mobile strategy that seeks alternatives to the dominant structure of capitalist world-system." Goodman, *Translating Southwestern Landscapes* (Tucson: University of Arizona Press, 2000), 167.

54. Martin Heidegger, "Conversation on a Country Path about Thinking," in *Discourse on Thinking* (New York: Harper Torchbooks, 1966), 66–67.

55. Soja, *Postmodern Geographies*, 189.

56. Soja spells the concept as one word, and I will follow this convention. However, other critics, such as Homi Bhabha, use two words.

57. Soja, *Thirdspace*, 1.

58. Soja, *Thirdspace*, 5, 3, 5.

59. I am grateful to Victor Burgin's helpful book *In/Different Spaces* (Berkeley: University of California Press, 1996), 26–28, for his discussion of Lefebvre's and Soja's work.

60. Quoted in Soja, *Thirdspace*, 10.

61. Homi Bhabha, "The Third Space," in *Identity, Community, Culture, Difference*, ed. Jonathan Rutherford (London: Lawrence and Wishart, 1990), 211.

62. A key figure here is Paul Vidal de la Blache (1845–1918), who founded *Annales de Geographie* and was committed to intensive regional geography, believing that the physical environment and human activity were intimately connected and that one should study the "genre de vie" (a way of living) in all its elements. Such thinking was immensely influential on Jackson.

63. Richard Hoggart's *The Use of Literacy* (1957) and Raymond Williams's *Culture and Society* (1958) are seen as inaugural texts in British cultural studies, but Jackson's *Landscape* was launched in 1951. However, Jackson's work responded to earlier European work in France in the 1930s and later via the British Independent Group (itself responding to U.S. popular culture). These circuits of exchange and influence are vital to understanding Jackson and his inevitable resistance to any essentialist label. He studies America—the West—but without an inwardness.

64. For example, Jackson wrote specifically on Santa Fe, New Mexico, Optimo City (an invented western space), Chihuahua, and many other western landscapes.

65. Quoted in Paul Groth and Chris Wilson, eds., *Everyday America* (Berkeley: University of California Press, 2003), 9.

66. I borrow the term "everyday regionalisms" from Matt Herman, "Literature, Growth, and Criticism in the New West," *Western American Literature* 38, no. 1 (2003): 67. Krista Comer developed the term in "Everyday Regionalisms in Contemporary Critical Practice," in *Postwestern Cultures: Literature, Theory, Space*, ed. Susan Kollin (Lincoln: University of Nebraska Press, 2007), 30–58. For Jackson on the "vernacular" see his "The Vernacular City" in *Landscape in Sight: Looking at America*, ed. H. L. Horowitz (New Haven: Yale University Press, 1997), 246.

67. John Brinckerhoff Jackson, *Discovering the Vernacular Landscape* (New Haven: Yale University Press, 1984), xi; and Jackson, "High Plains," in Horowitz, *Landscape in Sight*, 160.

68. See the introduction for a brief discussion of genealogy. Jackson was known both to the founder of New Western history, Patricia Nelson Limerick, and to her architect husband, Jeffrey, and both have written about him. Patricia Limerick refers to him as a "personal trainer, who takes us through callisthenics that trick us into revealing unexpected reservoirs of stamina and agility and who gives us a chance to rethink the rules of the game" (see Wilson and Groth, *Everyday America*, 36).

69. Donald Worster, *Under Western Skies: Nature and History in the American West* (New York: Oxford University Press, 1992), 12.

70. Gilles Deleuze and Félix Guattari, *Kafka: Toward a Minor Literature* (Minneapolis: University of Minnesota Press, 1986), 18; and Gilles Deleuze and Félix Guattari, *A Thousand Plateaus* (London: Athlone Press, 1996), 7. Of course, the word "vernacular" carries with it the sense of a language that is native and local, but like Deleuze and Guattari's concept of the "minor," Jackson's use of "vernacular" is wider and more complex.

71. Gilles Deleuze, *Essays Critical and Clinical* (London: Verso, 1998), lv.

72. Grady Clay, "From Crossing the American Grain for Broadcast on Public Radio WFPL December 18, 1996," *Landscape Journal* 16, no. 1 (1997): 19.

73. Deleuze, *Essays Critical and Clinical*, 57.

74. John Brinckerhoff Jackson, *Landscapes: Selected Writings*, ed. Ervin H. Zube (Amherst: University of Massachusetts Press, 1970), 68.

75. Michel Foucault, *Language, Counter-Memory, Practice: Selected Essays and Interviews* (Ithaca: Cornell University Press), 1993, 161; Jackson, *Discovering the Vernacular Landscape*, 85. Jackson had read Foucault, quoting him, for example, in *The Necessity for Ruins* (Amherst: University of Massachusetts Press, 1980), 5–6.

76. Jackson, *Discovering the Vernacular Landscape*, xiii, x.

77. Jackson in Horowitz, *Landscape in Sight*, 26; and in Jackson, *Discovering the Vernacular Landscape*, 141.

78. Zelinsky quoted in Rick Van Noy, *Surveying the Interior: Literary Cartographers and the Sense of Place* (Reno: University of Nevada Press, 2003) 15. Jackson discusses territoriality at some length in "The Accessible Landscape" (in Horowitz, *Landscape in Sight*, 69–71).

79. Jackson, *Landscapes*, 142.

80. Jackson in Horowitz, *Landscape in Sight*, 167.

81. John Brinckerhoff Jackson, *A Sense of Time, A Sense of Place* (New Haven: Yale University Press, 1994), 153, 154.

82. See the introduction's discussion of grid theory in the work of Rosalind Krauss, Rem Koolhaas, Bernard Tschumi, Rick Van Noy, and William L. Fox.

83. Stilgoe quoted in Van Noy, *Surveying the Interior*, 16; Jackson, *A Sense of Time*, 6, 4, 6. As I have argued elsewhere, Jackson's work has to be seen as related to the Beat and counterculture of the 1950s and 1960s and in particular their questioning of the centripetal forces of consensus, suburbia, consumerism, and containment. See Neil Campbell, "'Much Unseen Is Also Here': John Brinckerhoff Jackson's New Western Roadscapes," *European Journal of American Culture* 23, no. 3 (2004): 173–85.

84. Deleuze and Guattari, *A Thousand Plateaus*, 361–62, xiii.

85. Jackson, *Discovering the Vernacular Landscape*, 67, 119, and Jackson quoted in Horowitz, *Landscape in Sight*, 260, 263–64. See Antonio Gramsci's work on Fordism and hegemony, *Selections from the Prison Notebooks* (New York: Lawrence and Wishart, 1971).

86. See Horowitz, *Landscape in Sight*, xiv; Gilles Deleuze, *The Fold: Leibniz and the Baroque* (Minneapolis: University of Minnesota Press, 1993), 3. Another connection from Jackson to Robert Venturi and Denise Scott Brown is through a shared interest in the baroque; see Robert Venturi, *Complexity and Contradiction in Architecture* (New York: MOMA, 1966), 13.

87. Jackson, *Landscapes*, 66.

88. John Rajchman, *Constructions* (Cambridge: MIT Press, 1998), 26.

89. Jackson in Horowitz, *Landscape in Sight*, 352.

90. Kathleen Stewart, *A Space on the Side of the Road: Cultural Poetics in an "Other" America* (Princeton: Princeton University Press, 1996), 3. Again the idea of "becoming" is borrowed from Deleuze and Guattari.

91. Stewart, *A Space*, 3.

92. Jackson, *A Sense of Time*, 180; Jackson in Horowitz, *Landscape in Sight*, 291.

93. Homi Bhabha, *The Location of Culture* (London: Routledge, 1994), 37.

94. Jackson, *The Necessity for Ruins*, 11.

95. The phrase "regional nationalism" is used by Matt Herman in "Literature, Growth, and Criticism in the New West," 71; Jackson, *The Necessity for Ruins*, 11.

96. Jackson, *Discovering the Vernacular Landscape*, xii.

97. Lefaivre and Tzonis, *Critical Regionalism*, 20.

98. Mumford quoted in Lefaivre and Tzonis, *Critical Regionalism*, 39.

99. Jackson in Horowitz, *Landscape in Sight*, 223, and Jackson, *Discovering the Vernacular Landscape*, 152–55.

100. Deleuze and Guattari, *A Thousand Plateaus*, 474.

101. Jackson, *Discovering the Vernacular Landscape*, 154, 155; Burgin, *In/Different Spaces*, 185.

102. Jackson, *Landscapes*, 58; P. Groth and T. Bressi, eds., *Understanding Ordinary Landscapes* (Berkeley: University of California Press, 1997), 153; Jackson, *Discovering the Vernacular Landscape*, 157.

103. Jackson in Horowitz, *Landscape in Sight*, 207–8; Jackson, *Landscapes*, 149, 149–50. In this respect Jackson has something in common with Paul Virilio's exploration of how speed and acceleration in the modern world rob humanity of its contacts with life.

104. Jackson, *Landscapes*, 149–50.

105. Jackson, *Landscapes*, 150, 9; Jackson in Horowitz, *Landscape in Sight*, 23–27, 69. Susan Naremore Maher's article "Deep Mapping the Great Plains: Surveying the Literary Cartography of Place," *Western American Literature* 36, no. 1 (2001): 4–24, was a provocative source for some of these ideas. William Least Heat-Moon, whom Maher discusses, mentions Jackson seven times in the "From the Commonplace Book" section of *PrairyErth*.

106. Jackson is often criticized as nonpolitical; see Richard Walker, "Unseen and Disbelieved: A Political Economist among Cultural Geographers," in Groth and Bressi, *Understanding Ordinary Landscapes*, 162–79. Although I would agree that Jackson does not consider issues of race and gender in the manner of recent cultural studies, he is very aware of the presence of class, political control, and forms of spatial "apartheid." Jackson is not, as Walker states, "too respectful" (172), but he is more observant and astute in his ideological analysis than is often credited. His recognition of poverty as a major factor in spatiality is a very important breakthrough and ties his ideas in with those of Michael Harrington (see Campbell, "'Much Unseen Is Also Here'").

107. Jackson, *Discovering the Vernacular Landscape*, 150.

108. Michel De Certeau, *The Practice of Everyday Life* (Berkeley: University of California Press, 1984).

NOTES TO PAGES 70–79

109. Jackson, "The House in the Vernacular Landscape," in *The Making of the American Landscape*, ed. Michael Conzen (London: Routledge, 1990), 368.

110. Jackson, *Landscapes*, 72, 111, 138, 143; Jackson in Conzen, *Making of the American Landscape*, 368. Again I see Jackson as working ahead of urbanist Mike Davis, whose work on public space is prefigured in many of these essays and ideas.

111. Jackson, *Landscapes*, 111, 9; Jackson, *Discovering the Vernacular Landscape*, 148.

112. Jackson in Horowitz, *Landscape in Sight*, 162, 77.

113. Deleuze and Guattari, *Kafka*, 24, 25, 26, 27, 27.

114. Deleuze and Guattari, *A Thousand Plateaus*, 8, 98.

115. Denise Scott Brown, "Learning from Brinck," in Groth and Wilson, *Everyday America*, 56.

116. Bhabha, *The Location of Culture*, 38.

117. Jackson, *Landscapes*, 147.

118. Bhabha, *The Location of Culture*, 38–39.

119. Jackson in Horowitz, *Landscape in Sight*, 205.

120. Jackson in Horowitz, *Landscape in Sight*, 368.

121. Comer, "Everyday Regionalisms," 32.

122. Jackson, *Discovering the Vernacular Landscape*, 148, 155, xi.

2. Feasts of Wire

1. José David Saldívar, *Border Matters: Remapping American Cultural Studies* (Berkeley: University of California Press, 1997), ix. Saldívar comments on Gilroy's influence (12). See also how the term "transnational imaginary" is defined and used in Ramón Saldívar, *The Borderlands of Culture: Américo Paredes and the Transnational Imaginary* (Durham: Duke University Press, 2006).

2. Donald Pease, ed., *Revisionary Interventions into the Americanist Canon* (Durham: Duke University Press, 1994), 11.

3. J. D. Saldívar quoting Amy Kaplan in *Border Matters*, xiii.

4. J. D. Saldívar, *Border Matters*, 13–14.

5. Deleuze in Gilles Deleuze and Claire Parnet, *Dialogues II* (London: Continuum, 2002), 131–32.

6. J. D. Saldívar, *Border Matters*, 13–14.

7. Paul Giles, *Virtual Americas* (Durham: Duke University Press, 2003), 63, 65.

8. Giles, *Virtual Americas*, 72.

9. Paul Gilroy, *The Black Atlantic* (London: Verso, 1993), x, xi, 2, 1.

10. Gilroy, *The Black Atlantic*, 2–3.

11. Gilroy, *The Black Atlantic*, 3.

12. Giles, *Virtual Americas*, 271.

13. Gilroy, *The Black Atlantic*, 4. Gilroy's direct reference to Deleuze and Guattari is limited to one citation in *The Black Atlantic* (31), in reference to Edouard

Glissant. However, it is apparent that his work is informed by their ideas, in particular the concept of the rhizome.

14. Rubén Martinez, interview with author, July 7, 2005.

15. R. Saldívar, *The Borderlands of Culture*, 28.

16. Gloria Anzaldúa, *Borderlands/La Frontera* (San Francisco: Aunt Lute Books, 1987), n.p., 22.

17. Gloria Anzaldúa, "La prieta," in *This Bridge Called My Back: Writings by Radical Women of Color*, ed. C. Moraga and Gloria Anzaldúa (San Francisco: Aunt Lute Books, 1981), 208–9.

18. Charles Bowden with Virgil Hancock, *Chihuahua: Pictures from the Edge* (Albuquerque: University of New Mexico Press, 1996), refers to the borderlands as the "Edge. The sound is a blade that cuts" (4).

19. Anzaldúa, *Borderlands*, 49, 79–82, 46. "Coatlicue" is Anzaldúa's term for everyday ruptures, contradictions, the fusion of opposites that act as a jarring prelude to "crossing over," change, and transformation.

20. Renato Rosaldo, *Culture and Truth* (Boston: Beacon Press, 1993), 216.

21. Anzaldúa, *Borderlands*, 82.

22. Iain Chambers, *Migrancy, Culture, Identity* (London: Routledge, 1994), 6.

23. Urrea credits Martinez in his *The Devil's Highway: A True Story* (New York: Little Brown, 2004), acknowledging *Crossing Over* as "a classic of border literature" and writing that "Anyone who wants to understand the world of the undocumented entrant could do worse than start here" (228). In return, Martinez credits Urrea in *The New Americans* (New York: The New Press, 2004): "whose work on many of the themes in this book precedes mine" (vii).

24. Martinez interview with author, July 7, 2005.

25. Urrea refers to his books as a "series" in *By the Lake of Sleeping Children* (New York: Anchor Books, 1996), 7. His first book, *Across the Wire* (New York: Anchor Books, 1993), was published the year after Martinez's *The Other Side* (New York: Vintage, 1992). Urrea has lived in Tijuana, Mexico City, Colorado, Illinois, California, Massachusetts, Arizona, Louisiana.

26. Luis Alberto Urrea, *Nobody's Son: Notes from an American Life* (Tucson: University of Arizona Press, 1998), 58.

27. Gilroy, *The Black Atlantic*, xi.

28. Urrea, *Nobody's Son*, 76, 10, 11, 12. Urrea makes this comment first in *By the Lake of Sleeping Children*, 4.

29. Urrea, *Nobody's Son*, 12, 58.

30. Guillermo Gómez-Pena, *Dangerous Border Crossers* (London: Routledge, 2000), 10. See the similar discussion of Native American Chris Eyre's notion of home in chapter 6.

31. Luis Alberto Urrea, *Wandering Time* (Tucson: University of Arizona Press, 1999), 11. Ghosts recur throughout Urrea's work; see, for example, *The Devil's Highway*, 24, 25.

32. Luis Alberto Urrea, *Six Kinds of Sky* (El Paso: Cinco Puntos Press, 2002), 145. In *Nobody's Son*, Urrea writes, "We're all restless out here. Americans hurrying away. That seems the quintessential American direction: away" (172).

33. Luis Alberto Urrea, *In Search of Snow* (New York: Harper Perennial, 1994), 199.

34. Urrea, *Nobody's Son*, 184.

35. Urrea, *The Devil's Highway*, 11, 7; Bowden with Hancock, *Chihuahua*, 7. Bowden also refers to the border as "two ghost ships" (7–8). Bowden is often cited by Urrea (*By the Lake of Sleeping Children*, xv; *The Devil's Highway*, 56) and is acknowledged as an "invaluable source of border/desert information" (*The Devil's Highway*, 228). In return, Bowden is quoted on the cover of *The Devil's Highway*.

36. Urrea, *Across the Wire*, 2. Américo Paredes invented the idea of Greater Mexico as "an imaginary social space consisting in transnational communities of shared fates" (R. Saldívar, *The Borderlands of Culture*, 59). It is used to signify the extraterritorial Mexican spaces that lie outside the national boundaries of Mexico where millions of migrant or diasporic Mexicans live and work. As Martinez and Urrea show, the extent of Greater Mexico is growing as Mexicans move further into the U.S. hinterland. For other work by Montoya see http://www.malaquiasmontoya.com.

37. J. D. Saldívar, *Border Matters*, 139, quoting James Clifford, *Person and Myth: Maurice Leenhardt in the Melanesian World* (Durham: Duke University Press, 1992), 126.

38. Luis Alberto Urrea, "Ghost Sickness 14" (original in Spanish), in *Ghost Sickness* (El Paso: Cinco Puntos Press, 1997), 25, 93.

39. Urrea, *Ghost Sickness*, 14; Urrea, *Wandering Time*, 8, 13, 24–25. "Walking" is the word Urrea uses to describe migrant movement across the border in *The Devil's Highway*.

40. Urrea, *Six Kinds of Sky*, 141.

41. It is clear from Martinez's work posted on the ZoneZero website that *Crossing Over* had its origins within the first "New Americans" project, which started around 1996 when he moved to Mexico City. The book for the first project was supposed to appear in 1998 but clearly evolved into two, *Crossing Over* and *The New Americans*. The latter had by then also become tied into a PBS television series of the same name.

42. Martinez, *The New Americans*, 237, 234; Rubén Martinez, *Crossing Over: A Mexican Family on the Migrant Trail* (New York: Picador, 2001), 164.

43. Martinez, *The New Americans*, 238.

44. Martinez, *The Other Side*, 3. In *The New Americans*, Martinez describes the rhetoric of consensus as based around notions of oneness combined with the giving up of names and beliefs (8–9).

45. Rubén Martinez, interview with Robert Birnbaum, http://www.identitytheory.com/people/birnbaum31.html.

46. Martinez was aligned with the Border Arts Workshop between 1986 and 1996 and collaborated on a number of projects, including "Danger Zone/Terreno Peligroso" in 1995. He translated Guillermo Gómez-Pena's essay "Documented/ Undocumented" in 1988 in *Multicultural Literacy: Opening the American Mind*, ed. Rick Simonson and Scott Walker (St. Paul: Graywolf Press, 1988), 127–34, and has three poems in Gómez-Pena's *Temple of Confessions* (1996). He refers to Gómez-Pena as a "mentor" in the "border aesthetic and activist art" (interview with author, August 22, 2005). Gómez-Pena in turn acknowledges Martinez in his *Warrior for Gringostroika* (St. Paul: Graywolf Press, 1993) as "my carnalisimo" (7).

47. Gómez-Pena, *Warrior for Gringostroika*, 16.

48. Gómez-Pena, *Warrior for Gringostroika*, 21; Gómez-Pena, "Documented/ Undocumented," 128–29, 130–31.

49. Gómez-Pena, *Dangerous Border Crossers*, 9.

50. Guillermo Gómez-Pena, *The New World Border* (San Francisco: City Lights Books, 1996), ii.

51. Martinez stated on his ZoneZero internet web diary that the "New Americans" project had various media marked out for its outcomes: book, articles, photographs, radio vignettes, exhibit, website postings, and live chats. "Perpetual Motion," http://www.zonezero.com/exposiciones/fotografos/newam/perpetual2.html.

52. Guillermo Gómez-Pena, "The New World (b)order: A Work in Progress," *Third Text* 21 (1992–93): 72; Martinez interview with author, September 22, 2005.

53. J. D. Saldívar, *Border Matters*, 140–45.

54. Martinez, *The New Americans*, 7, 4.

55. Martinez, *The Other Side*, 5. In *Warrior for Gringostroika* (18), Gómez-Pena claimed that he felt he was "crucified by the East, the West, the North and the South," and later, in 1994, he produced an art installation/performance with Roberto Sifuentes called "The Cruci-Fiction Project" (see *Temple of Confessions* [New York: Powerhouse Cultural Entertainment Books, 1996]).

56. Gloria Anzaldúa in *This Bridge We Call Home: Radical Visions for Transformation*, ed. Gloria Anzaldúa and Analouise Keating (London: Routledge, 2002), 549.

57. Gómez-Pena, *Warrior for Gringostroika*, 19.

58. Martinez, *The New Americans*, 218.

59. Rubén Martinez, "Perspective: The Mother's Eye," http://www.zonezero .com/exposiciones/fotografos/rodriquez/rubenmtz.html; Martinez, *The New Americans*, 219.

60. Quoted in Alicia Gaspar de Alba, *Chicano Art: Inside/Outside the Master's House. Cultural Politics and the CARA Exhibition* (Austin: University of Texas Press, 1998), 25.

61. Martinez, "Perpetual Motion"; Martinez, interview with author, September 22, 2005. The work of Robert Frank is discussed more in chapter 5.

62. Georg M. Gugelberger, ed., *The Real Thing: Testimonial Discourse and Latin America* (Durham: Duke University Press, 1996), 9.

63. Shoshana Felman and Dori Laub, eds., *Testimony: Crises of Witnessing in Literature, Psychoanalysis, and History* (New York: Routledge, 1992), 5.

64. Martinez, *Crossing Over*, 109. Claire F. Fox, *The Fence and the River: Culture and Politics at the U.S.-Mexico Border* (Minneapolis: University of Minnesota Press, 19990, refers to the "abstract grid" created by the border controls and quotes artist/musician Terry Allen—"You can't look at anything without a grid kind of being in front of you" (49).

65. Martinez, *The New Americans*, 217, 244.

66. Rosaldo, *Culture and Truth*, 44.

67. James Clifford, *Routes: Travel and Translation in the Late Twentieth Century* (Boston: Harvard University Press, 1997), 81.

68. Rosaldo, *Culture and Truth*, 20.

69. Martinez, *The New Americans*, 7; Gloria Anzaldúa, *Interviews/Entrevistas* (London: Routledge, 2000), 242.

70. Sonia Saldívar-Hull discusses "fictionalized literary testimonio" in "Women Hollering Transfronteriza Feminisms," *Cultural Studies* 13, no. 2 (1999): 251–62; Anzaldúa in Anzaldúa and Keating, *This Bridge We Call Home*, 544; Gómez-Pena, *Dangerous Border Crossers*, 207, also uses the earthquake to suggest cultural change.

71. Martinez, *The Other Side*, 19.

72. Anzaldúa, *Interviews*, 225–26, 268, 238–39. On this see Hamid Naficy's idea of "border consciousness" discussed in chapter 3.

73. Urrea, *Nobody's Son*, 58.

74. Martinez, *The Other Side*, 128.

75. Chambers, *Migrancy, Culture, Identity*, 5; Anzaldúa, *Interviews*, 238.

76. Gloria Anzaldúa, ed., *Making Face, Making Soul: Haciendo Caras* (San Francisco: Aunt Lute Books, 1990), xv; Anzaldúa, *Borderlands*, 37.

77. Martinez, *The Other Side*, 130. In this section, as in much of Martinez's work, one can see the influence of Mike Davis, whose *City of Quartz* (London: Verso, 1990) examined the myths and realities of the city. In the program Davis made for Channel 4 in the United Kingdom, "LA Wars: Junkyard of Dreams," Martinez appears working in a classroom with L.A. kids and performs his poem "Manifesto."

78. Martinez, *The Other Side*, 146, 132, 131, 132.

79. Martinez, *The Other Side*, 86.

80. Tomás Ybarra-Frausto, "Rasquachismo: A Chicano Sensibility," in *Chicano Aesthetics: Rasquachismo*, Exhibition catalog (Phoenix: MARS, 1989), 5–8.

81. Martinez, *The Other Side*, 136.

82. Martinez, *The Other Side*, 148, 168, 170.

83. Martinez, *Crossing Over*, 3–4. He had intended for this book to be more like

The Other Side, with "MTV-style editing seen from both sides of the border—not a linear narrative . . . I wanted to capture border culture in all its complexity" (Martinez interview with Robert Birnbaum). This is evident in the 1999 piece "The Manifesto of the Purepecha Plateau," http://zonezero.com/magazines/articles/martinez/manif.en.html.

84. This section draws on the work of Joseph Roach, whose *Cities of the Dead: Circum-Atlantic Performance* (New York: Columbia University Press, 1996) explores the complex cultural journeys undertaken in the performance of "blackness."

85. Roach, *Cities of the Dead*, 4–5.

86. Martinez, *Crossing Over*, 43, 9, 81, 160, 25.

87. Roach, *Cities of the Dead*, 5; Martinez, *Crossing Over*, 10.

88. Roach quoting James Clifford, *The Predicament of Culture* (Berkeley: University of California Press, 1988), 15, in Roach, *Cities of the Dead*, 192.

89. Martinez, *Crossing Over*, 139–40.

90. Martinez, *Crossing Over*, 18; Roach, *Cities of the Dead*, xiii.

91. Urrea, *Six Kinds of Sky*, 145.

92. Roach, *Cities of the Dead*, 50, 55.

93. Martinez uses the term "borderscape" in *The New Americans*, 179, in his discussion of Los Tigres Del Norte. The town of Chéran can be defined using Peggy Levitt's term "transnational village" as set out in *The Transnational Villagers* (Berkeley: University of California Press, 2001), 11. Martinez acknowledges Levitt in *The New Americans*, viii, and *Crossing Over*, 140, 30.

94. Martinez, *Crossing Over*, 259.

95. Martinez, *The New Americans*, 208, 9. Urrea, as we saw earlier, does a similar thing at the opening of *The Devil's Highway* linking the Yuma 14 to Coronado.

96. José F. Aranda Jr., *When We Arrive: A New Literary History of Mexican America* (Tucson: University of Arizona Press, 2003), 165, cites an interview in which Rivera tells of Steinbeck's influence. In the book blurb for *Crossing Over*, Urrea refers to Steinbeck as Martinez's "spiritual forbear."

97. Martinez, *Crossing Over*, 95. A "relación" is explained in *Crossing Over* as "a subjective history . . . based on the author's firsthand interviews with elders, so that it is often difficult to separate fact and myth" (52).

98. Deleuze and Parnet, *Dialogues II*, 36–37, 43, 27–28. Deleuze, like Martinez, often mentions his admiration for the work of Kerouac.

99. Hector Calderón, "Rereading Rivera's *Y no se lo trago la tierra*," in *Criticism in the Borderlands*, ed. Hector Calderón and José David Saldívar (Durham: Duke University Press, 1991), 104; Tomás Rivera, *. . . And the Earth Did Not Devour Him* (1971; Houston: Arté Publico Press, 1995), 95.

100. Rivera, *. . . And the Earth Did Not Devour Him*, 109.

101. Gilles Deleuze and Felix Guattari, *Kafka: Toward a Minor Literature* (Minneapolis: University of Minnesota Press, 1986), 19.

102. Rivera, *. . . And the Earth Did Not Devour Him*, 145.

103. Aranda, *When We Arrive*, xv.

104. Martinez, *The New Americans*, 211.

105. Martinez, *Crossing Over*, 17, 2, 198, 191–92.

106. Rivera, . . . *And the Earth Did Not Devour Him*, 151, 152.

107. Martinez, *Crossing Over*, 43, 46; Mike Davis, *Magical Urbanism: Latinos Reinvent the U.S. Big City* (London: Verso, 2000), 80.

108. Martinez, *Crossing Over*, 112, 295.

109. Davis, *Magical Urbanism*, 80.

110. Martinez, *Crossing Over*, 132; Davis, *Magical Urbanism*, 81.

111. Doreen Massey quoted in Stuart Hall, "New Cultures for Old," in *A Place in the World?* ed. Doreen Massey and Pat Jess (Oxford: Oxford University Press, 1995), 186; Hall, "New Cultures for Old," 193. Hall borrows the notion of contact zones from Mary Louise Pratt's *Imperial Eyes* (London: Routledge, 1992). See the introduction for more on these ideas.

112. Martinez, *Crossing Over*, 137.

113. Martinez, *Crossing Over*, 191.

114. Martinez, *Crossing Over*, 223.

115. Hall, "New Cultures for Old," 206.

116. Gilroy, *The Black Atlantic*, 198.

117. Urrea, *Nobody's Son*, 182–83.

118. Martinez, *Crossing Over*, 42, 190, 222; Martinez, *The New Americans*, 9.

119. Martinez, *Crossing Over*, 223; Martinez posted at http://www.zonezero .com/exposiciones/fotografos/newam/cowboys2.html.

120. Anzaldúa, *Borderlands*, 66.

121. Bowden with Hancock, *Chihuahua*, 54.

122. Martinez posted at http://www.zonezero.com/exposiciones/fotografos/ newam/cowboys2.html.

123. Bowden with Hancock, *Chihuahua*, 54.

124. Gómez-Pena, *The New World Border*, 12. Susan Stanford Friedman writes in *Mappings: Feminism and the Cultural Geographies of Encounter* (Princeton: Princeton University Press, 1998) that "Borders have a way of insisting on separation at the same time as they acknowledge connection. Like bridges. Bridges signify the possibility of passing over" (3).

125. Anzaldúa in Anzaldúa and Keating, *This Bridge We Call Home*, 541, 548–49, 560; Chela Sandoval, foreword, in Anzaldúa and Keating, *This Bridge We Call Home*, 23.

126. Martinez, *The New Americans*, 241; Charles Bowden, *Juarez: The Laboratory of Our Future* (New York: Aperture, 1998), 76. NAFTA lifted barriers on the movement of goods and services but excluded the free movement of labor, creating a more dangerous, militarized environment for those crossing. Operation Gatekeeper, introduced by President Clinton in 1995 and 1996, aimed to secure borders against such crossings. Together these have given rise to a "borderless

economy with a barricaded border." Teresa Carrillo, "Watching Over Greater Mexico," in *Alambrista and the U.S.-Mexico Border*, ed. Nicholas J. Cull and David Carrasco (Albuquerque: University of New Mexico Press, 2004), 103.

127. Martinez, *The New Americans*, 9.

128. Anzaldúa, *Borderlands*, 2–3.

129. Anzaldúa in Anzaldúa and Keating, *This Bridge We Call Home*, 4, 5, 549.

130. Anzaldúa in Anzaldúa and Keating, *This Bridge We Call Home*, 560, 561, 570, 573, 574.

131. Martinez, *The New Americans*, 248, 225.

132. Rosa Linda Fregoso, *meXicana Encounters: The Making of Social Identities on the Borderlands* (Berkeley: University of California Press, 2003), xvi. Historian Teresa Carrillo supports this view: "Greater Mexico projects a forward-looking transnational vision that is an odd contrast to a stale backdrop of nationalist notions and closed borders. . . . To anyone complacently lost in a nationalist past, Greater Mexico presents a challenge and a road map" ("Watching Over Greater Mexico," 119).

133. Quoted in Arthur Sal, "Running with the Devil," *Union-Tribune*, http://www.luisurrea.com/extras/articles/running_with_the_devil.htm.

134. Néstor Garcia Canclini, *Hybrid Cultures* (1989; Minneapolis: University of Minnesota Press, 1995), 233; Goméz-Pena, "Documented/Undocumented," 127.

135. Bowden with Hancock, *Chihuahua*, 6–7.

136. Bowden with Hancock, *Chihuahua*, 16.

137. Gómez-Pena, *Warrior for Gringostroika*, 56.

138. Bowden with Hancock, *Chihuahua*, 19, 17.

139. Bowden with Hancock, *Chihuahua*, 18; see also Bowden, *Juarez*; and Charles Bowden, *Down by the River: Drugs, Money, Murder, and Family* (New York: Simon and Schuster, 2004).

140. Bowden, *Juarez*, 49; Felman and Laub, *Testimony*, 5.

141. Bowden with Hancock, *Chihuahua*, 18–19, 20, 42, 47, 49.

142. Gilles Deleuze and Félix Guattari, *A Thousand Plateaus* (London: Athlone Press, 1996), 9; Gilles Deleuze, *Essays Critical and Clinical* (London: Verso, 1998), 2; Gilles Deleuze, *Negotiations, 1972–1990* (New York: Columbia University Press, 1995), 45.

143. Deleuze, *Essays Critical and Clinical*, 4.

144. Martinez, "The Manifesto of the Purepecha Plateau"; Martinez, "Perpetual Motion."

145. Martinez, "Perpetual Motion" (posted February 1998).

3. Welcome to Westworld

1. Michel De Certeau, *The Practice of Everyday Life* (1984; Berkeley: University of California Press, 1988), xviii. De Certeau describes the established, dominant

systems as "gridding (*quadriller*)," a "framework" of "constructed, written, and pre-fabricated space," ordered by "strategy" but challenged by "tactics" (46, 34–35, 37).

2. Sergio Donati (co-scriptwriter) quoted in Christopher Frayling, *Sergio Leone: Once Upon a Time in Italy* (London: Thames and Hudson, 2005), 152.

3. In 1962 German producer Horst Wendlandt and director Harald Reinl made *The Treasure of Silver Lake*, based on the work of Karl May. Filmed in Yugoslavia and starring American actor Lex Barker and Frenchman Pierre Brice, this tongue-in-cheek adventure did well in Europe and opened the way for other films by German, Italian, and Spanish directors. Between 1960 and 1975, European film production companies made nearly six hundred Westerns.

4. Christopher Frayling, *Sergio Leone: Something to Do with Death* (London: Faber and Faber, 2000), 253.

5. Maxine Feifer, *Going Places: The Ways of the Tourist from Imperial Rome to the Present Day* (London: MacMillan, 1985), 270; Arjun Appadurai, *Modernity at Large: Cultural Dimensions of Modernity* (Minneapolis: University of Minnesota Press, 1996), 3.

6. Feifer, *Going Places*, 271.

7. Alex Cox, *Ten Thousand Ways to Die* (unpublished manuscript, 1978), 170, accessed from www.alexcox.com.

8. Nathaniel Lewis, *Unsettling the Literary West* (Lincoln: University of Nebraska Press, 2003), 6.

9. I examine the term "post-tourism" at length in "Producing America: Re-examining Post-tourism in the Global Media Age," in *The Media and the Tourist Imagination: Converging Cultures*, ed. D. Crouch, R. Jackson, and F. Thompson (London: Routledge, 2005). The term "cinema cinema" is Leone's as reported in Frayling, *Sergio Leone: Once Upon a Time in Italy*, 17.

10. Wim Wenders, *On Film: Essays and Conversations* (London: Faber and Faber, 2001), 28.

11. Leone interviewed in Frayling, *Sergio Leone: Once Upon a Time in Italy*, 86.

12. Leone quoted in Sarah Hill, "Sergio Leone and the Myth of the American West: *Once Upon a Time in America*," *Romance Languages Annual* 9 (1998): 204 (emphasis added).

13. Jim Kitses, *Horizons West* (London: BFI, 2004), 249. One prominent study of the Western, Richard Slotkin's trilogy, mentions Leone only once, in a passing reference to his influence on Clint Eastwood.

14. Baudrillard quoted in Frayling, *Sergio Leone: Something to Do with Death*, 492; Bertolucci quoted in Frayling, *Sergio Leone: Once Upon a Time in Italy*, 162.

15. Cox, *Ten Thousand Ways to Die*, 180.

16. John Storey, *An Introductory Guide to Cultural Theory and Popular Culture* (Hemel Hempstead: Harvester Wheatsheaf, 1993), 159.

17. Mikhail Bakhtin, *The Dialogic Imagination* (Austin: University of Texas Press, 1990), 421.

18. Hamid Naficy, *An Accented Cinema: Exilic and Diasporic Filmmaking* (Princeton: Princeton University Press, 2001), 22, 4, 32. I explored this notion of "border consciousness" in chapter 2.

19. Naficy, *An Accented Cinema*, 31.

20. Michel De Certeau, *The Writing of History* (New York: Columbia University Press, 1988), 79.

21. Modarressi quoted in Naficy, *An Accented Cinema*, 23.

22. See chapter 2 for a discussion of the notion of the border as a bridge. See also chapter 6 for a discussion of its use as a metaphor in Chris Eyre's work.

23. Naficy, *An Accented Cinema*, 31.

24. See John Fawell, *The Art of Sergio Leone's Once Upon a Time in the West* (London: McFarland, 2005), 135–37.

25. Quoted in Frayling, *Sergio Leone: Something to Do with Death*, 252.

26. Frayling, *Sergio Leone: Once Upon a Time in Italy*, 55.

27. Gilles Deleuze and Félix Guattari, *What Is Philosophy?* (London: Verso, 1994), 188.

28. Paul Smith, *Clint Eastwood: Cultural Production* (Minneapolis: University of Minnesota Press, 1993), 1, 4, 17.

29. Christopher Frayling, *Spaghetti Westerns: Cowboys and Europeans from Karl May to Sergio Leone* (London: RKP, 1981), 121–37; Krista Comer, *Landscapes of the New West* (Chapel Hill: University of North Carolina Press, 1999), 5.

30. Smith, *Clint Eastwood*, 4, 5.

31. Kobena Mercer, *Welcome to the Jungle: New Positions in Black Cultural Studies* (London: Routledge, 1994), 31.

32. Giuliana Muscio, "Invasion and Counterattack: Italian and American Film Relations in the Postwar Period," in *"Here, There and Everywhere": The Foreign Relations of American Popular Culture*, ed. Richard Wagnleitner and Elaine Tyler May (Hanover: University Press of New England, 2000), 128.

33. William L. Fox, *The Void, the Grid, and the Sign: Traversing the Great Basin* (Salt Lake City: University of Utah Press, 2000), 138, 131.

34. Patricia Nelson Limerick, *The Legacy of Conquest* (New York: Norton, 1987), 27.

35. Leone in Frayling, *Spaghetti Westerns*, 135.

36. De Certeau, *The Writing of History*, xxv–xxvi.

37. De Certeau, *The Writing of History*, 79.

38. De Certeau, *The Writing of History*, 98.

39. De Certeau, *The Writing of History*, 100.

40. Janet Walker, "Captive Images in the Traumatic Western: *The Searchers, Pursued, Once Upon a Time in the West*, and *Lone Star*," in *Westerns: Films through History*, ed. Walker (New York: Routledge, 2001), 239.

41. Lee Clark Mitchell, *Westerns* (Chicago: University of Chicago, 1996), 239.

42. In *Back in the Saddle Again: New Essays on the Western*, ed. Ed Buscombe and

Roberta Pearson (London: BFI, 1998), Rick Worland and Edward Countryman in "The New Western American Historiography and the Emergence of the New American Westerns" define Leone's films as "Marxist anti-Westerns" (188).

43. Philip French, *Westerns: Aspects of a Movie Genre* (London: Secker and Warburg, 1977/1973), 171.

44. Frayling, *Spaghetti Westerns*, 136 (emphasis in source).

45. Smith, *Clint Eastwood*, 22.

46. Jacques Derrida, "The Law of Genre," *Critical Inquiry* 7 (Autumn 1980): 59. Leone also uses the word "contamination" to describe the blending of European views with Hollywood Westerns (see Frayling, *Sergio Leone: Once Upon a Time in Italy*, 86).

47. Derrida in *A Derrida Reader*, ed. Peggy Kamuf (Hemel Hempstead: Harvester Wheatsheaf, 1991), 259.

48. Derrida, "The Law of Genre," 70.

49. Frayling, *Spaghetti Westerns*, 225.

50. These terms come from Deleuze's discussion of framing in *Cinema 1* (1983; London: Continuum Press, 2005).

51. Quoted in Frayling, *Sergio Leone: Something to Do with Death*, 272.

52. Roland Barthes, "The Death of the Author," in *Image/Music/Text* (1977; London: Fontana, 1979), 146, 148.

53. Roland Barthes, "From Work to Text," in *Image/Music/Text*, 160, 162–63, 164.

54. Roland Barthes, *The Semiotic Challenge* (Oxford: Blackwell, 1988), 292.

55. Victor Burgin, *The End of Art Theory: Criticism and Postmodernity* (London: MacMillan, 1986), 73. See James Goodwin, *Akira Kurosawa and Intertextual Cinema* (Baltimore: Johns Hopkins University Press, 1994), for a discussion of Kurosawa's intertextuality and its relationship to the work of Barthes and Bakhtin. Of course, Kurosawa's intertexts included Hollywood Westerns in films like *Yojimbo*, which in turn Leone used as an intertext for his own *Fistful of Dollars*.

56. Deleuze and Guattari, *What Is Philosophy?* 204.

57. Richard Slotkin, *Regeneration through Violence: The Mythology of the American Frontier, 1600–1860* (Middletown CT: Wesleyan University Press, 1973), 5.

58. Cox, *Ten Thousand Ways to Die*, 114.

59. Leone quoted in Frayling, *Sergio Leone: Something to Do with Death*, 252; and Frayling, *Spaghetti Westerns*, 194.

60. Leone quoted in Frayling, *Sergio Leone: Once Upon a Time in Italy*, 88.

61. Frayling, *Spaghetti Westerns*, xv.

62. Hill, "Sergio Leone and the Myth of the American West," 202.

63. Leone quoted in Frayling, *Sergio Leone: Something to Do with Death*, 256.

64. Frayling, *Sergio Leone: Something to Do with Death*, 257.

65. Roland Barthes, *The Pleasure of the Text* (1973; New York: Hill and Wang, 1975), 94, 36.

66. Bertolucci referred to "doing a film which gave pleasure to everyone, in the sense of Roland Barthes' *Plaisir du Texte*" (in Frayling, *Sergio Leone: Something to Do with Death*, 249).

67. Judith Butler, "Merely Cultural," *New Left Review*, no. 227 (1998): 34–35, quoted in Susan Kollin, "Genre and the Geographies of Violence: Cormac McCarthy and the Contemporary Western," *Contemporary Literature* 42, no. 3 (2001): 3.

68. Frayling, *Sergio Leone: Something to Do with Death*, 250.

69. Quoted in Frayling, *Sergio Leone: Once Upon a Time in Italy*, 25.

70. Frayling, *Sergio Leone: Something to Do with Death*, 256, 253, 258.

71. Wenders, *On Film*, 28–29.

72. Quoted in Frayling, *Spaghetti Westerns*, 158.

73. E. H. Gombrich, *The Story of Art* (1950; London: Phaidon, 1972), 344, 347, 349.

74. Gilles Deleuze, *The Fold: Leibniz and the Baroque* (Minneapolis: University of Minnesota Press, 1993), 3, 35. A number of critics refer to Leone's work as baroque—see David Thomson, "Leonesque," *American Film* 14, no. 10 (1989): 30; Adrian Martin, *Once Upon a Time in America* (London: BFI, 1998), 10—but none explore or develop this term. I examine the baroque in relation to J. B. Jackson's work in chapter 1 and the fold in the introduction.

75. Deleuze, *The Fold*, xii; Martin, *Once Upon a Time in America*, 10.

76. Quoted in Frayling, *Sergio Leone: Something to Do with Death*, 125.

77. Quoted in Frayling, *Sergio Leone: Once Upon a Time in Italy*, 87.

78. Quoted in Frayling, *Spaghetti Westerns*, 64.

79. Bertolucci in *Once Upon a Time in the West*, DVD documentary, "Something to Do with Death," 2003.

80. Smith, *Clint Eastwood*, 19, 20; Edward Said, *The World, the Text, the Critic* (London: Vintage, 1991), 226.

81. Marcia Landy, *Cinematic Uses of the Past* (Minneapolis: University of Minnesota Press, 1996,) 69–70.

82. Thomson, "Leonesque," 28.

83. Most notably, Sam Peckinpah, Clint Eastwood (whose *Unforgiven* is dedicated to "Sergio [Leone] and Don [Siegel]"), Alex Cox, Mario Van Peebles, Robert Rodriguez, Quentin Tarantino, Shane Meadows, and Tsui Hark. Alex Cox wrote his (abandoned) dissertation on the Italian Western *Ten Thousand Ways to Die* (available on his website, www.alexcox.com). See Frayling, "The Leone Legacy," in *Sergio Leone: Once Upon a Time in Italy*.

84. This is surely the central reason for Mario Van Peebles's references to Leone's work in *Posse* (1987), and especially for his use of Woody Strode as an iconic figure just as Leone did in *Once Upon a Time in the West*. Strode opens the film with a preface about injustice, racism, and the need for minority stories to be told. Throughout *Posse*, Van Peebles deliberately echoes Leone's work: creaking

sound track, topsy-turvy camera angles, bold close-ups, the use of a fob watch, the use of a flashback past slowly revealed, the railroad sequences, etc.

85. Martin, *Once Upon a Time in America*, 12–13.

86. Quoted in Frayling, *Spaghetti Westerns*, 65.

87. Quoted in E. Lomenzo, "A Fable for Adults," *Film Comment* 20, no. 4 (1984): 22.

88. Frayling, *Sergio Leone: Something to Do with Death*, 254.

89. Peter Hitchcock, *Imaginary States: Studies in Cultural Transnationalism* (Urbana: University of Illinois Press, 2003), 9.

90. Stuart Hall quoted in Hitchcock, *Imaginary States*, 20.

91. Gilles Deleuze, *Cinema 2* (1985; London: Athlone Press, 2000), 217, 216, 220, 217, 219, 223.

92. Claire Colebrook, *Gilles Deleuze* (London: Routledge, 2002), 121.

93. Deleuze, *Cinema 2*, 220.

94. De Certeau, *The Practice of Everyday Life*, 98.

95. Deleuze, *Cinema 2*, 217.

96. There are echoes here of Eastwood's *Unforgiven*, a film also concerned with legend and history and whose central figure, William Munny, comes into contact with a western writer/historian/dime novelist by the name of Beauchamp (echoing Beauregard?) trying to record the narratives of the dying West.

97. "Nobody" also travels back into U.S. cinematic Westerns in Jim Jarmusch's *Dead Man*, where the Native American character played by Gary Farmer is called this. As Michael K. Johnson has pointed out (Western Literature Association, 2003, Houston) this also refers to the Chris Eyre/Sherman Alexie film *Smoke Signals*, in which a young character whose father is played by Gary Farmer answers his father's question "Who is your favorite Indian?" with "Nobody." See chapters 4 and 6 for a discussion of both films.

98. Frayling, *Spaghetti Westerns*, 252.

99. Frayling, *Spaghetti Westerns*, 254–55.

100. See my discussion of *Heaven's Gate* in chapter 4.

101. Quoted in Frayling, *Sergio Leone: Something to Do with Death*, 24.

102. Roxanne Dunbar-Ortiz, "The Grid of History: Cowboys and Indians," *Monthly Review*, 2003, http://www.findarticles.com/p/articles/mi_m1132/is_3_55/ai_105368633/print.

4. "The 'Western' in Quotes"

1. André Bazin, "The Evolution of the Western," in *What Is Cinema?* vol. 2 (Berkeley: University of California Press, 1971), 152; Gilles Deleuze and Félix Guattari, *A Thousand Plateaus* (London: Athlone Press, 1996), 98. "Major" and "majority" here are not about quantity but signify "a constant, of expression or content, serving as a standard measure . . . [such as] adult-white-heterosexual-European-male-speaking . . . [and] assumes a state of power and domination" (105, 99).

2. Gilles Deleuze and Claire Parnet, *Dialogues II* (London: Continuum, 2002), 4; Deleuze and Guattari, *A Thousand Plateaus*, 105.

3. Robin Wood, *Hollywood from Vietnam to Reagan* (New York: Columbia University Press, 1986), 306, 303, 305. One is reminded here of Leone's "cinematic fresco" in *Once Upon a Time in the West* and of how Leone saw this project as "my version of the story of the birth of a nation" (see chapter 3). There are many links between Cimino's film and Leone's—their use of trains and immigrants, for example, and most obviously in both using the town name Sweetwater. Both directors have been viewed as Marxist for their interest in class, economics, and alternative forms of community.

4. See Claire Colebrook, *Gilles Deleuze* (London: Routledge, 2002), 53; see also Daniel Frampton, *Filmosophy* (London: Wallflower Press, 2006), for a development in rethinking cinema from Deleuze.

5. Gilles Deleuze, *Cinema 1* (1992; London: Continuum, 2005), 215; Gilles Deleuze and Félix Guattari, *What Is Philosophy?* (London: Verso, 2003), 176.

6. Wood, *Hollywood from Vietnam to Reagan*, 306.

7. This can been seen again in the political furor over *The West as America* exhibition in 1992.

8. Wood, *Hollywood from Vietnam to Reagan*, 314.

9. Patrick McGee, *From Shane to Kill Bill: Rethinking the Western* (Oxford: Blackwell, 2006), 233.

10. Jim Jarmusch, "Ghost Dancer," *Uncut DVD*, November–December 2005, 78.

11. Jarmusch in *Jim Jarmusch Interviews*, ed. L. Hertzberg (Jackson: University of Mississippi, 2001), 161.

12. See my discussion of some of these films in *The Cultures of the American New West* (Edinburgh: Edinburgh University Press, 2000).

13. Jarmusch appears in Cox's punk Western *Straight to Hell*. Sy Richardson, a regular in Cox's films, scripted *Posse*. See Alexander Keller, "Generic Subversion as Counterhistory: Mario Van Peebles' *Posse*," in *Westerns: Films through History*, ed. Janet Walker (London: Routledge, 2001), 27–46.

14. Jarmusch quoted in Jacquelyn Kilpatrick, *Celluloid Indians: Native Americans and Film* (Lincoln: University of Nebraska Press, 1999), 170; "An Interview with Mili Avital and Jim Jarmusch," http://www.thei.aust.com/isite/celldeadman,html; Jarmusch in Hertzberg, *Jarmusch Interviews*, 204.

15. This interrogation of genres is something Jarmusch's work shares with Robert Altman's and, as we will see in this section, with the "eclectic," genre-jumping work of both Michael Winterbottom and Ang Lee.

16. Dick Hebdige, *Subculture: The Meaning of Style* (London: Routledge, 1979), 103; John Fiske, *Understanding Popular Culture* (London: Unwin, 1989), 150.

17. Greg Rickman, "The Western under Erasure," in *The Western Reader*, ed. Jim Kitses and Greg Rickman (New York: Limelight Editions, 1999); Jacques

Derrida, *Of Grammatology* (Baltimore: Johns Hopkins University Press, 1974), 23; Jarmusch, "Ghost Dancer," 78. As we will see, Annie Proulx has used the same sense of layers to discuss how her fiction works.

18. See Nicholas Rombes, ed., *New Punk Cinema* (Edinburgh: Edinburgh University Press, 2005), 11, for Jarmusch's comments on punk and film. His friendship with Alex Cox (the "punk film phenomenon"—193), appearing in the latter's spaghetti Western *Straight to Hell*, further testifies to this important cultural connection. See chapter 3 for more on Cox and Leone.

19. Gilles Deleuze, *Foucault* (London: Athlone Press, 1988), 87.

20. Deleuze, *Foucault*, 87. I think the word "mutation" best explains the genre hybridity of the film and accounts for the endless speculation about what kind of a film it is—see Rickman's discussion of "acid" and "comic," for example, in "The Western under Erasure." My point is that it is all these amid the "layers" of the film.

21. Jarmusch in Hertzberg, *Jarmusch Interviews*, 193.

22. Jarmusch is a huge fan of Robert Frank's work as photographer and filmmaker and has spoken of how Wenders inspired him. Jarmusch in Hertzberg, *Jarmusch Interviews*, 136, 191, 86, 205.

23. Hertzberg, *Jarmusch Interviews*, 15, 208. In terms of literature, Jarmusch compares this disorientation of travel with reading William Burroughs's "cut-up" fiction as a teenager. The tenderfoot is a stock Western figure and in literary terms is best associated with Owen Wister's *The Virginian* (1902).

24. Susan Kollin, "Dead Man, Dead West," *Arizona Quarterly* 56 (Autumn 2000): 131.

25. Hertzberg, *Jarmusch Interviews*, 34.

26. Geoff Andrew, *Stranger Than Paradise: Maverick Film-makers in Recent American Cinema* (London: Prion Books, 1998), 161.

27. Homi Bhabha, *The Location of Culture* (London: Routledge, 1994), 86, 88–89.

28. Gerald Vizenor and A. Robert Lee, *Postindian Conversations* (Lincoln: University of Nebraska, 1999), 84. For a more detailed examination of Vizenor see chapter 6. Jarmusch cited in Kilpatrick, *Celluloid Indians*, 171. Kollin, "Dead Man, Dead West," 131.

29. In a nice touch of playful irony, Jarmusch does provide the classic Western "shoot-out" in his next film, *Ghost Dog*, in which the final scene is announced to the chimes of high noon—"This is the final shootout scene," the central character says just before his death. In a similar intertextual joke, in an earlier scene the hit man Ghost Dog is mistaken for an Indian, played by Gary Farmer (Nobody), who uses the same phrase as in *Dead Man* ("stupid fucking white man") to denounce his would-be assassins.

30. Jarmusch said that this was what the film was about—see "Ghost Dancer," 78.

31. Deborah Allison, "Michael Winterbottom," in *Senses of Cinema*, http://www
.sensesofcinema.com/contents/directors/05/winterbottom.html.

32. Winterbottom had already directed one Hardy film, *Jude* (1995), and has
since made films about the former Yugoslavia (*Welcome to Sarajevo*, 1997) and
about asylum seekers coming to England (*In This World*, 2002). His most recent
project was *The Road to Guantanamo*, which is about British Muslims taken to the
Cuban prison after 9/11. *The Claim* was filmed in Canada.

33. Paul Gilroy, *The Black Atlantic: Modernity and Double Consciousness* (1993; London: Verso, 1996), xi.

34. Gilroy, *The Black Atlantic*, 4; Krista Comer, "Postmodernism and the West:
Reflections on a Post-1989 Field Imaginary," unpublished conference paper,
Western Literature Association conference, Omaha, 2001, 1.

35. Thomas Hardy, *The Mayor of Casterbridge* (1886; London: Macmillan, 1969),
50.

36. Kinski was cast for her associations with another Hardy film, Roman
Polanski's *Tess*, and because of her father, Klaus Kinski, whom Winterbottom
admired for his part in Werner Herzog's epic *Fitzcarraldo* (referred to in *The Claim*
in the house-moving scene). She also forms an important connection to *Paris,
Texas*, where she was cast for her other associations to her father as a spaghetti
Western star (see *My Name Is Nobody*).

37. Hardy, *The Mayor of Casterbridge*, 31–32.

38. Patricia Nelson Limerick, *The Legacy of Conquest* (New York: Norton, 1987),
99–100.

39. Ronald Takaki, *Iron Cages: Race and Culture in Nineteenth-Century America*
(London: Athlone Press, 1979), 173.

40. Patricia Nelson Limerick, *Something in the Soil: Legacies and Reckonings in the
New West* (New York: Norton, 2000), 19–20.

41. Hardy, *The Mayor of Casterbridge*, 33.

42. Michael Winterbottom in S. Applebaum, "Winterbottom: The Claimant,"
http://www.netribution.co.uk/features/interviews/2001/michael_winterbot
tom/1.html. The HBO series *Deadwood* adopts a similar position with the Black
Hills of 1876 edging into Indian territory and so outside existing legal jurisdictions.

43. William Carlos Williams, *In the American Grain* (1925; London: Peregrine,
1971), 55.

44. Winterbottom in Applebaum, "Winterbottom: The Claimant."

45. Michel De Certeau, *The Writing of History* (New York: Columbia University
Press, 1988), xxv–xxvi. See chapter 3 for more on this idea.

46. Prescient because it belongs to a chain of images signifying fire that will
culminate in the destruction of Dillon's dream at the climax of the film.

47. Susan Johnson, *Roaring Camp: The Social World of the California Gold Rush*
(New York: Norton, 2000), 12, 78.

48. The French title for the film was *Rédemption*.

49. There are a number of similarities between *The Claim* and *Eureka* (1982). Both begin in snowy wastes (California and the Yukon) and involve inordinate wealth from gold claims and the terrible pressure from the past brought to bear on the future as a result. Both are about "endeavor," as McCann calls it, but as he also says, "endeavor seemed to be a curse."

50. William L. Fox, *The Void, the Grid, and the Sign* (Reno: University of Nevada Press, 2000), 130.

51. Fox, *The Void*, 91, 95.

52. Walter Benjamin, "The Work of Art in the Age of Mechanical Reproduction," in *Illuminations* (1955; London: Fontana, 1992), 230.

53. Fox, *The Void*, 129.

54. Hardy, *The Mayor of Casterbridge*, book cover quotation, 296, 334.

55. Fox, *The Void*, 138.

56. This is similar again to *Deadwood*'s ambiguous representation of Al Swearengen and Cy Tolliver, its twin tyrants "building" the West (as America) through acts of immense horror *and* necessity.

57. Winterbottom in Applebaum, "Winterbottom: The Claimant."

58. Patricia Nelson Limerick, "Haunted by Rhyolite: Learning from the Landscape of Failure," *American Art* 6, no. 4 (1992): 23, 34.

59. Limerick, "Haunted by Rhyolite," 38.

60. Rebecca Murray, "Director Ang Lee Discusses *Brokeback Mountain*," http://movies.about.com/od/brokebackmountain/a/brokeback120605_p.htm.

61. Deleuze and Guattari, *A Thousand Plateaus*, 25.

62. Robert Ordona, "Brokeback Mountain—As Gay as It Gets: An Interview with Ang Lee," http://www.gay.com/content/tools/print.html?coll=pno_entertainment&sernum=1139.

63. Annie Proulx, "Getting Movied," in Annie Proulx, Larry McMurtry, and Diana Ossana, *Brokeback Mountain: Story to Screenplay* (New York: Harper Perennial, 2006), 134, 137; Larry McMurtry, "Adapting Brokeback Mountain," in Proulx, McMurtry, and Ossana, *Brokeback Mountain*, 140.

64. Annie Proulx, "Getting Movied," 133; "Interview with Annie Proulx," *Missouri Review* 22, no. 2 (1999), http://www.missourireview.com.

65. Larry McMurtry, *In a Narrow Grave: Essays on Texas* (New York: Touchstone, 1968), 140, 143.

66. Larry McMurtry, *Walter Benjamin at the Dairy Queen* (New York: Touchstone, 2001), 66.

67. Raymond L. Neinstein, *The Ghost Country: A Study of the Novels of Larry McMurtry* (Berkeley: Creative Arts Book Company, 1976), 24; McMurtry, *Walter Benjamin at the Dairy Queen*, 55.

68. McMurtry, "Adapting Brokeback Mountain," 141; Diana Ossana, "Climbing Brokeback Mountain," in Proulx, McMurtry, and Ossana, *Brokeback Mountain*, 150.

69. McMurtry uses the word "conflicted" to describe Ennis in his screenplay—see McMurtry, "Adapting Brokeback Mountain," 28.

70. Thomas Chau, "Interview: Ang Lee on Brokeback Mountain," http://www.cinecom.com/news.php?id=0512271; Murray, "Director Ang Lee Discusses Brokeback Mountain."

71. Matthew Testa, "At Close Range with Annie Proulx," http://www.planetjh.com/testa_2005_12_07_proulx.html.

72. Deleuze and Guattari, A Thousand Plateaus, 98. In "Climbing Brokeback Mountain," Ossana comments on Lee's choice of crew for the film as both multicultural and experienced in their work with, among others, "Robert Altman . . . Sergio Leone . . . and Jim Jarmusch" (149).

73. Quoted in John Douglas, "Easyriders," Uncut, January 2006, 129.

74. Proulx, "Getting Movied," 137; Ossana, "Climbing Brokeback Mountain," 148.

75. "Interview with Annie Proulx."

76. "Interview with Annie Proulx."

77. Annie Proulx, Close Range: Wyoming Stories (London: Fourth Estate, 1999), 9.

78. "Interview with Annie Proulx."

79. "Interview with Annie Proulx"; Annie Proulx, "Biography," http://www.annieproulx.com/bio.html. It is worth noting the influence of Braudel on Deleuze and De Certeau, whose ideas I utilize throughout this book.

80. Proulx, "Getting Movied," 130. There are similarities here with Cormac McCarthy's two young male protagonists in his border trilogy, Billy Parham and John Grady Cole, whose lives are defined in part by a desire to reterritorialize memory and live out the mythic past as the active present as a means of self-definition. See Campbell, The Cultures of the American New West, 26.

81. Proulx, Close Range, 284, 285, 286, 289; Proulx, "Biography."

82. Proulx, Close Range, 300.

83. From script in Proulx, McMurtry, and Ossana, Brokeback Mountain, 66.

84. "Interview with Annie Proulx."

85. Ordona, "Brokeback Mountain—As Gay as It Gets," 2.

86. Proulx, Close Range, 303.

87. Jane Tompkins, West of Everything (New York: Oxford University Press, 1992).

88. Proulx, Close Range, 285, 294, 313, 315, 289, 309.

89. This is made explicit in the story and the film through the story of two gay ranchers, one of whom is beaten to death and left in a ditch, a scene Ennis's father makes Ennis witness as a child. Jack's own death is possibly a similarly violent end. Proulx, "Getting Movied," 134.

90. Proulx, "Getting Movied," 137; Proulx, Close Range, 287, 291, 301.

91. Proulx, Close Range, 285.

92. Proulx, *Close Range*, 291, 292.

93. Proulx, *Close Range*, 292, 284, 302, 292.

94. "Annie Proulx Tells the Story behind *Brokeback Mountain*," http://www .advocate.com/print_article_ektid23486.asp; Proulx, *Close Range*, 307, 309, 286.

95. Blake Allmendinger, *Ten Most Wanted: The New Western Literature* (London: Routledge, 1998).

96. Proulx, *Close Range*, 316.

97. Proulx, *Close Range*, 283–84, 316.

98. Script in Proulx, McMurtry, and Ossana, *Brokeback Mountain*, 97; Stephen Hunter, "A Picture of Two Americas in Brokeback Mountain," http://www .washingtonpost.com/wp-dyn/content/article/2006/02/01/AR2006020201024.

99. Proulx, *Close Range*, 314. This realization is linked in the story to a memory of Jack's story about his father beating and urinating on him as a child—an exemplary tale of phallic patriarchal power that links in his mind to his own father taking him to see the beaten gay farmer as a child.

100. "Interview with Annie Proulx."

101. Proulx, *Close Range*, 310, 318.

5. Dialogical Landscapes

1. Meyerowitz is an important "thread" in my chain, since he worked with Tony Ray-Jones (see *Cape Light* [Boston: New York Graphic Society, 1978]) and has written of the two major influences on him as Robert Frank and Eugene Atget (see *Creating a Sense of Place* [Washington DC: Smithsonian Press, 1990]). Along with that of William Eggleston, Stephen Shore, and Joel Sternfeld, Meyerowitz's color work can be seen echoed in Ormerod's later work. Meyerowitz, *Creating a Sense of Place*, 17, 18.

2. Martha Sandweiss, *Print the Legend: Photography and the American West* (New Haven: Yale University Press, 2002), 7, 14.

3. Rosalind Krauss, "Grids," in *The Originality of the Avant-Garde and other Modernist Myths* (1986; Cambridge: MIT Press, 1991), 9.

4. Stupich quoted in Robert Dawson et al., eds., *Ansel Adams: New Light: Essays on His Legacy and Legend* (San Francisco: Friends of Photography, 1993), 95.

5. Mikhail Bakhtin, *The Dialogic Imagination* (Austin: University of Texas Press, 1990), 14–17.

6. Paul Giles, *Virtual Americas* (Durham: Duke University Press, 2002), 25.

7. Krauss, "Grids," 158.

8. David Robertson, *West of Eden* (Yosemite: Wilderness Press, 1984), 124.

9. Mikhail Bakhtin, *Speech Genres* (Austin: University of Texas Press 1986), 7, 22–23.

10. Mark Klett, "The Legacy of Ansel Adams: Debts and Burdens," *Aperture* 120 (Summer 1990): 72.

11. Roland Barthes, *Camera Lucida* (1980; London: Vintage, 1993), 41, 45, 49, 53, 55, 57–59.

12. Roland Barthes, *Image/Music/Text* (1977; London: Fontana, 1979), 53, 54.

13. Ann Jefferson, "Body Matters: Self and Other in Bakhtin, Sartre and Barthes," in *Bakhtin and Cultural Theory*, ed. Ken Hirshkop and David Shepherd (Manchester: Manchester University Press, 1989), 172–73.

14. See the discussion of "thirding" and "thirdspace" in chapter 1 and the introduction and note the connections here with discussions of "folding" throughout this book derived from the work of Deleuze and Guattari. Barthes, *Image/Music/Text*, 148.

15. Gilles Deleuze and Claire Parnet, *Dialogues II* (London: Continuum, 2002), viii.

16. Dorothea Lange and Paul Taylor's *An American Exodus* (New Haven: Yale University Press, 1969) includes a section entitled "Last West" and begins and ends with an open road—U.S. 54, Southern New Mexico—a photograph echoed by Frank in his "U.S. 285, New Mexico" in *The Americans*; Jack Kerouac, introduction to Robert Frank, *The Americans* (1958; Manchester: Cornerhouse, 1993), 5; Ann W. Tucker and Philip Brookman, eds., *Robert Frank: New York to Nova Scotia* (Boston: Little, Brown, 1986), 38.

17. Tucker and Brookman, *Robert Frank*, 38, 36–37, 40.

18. Mikhail Bakhtin, *Problems of Dostoevsky's Poetics* (Minneapolis: University of Minnesota Press, 1997), 30.

19. Jack Kerouac, *On the Road* (Harmondsworth: Penguin, 1985), 19–20.

20. Kerouac, introduction to *The Americans*, 5.

21. Kerouac, *On the Road*, 8, 14, 17.

22. Kerouac, introduction to *The Americans*, 9.

23. Tucker and Brookman, *Robert Frank*, 20, 31.

24. Sean O'Hagan, "The Big Empty," *The Observer*, October 24, 2004, 5.

25. Frank quoted in Brigitta Burger-Utzer and Stefan Grissemann, *Frank Films: The Film and Video Work of Robert Frank* (New York: Scalo, 2003), 176.

26. Alan Nadel, *Containment Culture: American Narratives, Postmodernism, and the Atomic Age* (Durham: Duke University Press, 1995), xii.

27. Sara Greenhough and Philip Brookman, eds., *Moving Out* (Washington DC: National Gallery of Art, 1994), 98.

28. Kerouac, *On the Road*, 230, 34, 51, 83, 239.

29. Unfortunately, I am unable to reproduce any of Robert Frank's images in this chapter; however, this image appears in Greenhough and Brookman, *Moving Out*, 96–97.

30. Sandra S. Phillips, "To Subdue the Continent: Photographs of the Developing West," in *Crossing the Frontier*, ed. Phillips et al. (San Francisco: Chronicle Books, 1996), 39.

31. In the *Robert Frank: Storylines* exhibition in London (2004) Frank's later

work was often arranged as series of square photographs or grids accompanied by fragments, suggesting his frustration with the very limits of photography to express, and his constant striving to find alternative, deframed methods.

32. Barthes, *Camera Lucida*, 57–59.

33. Gilles Deleuze and Félix Guattari, *What Is Philosophy?* (London: Verso, 1994), 188, 191. They in turn borrow much of this thinking from Bakhtin and reference him at this point (see 188–89). Jacques Derrida discusses the issue of framing in his *The Truth of Painting* (1978; Chicago: University of Chicago Press, 1987).

34. These ideas come from Gilles Deleuze, *Francis Bacon: The Logic of Sensation* (London: Continuum, 2004), 99–110.

35. Gilles Deleuze, *Negotiations, 1972–1990* (New York: Columbia University Press, 1995), 33; *Robert Frank: Storylines*, Tate Modern, London, October 28, 2004–January 23, 2005.

36. Greenhough and Brookman, *Moving Out*, 119.

37. Deleuze and Guattari, *What Is Philosophy?* 176.

38. Ginsberg quoted in Burger-Utzer and Grissemann, *Frank Films*, 82–84.

39. Greenhough and Brookman, *Moving Out*, 218.

40. Julia Kristeva, *Strangers to Ourselves* (New York: Columbia University Press, 1991), 5.

41. This image is in Frank, *The Americans*, 131.

42. Ed Ruscha, *Leave Any Information at the Signal: Writings, Interviews, Bits, Pages* (London: MIT Press, 2002), 278, 148. Ruscha has written about the trigger to his own photography: "When I grew up in Oklahoma, photographers were nerds . . . either nerds or pornographers, or both. Then I saw Robert Frank's *Americans*" (317). Ruscha, like Frank, also made films. He admires fellow American photographers Lewis Baltz, Stephen Shore, and William Eggleston (see 218). See chapter 1 for connections among Ruscha, Jackson, and Venturi.

43. Ruscha, *Leave Any Information at the Signal*, 342.

44. Dave Hickey and Peter Plagens, *The Works of Ed Ruscha* (New York: Hudson Hills Press, 1982), 24.

45. Robert Silberman, "Contemporary Photography and the Myth of the West," in *The American West: As Seen by Europeans and Americans*, ed. Rob Kroes (Amsterdam: Free University Press, 1989), 56.

46. Frank, *The Americans*, 139.

47. Greenhough and Brookman, *Moving Out*, 107.

48. Robert Frank, *Photofile* (London: Thames and Hudson, 1991), n.p.

49. Robert Venturi, *Complexity and Contradiction in Architecture* (New York: MOMA, 1966), 22.

50. William Jenkins, *New Topographics: Photographs of a Man-altered Landscape* (New York: International Museum of Photography, 1975), 5.

51. Jenkins, *New Topographics*, 7.

52. Robert Adams, *The New West* (1974; Cologne: Verlag der Buchhandlung Walther Konig, 2000), xiv.

53. Bakhtin, *Speech Genres*, 49–50.

54. Guy Blaisdell, ed., *Lewis Baltz: Rule without Exception* (Albuquerque: University of New Mexico, 1990), 80, 40.

55. Jeff Rian, *Lewis Baltz* (London: Phaidon, 2001), 8.

56. Bakhtin, *Speech Genres*, 28, 29, 32, 42.

57. Michel De Certeau, *The Practice of Everyday Life* (Berkeley: University of California Press, 1988), 108, 107.

58. Victor Burgin, ed., *Thinking Photography* (London: MacMillan, 1982), 153.

59. De Certeau, *The Practice of Everyday Life*, 109, 108, 200.

60. Shore's work, like Frank's and Ormerod's, is not only of the West but includes many images from Idaho, Wyoming, Texas, California, North Dakota, Arizona, Oregon, Utah, New Mexico, Washington, and Montana.

61. Quoted in Stephen Shore, *Uncommon Places* (New York: Aperture, 1982), 30.

62. Shore's presentation at Tate Modern, London, December 3, 2004, as part of the symposium on Robert Frank.

63. Vladimir Nabokov, *Lolita* (London: Corgi Books, 1961), 153–54, 161.

64. Shore, *Uncommon Places*, 63, 15.

65. Lefebvre quoted in Edward Soja, *Postmodern Geographies* (London: Routledge, 1989), 80.

66. Henri Lefebvre, *Critique of Everyday Life* (London: Verso, 1991), 134.

67. Michael Holquist, *Bakhtin* (London: Routledge, 1991), 31.

68. Lefebvre, *Critique of Everyday Life*, 132.

69. I borrow the term "astonished foreigner" from Max Kozloff's essay on John Gutmann in *The Restless Decade* (New York: Harry Abrams, 1996), 9.

70. Paul Gilroy, *The Black Atlantic* (London: Verso, 1993), 73.

71. Deleuze and Parnet, *Dialogues II*, 4–5.

72. Geoff Weston, interview with author, 2001.

73. Richard Hoggart, *The Uses of Literacy* (Harmondsworth: Penguin, 1957), 248. Born in 1957 myself, I remember the diet of TV Westerns on British television: *Bronco Lane*, *The Lone Ranger*, *Rawhide*, *Maverick*, *Wells Fargo*, *Laramie*, *Cheyenne*, *Wagon Train*, *Gunsmoke*, and *Bonanza*.

74. Peter Reyner Banham, *Design by Choice* (London: Academy Editions, 1981), 85. He was a fan of the work of J. B. Jackson (see Banham, *Scenes in America Deserta* [London: Thames and Hudson, 1982], 166, and chapter 1 in this book). Banham quoted in Duncan Webster, *Looka Yonder! The Imaginary America of Populist Culture* (London: Routledge, 1988), 247.

75. Banham quoted in Nigel Whiteley, *Reyner Banham: Historian of the Immediate Future* (Cambridge: MIT Press, 2002), 380; Banham quoted in Webster, *Looka Yonder!* 247.

76. See his *Los Angeles: The Architecture of Four Ecologies* (Harmondsworth: Penguin, 1971) and *Scenes in America Deserta*.

77. Banham, *Scenes in America Deserta*, 215, 159, 3, 227.

78. Whiteley, *Reyner Banham*, 400, 399.

79. Banham, *Scenes in America Deserta*, 168, 199–200.

80. Reyner Banham, "The Man-Mauled Desert," in Richard Misrach, *Desert Cantos* (Albuquerque: University of New Mexico Press, 1988), 1–2.

81. Banham, *Scenes in America Deserta*, 167.

82. Jean Baudrillard, *America* (London: Verso, 1991), 56, 70.

83. De Certeau, *The Practice of Everyday Life*, 201.

84. Baudrillard, *America*, 72; Geoff Dyer, *The Ongoing Moment* (New York: Pantheon, 1995), 141–42.

85. Barthes, *Camera Lucida*, 118.

86. Elizabeth Grosz, *Architecture from the Outside: Essays on Virtual and Real Space* (Cambridge: MIT Press, 2001), 58 (see the introduction).

87. Gilles Deleuze, *Cinema 2* (London: Athlone Press, 1994), 180, 187–88.

88. J. S. Keates, *Cartographic Design and Production* (Harlow: Longman, 1973), 67.

89. Peter Eisenman, *Inside Out: Selected Writings, 1963–1988* (New Haven: Yale University Press, 2004), 229, 233.

90. Graeme Gilloch, *Myth and Metropolis: Walter Benjamin and the City* (Cambridge: Polity, 1996), 124.

91. Walter Benjamin, *Illuminations* (London: Fontana, 1992), 216, 229–30, 214.

92. Susan Stewart, *On Longing: Narratives of the Miniature, the Gigantic, the Souvenir, the Collection* (Durham: Duke University Press, 1993), 30–31.

93. "He was a big fan of Hopper, especially when he moved into color, and there is a certain stillness and emptiness in some of Michael's pictures which is what people talk about in relation to Hopper's paintings, so I think he took something from that" (Weston interview).

94. Walter Benjamin, *The Arcades Project* (Boston: Belknap/Harvard Press, 1999), 474.

95. John Brinckerhoff Jackson, *The Necessity for Ruins* (Amherst: University of Massachusetts Press, 1980), 102.

96. Peter Stallybrass and Allon White, *The Politics and Poetics of Transgression* (Ithaca: Cornell University Press, 1986), 8, 9.

97. Henri Lefebvre, *The Production of Space* (Oxford: Blackwell, 1994), 373.

98. Deleuze, *Cinema 2*, 256.

99. Rudy Vanderlans, *Supermarket* (Corte Madera: Gingko Press, 2001), 34–35.

100. Berger quoted in Nick Waplington, *Living Room* (Manchester: Cornerhouse, 1991), n.p.

101. Nick Waplington, *Truth or Consequences* (London: Phaidon, 2001), n.p.

102. Nick Waplington, *The Indecisive Memento* (London: Booth-Chibbon, 1998), n.p. To heighten the "tourist" sensibility he includes time/date stamps within many of his images.

103. James Clifford, *Routes* (Cambridge: Harvard University Press, 1997), 3.

104. Janet Wolff, "On the Road Again: Metaphors of Travel in Cultural Criticism," *Cultural Studies* 7, no. 2 (1993): 226; Waplington, *The Indecisive Memento*, n.p.

105. Waplington, *The Indecisive Memento*, n.p.

106. Carlo McCormick, "The Indecisive Memento," in Waplington, *The Indecisive Memento*, n.p.

107. Kristeva, *Strangers to Ourselves*, 5, 11.

108. Clifford, *Routes*, 11.

109. Wim Wenders, *On Film: Essays and Conversations* (London: Faber and Faber, 2001), 130.

110. Wenders, *On Film*, 134, 417–18.

111. Doreen Massey, *Space, Place and Gender* (Cambridge: Polity, 1994), 154–55.

112. Wim Wenders, *Written in the West* (1987; Munich: Schirmer, 1997), 10; Wenders, *On Film*, 415. This comment parallels that of J. B. Jackson and his "askew" vision (see chapter 1).

113. John Slyce, "Introduction: In a Landscape of Quotation," in Waplington, *Truth or Consequences*, n.p.

114. Wenders, *On Film*, 440.

115. Slyce, introduction, n.p.

116. Stewart, *On Longing*, 19–20.

117. Stewart, *On Longing*, 19; Slyce, introduction, n.p.

118. This image echoes the work of William Eggleston most directly but also overlaps with images made by German Gerd Kittel of supermarket shelves in the United Kingdom. Ormerod was fascinated by U.S. supermarkets for their "alien" (and familiar) qualities.

119. Walter Benjamin, *Charles Baudelaire* (London: Verso, 1997), 169.

120. I have no knowledge of Waplington's awareness of Ormerod's work, but their projects clearly intersect. Both studied at some point at Trent Polytechnic, Nottingham.

121. Barthes, *Image/Music/Text*, 160, 161.

122. Umberto Eco, *Travels in Hyperreality* (1973; New York: Harcourt, 1986), 7.

123. Waplington, *The Indecisive Memento*, n.p.

124. Nathaniel Lewis, in *Unsettling the Literary West* (Lincoln: University of Nebraska Press, 2003), a study of western literature and the idea of authenticity, calls his first chapter "Truth or Consequences."

125. Frank, *The Americans*, 9.

126. Andrew Cross, *Along Some American Highways* (London: Black Dog, 2003),

n.p., quoting John Brinckerhoff Jackson, *A Sense of Place, A Sense of Time* (New Haven: Yale University Press, 1994), 190–91. Cross told me in a conversation that he was "not impressed" by Waplington's *Truth or Consequences*, finding it too "self-conscious."

127. Andrew Cross, "Artist Interview—John Hansard Gallery," www.hansard gallery.org.uk/exhibition/archive/2004/andrew_cross; Doreen Massey, "The A34," in Andrew Cross, *An English Journey* (Southampton: Film and Video Umbrella/John Hansard Gallery, 2004), n.p.

128. Cross, "Artist Interview—John Hansard Gallery." This emerges in Cross's recent work photographing and filming Rugby, England, and Rugby, North Dakota, where the latter is the "geographical centre of the USA" and the former very much in the centre of England. In these works Cross examines notions of "centre" in economic, geographical, and political terms through a distinctly transnational perspective. Marc Augé, *Non-Places: Introduction to an Anthropology of Supermodernity* (1992; London: Verso, 1995).

129. Augé, *Non-Places*, 109.

130. Arjun Appadurai, *Modernity at Large* (Minneapolis: University of Minnesota Press, 1996), 31.

131. Latour quoted in Massey, "The A34," n.p.; Andrew Cross, notes for the ICA/Beck's Futures Exhibition, 2004, n.p.

6. Strata and Routes

1. Vizenor quoted in A. Robert Lee, *Postindian Conversations* (Lincoln: University of Nebraska Press, 1999), 155.

2. The term "ethnic drag" is taken from Katrin Sieg, *Ethnic Drag: Performing Race, Nation, Sexuality in West Germany* (Ann Arbor: University of Michigan Press, 2002), 255, 85, 86.

3. Philip J. Deloria, *Playing Indian* (New Haven: Yale University Press, 1998), 183–85.

4. Vizenor quoted in Lee, *Postindian Conversations*, 155.

5. Louis Owens, *Mixedblood Messages: Literature, Film, Family, Place* (Norman: University of Oklahoma Press, 1998), 26.

6. Mary Louise Pratt, *Imperial Eyes: Travel Writing and Transculturation* (London: Routledge, 1992), 4, 7.

7. Owens, *Mixedblood Messages*, 26. Owens's notion of frontier is very similar to Gerald McMaster's idea of the "border zone" (see note 29 below). Note the parallels here with the discussion of the border in chapter 3.

8. Owens, *Mixedblood Messages*, 45, 27–28, 41.

9. Vizenor quoted in Louis Owens, *Other Destinies: Understanding the American Indian Novel* (Norman: University of Oklahoma Press, 1992), 233.

10. Anzaldúa in *This Bridge We Call Home: Radical Visions for Transformation*, ed.

Gloria Anzaldúa and Analouise Keating (London: Routledge, 2002), 560. See a further discussion of this in chapter 3.

11. Gerald Vizenor, *Manifest Manners: Postindian Warriors of Survivance* (Hanover: Wesleyan University Press, 1994), 5.

12. Vizenor, *Manifest Manners*, 6, 11; Gerald Vizenor, *Fugitive Poses* (Lincoln: University of Nebraska Press, 1998), 22.

13. Vizenor quoted in Elvira Pulitano, *Toward a Native American Critical Theory* (Lincoln: University of Nebraska Press, 2003), 175.

14. Vizenor, *Fugitive Poses*, 15.

15. Gilles Deleuze and Claire Parnet, *Dialogues II* (London: Continuum, 2002), 4–5.

16. Gilles Deleuze and Félix Guattari, *Kafka: Toward a Minor Literature* (Minneapolis: University of Minnesota Press, 1986), 16; Gilles Deleuze, *Cinema 2* (London: Continuum, 2000), 216–17.

17. Vizenor, *Fugitive Poses*, 55, 23. "Transmotion" is a Vizenor term meaning "native motion and active presence . . . survivance. . . . Native stories of survivance are the creases of transmotion and sovereignty." "Sovenance" is the term he prefers to "sovereignty" with its echoes of European colonialism and closed thinking (15). Deleuze uses the term "crease" in his discussion of "the fold" (*The Fold* [Minneapolis: University of Minnesota Press, 1993], 36). Similarly, Vizenor uses the term "fold" in *Fugitive Poses* (see 62, 64).

18. Deleuze, *The Fold*, 34.

19. Deleuze, *The Fold*, 35, 38. Vizenor echoes this metaphor with the "creative curve of stories" in *Fugitive Poses* (44).

20. John Rajchman, *Constructions* (Boston: MIT Press, 1998), 20.

21. Deleuze and Guattari, *Kafka*, 28.

22. Vizenor quoted in Jace Weaver, *That the People Might Live: Native American Literatures and Native American Community* (New York: Oxford University Press, 1997), 141.

23. Pulitano, *Toward a Native American Critical Theory*, 170, 185.

24. Vizenor, *Fugitive Poses*, 37, 50.

25. Vizenor, *Fugitive Poses*, 55; Gerald Vizenor, "Imagic Moments: Native Identities and Literary Modernity," *Third Text* 46 (Spring 1999): 27.

26. Vizenor, *Fugitive Poses*, 87.

27. "Severance" is Vizenor's term for the function of the reservation (*Fugitive Poses*, 87); Gerald McMaster, "Living on Reservation X," in *Reservation X: The Power of Place in Aboriginal Contemporary Art*, ed. McMaster (Seattle: University of Washington Press and Canadian Museum of Civilization, 1998), 19.

28. McMaster, "Living on Reservation X," 20, 21, 22, 23.

29. Gerald McMaster, "Border Zones: The 'Injun-uity' of Aesthetic Tricks," *Cultural Studies* 9, no. 1 (1995): 74–90; McMaster, "Living on Reservation X," 28.

30. McMaster, "Border Zones," 75.

31. Charlotte Townsend-Gault, "Let X = Audience," in McMaster, *Reservation X*, 41, 51.

32. Gerald McMaster, "Mary Longman: Strata and Routes—There Is No Fixed Address for Reservation X," in McMaster, *Reservation X*, 67, 69, 70.

33. Stuart Hall, "New Cultures for Old," in *A Place in the World?* ed. Doreen Massey and Pat Jess (Oxford: Oxford University Press, 1995), 206, 207.

34. Longman quoted in McMaster, "Mary Longman," 74.

35. Gilles Deleuze and Félix Guattari, *A Thousand Plateaus* (London: Athlone Press, 1996), 14, 16, 5.

36. Deleuze and Guattari, *A Thousand Plateaus*, 212, 213. The molar relates to the "rooted" and the molecular to the "routed" here.

37. Pulitano, *Toward a Native American Critical Theory*, 7.

38. Pulitano, *Toward a Native American Critical Theory*, 13. Susan Bernardin takes up many of the debates surrounding issues of authenticity in lucid detail in her essay "The Authenticity Game" in *True West*, ed. William R. Handley and Nathaniel Lewis (Lincoln: University of Nebraska, 2004).

39. Craig Womack, *Red on Red: Native American Literary Separatism* (Minneapolis: University of Minnesota Press, 1999), 5, 12, 6–7, 11.

40. Pulitano, *Toward a Native American Critical Theory*, 62 (citing Bill Ashcroft).

41. Womack, *Red on Red*, 59, 12.

42. Pulitano, *Toward a Native American Critical Theory*, 12, 83. I adopt the lowercase "indian" as Gerald Vizenor does in his work (see below).

43. Womack, *Red on Red*, 64.

44. Vizenor, *Fugitive Poses*, 87–88.

45. Womack quoted in Pulitano, *Toward a Native American Critical Theory*, 85, 15.

46. Craig Womack interview, "Indian English Spoken Here," September 21, 2005, http://blogcritics.org/archives/2005/09/21/121220.php.

47. Womack, *Red on Red*, 65, 260, 224–25, 227, 233.

48. Ward Churchill, *Fantasies of the Master Race: Literature, Cinema, and the Colonization of American Indians* (San Francisco: City Lights, 1998), 175.

49. Vizenor quoted in Lee, *Postindian Conversations*, 157.

50. Womack, *Red on Red*, 20–21, 23–24.

51. Womack, *Red on Red*, 14. Note that when Deleuze and Guattari define the characteristics of "minor literature" they assert it is always, "political," "collective," and "deterritorializing" (*Kafka*, 16–17).

52. Deleuze and Guattari, *Kafka*, 18.

53. Womack, "Indian English Spoken Here," 5.

54. Deleuze and Guattari, *A Thousand Plateaus*, 105–6 (emphasis in original), 110.

55. McMaster, "Border Zones," 84; Michel De Certeau, *The Practice of Everyday Life* (Berkeley: University of California Press, 1988), 26.

56. McMaster, "Border Zones," 85, 87.

57. The phrase "insurgent Native American cinema" is taken from Susan Kollin, "Dead Man, Dead West," *Arizona Quarterly* 56, no. 3 (2000): 142; Vizenor, *Manifest Manners*, 6.

58. Vizenor, *Fugitive Poses*, 145, 155, 157.

59. Churchill, *Fantasies of the Master Race*, 167, 172, 186.

60. Weaver, *That the People Might Live*, 4.

61. Leslie Fiedler, *The Return of the Vanishing American* (London: Paladin, 1972), 10.

62. Ward Churchill, "Smoke Signals in Context: An Historical Overview," http://www.zmag.org/articles/nov98ward.htm.

63. Robert Warrior, preface to Beverly R. Singer, *Wiping the War Paint Off the Lens* (Minneapolis: University of Minnesota Press, 2001), vii, xiii; Jacquelyn Kilpatrick, *Celluloid Indians: Native Americans and Film* (Lincoln: University of Nebraska Press, 1999), 228–32. Singer is quick to point out that *Smoke Signals* was preceded by other Native films, such as Victor Masayesva's *Hopiit* and Arlene Bowman's *Navajo Talking Picture*, but none were distributed by Miramax or winners at Sundance.

64. Weaver, *That the People Might Live*, xii, xiii.

65. Bhabha quoted in Weaver, *That the People Might Live*, 43, from Homi Bhabha, *Location of Culture* (London: Routledge, 1994), 3.

66. Bhabha, *Location of Culture*, 4.

67. Chris Eyre interview transcript, September 2002, http://centerstage.net/stumped/Interviews/chris-eyre-transcript.html.

68. Chris Eyre interview, http://filmfreakcentral.net/notes/ceyreinterview.htm.

69. Dennis West and Joan M. West, "Sending Cinematic Smoke Signals: An Interview with Sherman Alexie," *Cineaste* 23, no. 4 (1998), http://www.berkeley.edu/MRC/alexie.html.

70. "Alien Nation—Michael Jones Talks with Chris Eyre and Sherman Alexie," in *Filmmaker: The Magazine of Independent Film*, Winter 1998, http://www.filmmakermagazine.com/winter1998/aliennation.php.

71. Vizenor, *Fugitive Poses*, 170, 175. See the introduction for an extensive discussion of these ideas.

72. Chris Eyre interview, http://www.minireviews.com/interviews/eyre.htm.

73. Eyre quoted in Dale Reynolds, "Contextual Clues," *A&U: America's AIDS Magazine*, http://www.aumag.org/coverstory/jan03cover.html.

74. "Alien Nation—Michael Jones Talks with Chris Eyre and Sherman Alexie."

75. Julien Fielding, "Native American Religion and Film: Interviews with Chris Eyre and Sherman Alexie," *Journal of Religion and Film* 7, no. 1 (April 2003), http://www.unomaha.edu/jrf/Vol7No1/nativefilm.htm.

76. Vizenor quoted in Lee, *Postindian Conversations*, 84; Vizenor, *Manifest Manners*, 171.

77. Vizenor, *Manifest Manners*, 70–71.

78. Vizenor quoted in Pulitano, *Toward a Native American Critical Theory*, 161.

79. Vizenor, *Fugitive Poses*, 179, 182, 183, 188–89, 178.

80. Pulitano, *Toward a Native American Critical Theory*, 161.

81. Eyre interview (see n. 73).

82. West and West, "Sending Cinematic Smoke Signals," 6, 7.

83. Owens, *Mixedblood Messages*, 72.

84. Kilpatrick, *Celluloid Indians*, 230.

85. Eyre interview transcript, September 2002.

86. Gerald Vizenor, introduction to *Narrative Chance: Postmodern Discourse on Native American Indian Literatures*, ed. Vizenor (Norman: University of Oklahoma Press, 1989), 6.

87. These political concerns even persist in the entertainment television films made for the PBS American Mystery Special strand, *Skinwalkers* and *The Thief of Time*, dealing with issues such as archaeological theft of Indian artifacts, pollution of Native lands, and religious corruption.

88. Owens, *Mixedblood Messages*, 19.

89. Elizabeth Cook-Lynn, *Anti-Indianism in Modern America: A Voice from Tatekeya's Earth* (Urbana: University of Illinois Press, 2001), 15–16.

90. Chris Eyre interview, http://filmfreakcentral.net/notes/ceyreinterview.htm.

91. Eyre interview transcript, September 2002.

92. Eyre quoted in Tania Casselle, "Eyre Exposes the Heart and Muscle beneath *Skins*," *Indian Country Today*, September 10, 2002, http://www.indiancountry.com/content.cfm?id=1031666942.

93. Alexie quoted in Robert Capriccioso, "Sherman Alexie," http://www.identitytheory.com/printpage.php.

94. Alexie quoted in Capriccioso, "Sherman Alexie."

95. Eyre quoted in Reynolds, "Contextual Clues."

96. Chris Eyre, interview on DVD *Skins* (First Look Home Entertainment, 2002).

97. Eyre interview, http://filmfreakcentral.net/notes/ceyreinterview.htm.

98. Deloria quoted in Owens, *Other Destinies*, 239.

99. Eyre quoted in http://www.indiancountry.com/content.cfm?id=1031666942.

100. Eyre interview transcript, September 2002.

101. Mikhail Bakhtin, *The Dialogic Imagination* (Austin: University of Texas Press, 1990), 23.

102. Cook-Lynn, *Anti-Indianism in Modern America*, 27.

103. Eyre uses the word "hypocrisy" in describing Mount Rushmore; see interview at http://filmfreakcentral.net/notes/ceyreinterview.htm.

104. I borrow the phrase "end in motion" from Susan Bernardin's comments on Owens's *Dark River* in "The Authenticity Game," 170.

105. Churchill's essay can be accessed with other documents from http://www.democracynow.org.

106. Cherrie Moraga and Gloria Anzaldúa, eds., *This Bridge Called My Back* (New York: Kitchen Table Press, 1981), 205. These ideas are also discussed in chapter 2.

107. Anzaldúa and Keating, *This Bridge We Call Home*, 1.

108. Owens, *Mixedblood Messages*, 26 (see earlier discussion of these ideas).

109. Weaver, *That the People Might Live*, xii.

110. Anzaldúa in Anzaldúa and Keating, *This Bridge We Call Home*, 3.

111. The film was originally to be called *Shiprock*, but because of problems over use of tribal land, the film was finally located in Salt Lake City, Utah.

112. Tapahonso quoted in Weaver, *That the People Might Live*, 44.

113. Anzaldúa quoted in Weaver, *That the People Might Live*, 4.

114. Film publicity "'A Thousand Roads': Exploring the Lives of Native Peoples of the Americas," http://voanews.com/specialenglish/archive/2005–06/2005–06–10-voal.cfm?rend.

115. Chris Eyre statement for Native Networks, http://www.nativenetworks.si.edu/ENG/rose/eyre_c.htm.

116. Gloria Anzaldúa, *Interviews/Entrevistas* (London: Routledge, 2000), 254, 185, 254.

117. Anzaldúa in Anzaldúa and Keating, *This Bridge We Call Home*, 549.

118. Weaver, *That the People Might Live*, 163; Anzaldúa in Anzaldúa and Keating, *This Bridge We Call Home*, 556.

7. Postwestern Generations?

1. Mike Davis, *Dead Cities* (New York: The New Press, 2002), 30–31.

2. I am suggesting in this section the important relationship between Ellis's novel and Coupland's work, and with this in mind it is worth noting that the latter has named Didion's novel as one of his favorites, calling it "Glamorously bleak. Reading Joan Didion makes you feel like somebody's smashing windows inside your head. In a good way." Coupland, "10 Recommended Books," www.geocities.com/Sotto/Gallery/5560/nrl.

3. Bret Easton Ellis, *Less Than Zero* (London: Picador, 1985), 206.

4. Ellis, *Less Than Zero*, 114, 207, 168.

5. Ellis, *Less Than Zero*, 207, 208. Reflection is something rare in Ellis's L.A. world of accelerated surfaces and "blank" looks. In Coupland's work it will become a vital characteristic of his post-Ellis West.

6. *The Twilight Zone* is referred to a lot in the novel and often in conjunction with Clay's recollections of Palm Springs. Ellis, *Less Than Zero*, 138.

7. Douglas Coupland, *Generation X* (1991; London: Abacus, 1992), 56. There is no space here to develop the connections between Coupland and filmmaker

Richard Linklater, who as a westerner (from Austin, Texas) has also built a career around the examination of a "slacker" culture and existential questioning, where, as one of his characters puts it, "withdrawing in disgust is not the same as apathy."

8. Ellis, *Less Than Zero*, 63.

9. Douglas Rushkoff, ed., *The GenX Reader* (New York: Ballantine, 1994), 5.

10. Douglas Coupland, *Girlfriend in a Coma* (London: Flamingo, 1998), 5.

11. Coupland, *Girlfriend in a Coma*, 5; Rob Shields, *The Virtual* (London: Routledge, 2003), 43.

12. Shields, *The Virtual*, 206. See the introduction's discussion of Paul Giles's work on this too.

13. Douglas Coupland, *Life after God* (1994; London: Scribner, 1999), 220–21.

14. Coupland quoted in Euan Ferguson, "Generation Next," *The Observer Magazine*, May 28, 2006, 28–33, 32.

15. Robert Kroetsch, "Reading across the Border," in *Studies on Canadian Literature*, ed. Arnold E. Davidson (New York: MLA, 1990), 339; Alexander Laurence, "Interview with Douglas Coupland" (1994), http://www.altx.com/int2/douglas.coupland.html.

16. Paul Giles, *Virtual Americas: Transnational Fictions and the Transatlantic Imaginary* (Durham: Duke University Press, 2002), 14.

17. Coupland, *Life after God*, 220. *Melrose Place* is a particular favorite of characters in Coupland's *Microserfs* (1995; London: Harper Perennial, 2004), 65.

18. Coupland, *Generation X*, 7.

19. Douglas Coupland, *Polaroids from the Dead* (London: Flamingo, 1997), 23.

20. Coupland, *Life after God*, 220–21.

21. Rushkoff, *The GenX Reader*, 6.

22. Coupland, *Generation X*, 15.

23. Douglas Coupland, *Miss Wyoming* (London: Flamingo, 2000), 260.

24. Coupland, *Generation X*, 11, 25.

25. Coupland, *Polaroids from the Dead*, 157.

26. Douglas Coupland, *Shampoo Planet* (London: Simon and Schuster, 1993), 5; Coupland, *Polaroids from the Dead*, 163; Coupland, *Miss Wyoming*, 103. It is noticeable how in the drawings for *Life after God*, Coupland often uses grids or patterns of enclosure to illustrate the stories (see 7, 75, 82, 83, 95).

27. Coupland, *Polaroids from the Dead*, 162, 164, 168.

28. Linklater quoted in John M. Ulrich and Andrea L. Harris, eds., *GenXegesis: Essays on Alternative Youth (Sub)Culture* (Madison: University of Wisconsin Press, 2003), 17–18.

29. Coupland, *Life after God*, 223.

30. Coupland, *Polaroids from the Dead*, 23.

31. Arjun Appadurai, *Modernity at Large: Cultural Dimensions of Globalization* (Minneapolis: University of Minnesota Press, 1996), 7–8, 31.

32. Coupland, *Life after God*, 80; Coupland, *Polaroids from the Dead*, 180.

33. Coupland, *Polaroids from the Dead*, 186.

34. Coupland, *Generation X*, 16, 39.

35. See Graeme Gilloch, *Myth and Metropolis: Walter Benjamin and the City* (Cambridge: Polity, 1996). This, as we will see, is true in different ways in *Girlfriend in a Coma* and *Miss Wyoming* and relates closely to the final word of *Shampoo Planet*, "Wake up!—the world is alive."

36. Coupland, *Generation X*, 8. There is an echo here of Jean Baudrillard's *Cool Memories* (1990), a work that resists the possibility of any coherent "story" in favor of a fragmented string of "memories" and impressions of the desert West.

37. Gilloch, *Myth and Metropolis*, 173.

38. Gilles Deleuze, *Essays Critical and Clinical* (London: Verso, 1998), 63.

39. Coupland, *Shampoo Planet*, 97, 120.

40. Deleuze, *Essays Critical and Clinical*, 65.

41. Deleuze, *Essays Critical and Clinical*, 1–2, 4.

42. Coupland, *Life after God*, 269.

43. Rushkoff, *The GenX Reader*, 7.

44. John Rajchman, *The Deleuze Connections* (Cambridge: MIT Press, 2000), 11.

45. Coupland, *Generation X*, 59, 41, 36.

46. Coupland, *Miss Wyoming*, 72.

47. Coupland, *Miss Wyoming*, 48. Both characters have had cosmetic surgery. The first time Susan Colgate is described, we are told "Her face was flawless made up and her hair was cut in the style of the era . . . a woman on a magazine cover . . . but locked in time and space" (3). We are also told that the Johnson family's wealth was from "pesticides originally, and then all forms of agrichemicals, plastics and pharmaceuticals, eventually forming a monster that spat out everything from mousetraps to orange juice to nuclear weapons components" (66).

48. Coupland, *Miss Wyoming*, 16.

49. Coupland, *Shampoo Planet*, 170.

50. Jean-François Lyotard, *The Postmodern Explained* (Minneapolis: University of Minnesota Press, 1993), 84.

51. Coupland, *Miss Wyoming*, 52. Katie Mills, "'Await Lightning': How Generation X Remaps the Road Story," in Ulrich and Harris, *GenXegesis*, 221–48, argues for Coupland's reworking of the road story in *Generation X*.

52. Coupland, *Miss Wyoming*, 78.

53. Coupland, *Generation X*, 151.

54. Coupland, *Polaroids from the Dead*, 180.

55. Coupland, *Shampoo Planet*, 252–53.

56. Mike Davis, *City of Quartz* (London: Verso, 1990), 375.

57. Davis, *City of Quartz*, 398–99, 434–35.

58. Gilloch, *Myth and Metropolis*, 166.

59. Coupland, *Shampoo Planet*, 286. In *Girlfriend in a Coma*, Coupland fictionalizes an apocalypse.

60. Coupland, *Generation X*, 171. Mike Davis's *Magical Urbanism* (London: Verso, 2000) suggests that Mexicans contributed to the "reinvention" of Los Angeles through a process of transnational "urban-genetic exchange" (30). See also essays in R. Homero Villa and G. J. Sanchez, eds., *Los Angeles and the Future of Urban Cultures* (Baltimore: Johns Hopkins University Press, 2005).

61. Coupland, *Generation X*, 171.

62. Elizabeth Grosz, *Architecture from the Outside: Essays on Virtual and Real Space* (Cambridge: MIT Press, 2001), 61.

63. In *Girlfriend in a Coma* the chapter titles act as a kind of choric commentary on the novel's events, offering quirky asides and slogans that are connected at different levels with the novel's themes. Headings include ". . . and after America?" "Nation or Ant Colony?" "Progress Is Over," and "It's All Fake" and touch on recurring notions about thought, fakery, lies, the future, artifice, destiny, and identity.

64. Coupland, *Generation X*, 173, 171.

65. Grosz, *Architecture from the Outside*, 58–59.

66. Rajchman, *The Deleuze Connections*, 99–100.

67. See Grosz, *Architecture from the Outside*, 63–64.

68. John Steinbeck, *The Grapes of Wrath* (1939; Harmondsworth: Penguin, 1972), 209.

69. George P. Lainsbury, "Generation X and the End of History," in Ulrich and Harris, *GenXegesis*, 193.

70. Coupland, *Generation X*, 179.

71. See Mark Forshaw, "Douglas Coupland: In and Out of 'Ironic Hell,'" *Critical Survey* 12, no. 3 (2000): 39–58; and William H. Katerberg, "Western Myth and the End of History in the Novels of Douglas Coupland," *Western Literature* 40, no. 3 (2005): 272–99. The latter is an excellent essay on Coupland's West and one with whose ideas I often cohere in this chapter. Ulrich, introduction, in Ulrich and Harris, *GenXegesis*, 16. This last phrase ("value of narrative") is a deliberate reference to Fredric Jameson's definition of postmodernism as, in part, the "waning of affect" (*Postmodernism or, The Cultural Logic of Late Capitalism* [London: Verso, 1991], 10).

72. Coupland, *Life after God*, 22.

73. Jameson, *Postmodernism*, 6, 9, 18–19.

74. Coupland, *Life after God*, 40.

75. Coupland, *Life after God*, 115; Coupland, *Girlfriend in a Coma*, 186.

76. Coupland, *Life after God*, 181, 37, 67.

77. Coupland, *Life after God*, 135, 136.

78. Coupland, *Polaroids from the Dead*, 112; Coupland, *Life after God*, 140.

79. Katerberg, "Western Myth and the End of History," 284.

80. Edward Said, "Reflections on Exile," in *Out There*, ed. R. Ferguson et al. (Cambridge: MIT Press, 1990), 359.

81. Iain Chambers, *Migrancy, Culture, Identity* (London: Routledge, 1994), 4.

82. Said, "Reflections on Exile," 365, 366.

83. Jean-François Lyotard, *Pacific Wall* (Venice: The Lapis Press, 1989/1979), 28.

84. Lyotard, *Pacific Wall*, 55.

85. Rubén Martinez, *Crossing Over* (New York: Picador, 2001), 223. See chapter 3 for a detailed discussion of his work.

86. Coupland, *Life after God*, 144.

87. Coupland, *Life after God*, 173.

88. Coupland, *Microserfs*, 61.

89. Coupland, *Miss Wyoming*, 310.

90. Coupland, *Miss Wyoming*, 62, 310–11.

91. Coupland, *Miss Wyoming*, 103, 311.

92. Coupland, *Shampoo Planet*, 76.

93. Ulrich introduction, 19.

94. Coupland, *Girlfriend in a Coma*, 236, 265, 256, 94, 270–71, 281.

95. Rajchman, *The Deleuze Connections*, 13.

96. Laurence, "Interview with Douglas Coupland."

97. Douglas Coupland, "Shannon Belkin: Nature's Prozac," 2001, http://www .dianefarrisgallery.com/artist/belkin/ex01/coupland.html.

98. Coupland, *Girlfriend in a Coma*, 279 (emphasis in source).

99. Coupland, *Generation X*, 150–51.

100. Coupland, *Shampoo Planet*, 299.

101. Michel Foucault, *The Order of Things* (1966; London: Routledge, 1997), xvii–xix.

102. Michel Foucault, "Of Other Spaces," in *Rethinking Architecture*, ed. Neil Leach (London: Routledge, 1997), 354.

103. Nathaniel Lewis, *Unsettling the Literary West: Authenticity and Authorship* (Lincoln: University of Nebraska Press, 2003), 246.

104. Lewis, *Unsettling the Literary West*, 246–47; Coupland, *Life after God*, 108; Laurence, "Interview with Douglas Coupland."

105. Coupland, *Shampoo Planet*, 371.

106. Jacques Derrida, "Point de folie: Maintenant l'architecture," in Leach, *Rethinking Architecture*, 330–31, 335, 328; see also Bernard Tschumi, *Architecture and Disjunction* (Cambridge: MIT Press, 1996).

107. John Rajchman, *Constructions* (Cambridge: MIT Press, 1997), 15–16, 18.

108. Coupland, *Generation X*, 16.

109. Ulrich introduction, 16.

110. Rajchman, *Constructions*, 119.

Conclusion

1. Jean-François Lyotard, *Pacific Wall* (1979; Venice: The Lapis Press, 1989), 2–3; Mark C. Taylor, *Hiding* (Chicago: University of Chicago Press, 1997), 250.

2. Lyotard, *Pacific Wall*, 33, 29; J-P. Mathy, *Extreme-Occident: French Intellectuals and America* (Chicago: University of Chicago Press, 1993), 191–92.

3. Mathy, *Extreme-Occident*, 192; Lyotard, *Pacific Wall*, 28, 31, 30–31.

4. John Rajchman, *Constructions* (Cambridge: MIT Press, 1998), 81; Lyotard, *Pacific Wall*, 55. I take the phrase "safety of sameness" from Paul Gilroy, *Between Camps: Nations, Cultures, and the Allure of Race* (London: Penguin, 2000), 107. The idea is that Piranesi represents labyrinthine forms, folds, and rhizomatic lines of flight, whereas Mondrian was the master of modernist grids. Mark Taylor compares the work of Bernard Tschumi (see introduction) with Piranesi's Carceri because of his love of labyrinthine structures (see *Hiding*, 262).

5. Tschumi quoted in Taylor, *Hiding*, 241; see also Mark C. Taylor, *Disfiguring: Art, Architecture, Religion* (Chicago: University of Chicago Press, 1992), 240–67.

6. Gilles Deleuze and Félix Guattari, *A Thousand Plateaus* (London: Athlone Press, 1996), 7.

7. Taylor, *Hiding*, 243.

8. Bernard Tschumi, *Architecture and Disjunction* (Cambridge: MIT Press, 1996), 166.

9. Tschumi quoted in Taylor, *Hiding*, 239.

10. Tschumi, *Architecture and Disjunction*, 196–97.

11. Taylor, *Disfiguring*, 247, 248.

12. Jacques Derrida, "Point de folie: Maintenant l'architecture" in *Rethinking Architecture*, ed. Neil Leach (London: Routledge, 1997), 328, 331.

13. Derrida, "Point de folie," 328, 326.

14. Tschumi, *Architecture and Disjunction*, 198, 204; Tschumi quoted in Taylor, *Disfiguring*, 242.

15. Derrida, "Point de folie," 326, 328.

16. Tschumi quoted in Taylor, *Disfiguring*, 251.

17. Tschumi, *Architecture and Disjunction*, 201, 205; see Derrida in Leach, *Rethinking Architecture*, 332, on deconstruction and construction; Gloria Anzaldúa, *Borderlands/La Frontera* (San Francisco: Aunt Lute Books, 1987), 82.

18. "Promenade cinématique" is Tschumi's phrase, quoted in Taylor, *Hiding*, 251. See William L. Fox, *In the Desert of Desire: Las Vegas and the Culture of Spectacle* (Reno: University of Nevada Press, 2005), for a similar discussion of Las Vegas spectacles.

19. Taylor, *Hiding*, 243. The experience of Las Vegas has been referred to as "cinematic tourism." See Norman Klein, "Scripting Las Vegas," in *The Grit beneath the Glitter*, ed. Hal K. Rothman (Berkeley: University of California Press), 2002, 29.

20. Bernard Tschumi, *Event-Cities 2* (Cambridge: MIT Press, 2000), 70.

21. Taylor, *Hiding*, 253.

22. Derrida, "Point de folie," 330. Taylor seems to borrow this form, in part, from Derrida's *Glas* (Lincoln: University of Nebraska Press, 1986), with its grids and blocks of text shifting the reader between his own words and those of Hegel and Jean Genet (among others). The book itself comments on the form it employs, providing a clue also of Taylor's work: "Two unequal columns . . . each of which—envelop(e)(s) or sheath(es), incalculably reverses, turns inside out, replaces, remarks, overlaps [*recoupe*] the other" (1). Derrida writes that "The art of this text is the air it causes to circulate between its screens. The chainings are invisible, everything seems improvised or juxtaposed. This text induces by agglutinating rather than demonstrating, by coupling and decoupling, gluing and ungluing . . . rather than by exhibiting the continuous, and analogical, instructive, suffocating necessity of discursive rhetoric" (75).

23. Taylor, *Hiding*, 262, 264, 267.

24. Derrida, "Point de folie," 332.

25. Dave Hickey, *Air Guitar* (Los Angeles: Art Issues, 1997), 23, 175–76.

26. Marcus Doel, "Un-glunking Geography: Spatial Science after De Seuss and Gilles Deleuze," in *Thinking Space*, ed. M. Crang and N. Thrift (London: Routledge, 2000), 131.

27. Tschumi, *Architecture and Disjunction*, 258; Tschumi quoted in Edward Casey, *The Fate of Place* (Berkeley: University of California, 1998), 318; Derrida, "Point de folie," 325.

28. Casey, *The Fate of Place*, 315.

29. Rajchman, *Constructions*, 20.

30. Taylor, *Hiding*, 258, 264.

31. Derrida, "Point de folie," 325; Jacques Derrida and Peter Eisenman, *Chora L Works* (New York: Monacelli Press, 1997), 97.

32. Paul Gilroy, *The Black Atlantic* (1993; London: Verso, 1996), 73.

33. Gilroy, *The Black Atlantic*, 75; George Lipsitz, *Time Passages* (1990; Minneapolis: University of Minnesota Press, 2000), 261.

34. Convertino quoted in John Mulvey, "The Scorched Earth," *Uncut*, April 2003, 86.

35. Burns interview, http://www.sa-wa-ro.com/Calexico-Pages/calexico-inerviews.htm; Burns quoted in Michael Barclay, "Calexico: The Expatriate Files," http://www.exclaim.ca/index.asp?layid=227csidi=1422. I am choosing Calexico as my case study, but others have explored different bands, most notably George Lipsitz's work on Los Lobos (in *Time Passages*) and José David Saldívar's on Los Tigres del Norte and El Vez (in *Border Matters*). Dave Alvin's band The Blasters invited Los Lobos to open their live shows in the 1980s (see Lipsitz, *Time Passages*, 150).

36. Joshua Garrett-Davis, "Composing the New Western," *High Country News*, September 13, 2004, http://www.hcn.org.

37. Lipsitz, *Time Passages*, 151, 150.

38. Arjun Appadurai, "Grassroots Globalization and the Research Imagination," *Public Culture* 12, no. 1 (2000): 5.

39. Rob Wilson and Wimal Dissanayake, eds., introduction, *Global/Local: Cultural Production and the Transnational Imaginary* (Durham: Duke University Press, 1996), 6.

40. Ramón Saldívar, *The Borderlands of Culture: Américo Paredes and the Transnational Imaginary* (Durham: Duke University Press, 2006), 9–10.

41. Saldívar, *The Borderlands of Culture*, 436.

42. Iain Chambers, *Culture after Humanism* (London: Routledge, 2001), 117–18, 118–19; see also Iain Chambers, *Migrancy, Culture, Identity* (London: Routledge, 1994), chapter 5.

43. Chambers, *Culture after Humanism*, 120.

44. Burns quoted in Siddhartha Mitter, "An Original Sound Keeps Evolving," *Boston Globe*, June 23, 2006, http://www.boston.com/ae/music/articles/2006/06/23/. The title may also refer to the Holocaust survivors' memorial stories via the book *From a Ruined Garden* (ed. J. Kugelmass and J. Boyarin [Bloomington: Indiana University Press, 1998]), or indeed to Charles Baudelaire's poem "The Ruined Garden" from his *Fleurs du Mal* (*Flowers of Evil*), which speaks of "what survives" after "flooded grounds" and of the need "to throw fresh seeds out" (see http://www.geocities.com/Paris/Arc/5340/bflowers.htm for a translation).

45. Chambers, *Culture after Humanism*, 123.

46. Chambers, *Culture after Humanism*, 124, and Chambers quoting Edward Said, 123.

47. Chambers, *Migrancy, Culture, Identity*, 79, 81.

48. Burns interview, http://www.sa-wa-ro.com/Calexico-Pages/calexico-interviews.htm.

49. Deleuze and Guattari, *A Thousand Plateaus*, 60, 49.

50. Carlos Fuentes, *The Crystal Frontier* (1995; London: Bloomsbury, 1999), 25.

51. Fuentes, *The Crystal Frontier*, 179, 188–89.

52. Fuentes, *The Crystal Frontier*, 253, 266. In the song "Across the Wire" Calexico refers to being "so far away and so near."

53. Burns interview, http://www.sa-wa-ro.com/Calexico-Pages/calexico-interviews.htm.

54. Burns quoted in Linda Ray, "Come Together," *No Depression*, March–April 2006, 66; Burns interview, "Questions of Doom" (2005), http://www.poptones.co.uk.

55. Chambers, *Culture after Humanism*, 118; Burns interview, "Questions of Doom."

56. Sylvie Simmons, "Calexico," http://www.sa-wa-ro.com/Calexico-Pages/calexico-interviews.htm.

57. Burns interview, http://suicidegirls.com/words/calexico; Burns talking to *Uncut*, June 2000, 37; Burns interview, "Questions of Doom."

58. Space forbids a detailed examination of these intertextualities, but in their interviews Calexico regularly discuss writers such as those listed, along with Mike Davis, Carlos Fuentes, Alex Shoumatoff, Mitch Cullin, Harry Crews, and most interestingly Lawrence Clark Powell, whose writings they set to music at the Singing Wind Bookstore in Benson, Arizona, and sampled on *Aerocalexico*'s track "Blacktop." Burns even discusses the work of Karl May, whose German "Old Shatterhand" stories were so influential on the global, mythic vision of the West that resurfaced as spaghetti Westerns in the 1960s (see Barclay, "Calexico: The Expatriate Files").

59. Burns quoted in Mulvey, "The Scorched Earth," 84.

60. Burns interview, http://www.sa-wa-ro.com/Calexico-Pages/calexico-inter views.htm.

61. Charles Bowden, *Blood Orchid: An Unnatural History of America* (New York: Random House, 1995), n.p.

62. Liane Lefaivre and Alexander Tzonis, *Critical Regionalism: Architecture and Identity in a Globalized World* (New York: Prestel Verlag, 2003), 34. See chapter 1 for more on this.

63. Joey Burns speaking in the DVD *Calexico: World Drifts In: Live at the Barbican* (City Slang, 2004).

64. Burns quoted in Barclay, "Calexico: The Expatriate Files." Calexico even "mirrors" the *Double Nickels* cover shot on their own CD *Aerocalexico*, which shows Burns and Convertino driving. "Reinvention" is a word approved of by John Convertino in an interview given to *Tape Op*, issue 13, http://www.prosoundweb .com/recording/tapeop/calexico/calexico_13_1.shtml.

65. Chambers, *Migrancy, Culture, Identity*, 83.

66. Burns quoted in Mulvey, "The Scorched Earth," 86.

67. Volker Zander sleeve notes to DVD *Calexico World Drifts In* (2004).

68. J. Convertino speaking on DVD *Calexico: World Drifts In*.

69. Burns interview, http://suicidegirls.com/words/calexico.

70. Burns interview, "Questions of Doom." Burns met Gastelum in 1989 while working for punk label SST Records. The cover art is a vital component of the Calexico western "aura" I am describing here, ranging from Gastelum's work, to a number of archive photographs of Calexico 1917, to contemporary cultural geography images of motels and landmarks, and in the reworking of the Western *The Professionals* poster for *Aerocalexico*.

71. Victor Gastelum, Artist's Statement, http://latinoartcommunity.org/com munity/ChicArt/ArtistDir/VicGas.html.

72. Burns interview, http://suicidegirls.com/words/calexico. Burns claimed in an interview that "travelling I think has a big influence on us . . . it's great to

talk to people over there [in Europe]" (http://www.publicbroadcasting.net/kxci/arts.artsmain/).

73. Burns, "Questions of Doom." The "world drifts in" is a phrase from the song "Quattro" on *Feast of Wire* and the subtitle of their DVD *Live at the Barbican*.

74. Mikhail Bakhtin, *The Dialogic Imagination* (Austin: University of Texas Poress, 1990), 368, 370.

75. Burns interview, http://www.publicbroadcasting.net/kxci/arts.artsmain/.

76. Gloria Anzaldúa in Analouise Keating, ed., *Interviews/Entrevistas* (London: Routledge, 2000), 185–86, 215.

77. Anzaldúa in Keating, *Interviews/Entrevistas*, 215.

78. Deleuze and Guattari, *A Thousand Plateaus*, 11–12.

79. Burns interview within R. Patterson, "Calexico: Raising Arizona," http://harpmagazine.com/articles/detail.cfm?article_id=3991.

80. Anzaldúa in Keating, *Interviews/Entrevistas*, 254.

81. Deleuze and Guattari, *A Thousand Plateaus*, 271. Calexico has recorded a number of live CDs that are sold on tour or through their website only, such as *Scraping* (2000), which recasts songs recorded elsewhere, such as "Crystal Frontier" and "Sonic Wind."

82. Burns interview, http://suicidegirls.com/words/calexico.

83. Convertino quoted from http://www.billions.com/artists/calexico.

84. Dave Alvin, *West of the West* (Yep Roc records, Chapel Hill, North Carolina, 2006). Alvin has written many songs about the borderlands as a cultural mix, in particular "Border Radio" with its echoes of Rubén Martinez's point about the hybrid nature of border radio (see chapter 3).

85. Gilroy, *The Black Atlantic*, 198.

86. Doe quoted in Brian Hinton, *South by Southwest: A Road Map to Alternative Country* (London: Sanctuary, 2003), 124.

87. In his book on "alternative country" music, *South by Southwest*, Hinton typifies the failure to comprehend Calexico's and Alvin's points about the "cosmic" or global turn in "Americana," structuring his book in an "arborial" manner (as Deleuze and Guattari term it), presenting a "road map" with sections called, rather predictably, "Roots," "Branches," and "New Blossoms"!

88. Lipsitz, *Time Passages*, 7.

89. Chambers, *Culture after Humanism*, 63.

90. Gilles Deleuze and Félix Guattari, *What Is Philosophy?* (1991; London: Verso, 2003), 189, 191.

91. Deleuze and Guattari, *A Thousand Plateaus*, 311.

92. Ronald Bogue, *Deleuze on Music, Painting, and the Arts* (London: Routledge, 2003), 188.

93. Russ Castronovo, "Compromised Narratives along the Border: The Mason-Dixon Line, Resistance, and Hegemony," in *Border Theory: The Limits of Cul-*

tural Politics, ed. S. Michaelsen and D. E. Johnson (Minneapolis: University of Minnesota Press, 1997), 216.

94. Deleuze and Guattari, *A Thousand Plateaus*, 49.

95. Deleuze and Guattari, *A Thousand Plateaus*, 60.

96. Deleuze and Guattari, *A Thousand Plateaus*, 349.

97. Deleuze and Guattari, *A Thousand Plateaus*, 350.

98. Deleuze and Guattari, *A Thousand Plateaus*, 349; Gilles Deleuze, *Essays Critical and Clinical* (London: Verso, 1998), 63.

99. Deleuze, *Essays Critical and Clinical*, 63.

100. Deleuze and Guattari, *A Thousand Plateaus*, 329.

INDEX

In the Postwestern Horizons series

Dirty Wars: Landscape, Power, and Waste in Western American Literature
John Beck

The Rhizomatic West
Representing the American West in a Transnational, Global, Media Age
Neil Campbell

True West
Authenticity and the American West
Edited by William R. Handley and Nathaniel Lewis

Postwestern Cultures
Literature, Theory, Space
Susan Kollin

Manifest and Other Destinies
Territorial Fictions of the
Nineteenth-Century United States
By Stephanie LeMenager

Unsettling the Literary West
Authenticity and Authorship
By Nathaniel Lewis

María Amparo Ruiz de Burton
Critical and Pedagogical Perspectives
Edited by Amelia María de la Luz Montes
and Anne Elizabeth Gol

To order or obtain more information on these or other University of Nebraska Press titles, visit www.nebraskapress.unl.edu

CPSIA information can be obtained at www.ICGtesting.com
Printed in the USA
LVOW040219181212

312130LV00002B/48/P

9 780803 243934